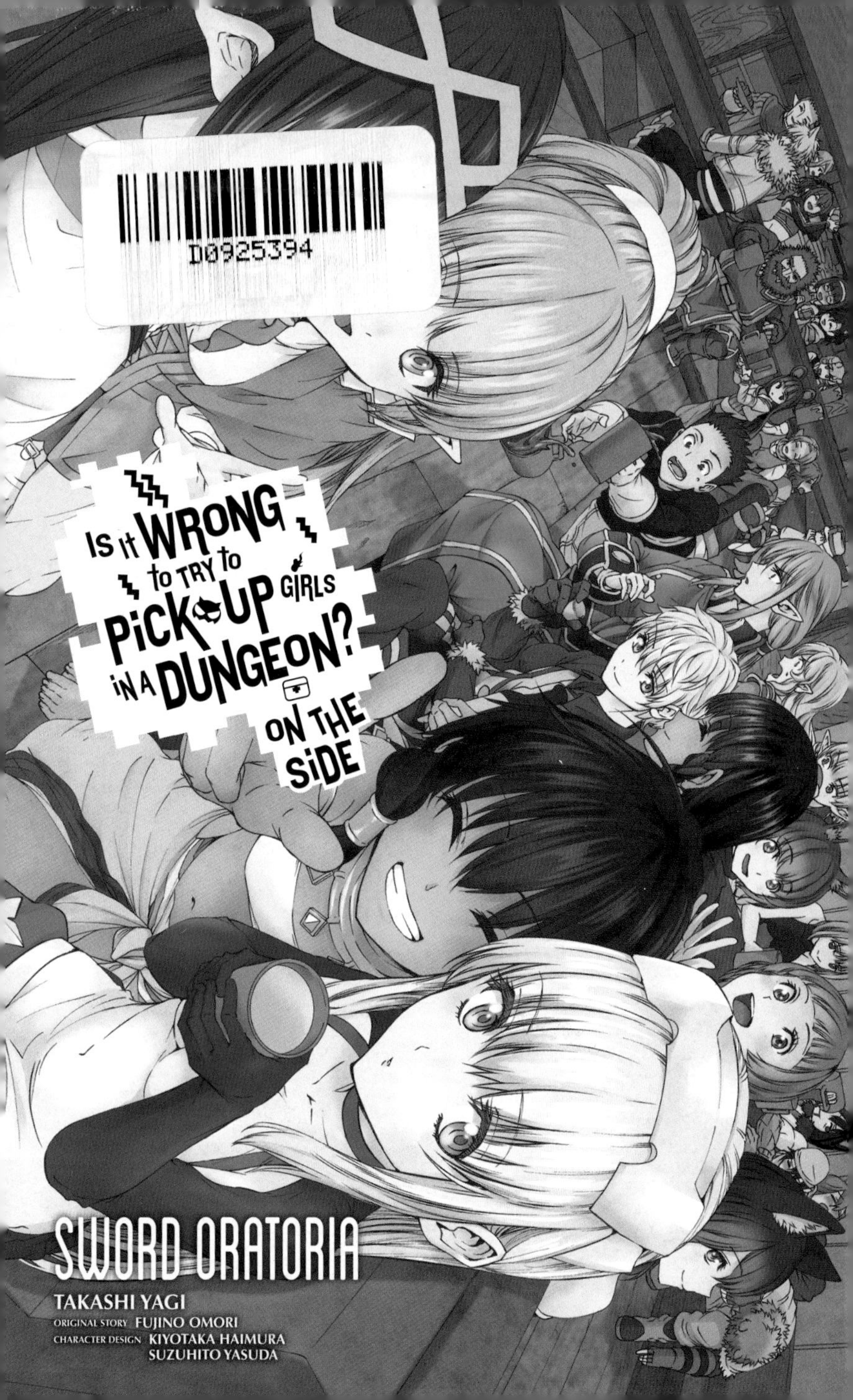
D0925394
Is it WRONG to TRY to PiCK UP GIRLS iN A DUNGEON?
ON THE SiDE
SWORD ORATORIA
TAKASHI YAGI
ORIGINAL STORY FUJINO OMORI
CHARACTER DESIGN KIYOTAKA HAIMURA
SUZUHITO YASUDA

16
SWORD ORATORIA

CONTENTS

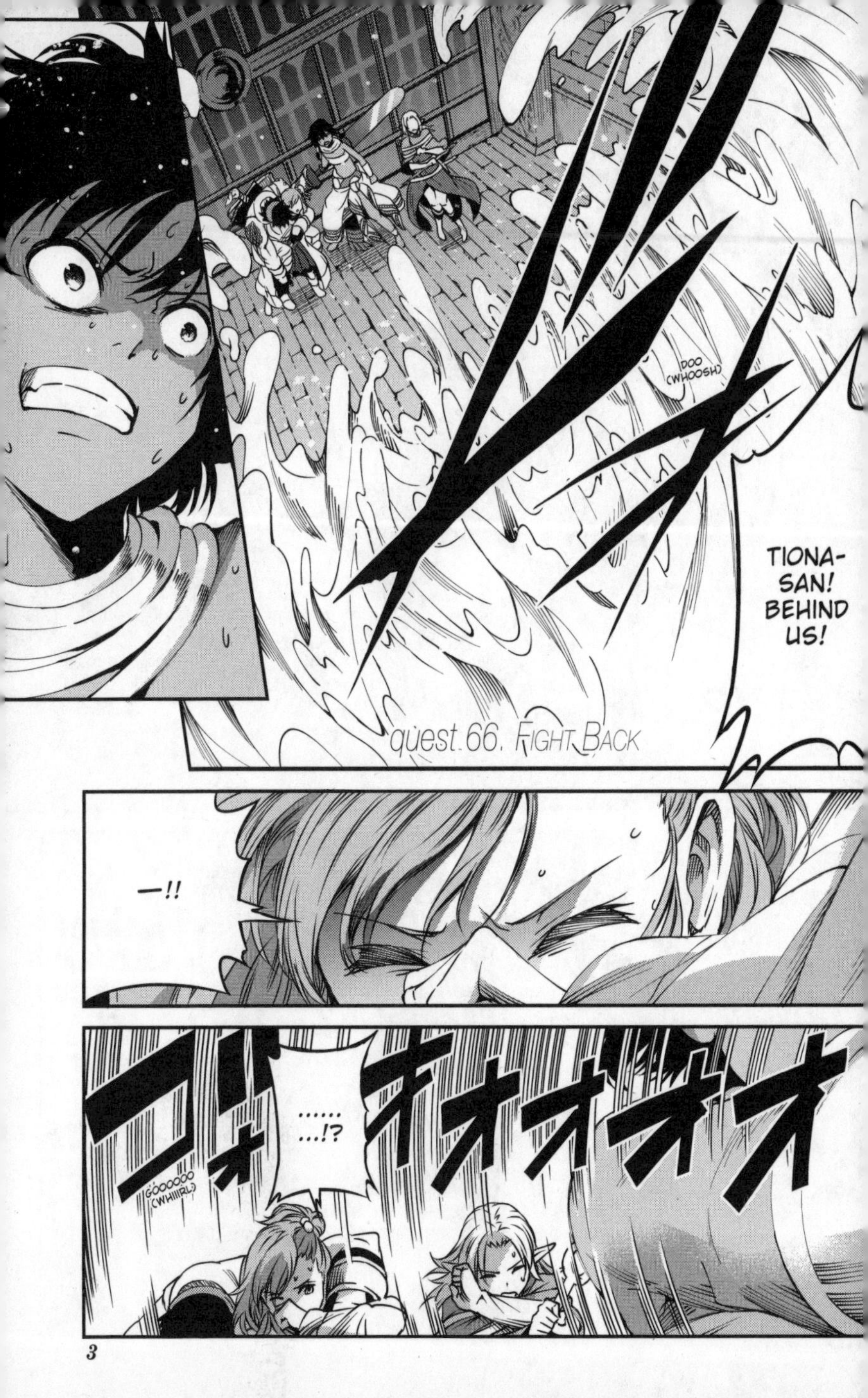
TIONA-SAN! BEHIND US!
DOO (WHOOSH)
quest.66. Fight Back
—!!
ゴォオオオオ
……
…!?
GOOOOOO (WHIIRL)

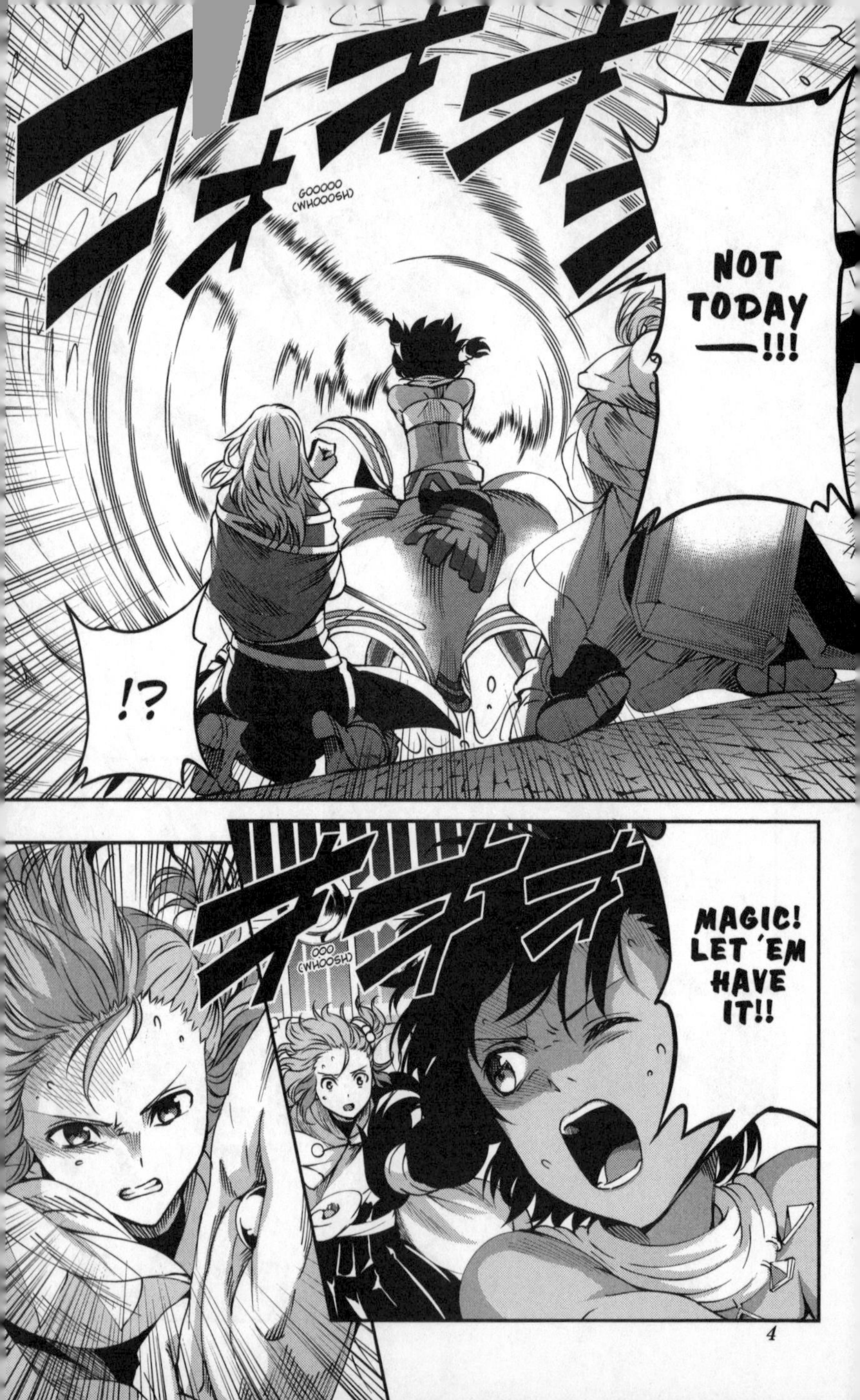
NOT TODAY —!!!
GOOOOO (WHOOOSH)
!?
MAGIC! LET 'EM HAVE IT!!
OOO (WHOOSH)

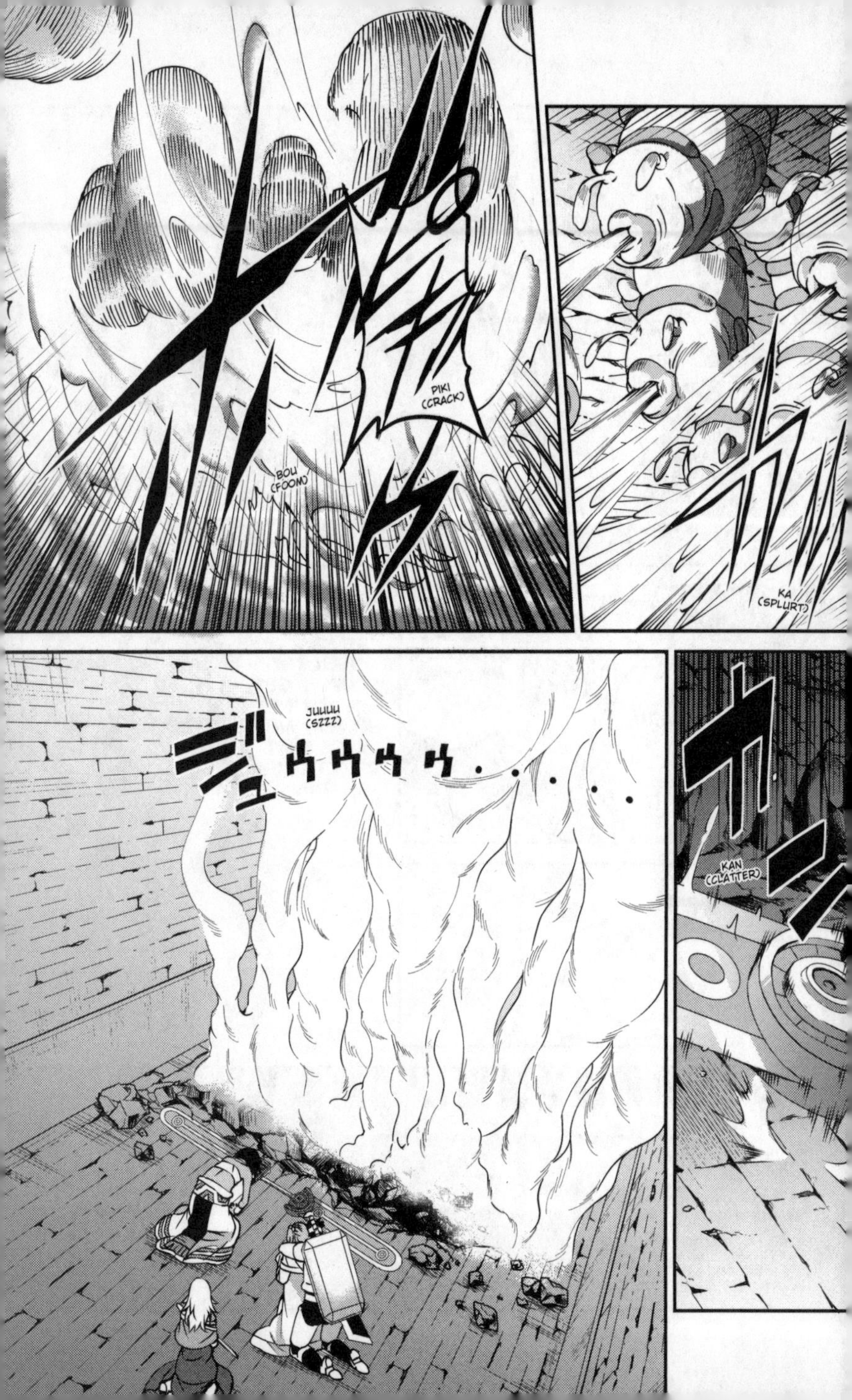
KA
(SPLURT)
PIKI
(CRACK)
BOU
(FOOM)
KAN
(CLATTER)
JUUUU
(SZZZ)

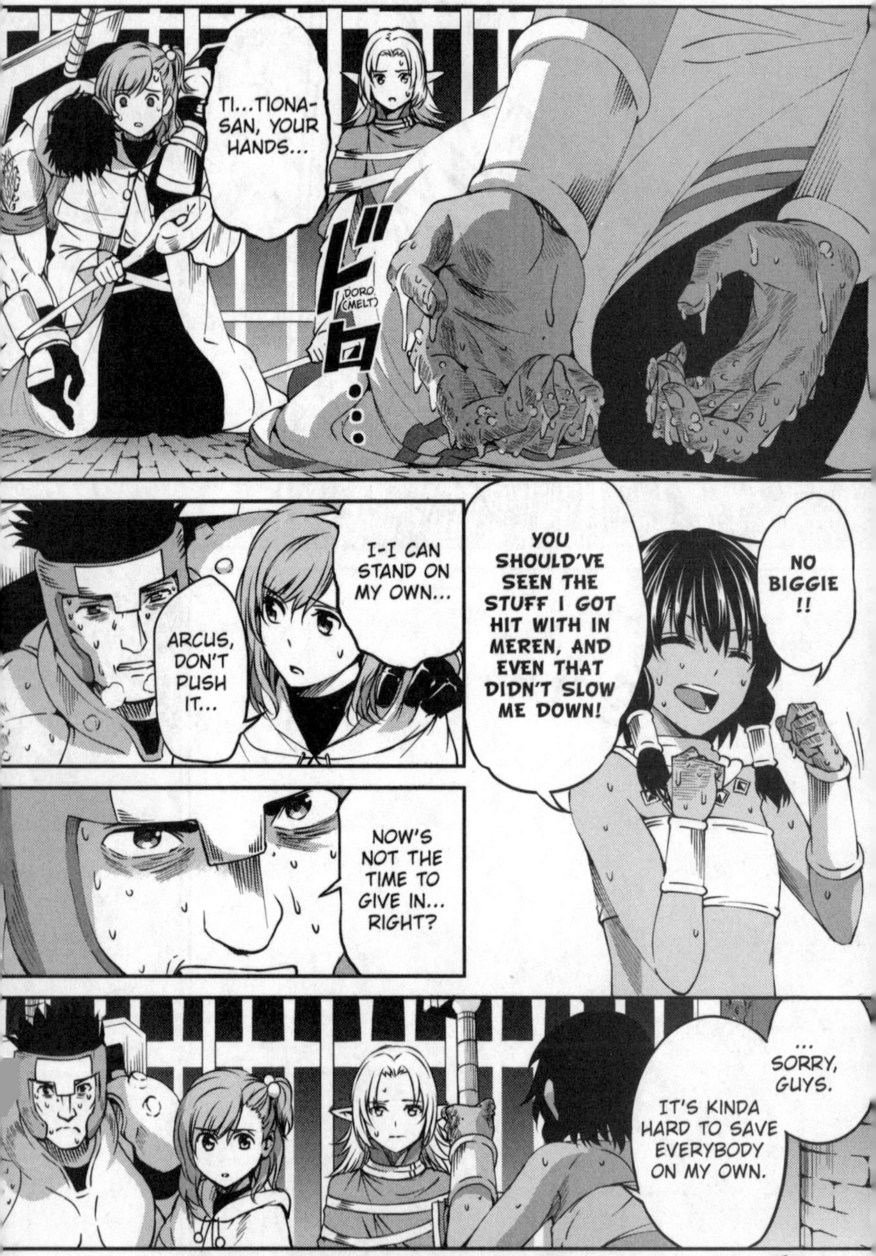
TI...TIONA-SAN, YOUR HANDS...
ドロ
DORO (MELT)
NO BIGGIE!!
YOU SHOULD'VE SEEN THE STUFF I GOT HIT WITH IN MEREN, AND EVEN THAT DIDN'T SLOW ME DOWN!
I-I CAN STAND ON MY OWN...
ARCUS, DON'T PUSH IT...
NOW'S NOT THE TIME TO GIVE IN... RIGHT?
... SORRY, GUYS.
IT'S KINDA HARD TO SAVE EVERYBODY ON MY OWN.

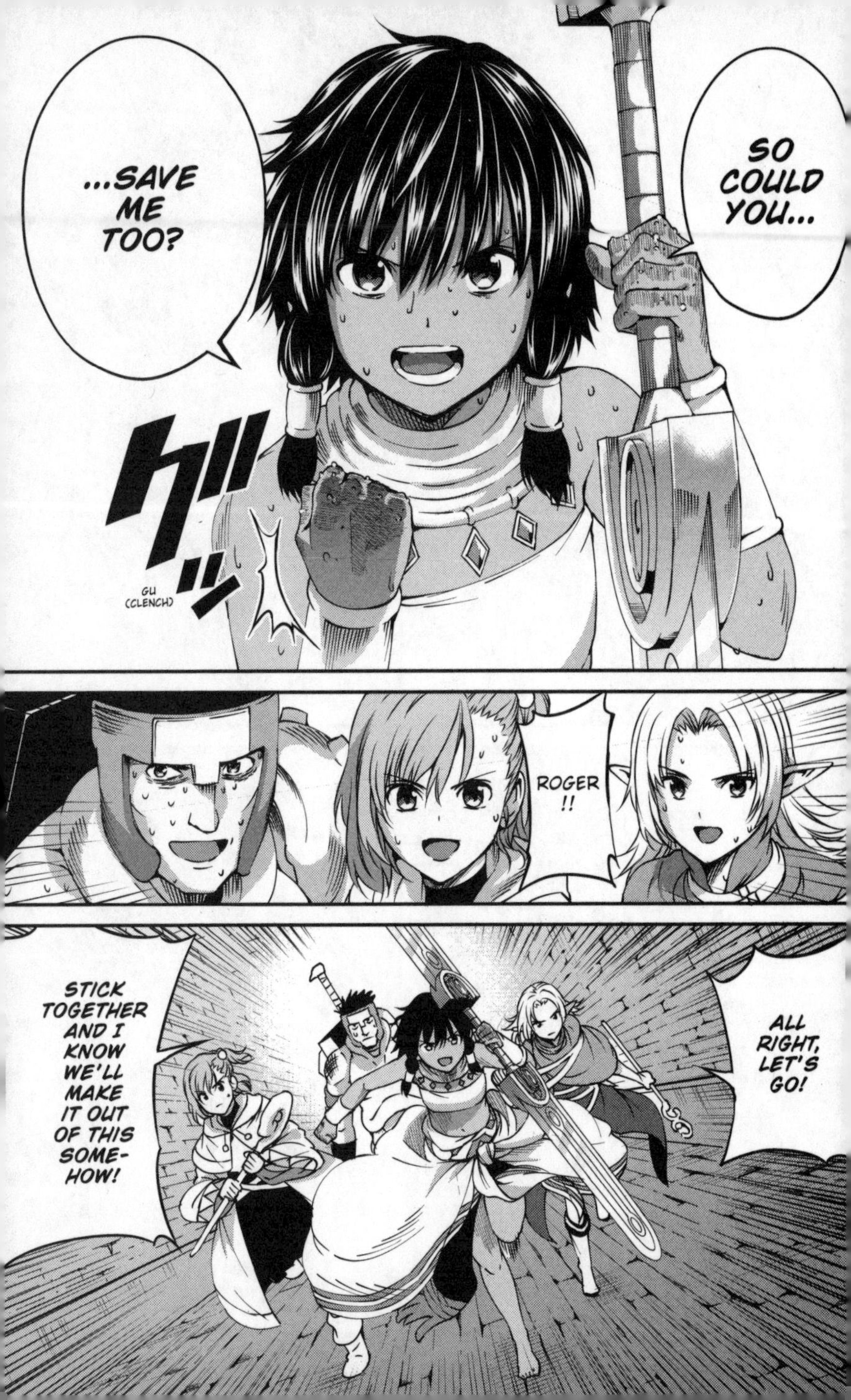
SO COULD YOU...
...SAVE ME TOO?
グッ
GU (CLENCH)
ROGER!!
ALL RIGHT, LET'S GO!
STICK TOGETHER AND I KNOW WE'LL MAKE IT OUT OF THIS SOME-HOW!

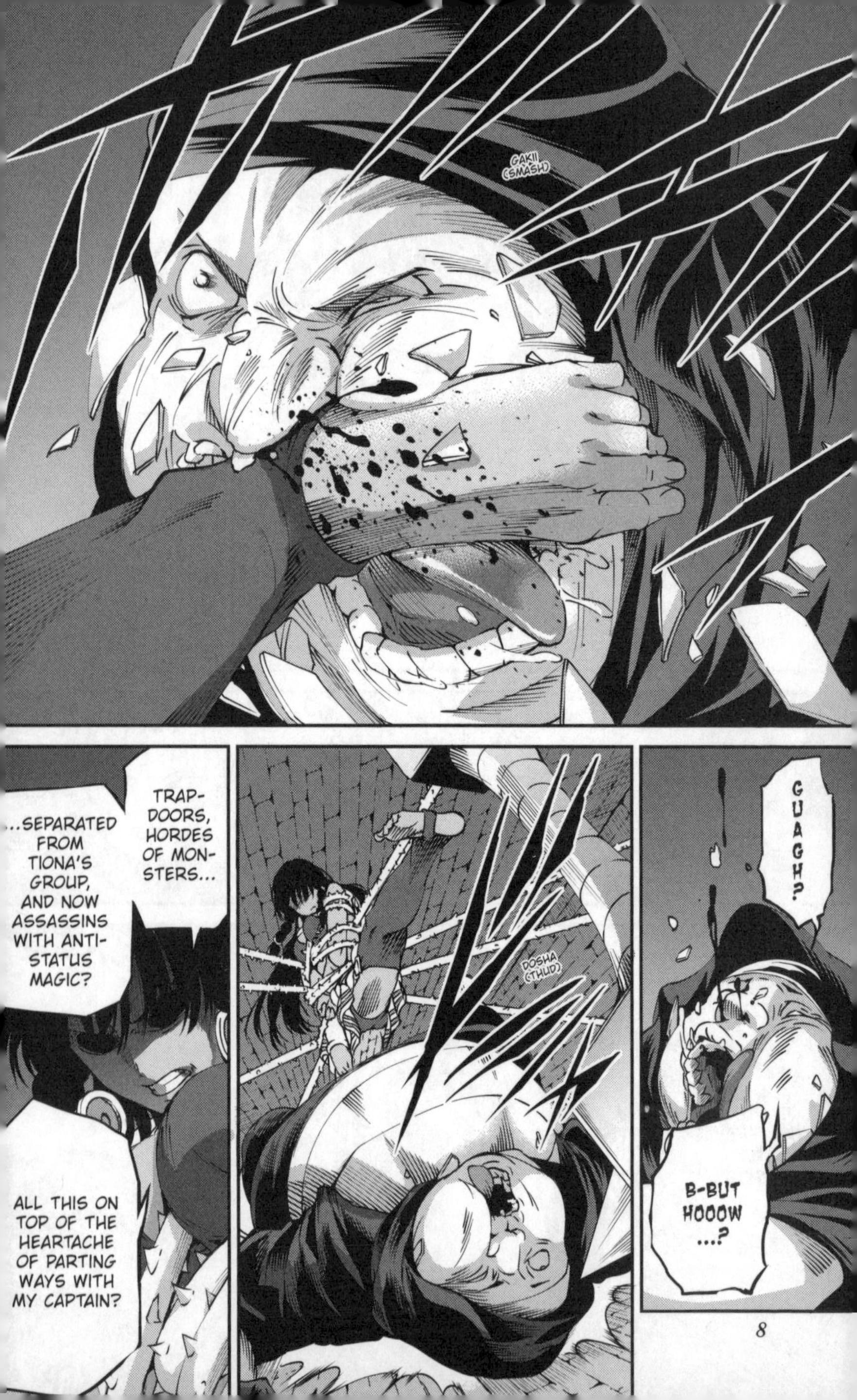
GAKII (SMASH)
GUAGH?
B-BUT HOOOW ...?
TRAP-DOORS, HORDES OF MON-STERS...
DOSHA (THUD)
...SEPARATED FROM TIONA'S GROUP, AND NOW ASSASSINS WITH ANTI-STATUS MAGIC?
ALL THIS ON TOP OF THE HEARTACHE OF PARTING WAYS WITH MY CAPTAIN?

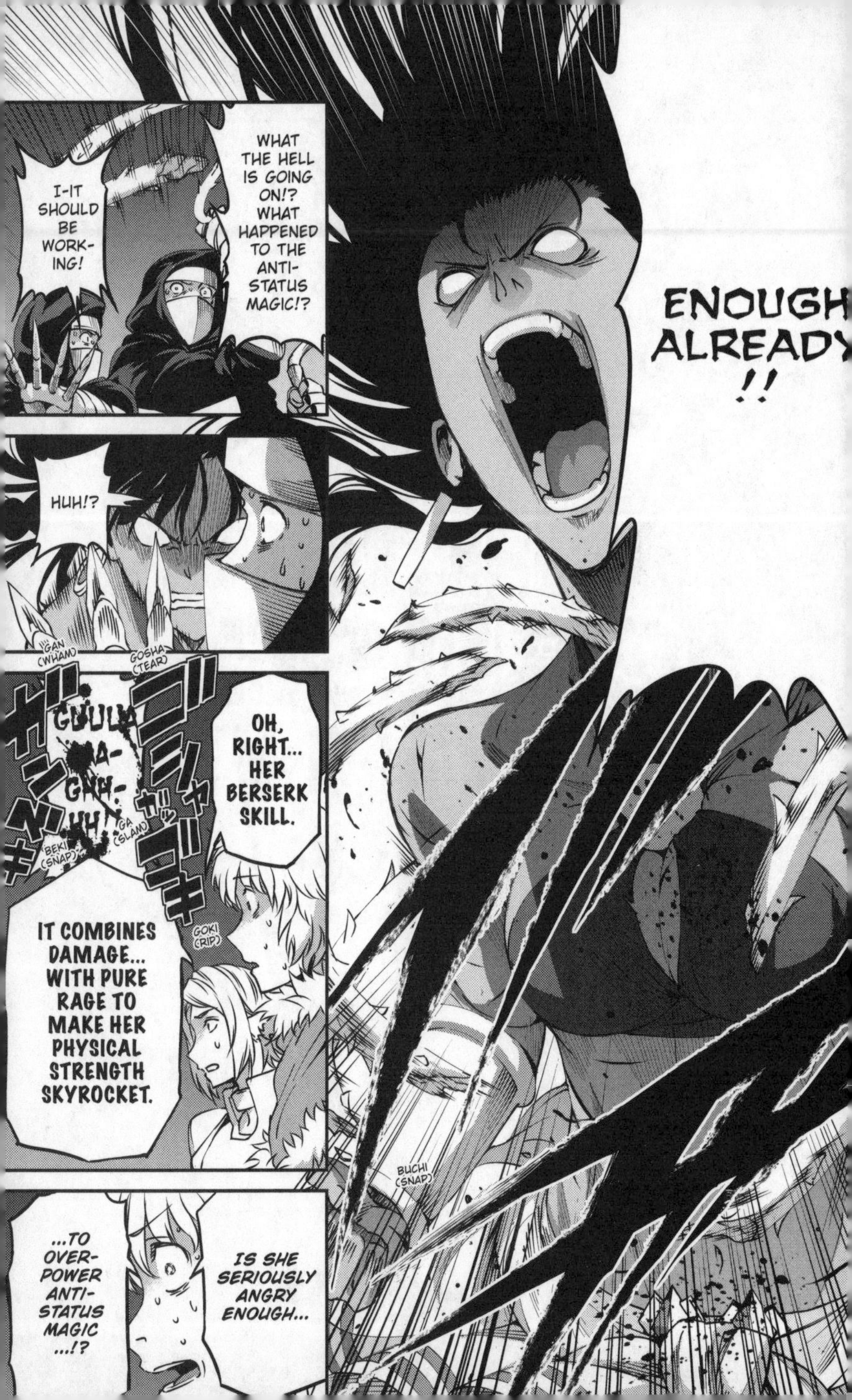

ENOUGH ALREADY!!
BUCHI (SNAP)
WHAT THE HELL IS GOING ON!? WHAT HAPPENED TO THE ANTI-STATUS MAGIC!?
I-IT SHOULD BE WORK-ING!
HUH!?
GAN (WHAM)
GOSHA (TEAR)
GA (SLAM)
GUULA A- GHH- UH!
BEKI (SNAP)
GOKI (RIP)
OH, RIGHT... HER BERSERK SKILL.
IT COMBINES DAMAGE... WITH PURE RAGE TO MAKE HER PHYSICAL STRENGTH SKYROCKET.
IS SHE SERIOUSLY ANGRY ENOUGH...
...TO OVER-POWER ANTI-STATUS MAGIC ...!?

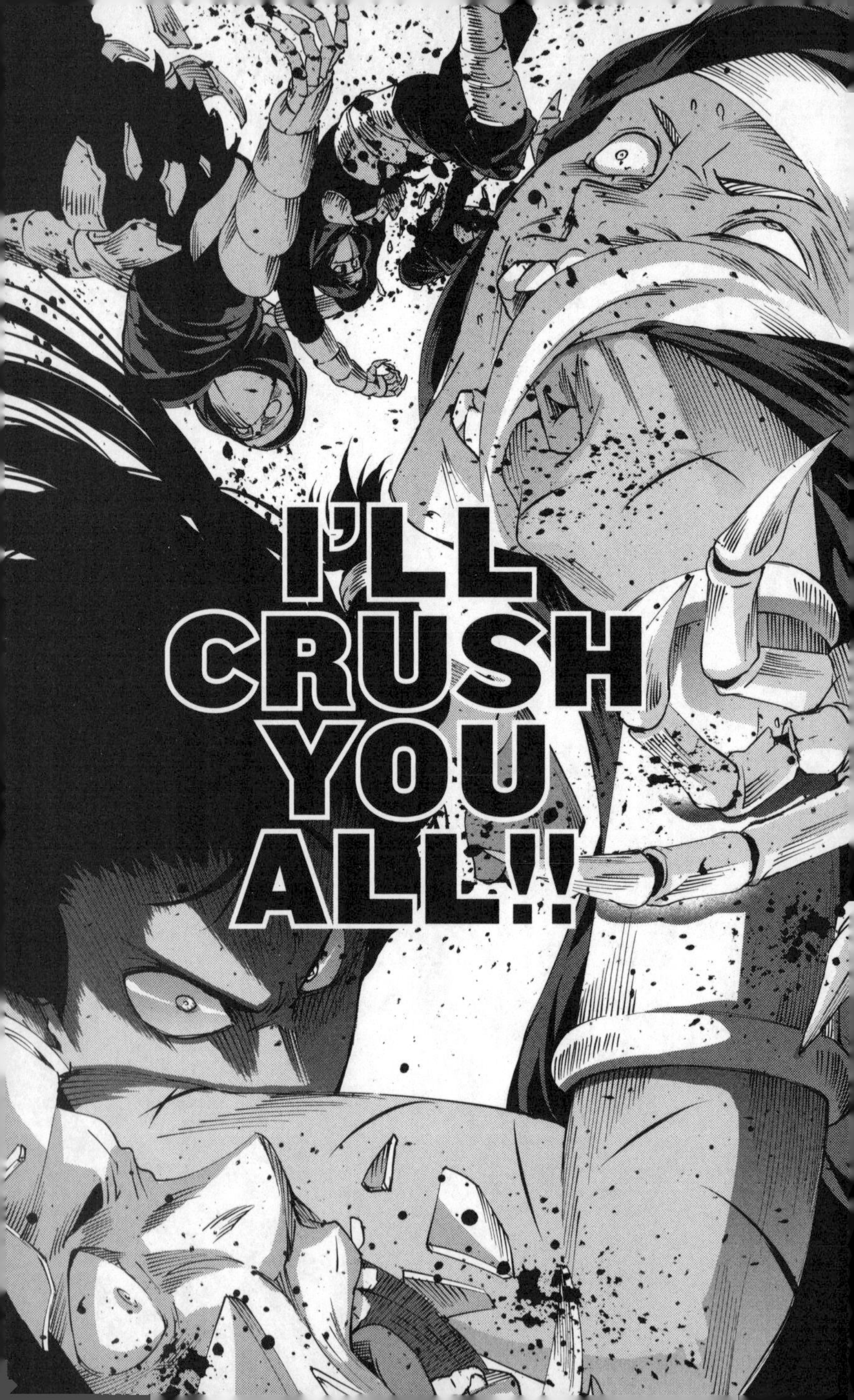
I'LL CRUSH YOU ALL!!

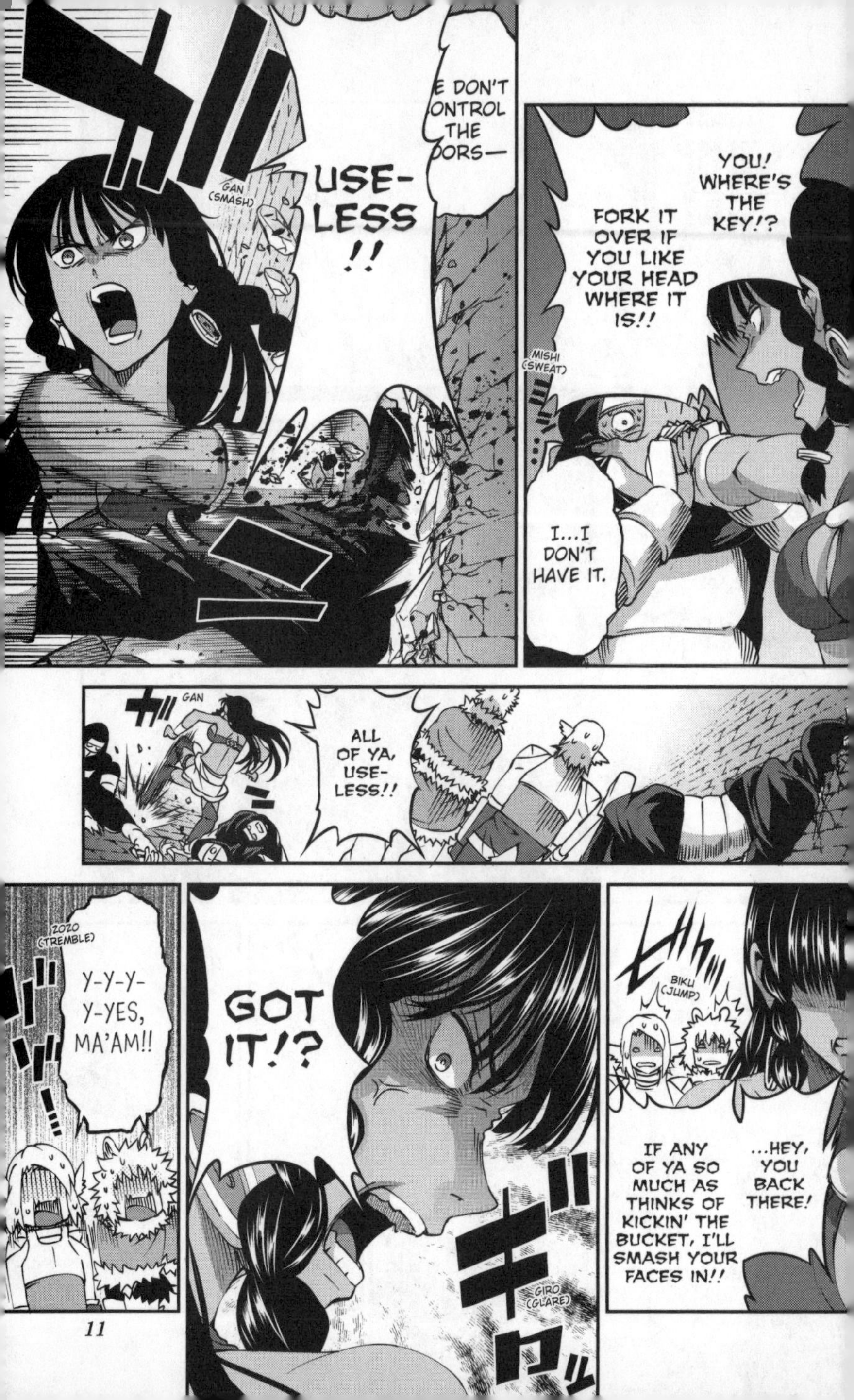
YOU! WHERE'S THE KEY!?
FORK IT OVER IF YOU LIKE YOUR HEAD WHERE IT IS!!
MISHI (SWEAT)
I...I DON'T HAVE IT.
E DON'T ONTROL THE ORS—
GAN (SMASH)
USE-LESS!!
ALL OF YA, USE-LESS!!
GAN
BIKU (JUMP)
...HEY, YOU BACK THERE!
IF ANY OF YA SO MUCH AS THINKS OF KICKIN' THE BUCKET, I'LL SMASH YOUR FACES IN!!
GOT IT!?
GIRO (GLARE)
ZOZO (TREMBLE)
Y-Y-Y-Y-YES, MA'AM!!

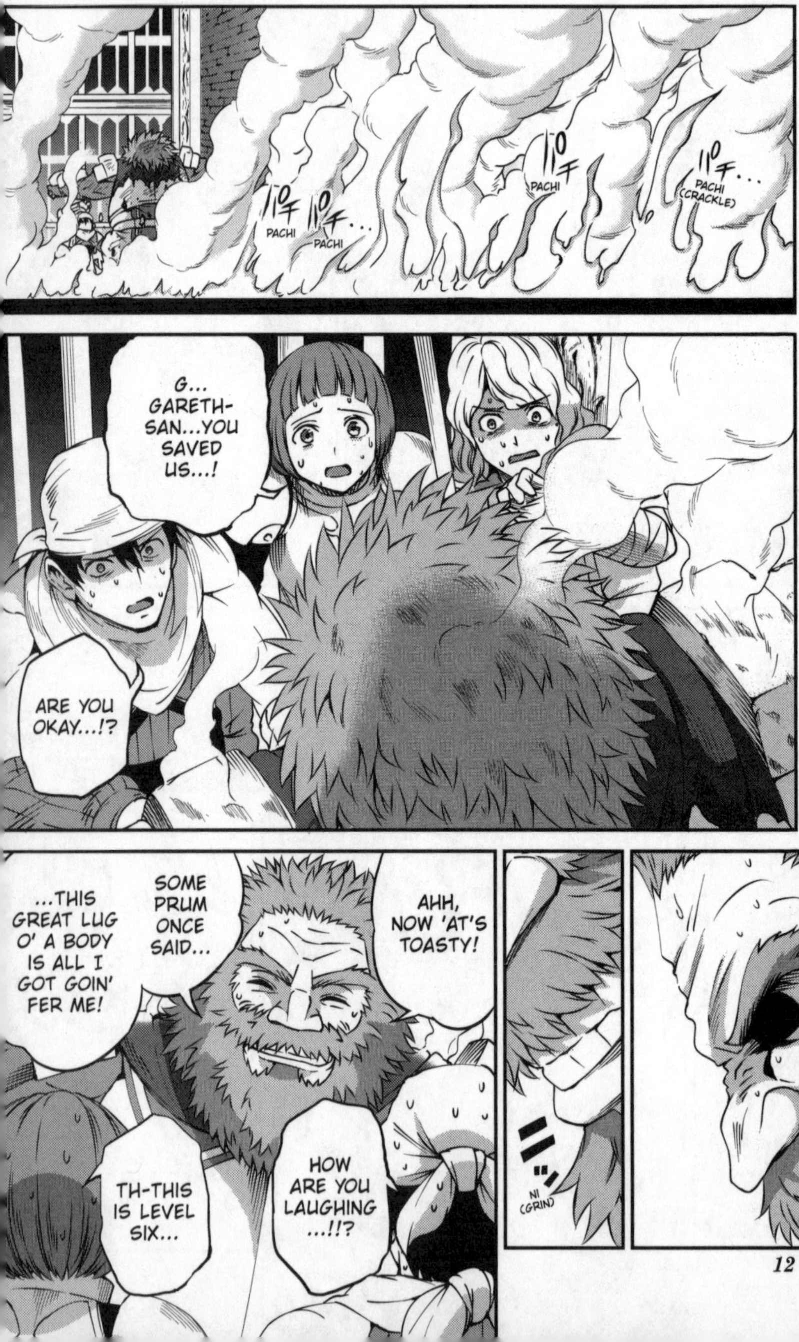

パチ…
PACHI (CRACKLE)
パチ
PACHI
パチ パチ…
PACHI PACHI
G... GARETH-SAN...YOU SAVED US...!
ARE YOU OKAY...!?
ニ
NI (GRIN)
AHH, NOW 'AT'S TOASTY!
SOME PRUM ONCE SAID...
...THIS GREAT LUG O' A BODY IS ALL I GOT GOIN' FER ME!
HOW ARE YOU LAUGHING ...!!?
TH-THIS IS LEVEL SIX...

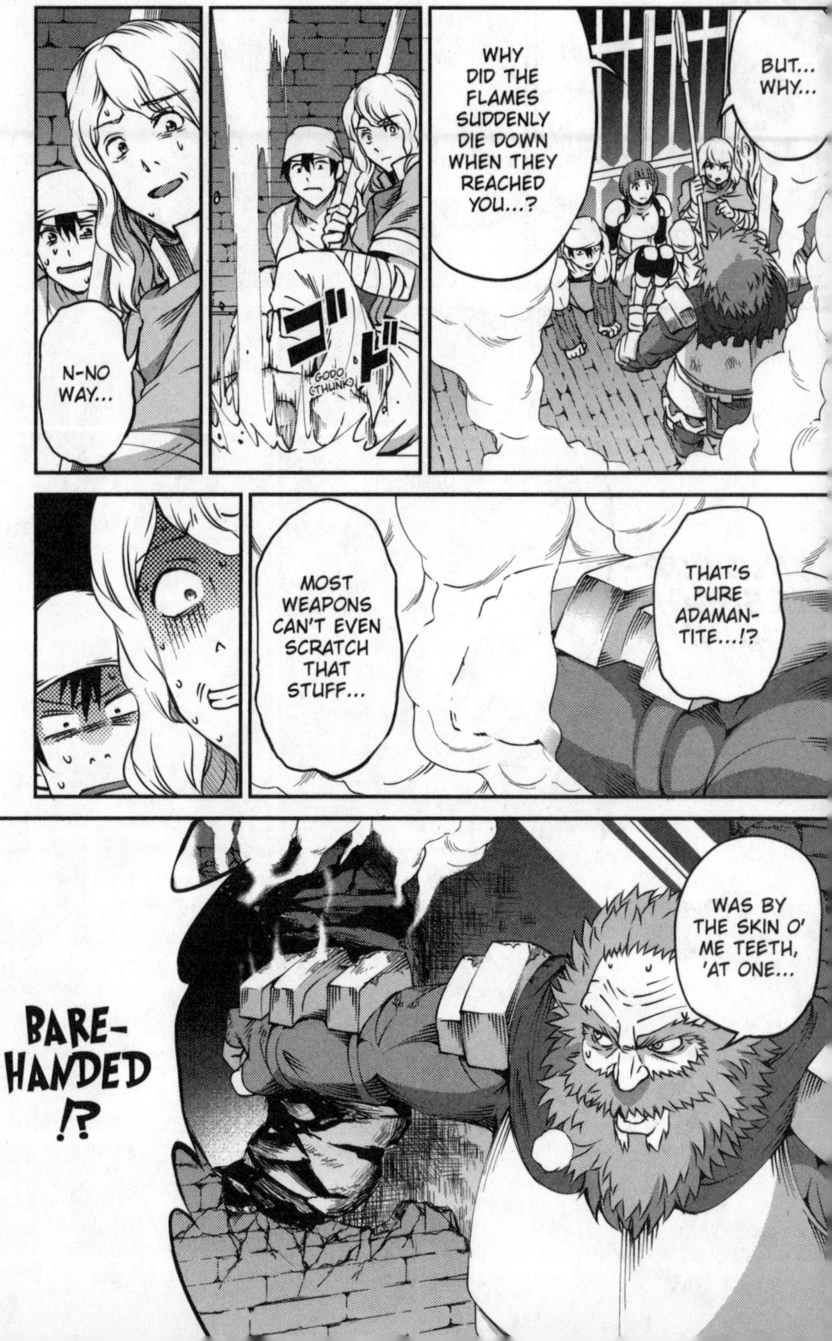
BUT... WHY...
WHY DID THE FLAMES SUDDENLY DIE DOWN WHEN THEY REACHED YOU...?
ゴド
GODO (THUNK)
N-NO WAY...
THAT'S PURE ADAMANTITE...!?
MOST WEAPONS CAN'T EVEN SCRATCH THAT STUFF...
WAS BY THE SKIN O' ME TEETH, 'AT ONE...
BARE-HANDED!?

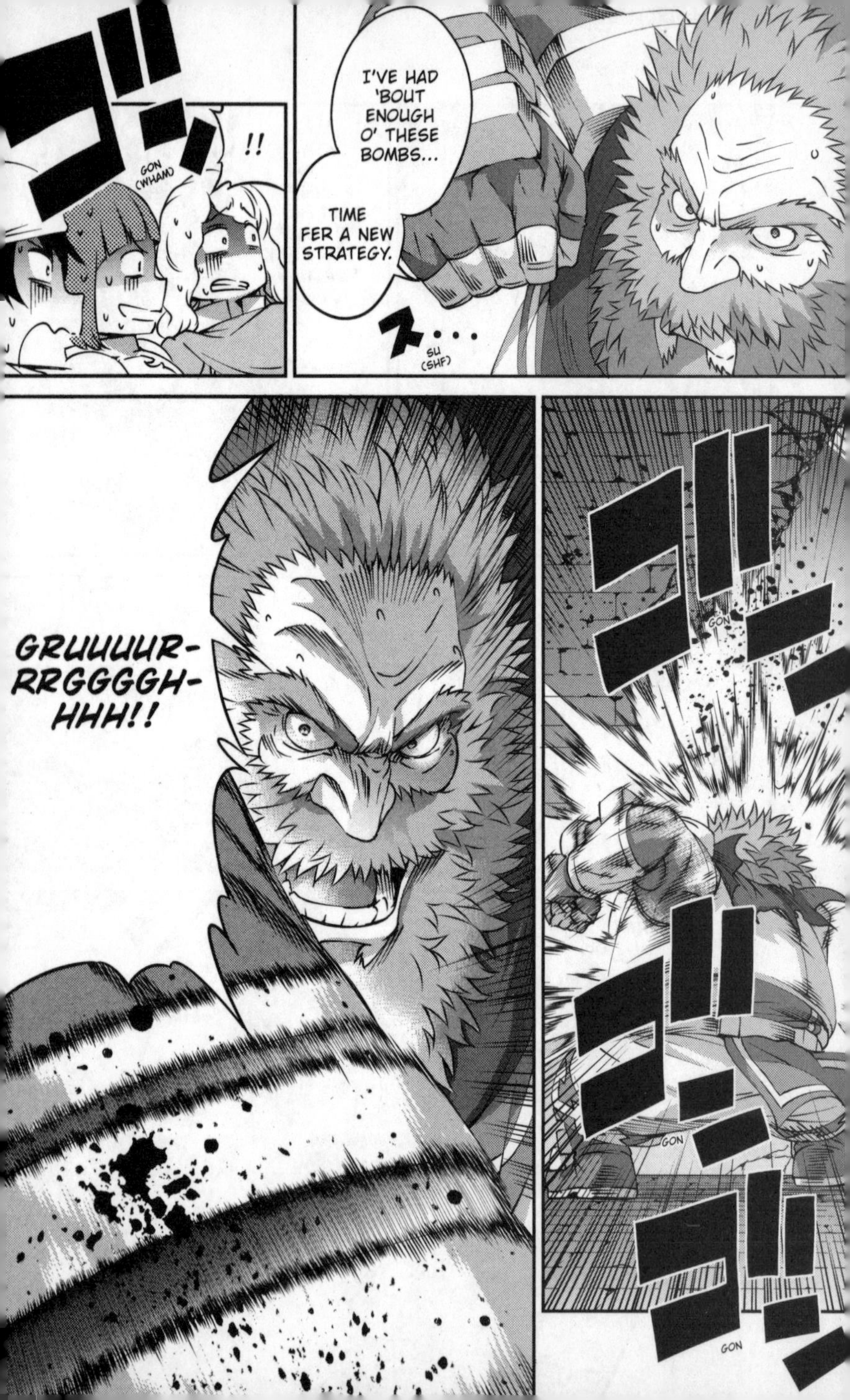

I'VE HAD 'BOUT ENOUGH O' THESE BOMBS...
TIME FER A NEW STRATEGY.
SU (SHF)
!!
GON (WHAM)
GON
GON
GON
GRUUUUR-RRGGGGH-HHH!!

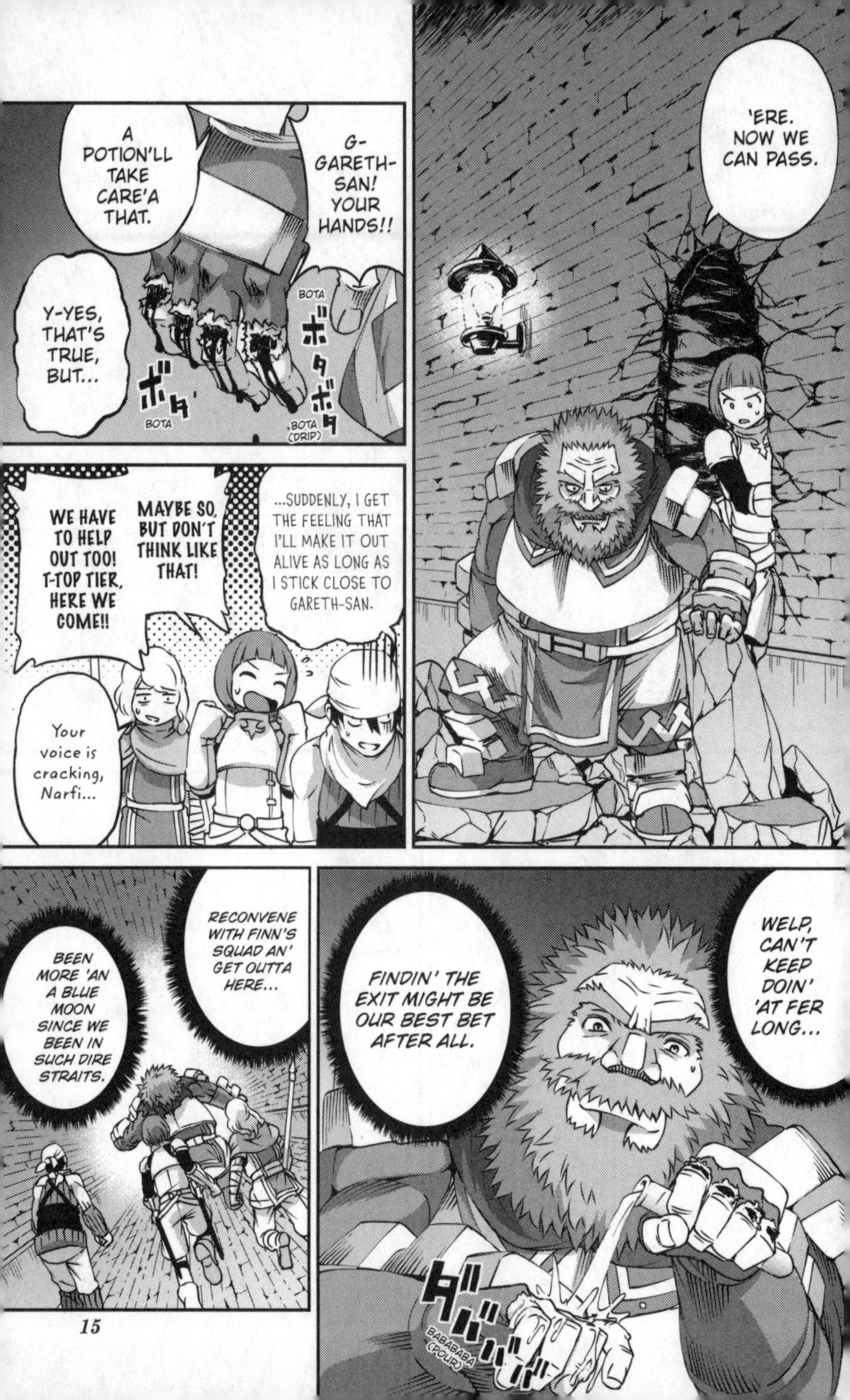

'ERE. NOW WE CAN PASS.
G-GARETH-SAN! YOUR HANDS!!
A POTION'LL TAKE CARE'A THAT.
ボタ BOTA
ボタボタ BOTA (DRIP)
ボタ BOTA
Y-YES, THAT'S TRUE, BUT...
...SUDDENLY, I GET THE FEELING THAT I'LL MAKE IT OUT ALIVE AS LONG AS I STICK CLOSE TO GARETH-SAN.
MAYBE SO, BUT DON'T THINK LIKE THAT!
WE HAVE TO HELP OUT TOO! T-TOP TIER, HERE WE COME!!
Your voice is cracking, Narfi...
WELP, CAN'T KEEP DOIN' 'AT FER LONG...
FINDIN' THE EXIT MIGHT BE OUR BEST BET AFTER ALL.
ダバババ BABABABA (POUR)
RECONVENE WITH FINN'S SQUAD AN' GET OUTTA HERE...
BEEN MORE 'AN A BLUE MOON SINCE WE BEEN IN SUCH DIRE STRAITS.

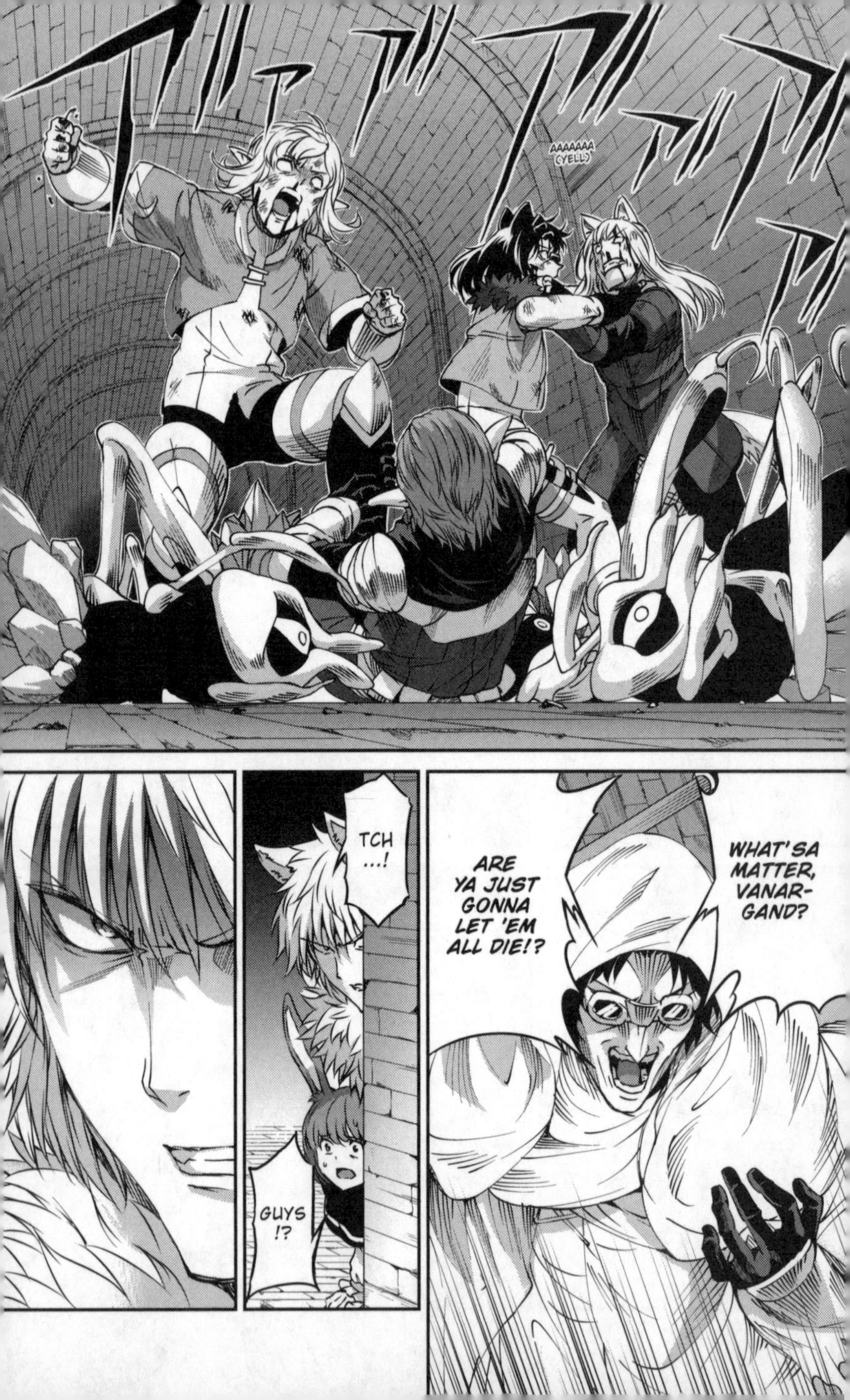
AAAAAAA (YELL)
WHAT'SA MATTER, VANARGAND?
ARE YA JUST GONNA LET 'EM ALL DIE!?
TCH ...!
GUYS !?

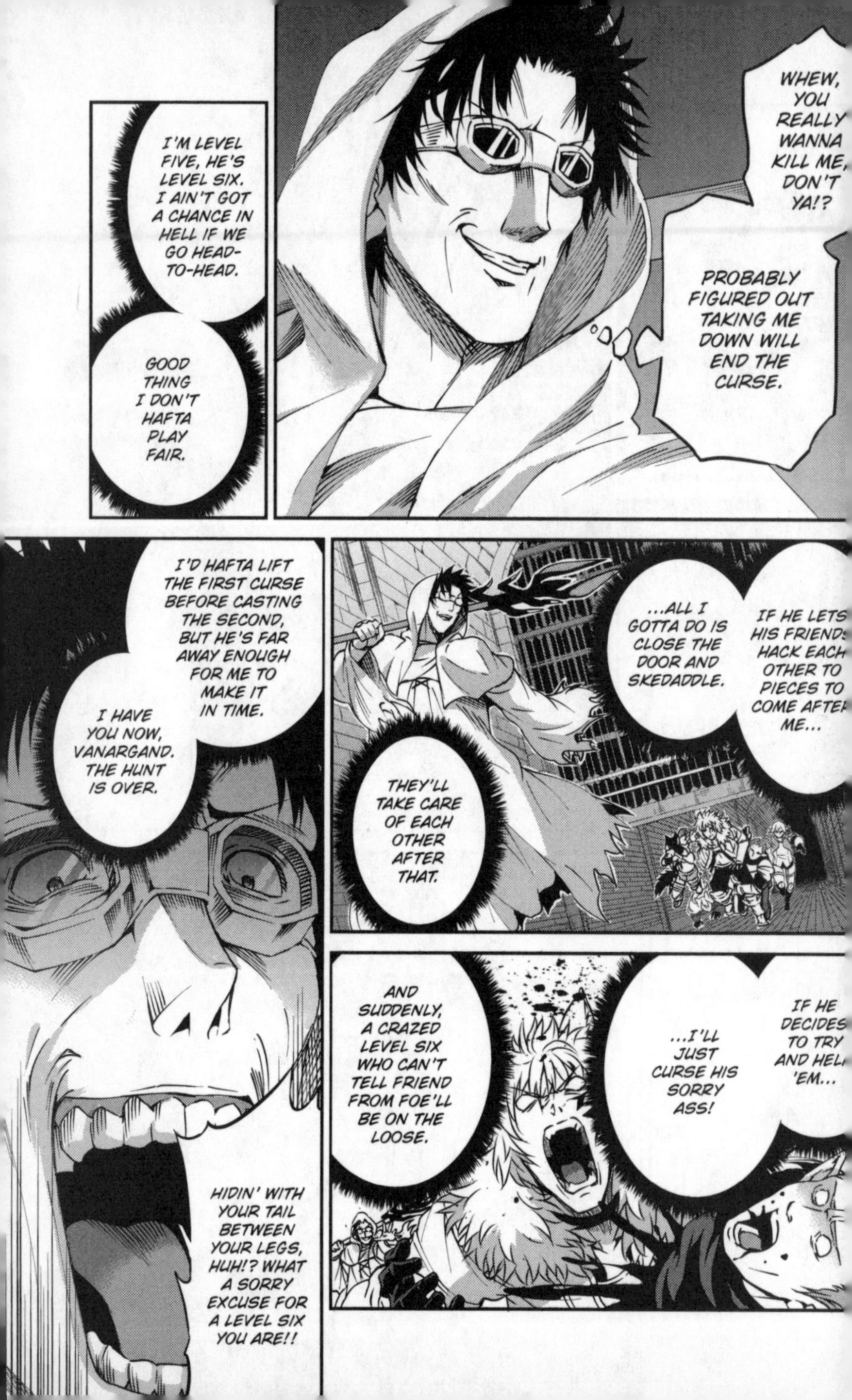
WHEW, YOU REALLY WANNA KILL ME, DON'T YA!?
PROBABLY FIGURED OUT TAKING ME DOWN WILL END THE CURSE.
I'M LEVEL FIVE, HE'S LEVEL SIX. I AIN'T GOT A CHANCE IN HELL IF WE GO HEAD-TO-HEAD.
GOOD THING I DON'T HAFTA PLAY FAIR.
IF HE LETS HIS FRIENDS HACK EACH OTHER TO PIECES TO COME AFTER ME...
...ALL I GOTTA DO IS CLOSE THE DOOR AND SKEDADDLE.
THEY'LL TAKE CARE OF EACH OTHER AFTER THAT.
IF HE DECIDES TO TRY AND HELP 'EM...
...I'LL JUST CURSE HIS SORRY ASS!
AND SUDDENLY, A CRAZED LEVEL SIX WHO CAN'T TELL FRIEND FROM FOE'LL BE ON THE LOOSE.
I'D HAFTA LIFT THE FIRST CURSE BEFORE CASTING THE SECOND, BUT HE'S FAR AWAY ENOUGH FOR ME TO MAKE IT IN TIME.
I HAVE YOU NOW, VANARGAND. THE HUNT IS OVER.
HIDIN' WITH YOUR TAIL BETWEEN YOUR LEGS, HUH!? WHAT A SORRY EXCUSE FOR A LEVEL SIX YOU ARE!!

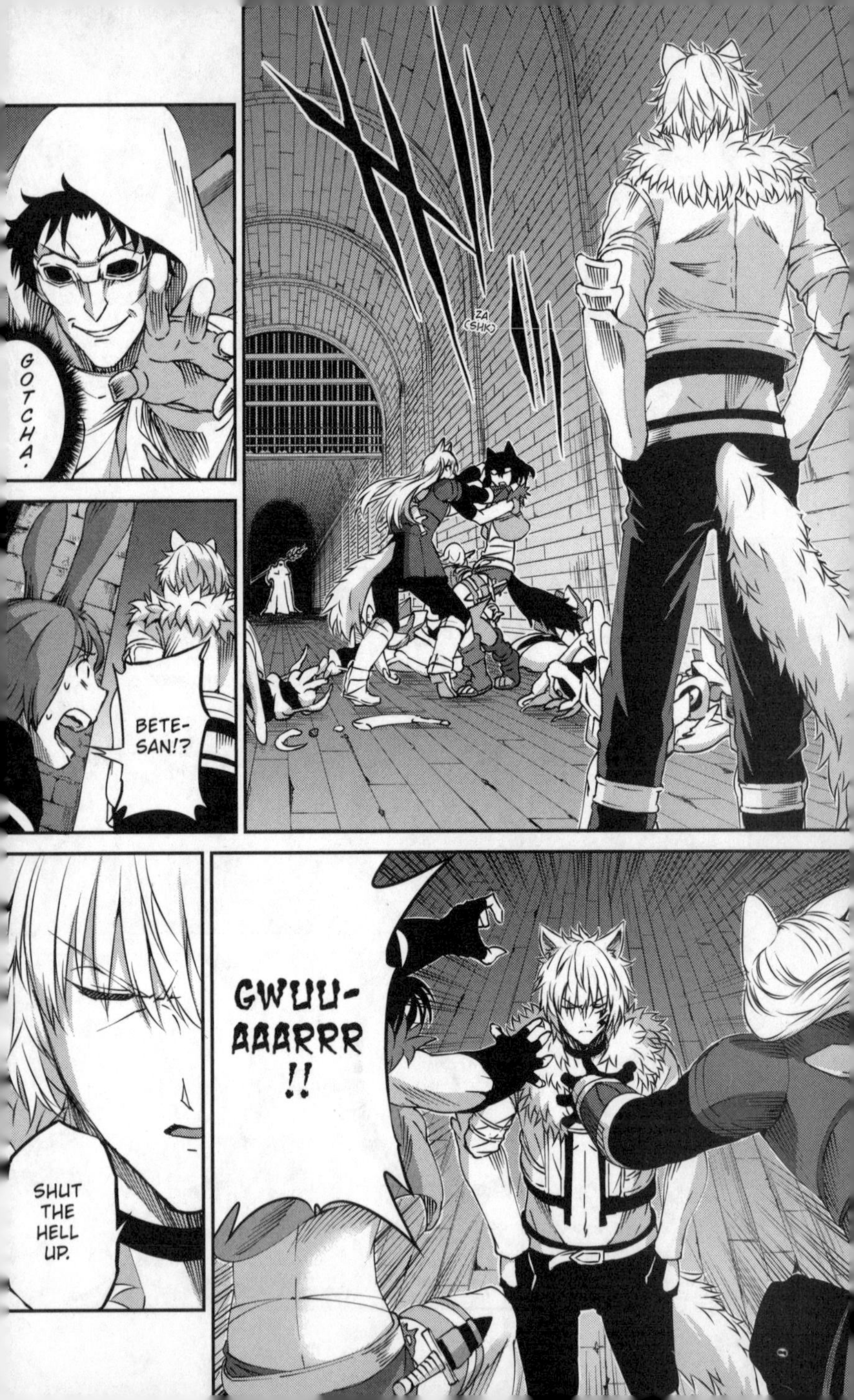
ZA (SHK)
GOTCHA.
BETE-SAN!?
GWUU-AAARRR!!
SHUT THE HELL UP.

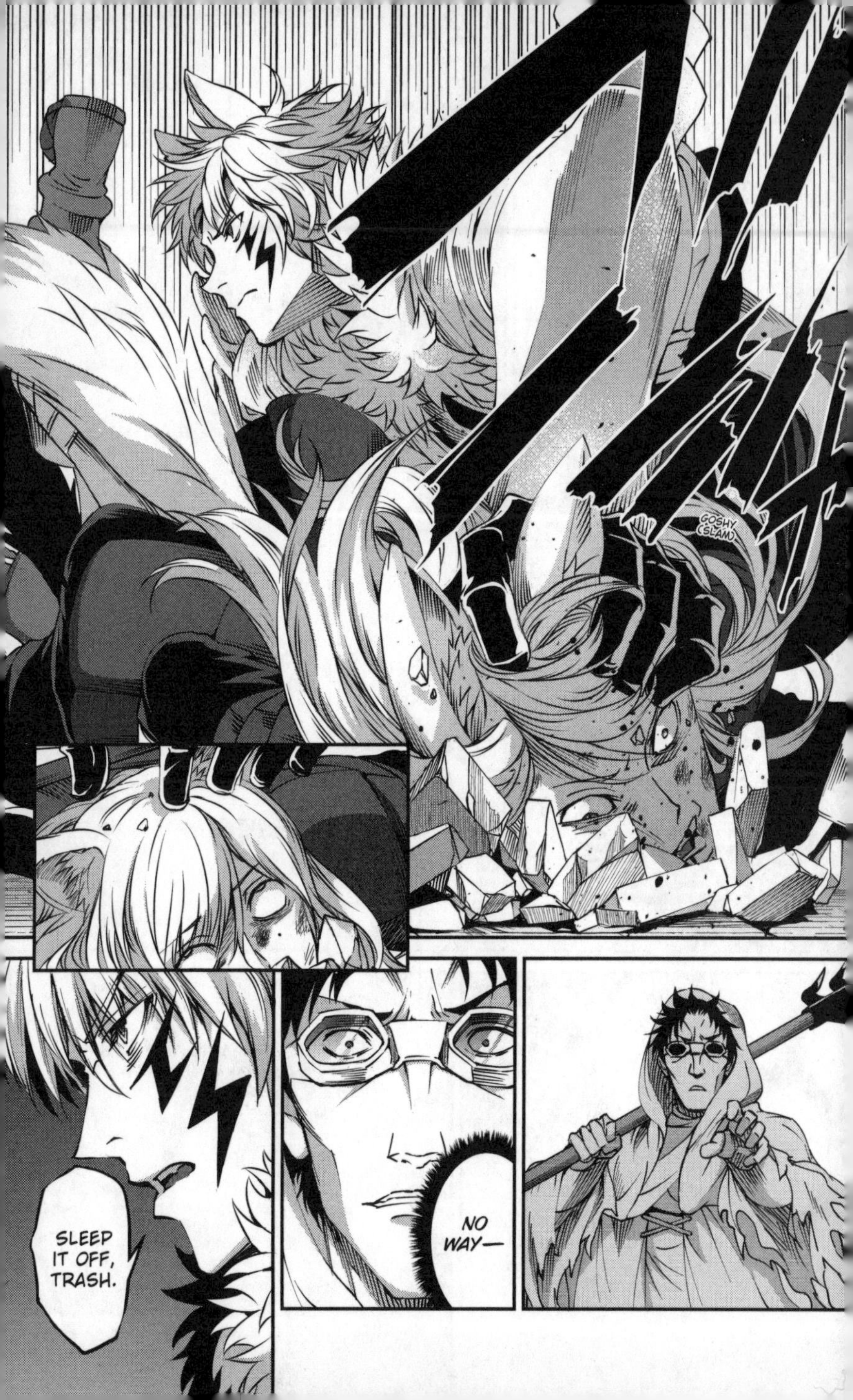
GOSHY (SLAM)
NO WAY—
SLEEP IT OFF, TRASH.

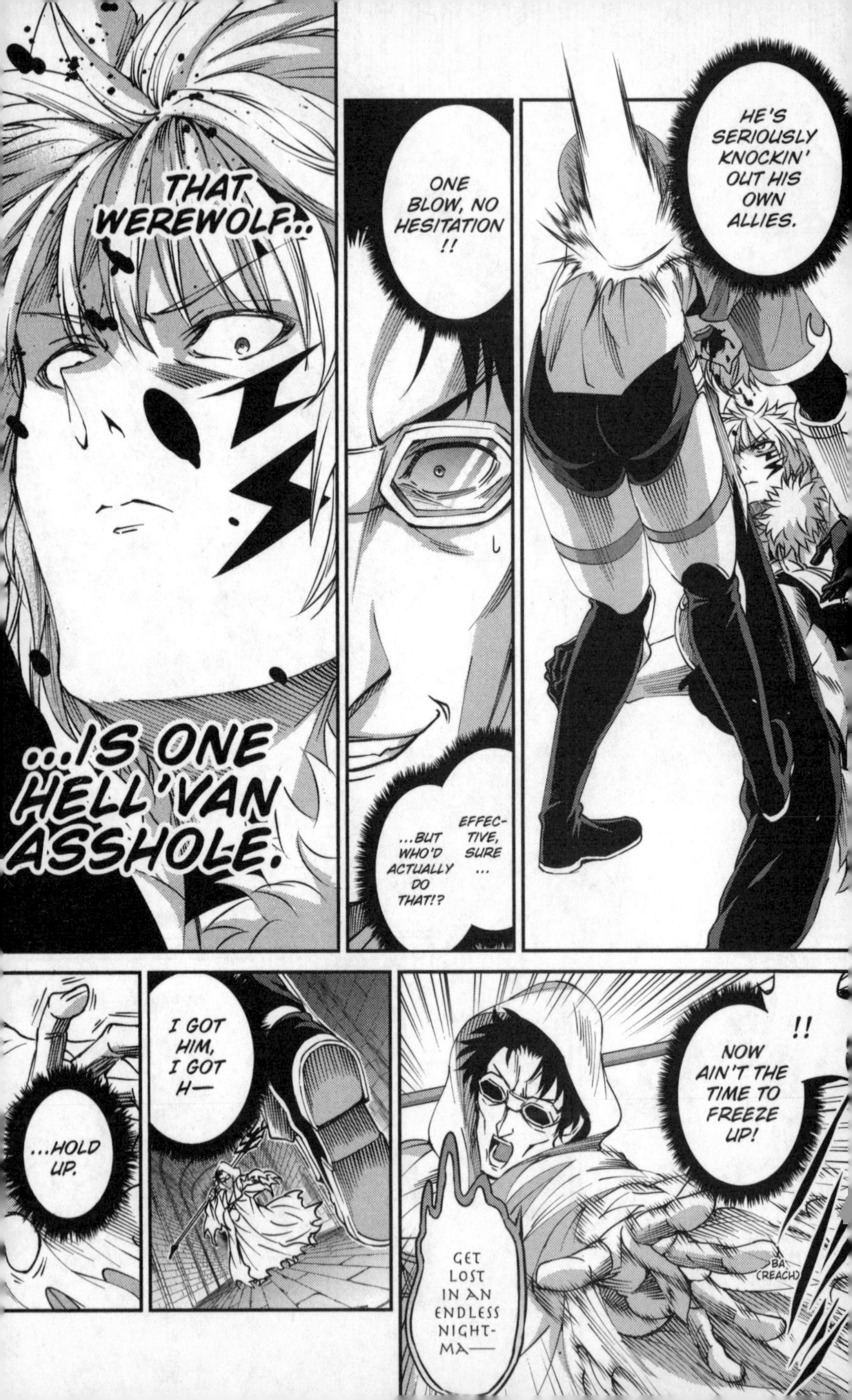
HE'S SERIOUSLY KNOCKIN' OUT HIS OWN ALLIES.
ONE BLOW, NO HESITATION !!
EFFEC-TIVE, SURE ...
...BUT WHO'D ACTUALLY DO THAT!?
THAT WEREWOLF...
...IS ONE HELL'VAN ASSHOLE.
!!
NOW AIN'T THE TIME TO FREEZE UP!
BA (REACH)
GET LOST IN AN ENDLESS NIGHT-MA—
I GOT HIM, I GOT H—
...HOLD UP.

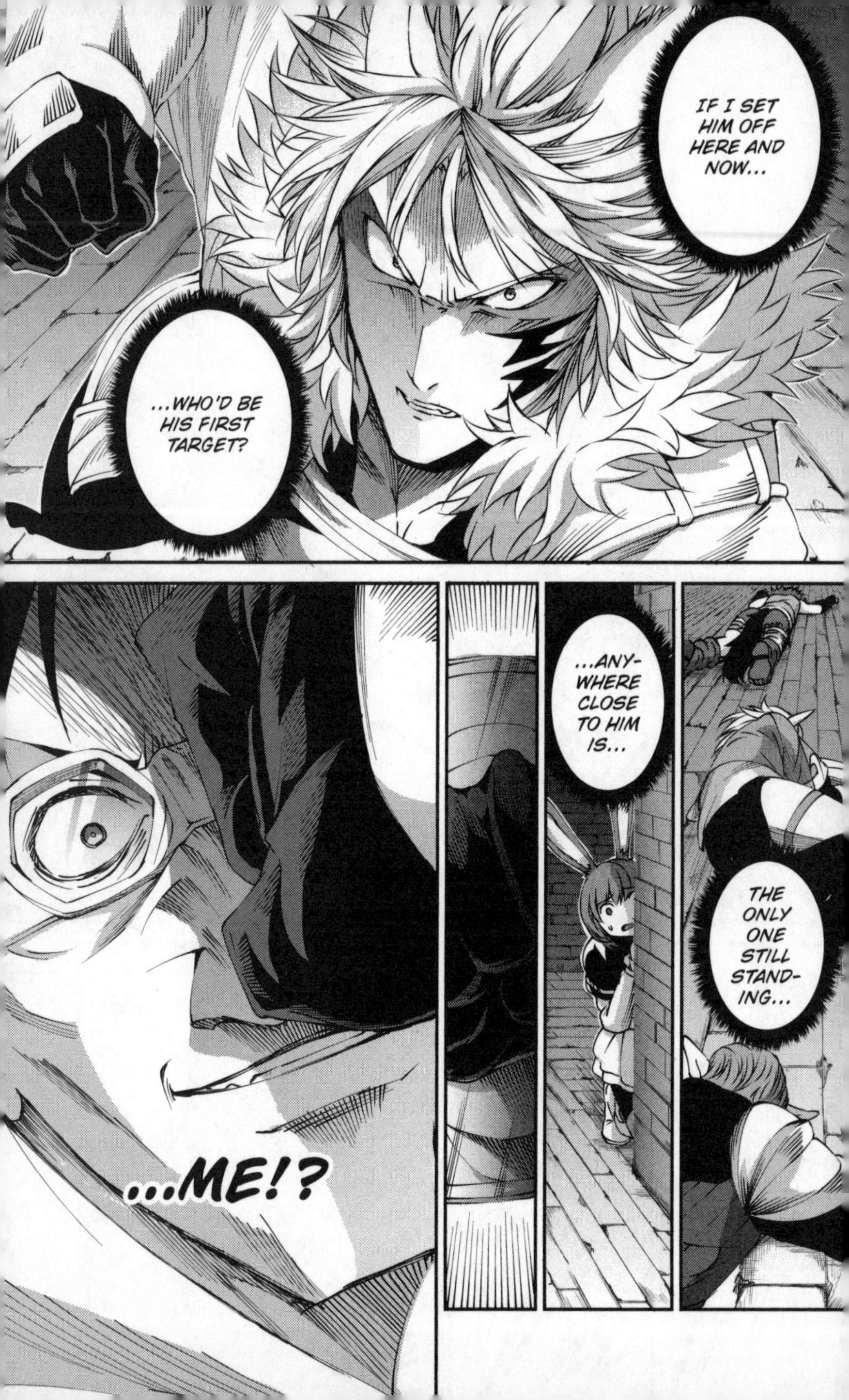
IF I SET HIM OFF HERE AND NOW...
...WHO'D BE HIS FIRST TARGET?
THE ONLY ONE STILL STAND-ING...
...ANY-WHERE CLOSE TO HIM IS...
...ME!?

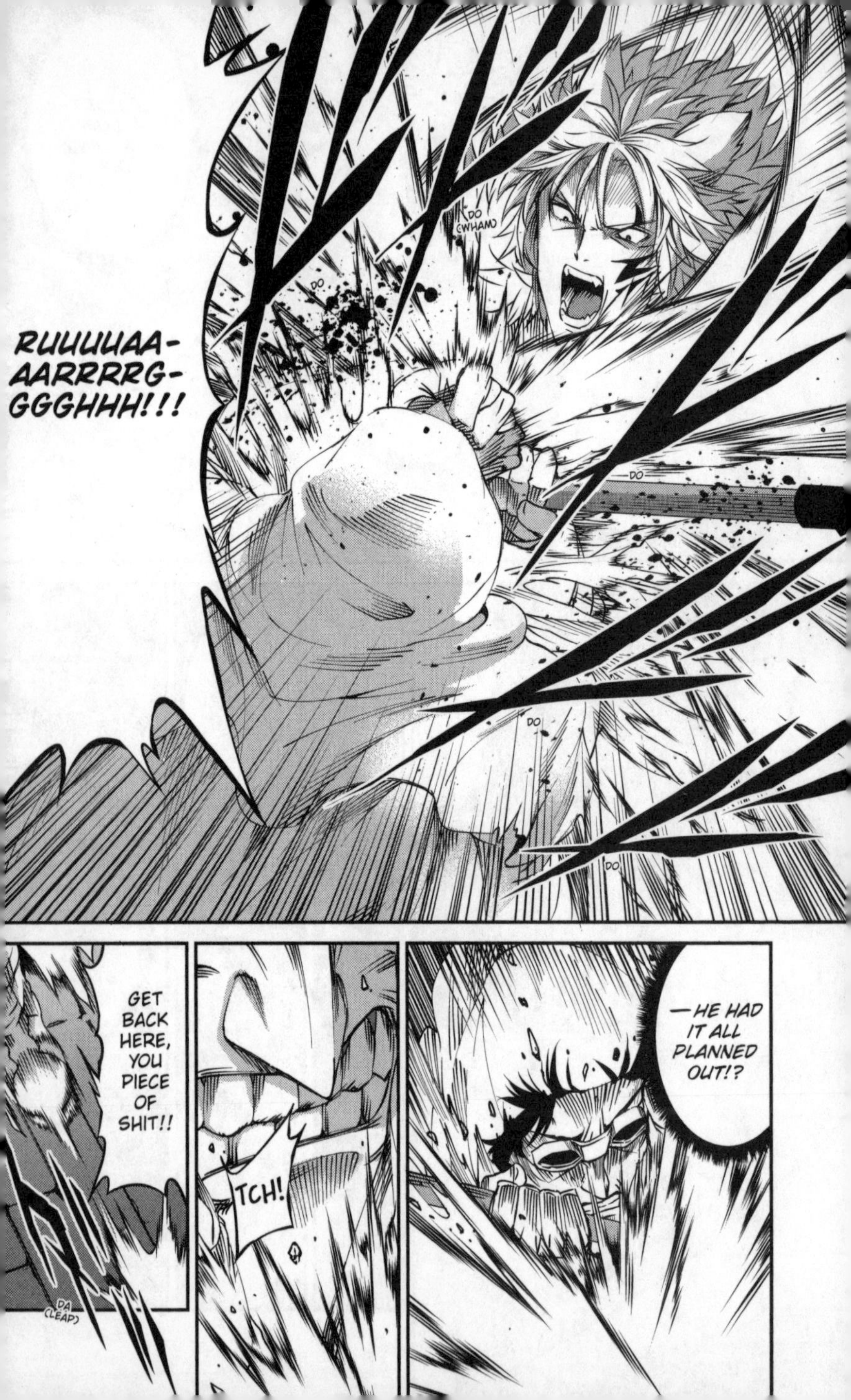
DO (WHAM)
DO
DO
RUUUUAA-AARRRRG-GGGHHH!!!
DO
DO
—HE HAD IT ALL PLANNED OUT!?
TCH!
GET BACK HERE, YOU PIECE OF SHIT!!
DA (LEAP)

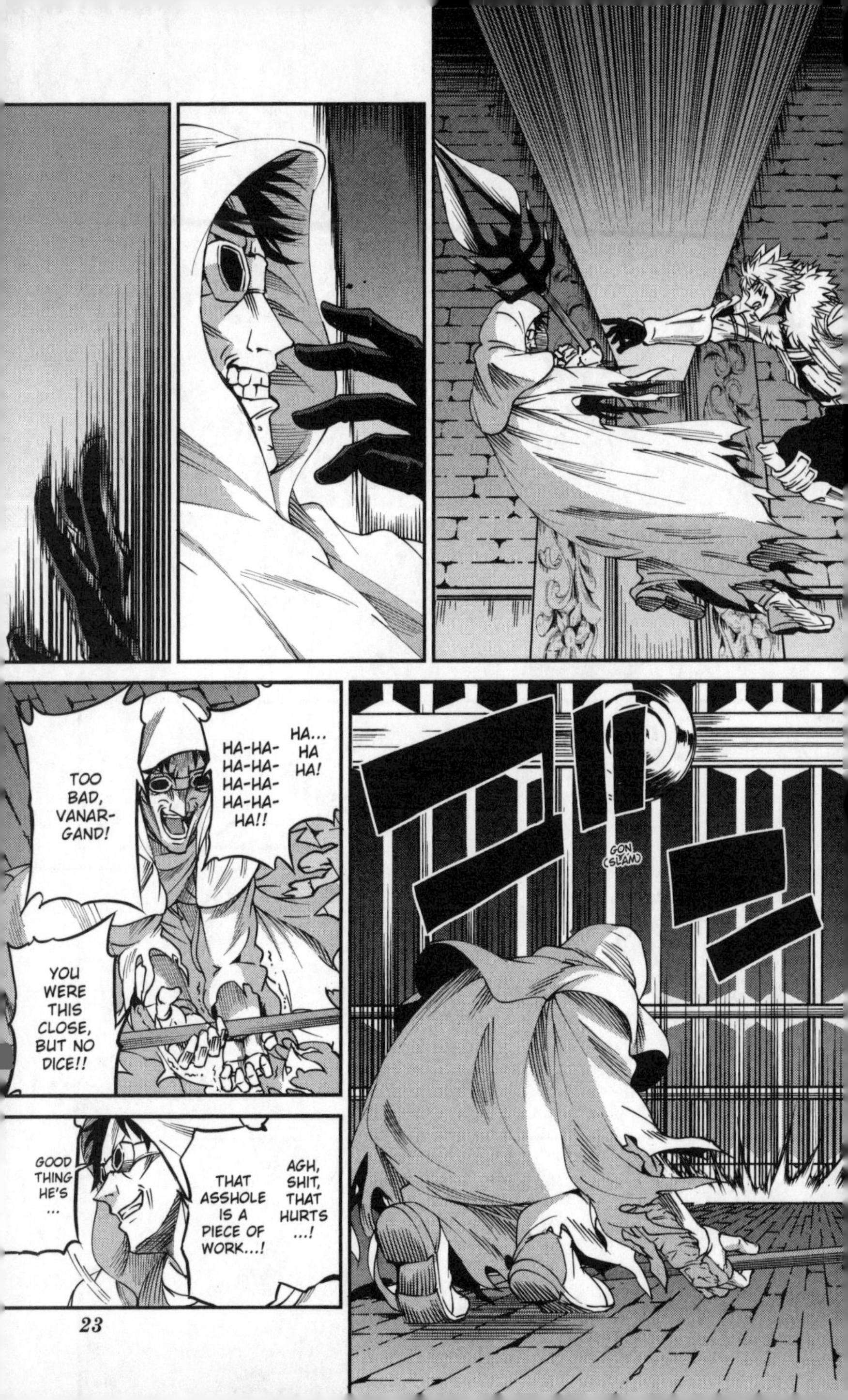
GON (SLAM)
HA... HA HA!
HA-HA-HA-HA-HA-HA-HA-HA-HA!!
TOO BAD, VANARGAND!
YOU WERE THIS CLOSE, BUT NO DICE!!
AGH, SHIT, THAT HURTS ...!
THAT ASSHOLE IS A PIECE OF WORK...!
GOOD THING HE'S ...

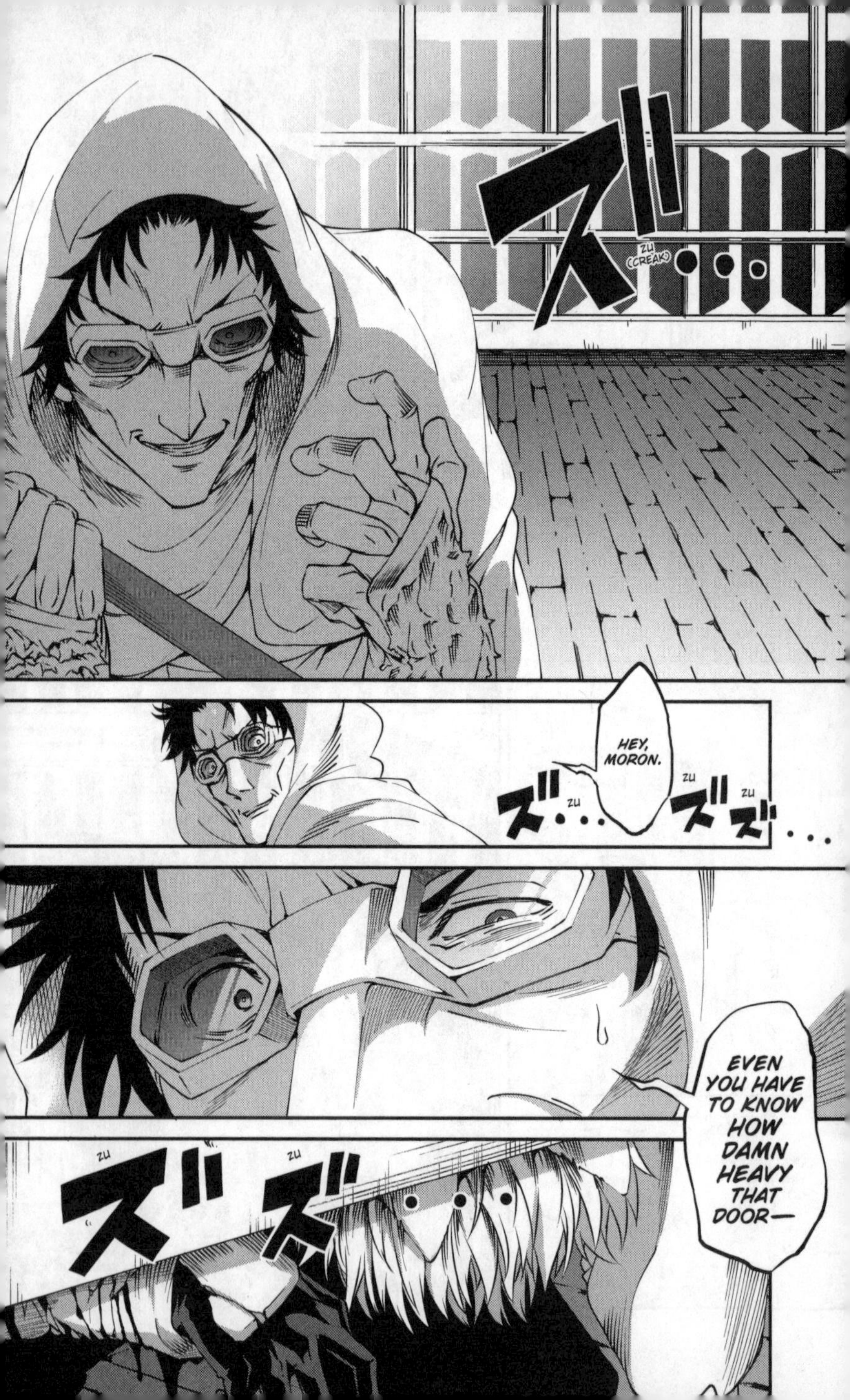
ZU
(CREAK)
HEY, MORON.
ZU
ZU
ZU
EVEN YOU HAVE TO KNOW HOW DAMN HEAVY THAT DOOR—
ZU
ZU

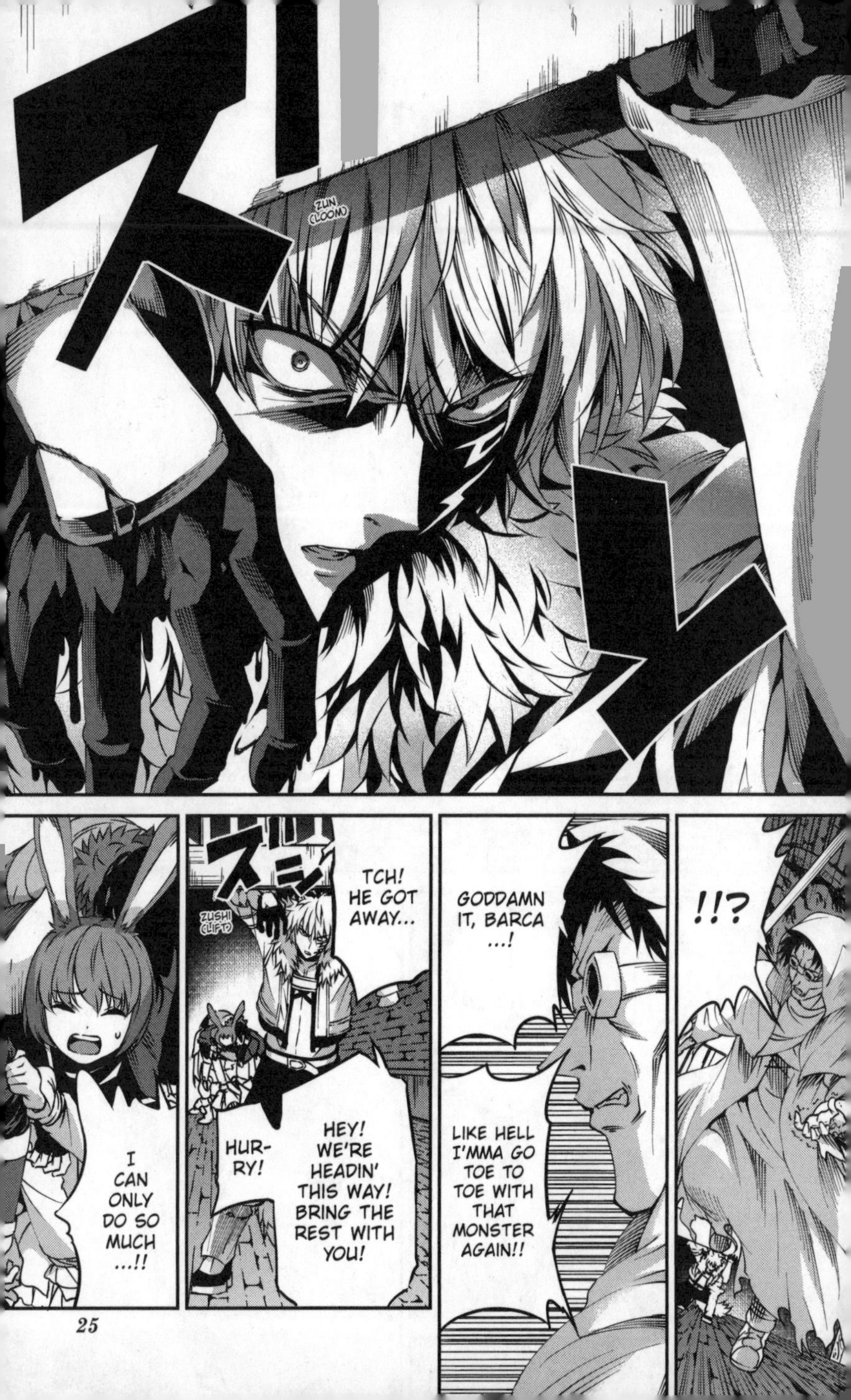
ZUN (LOOM)
!!?
GODDAMN IT, BARCA ...!
LIKE HELL I'MMA GO TOE TO TOE WITH THAT MONSTER AGAIN!!
TCH! HE GOT AWAY...
ZUSHI (LIFT)
HEY! WE'RE HEADIN' THIS WAY! BRING THE REST WITH YOU!
HUR-RY!
I CAN ONLY DO SO MUCH ...!!

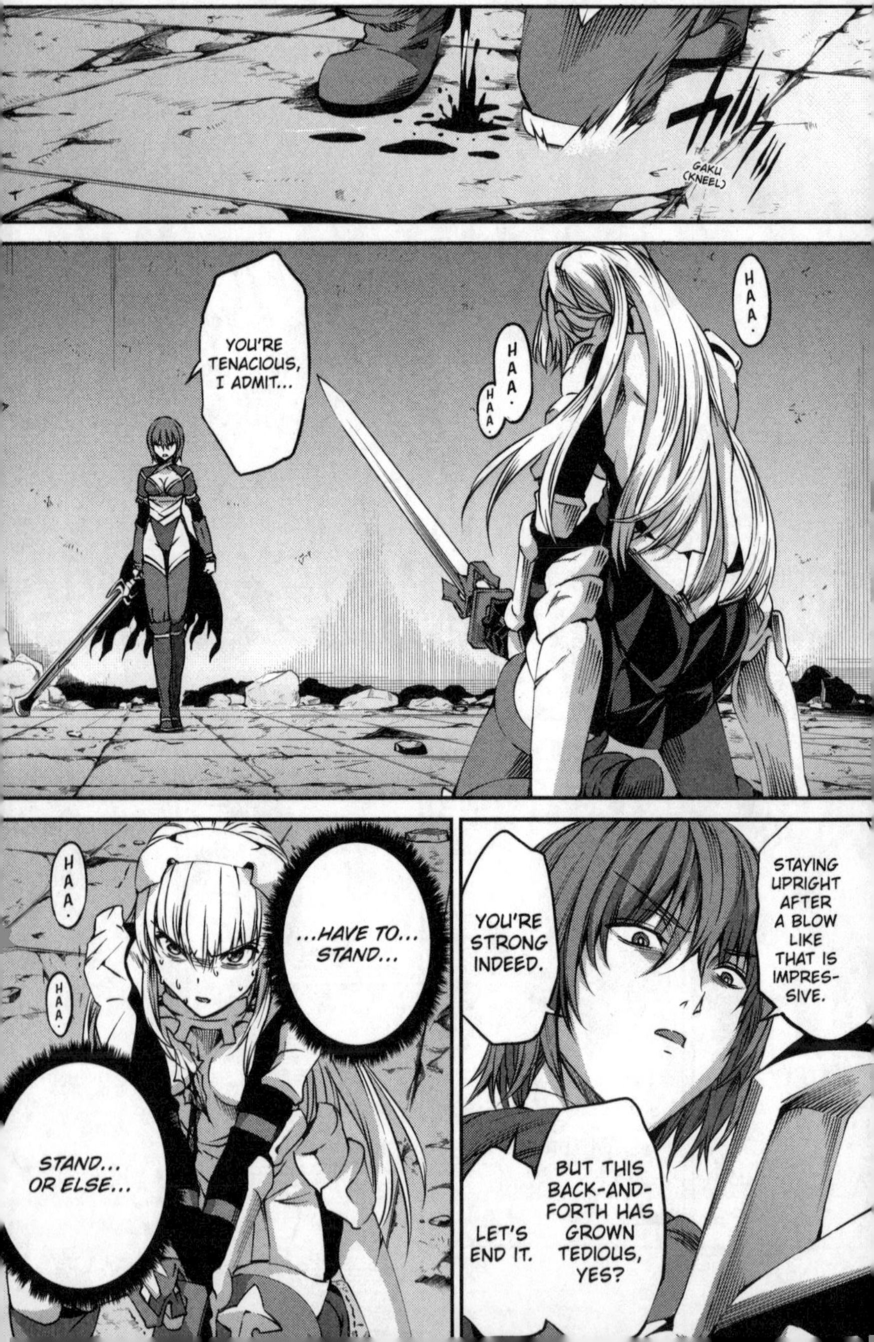
GAKU (KNEEL)
HAA.
HAA.
HAA.
YOU'RE TENACIOUS, I ADMIT...
STAYING UPRIGHT AFTER A BLOW LIKE THAT IS IMPRESSIVE.
YOU'RE STRONG INDEED.
BUT THIS BACK-AND-FORTH HAS GROWN TEDIOUS, YES?
LET'S END IT.
...HAVE TO... STAND...
HAA.
HAA.
STAND... OR ELSE...

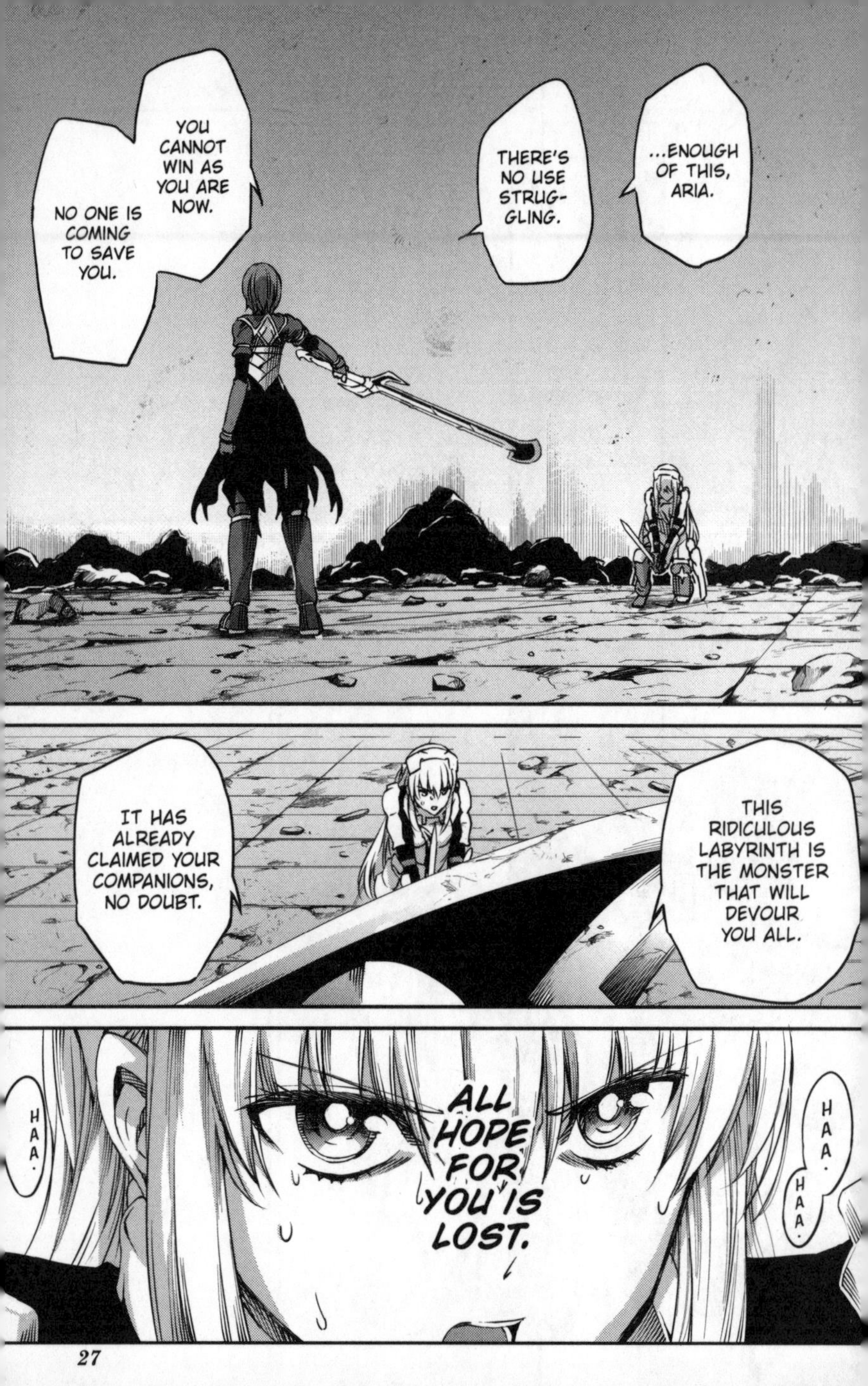
...ENOUGH OF THIS, ARIA.
THERE'S NO USE STRUG-GLING.
YOU CANNOT WIN AS YOU ARE NOW.
NO ONE IS COMING TO SAVE YOU.
THIS RIDICULOUS LABYRINTH IS THE MONSTER THAT WILL DEVOUR YOU ALL.
IT HAS ALREADY CLAIMED YOUR COMPANIONS, NO DOUBT.
HAA. HAA.
ALL HOPE FOR YOU IS LOST.
HAA.

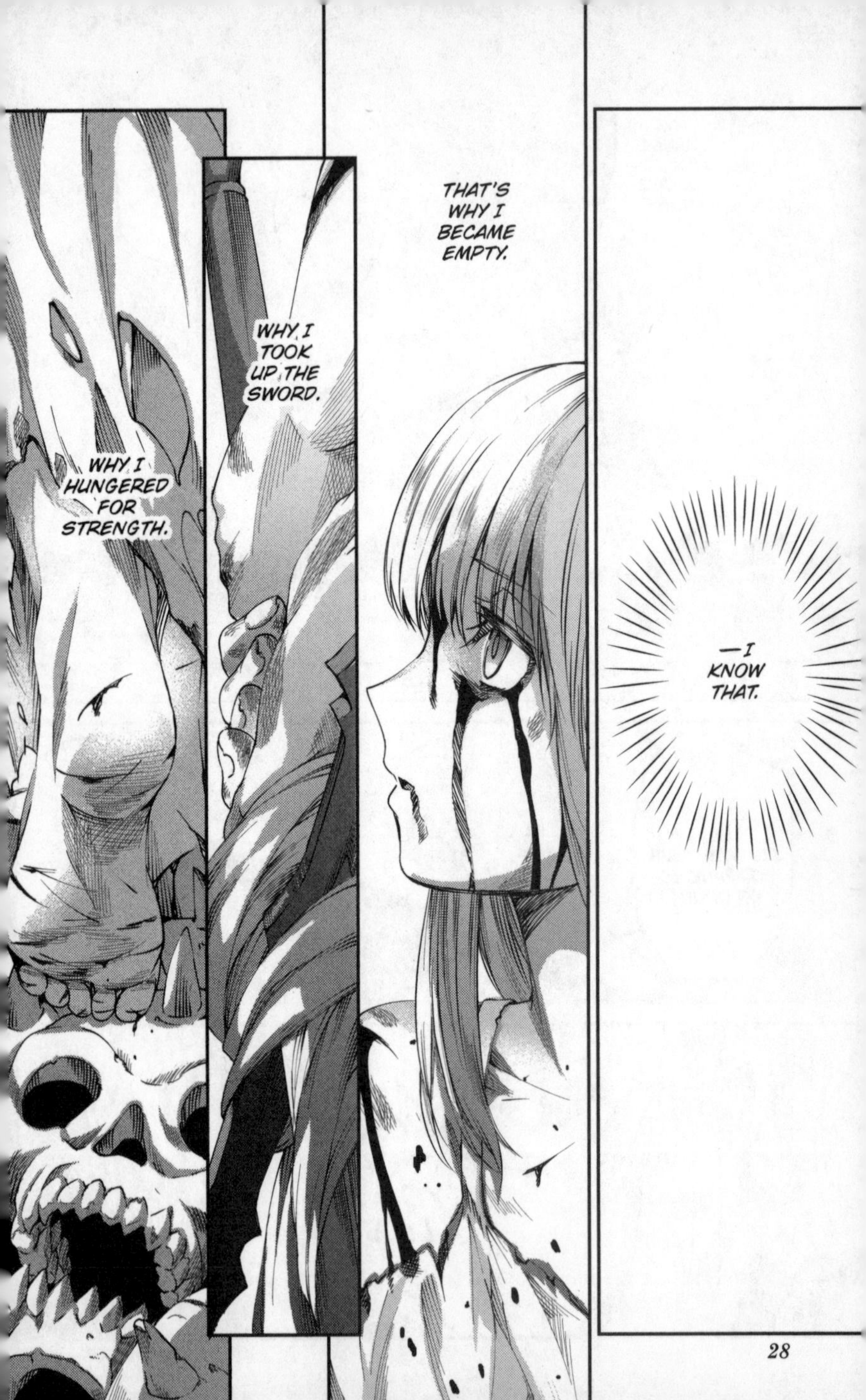
—I KNOW THAT.
THAT'S WHY I BECAME EMPTY.
WHY I TOOK UP THE SWORD.
WHY I HUNGERED FOR STRENGTH.

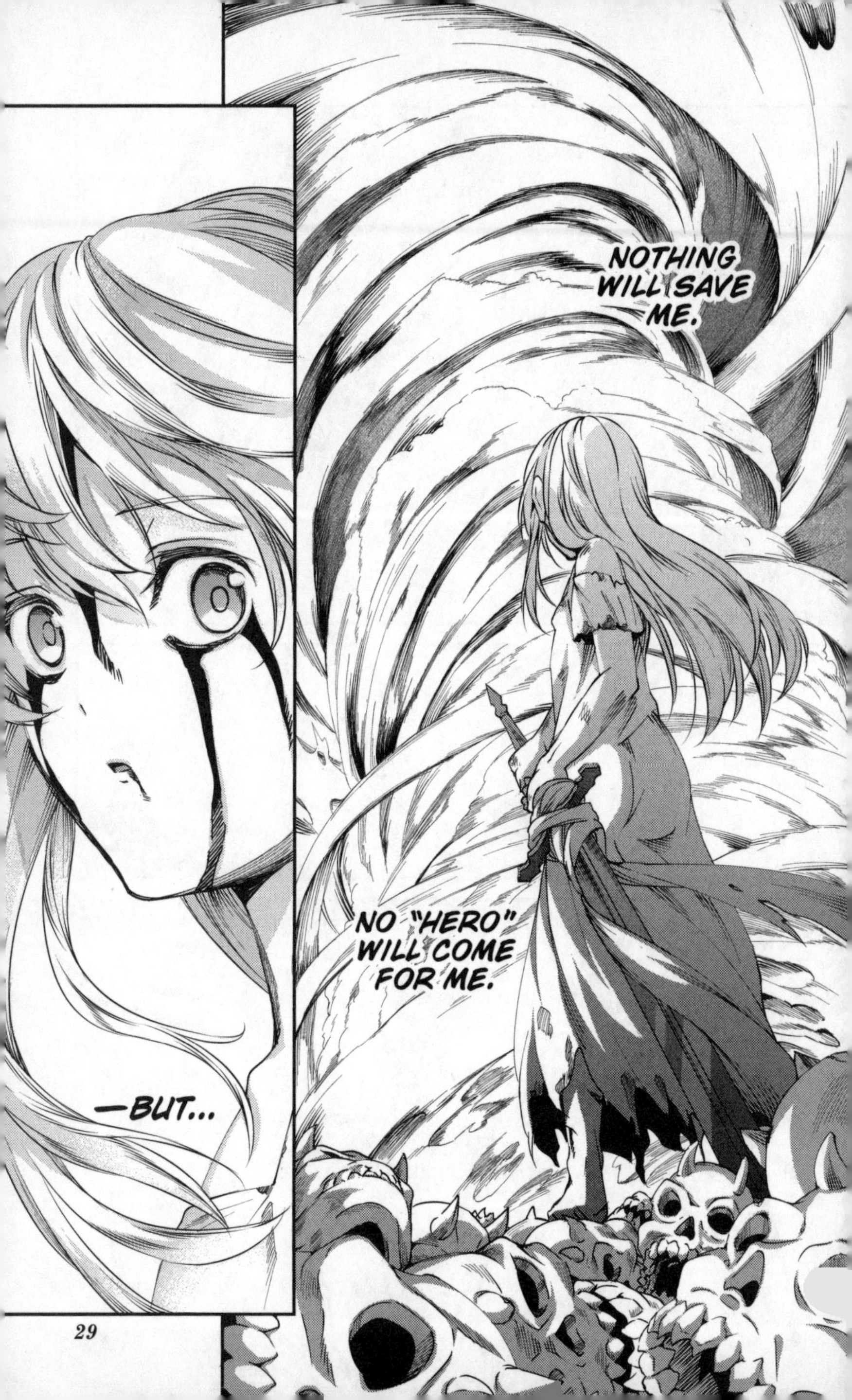
NOTHING WILL SAVE ME.
NO "HERO" WILL COME FOR ME.
—BUT...

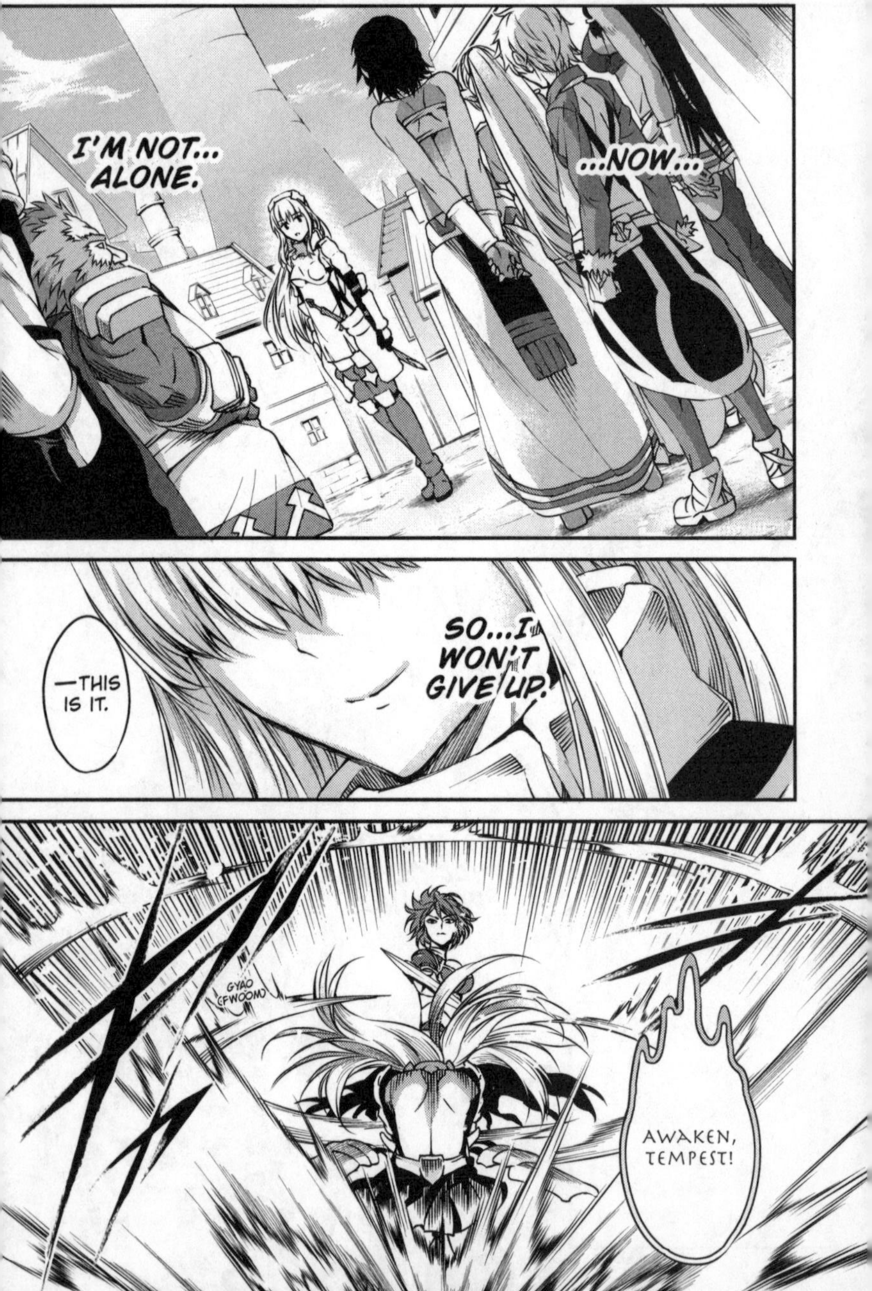
I'M NOT... ALONE.
...NOW...
SO...I WON'T GIVE UP.
—THIS IS IT.
AWAKEN, TEMPEST!
GYAO (FWOOM)

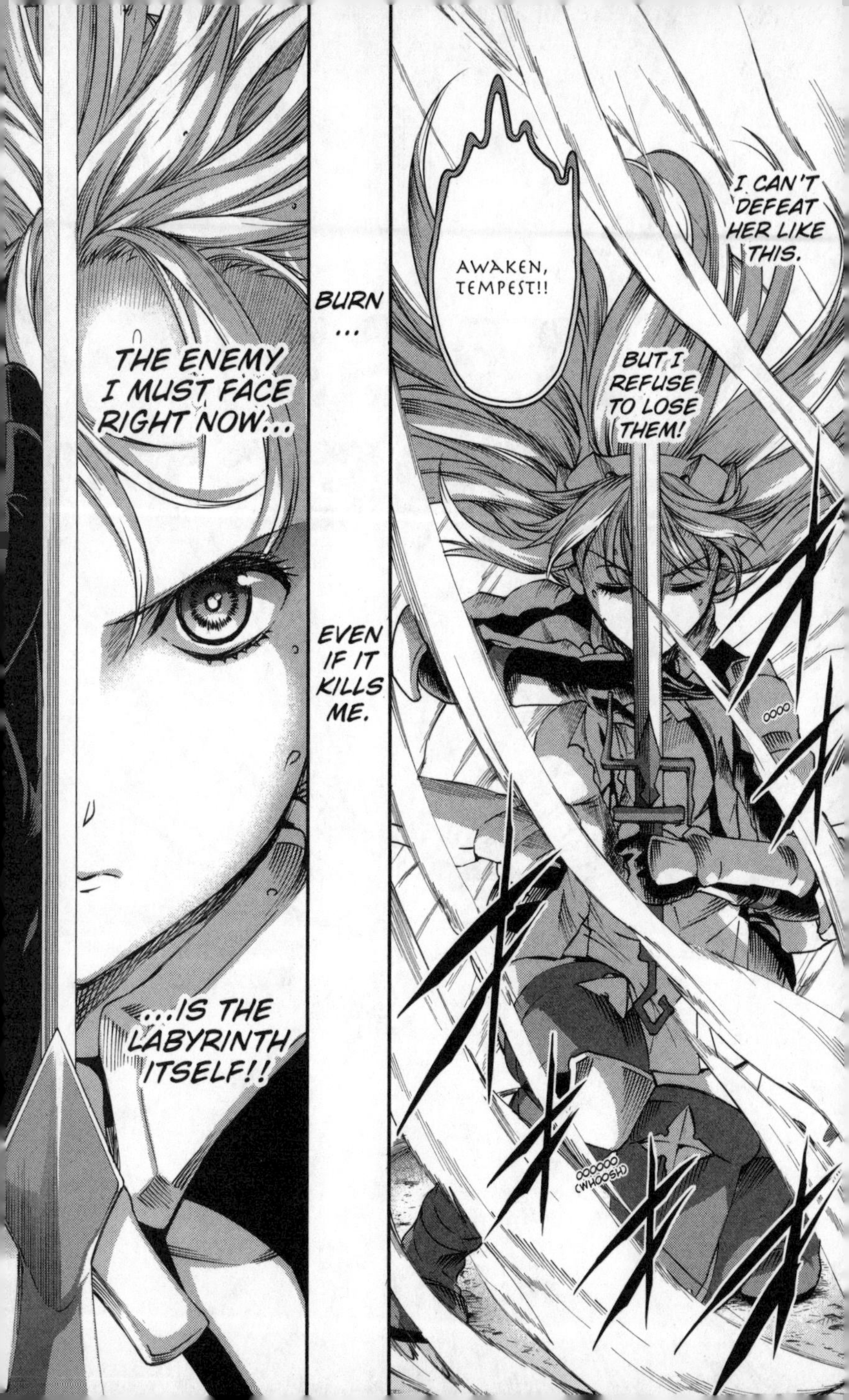

I CAN'T DEFEAT HER LIKE THIS.
BUT I REFUSE TO LOSE THEM!
AWAKEN, TEMPEST!!
OOOOOO (WHOOSH)
BURN...
EVEN IF IT KILLS ME.
THE ENEMY I MUST FACE RIGHT NOW...
...IS THE LABYRINTH ITSELF!!

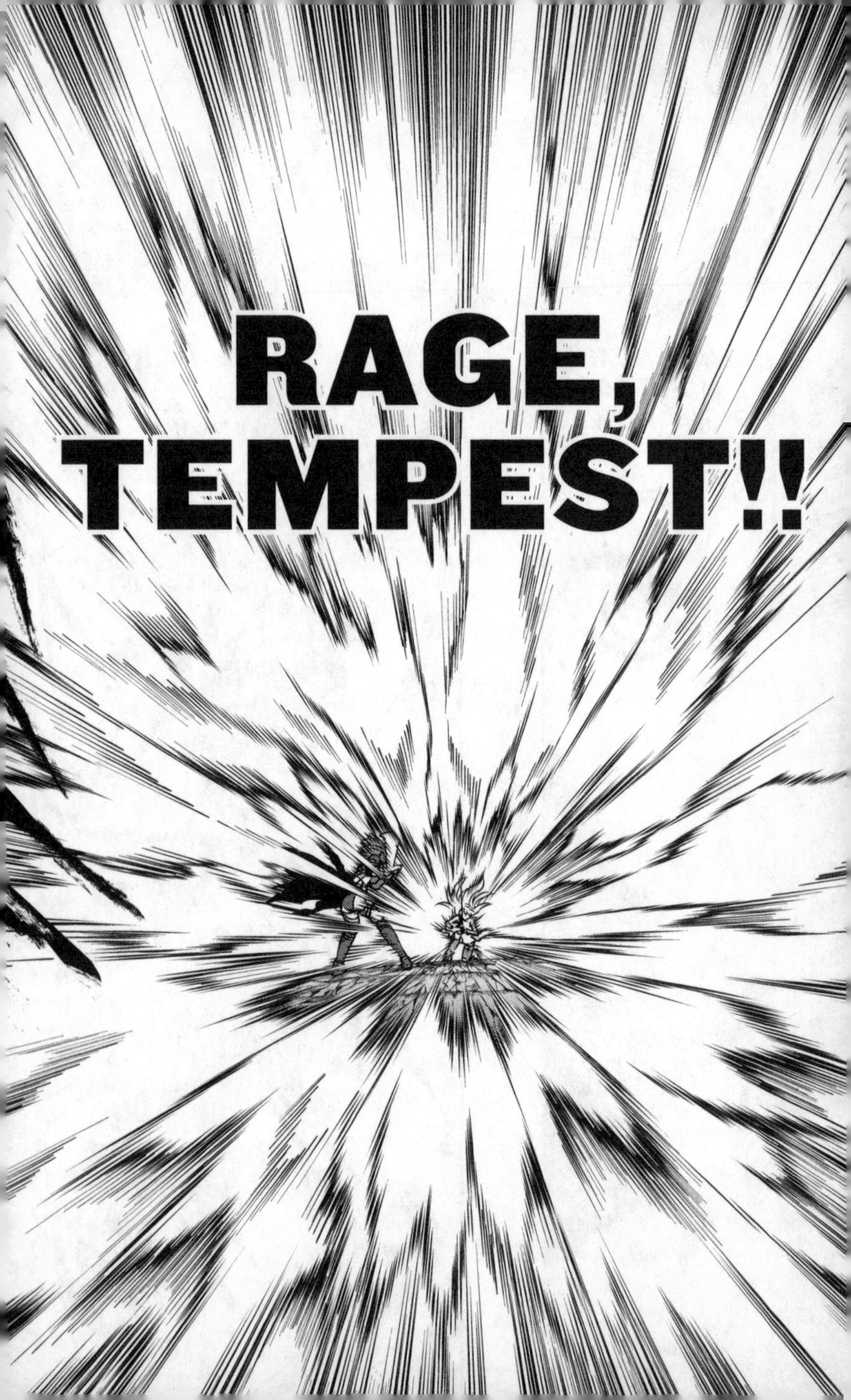
RAGE, TEMPEST!!

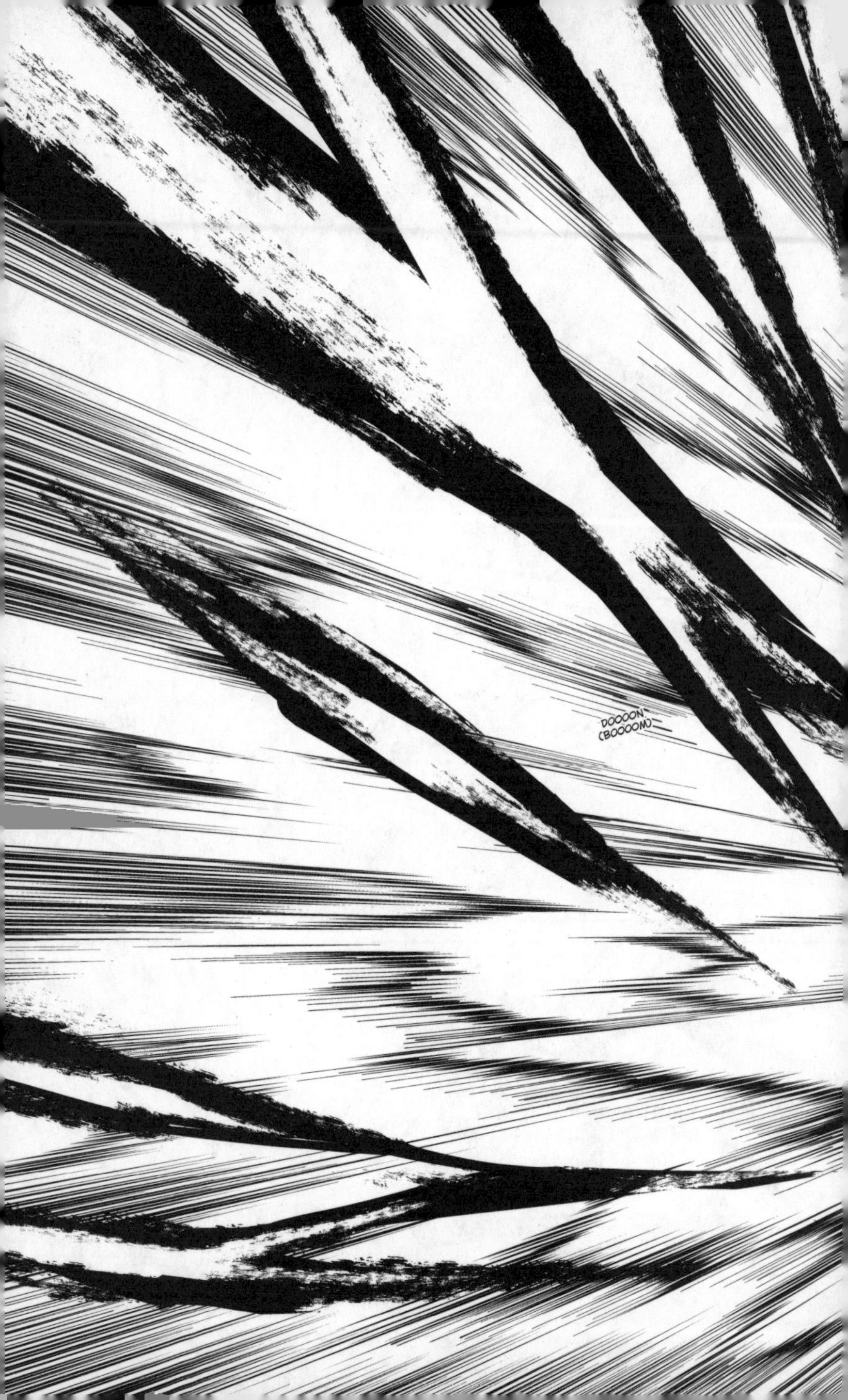
DOOOON
(BOOOOM)

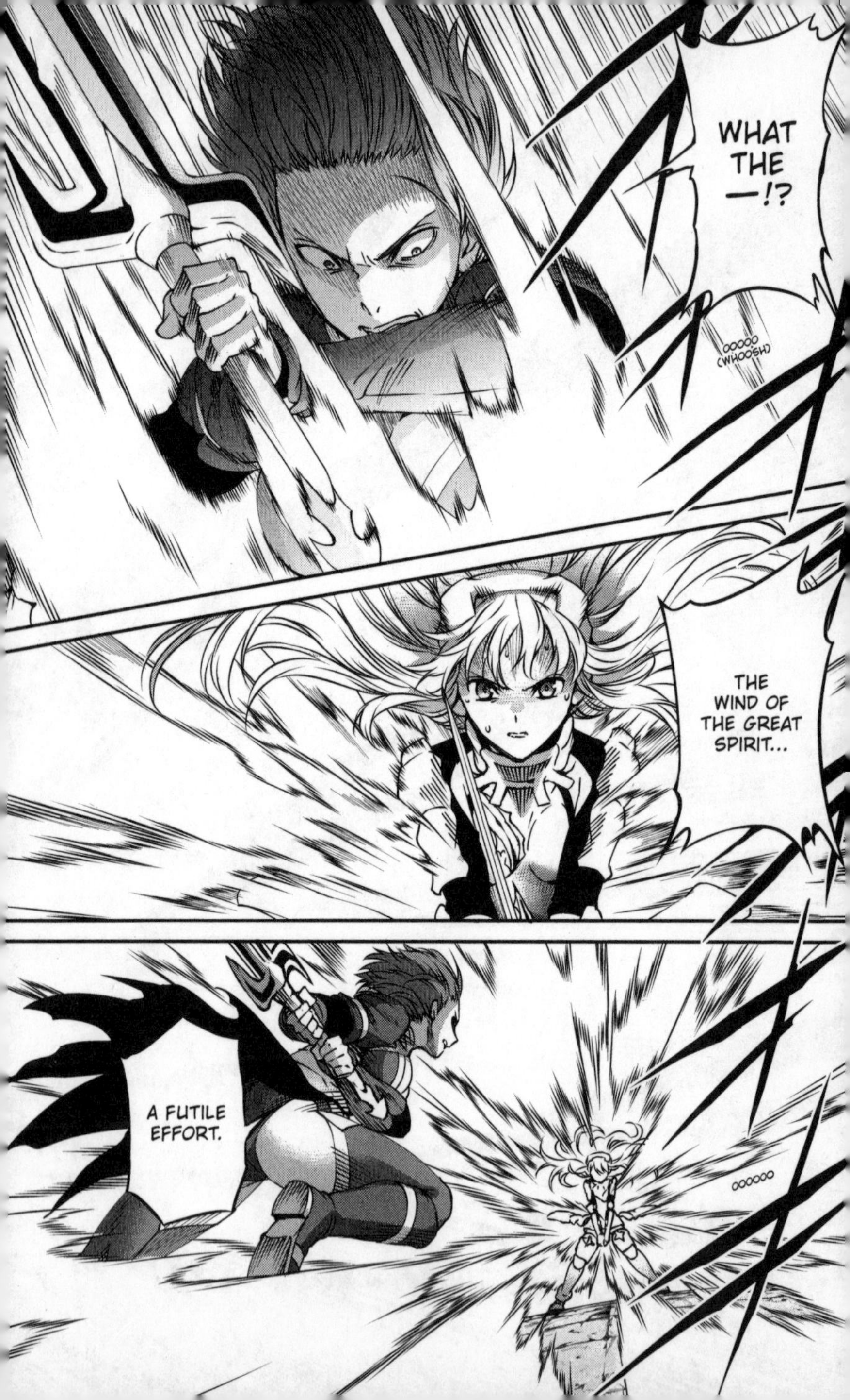
WHAT THE—!?
OOOOO (WHOOSH)
THE WIND OF THE GREAT SPIRIT...
OOOOOO
A FUTILE EFFORT.

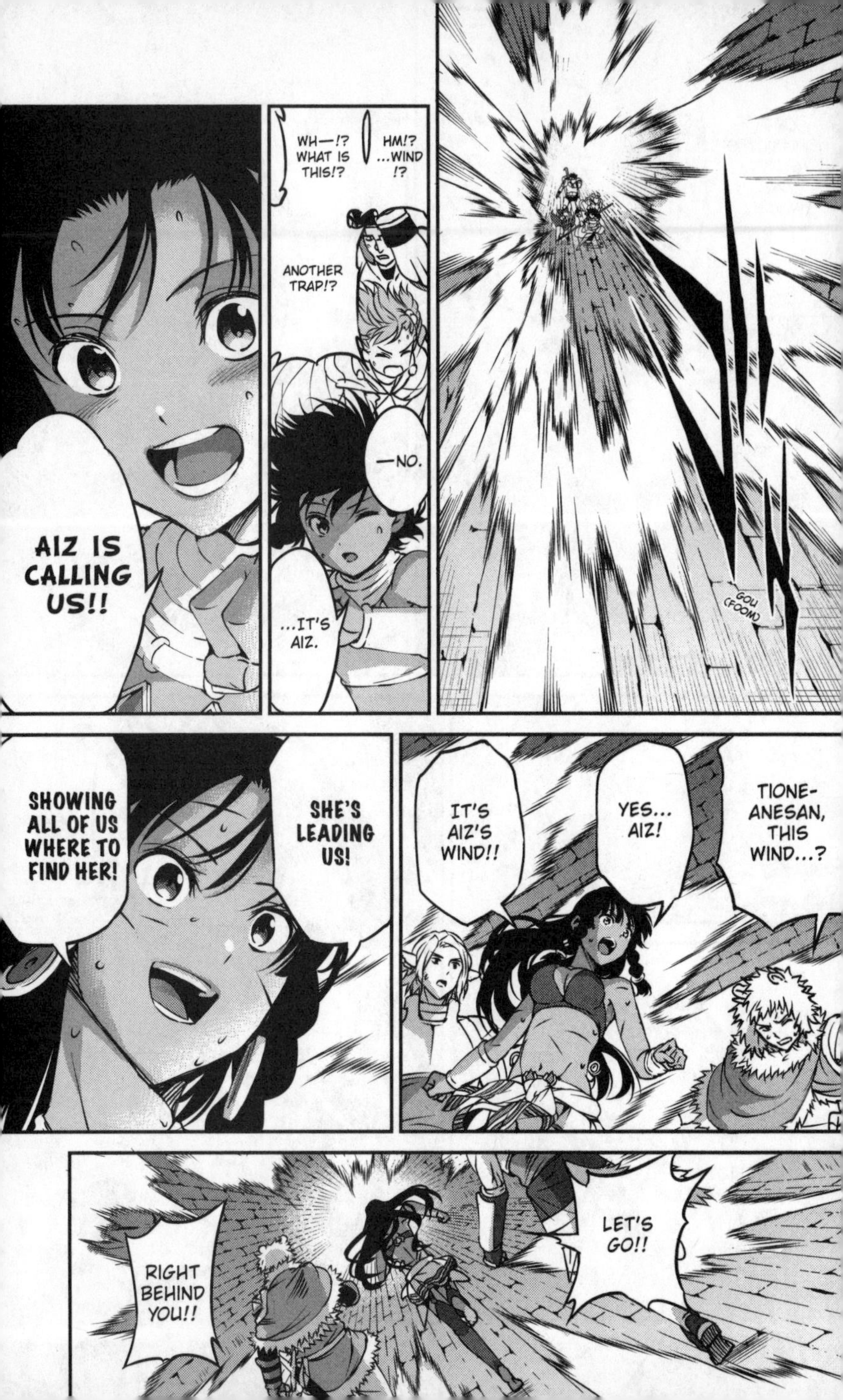
GOU (FOOM)
HM!? ...WIND!?
WH—!? WHAT IS THIS!?
ANOTHER TRAP!?
—NO.
...IT'S AIZ.
AIZ IS CALLING US!!
TIONE-ANESAN, THIS WIND...?
YES... AIZ!
IT'S AIZ'S WIND!!
SHE'S LEADING US!
SHOWING ALL OF US WHERE TO FIND HER!
LET'S GO!!
RIGHT BEHIND YOU!!

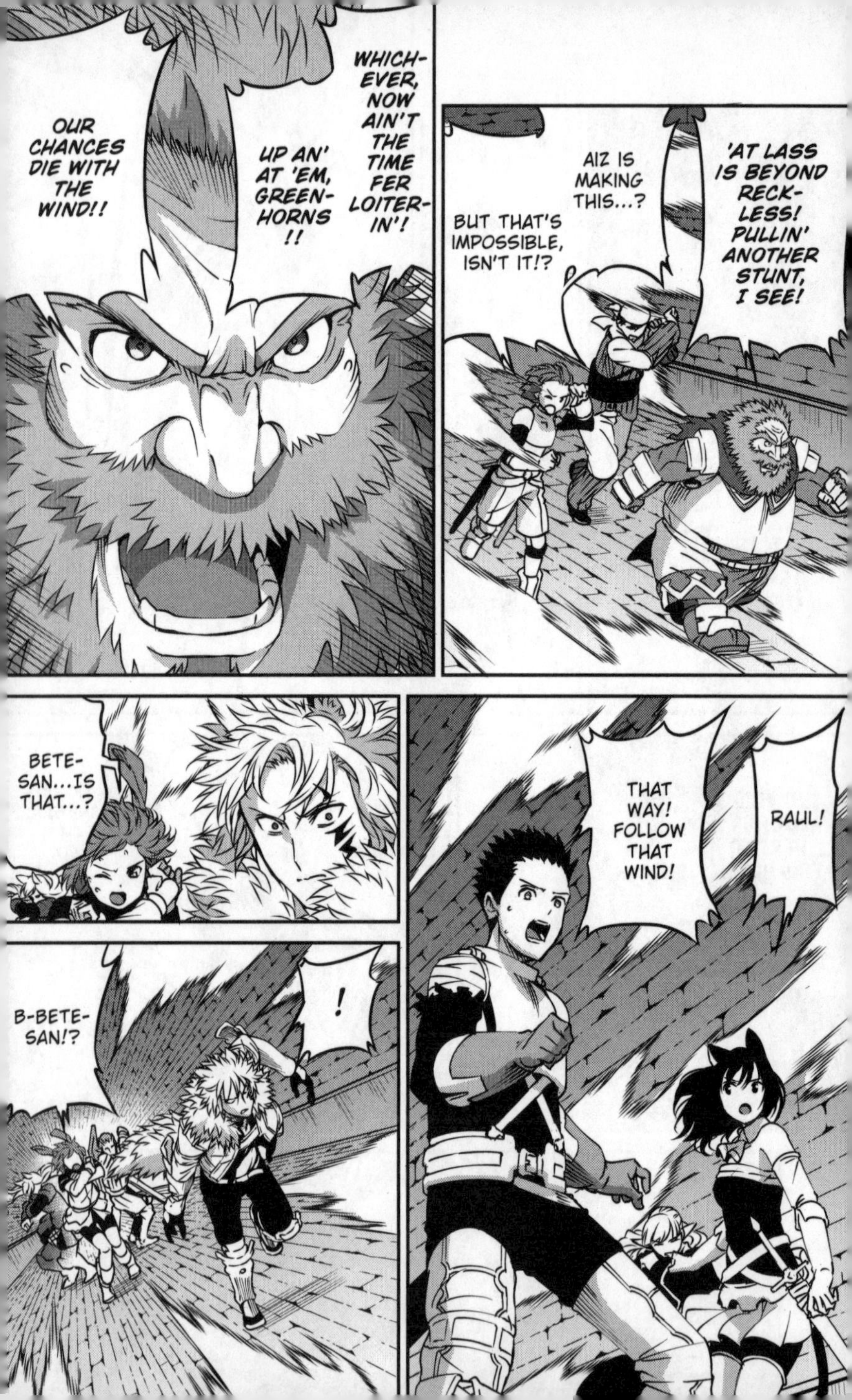
'AT LASS IS BEYOND RECK-LESS! PULLIN' ANOTHER STUNT, I SEE!
AIZ IS MAKING THIS...?
BUT THAT'S IMPOSSIBLE, ISN'T IT!?
WHICH-EVER, NOW AIN'T THE TIME FER LOITER-IN'!
UP AN' AT 'EM, GREEN-HORNS!!
OUR CHANCES DIE WITH THE WIND!!
RAUL!
THAT WAY! FOLLOW THAT WIND!
BETE-SAN...IS THAT...?
!
B-BETE-SAN!?

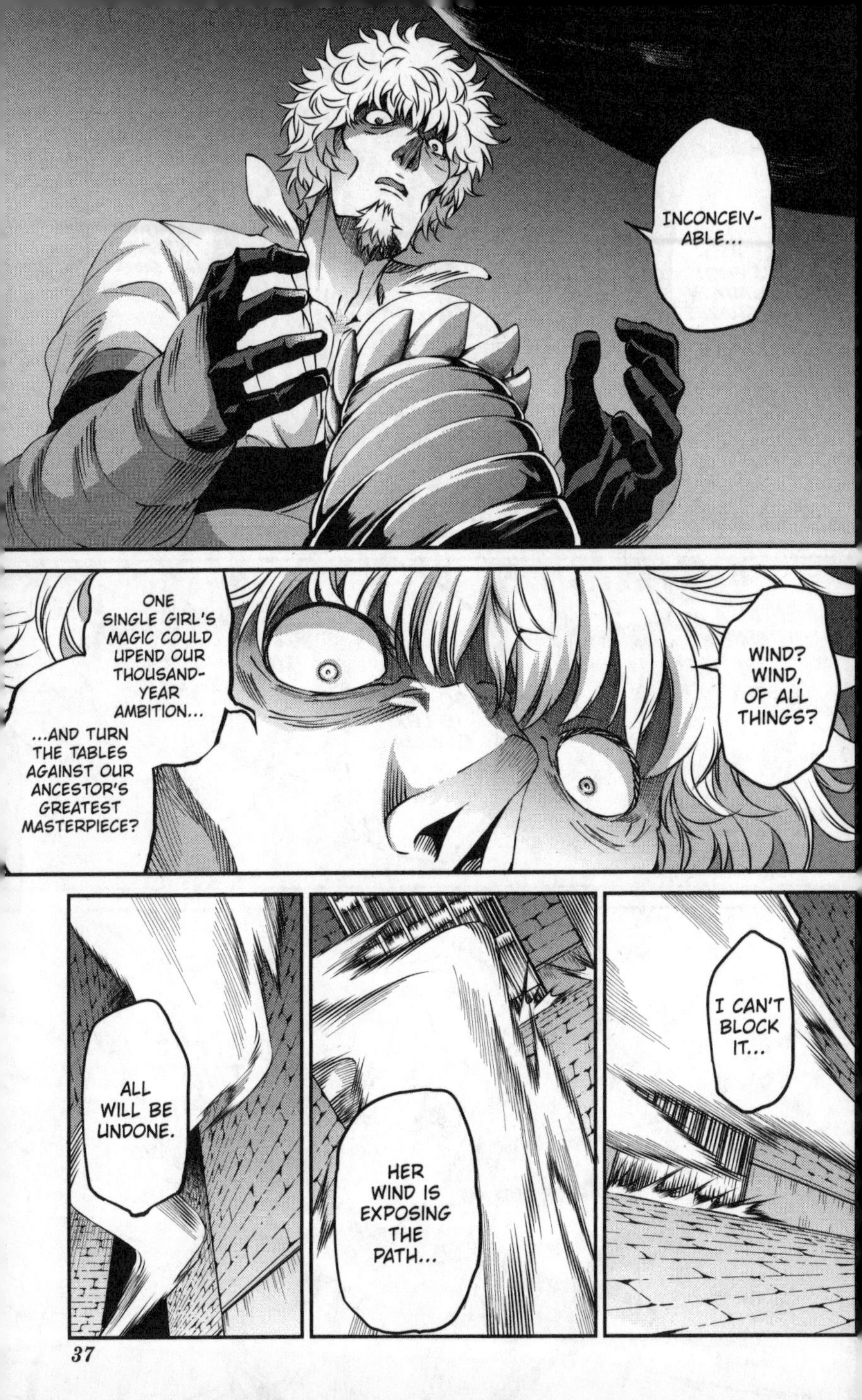
INCONCEIV-ABLE...
WIND? WIND, OF ALL THINGS?
ONE SINGLE GIRL'S MAGIC COULD UPEND OUR THOUSAND-YEAR AMBITION...
...AND TURN THE TABLES AGAINST OUR ANCESTOR'S GREATEST MASTERPIECE?
I CAN'T BLOCK IT...
HER WIND IS EXPOSING THE PATH...
ALL WILL BE UNDONE.

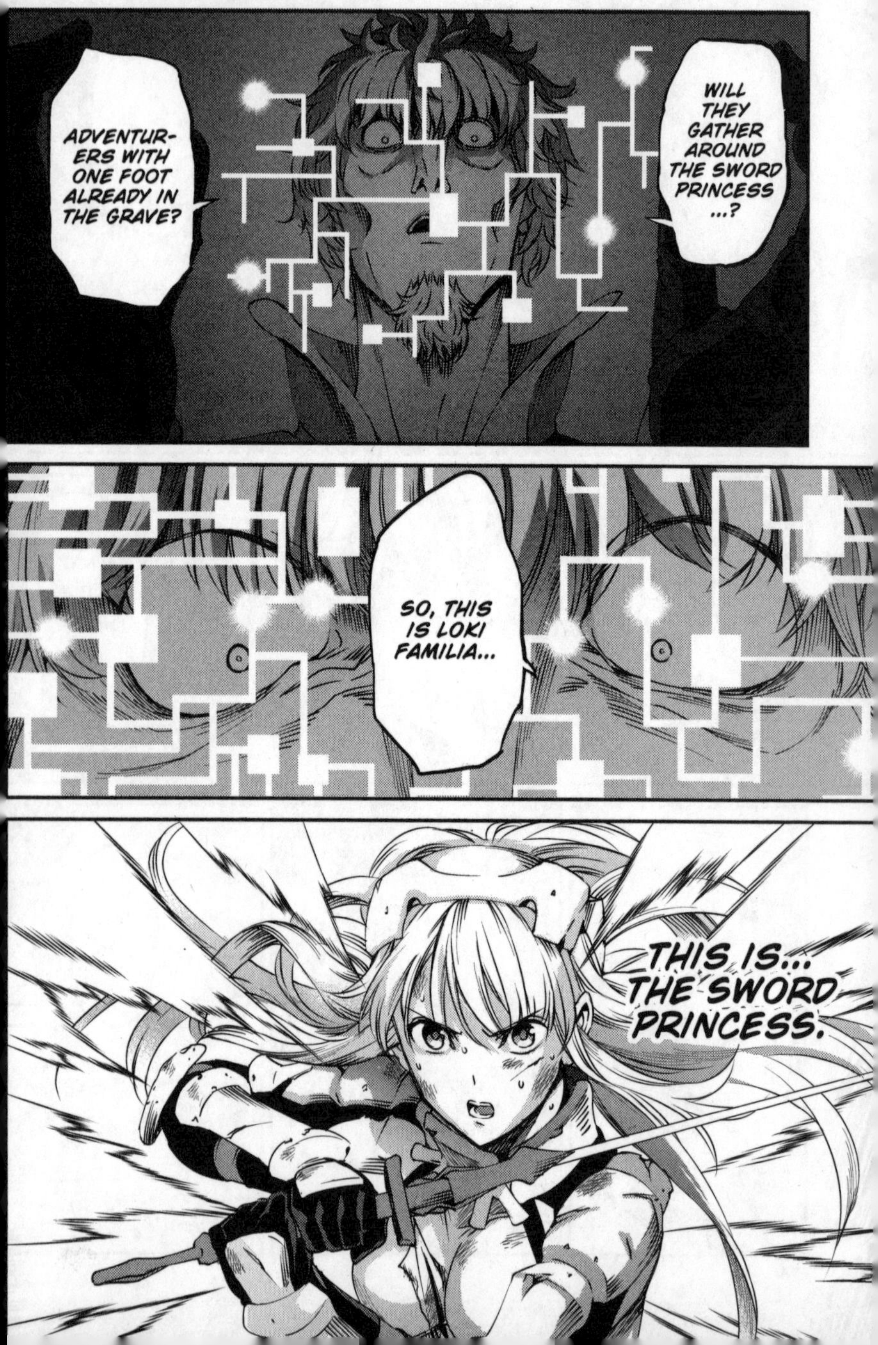

WILL THEY GATHER AROUND THE SWORD PRINCESS ...?
ADVENTURERS WITH ONE FOOT ALREADY IN THE GRAVE?
SO, THIS IS LOKI FAMILIA...
THIS IS... THE SWORD PRINCESS.

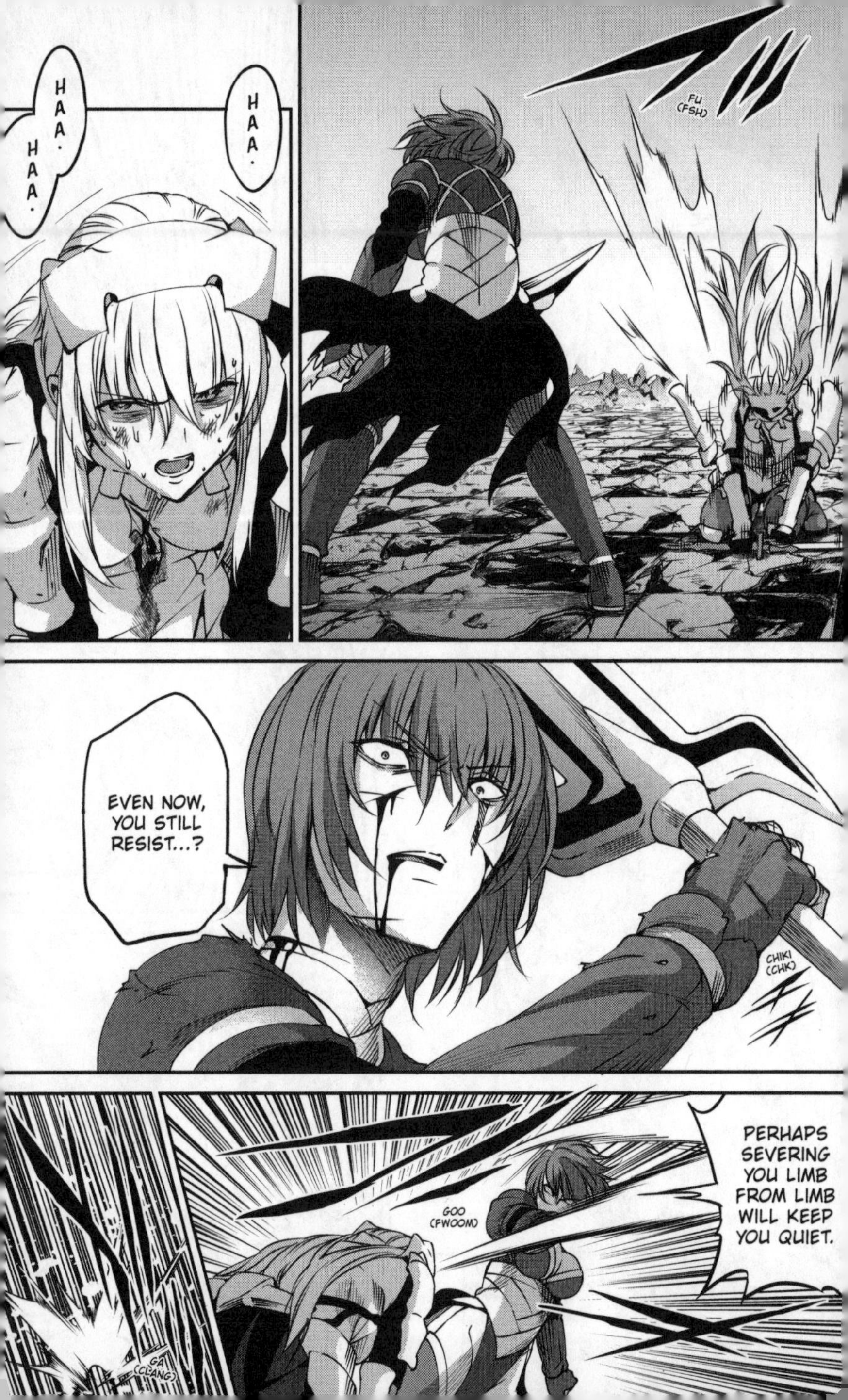

FU (FSH)
HAA. HAA.
HAA. HAA.
EVEN NOW, YOU STILL RESIST...?
CHIKI (CHK)
PERHAPS SEVERING YOU LIMB FROM LIMB WILL KEEP YOU QUIET.
GOO (FWOOM)
GA (CLANG)

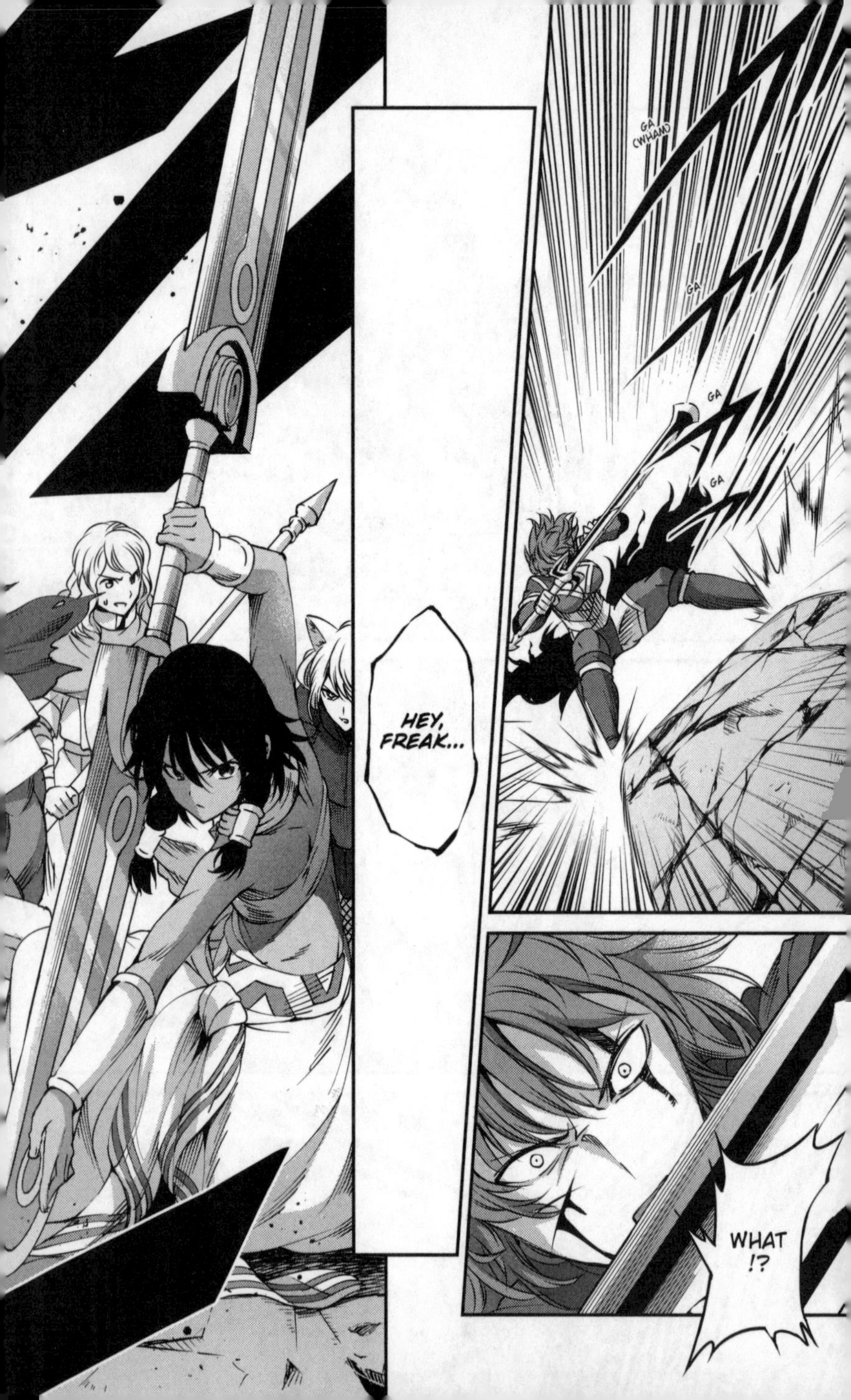
GA (WHAM)
GA
GA
GA
WHAT !?
HEY, FREAK...

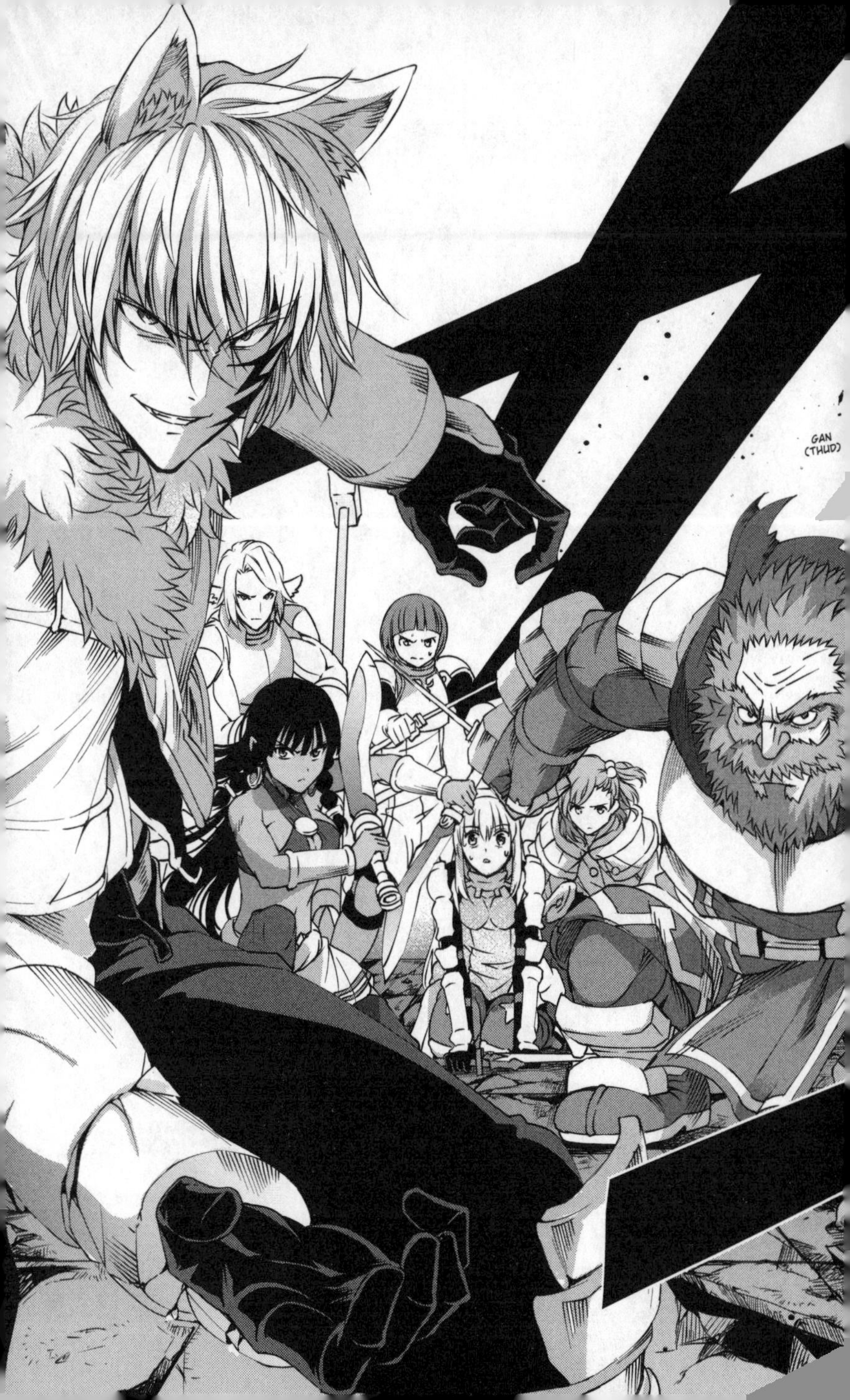
GAN
(THUD)

Is it WRONG to TRY to PICK UP GIRLS IN A DUNGEON? ON THE SIDE

Sword Oratoria

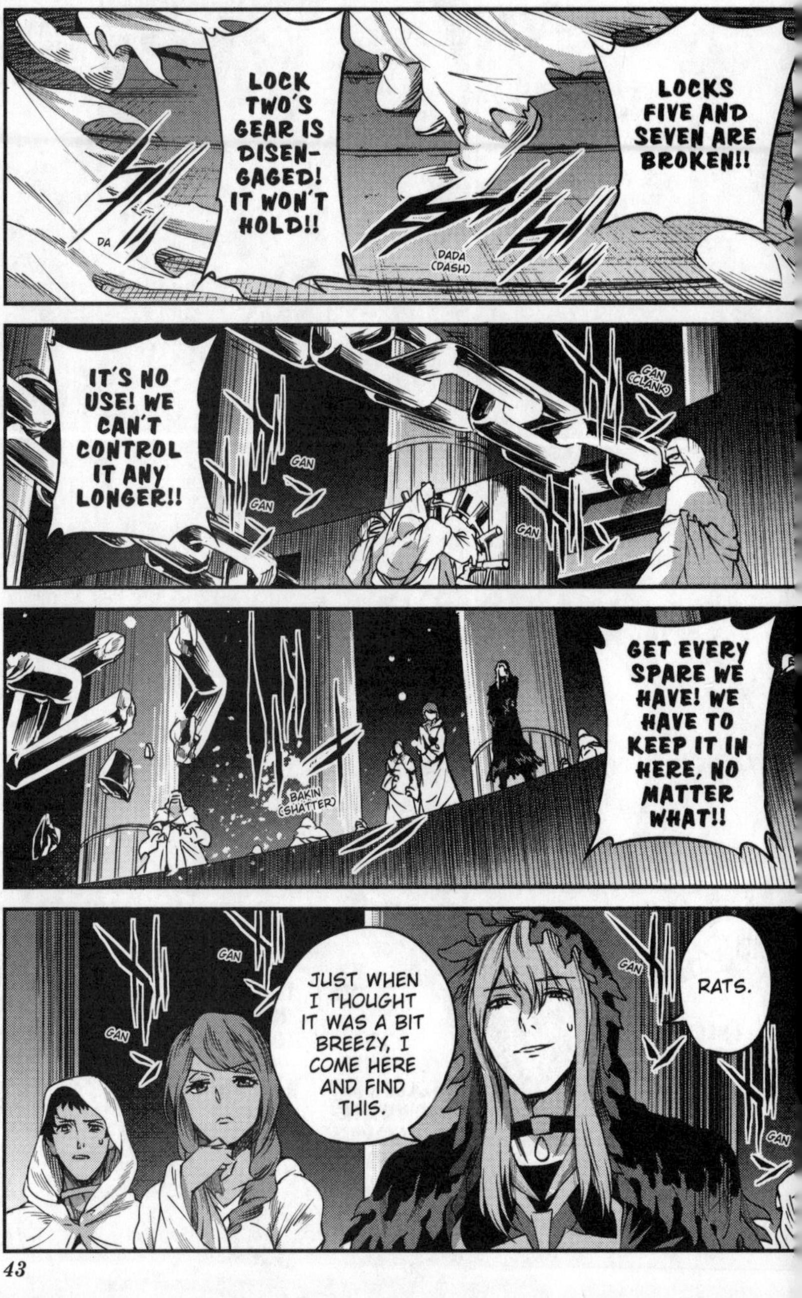
LOCKS FIVE AND SEVEN ARE BROKEN!!
DADA (DASH)
LOCK TWO'S GEAR IS DISEN-GAGED! IT WON'T HOLD!!
DA
GAN (CLANK)
GAN
GAN
GAN
IT'S NO USE! WE CAN'T CONTROL IT ANY LONGER!!
GET EVERY SPARE WE HAVE! WE HAVE TO KEEP IT IN HERE, NO MATTER WHAT!!
BAKIN (SHATTER)
GAN
RATS.
GAN
JUST WHEN I THOUGHT IT WAS A BIT BREEZY, I COME HERE AND FIND THIS.
GAN
GAN

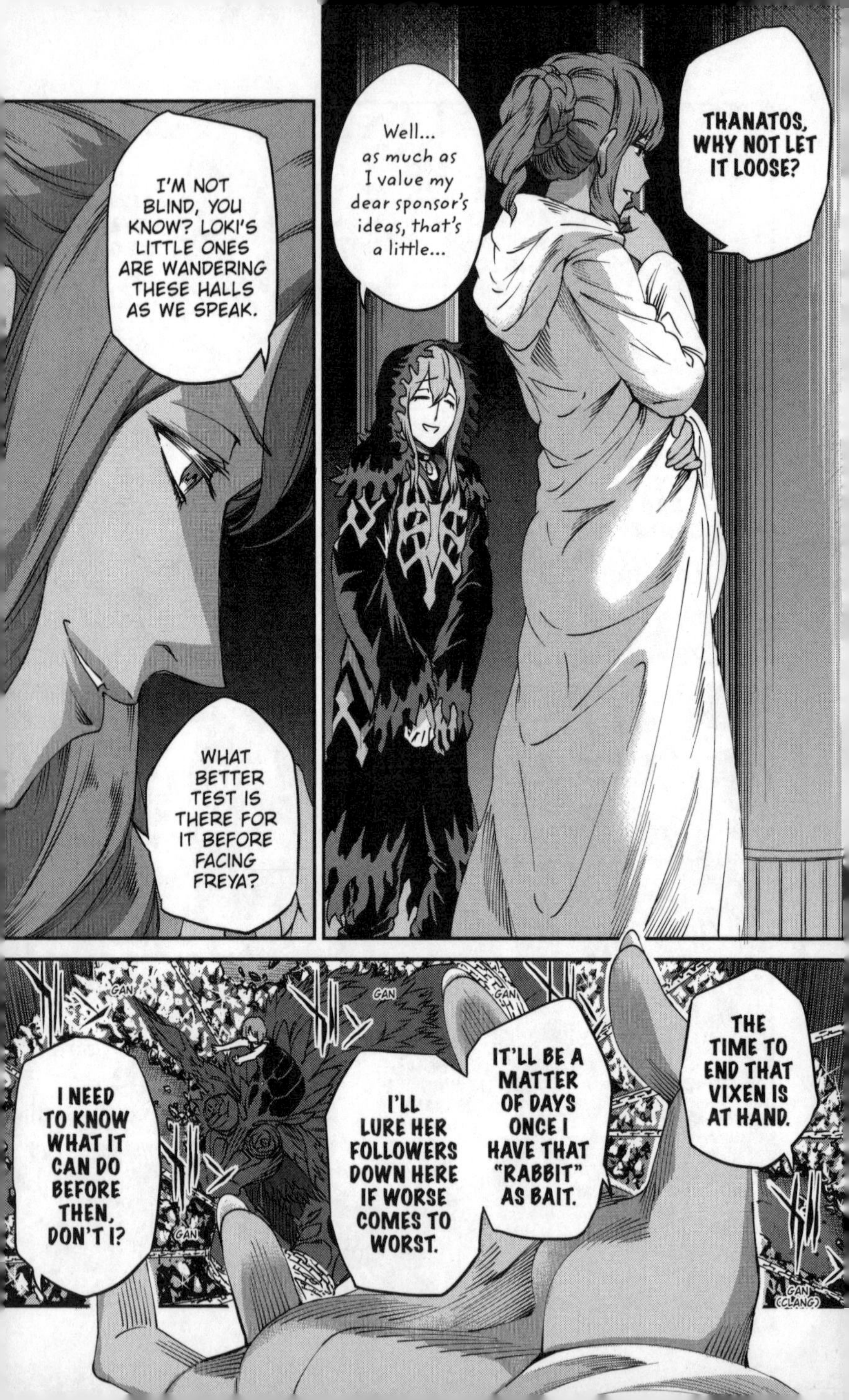
THANATOS, WHY NOT LET IT LOOSE?
Well... as much as I value my dear sponsor's ideas, that's a little...
I'M NOT BLIND, YOU KNOW? LOKI'S LITTLE ONES ARE WANDERING THESE HALLS AS WE SPEAK.
WHAT BETTER TEST IS THERE FOR IT BEFORE FACING FREYA?
GAN
GAN
GAN
THE TIME TO END THAT VIXEN IS AT HAND.
IT'LL BE A MATTER OF DAYS ONCE I HAVE THAT "RABBIT" AS BAIT.
I'LL LURE HER FOLLOWERS DOWN HERE IF WORSE COMES TO WORST.
I NEED TO KNOW WHAT IT CAN DO BEFORE THEN, DON'T I?
GAN
GAN (CLANG)

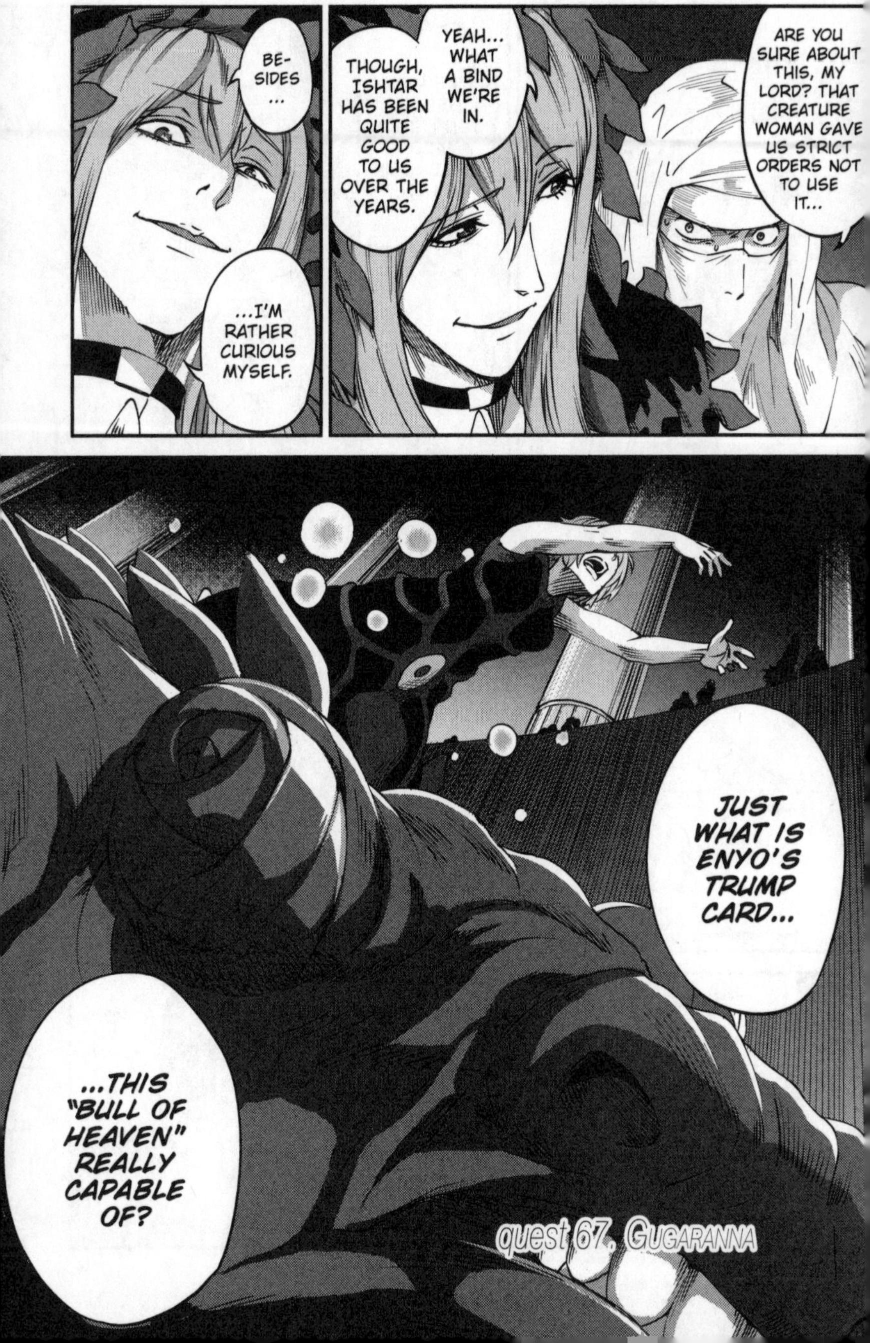
ARE YOU SURE ABOUT THIS, MY LORD? THAT CREATURE WOMAN GAVE US STRICT ORDERS NOT TO USE IT...
YEAH... WHAT A BIND WE'RE IN.
THOUGH, ISHTAR HAS BEEN QUITE GOOD TO US OVER THE YEARS.
BE-SIDES...
...I'M RATHER CURIOUS MYSELF.
JUST WHAT IS ENYO'S TRUMP CARD...
...THIS "BULL OF HEAVEN" REALLY CAPABLE OF?
quest 67. Gugaranna

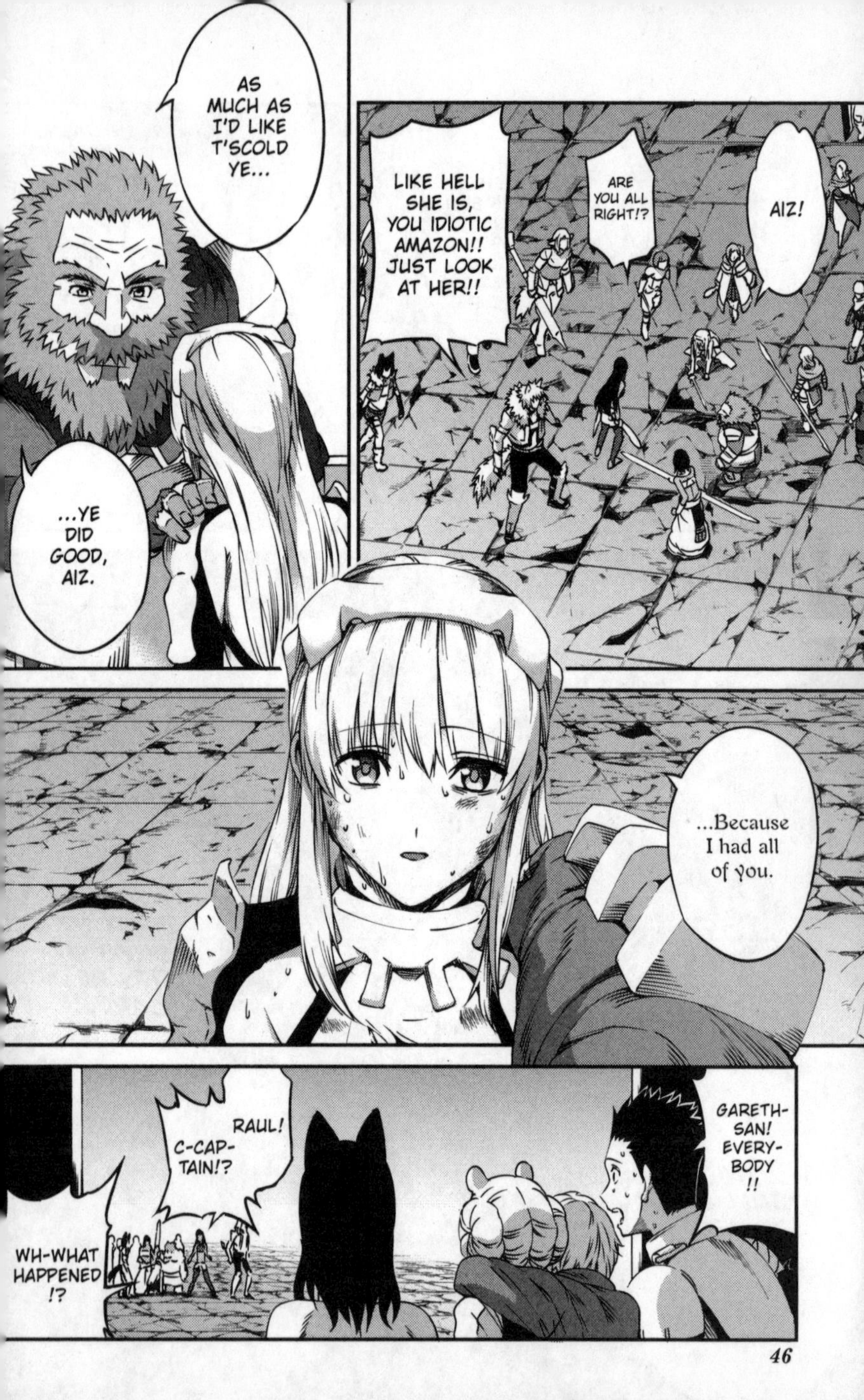
AIZ!
ARE YOU ALL RIGHT!?
LIKE HELL SHE IS, YOU IDIOTIC AMAZON!! JUST LOOK AT HER!!
AS MUCH AS I'D LIKE T'SCOLD YE...
...YE DID GOOD, AIZ.
...Because I had all of you.
GARETH-SAN! EVERYBODY!!
RAUL!
C-CAPTAIN!?
WH-WHAT HAPPENED!?

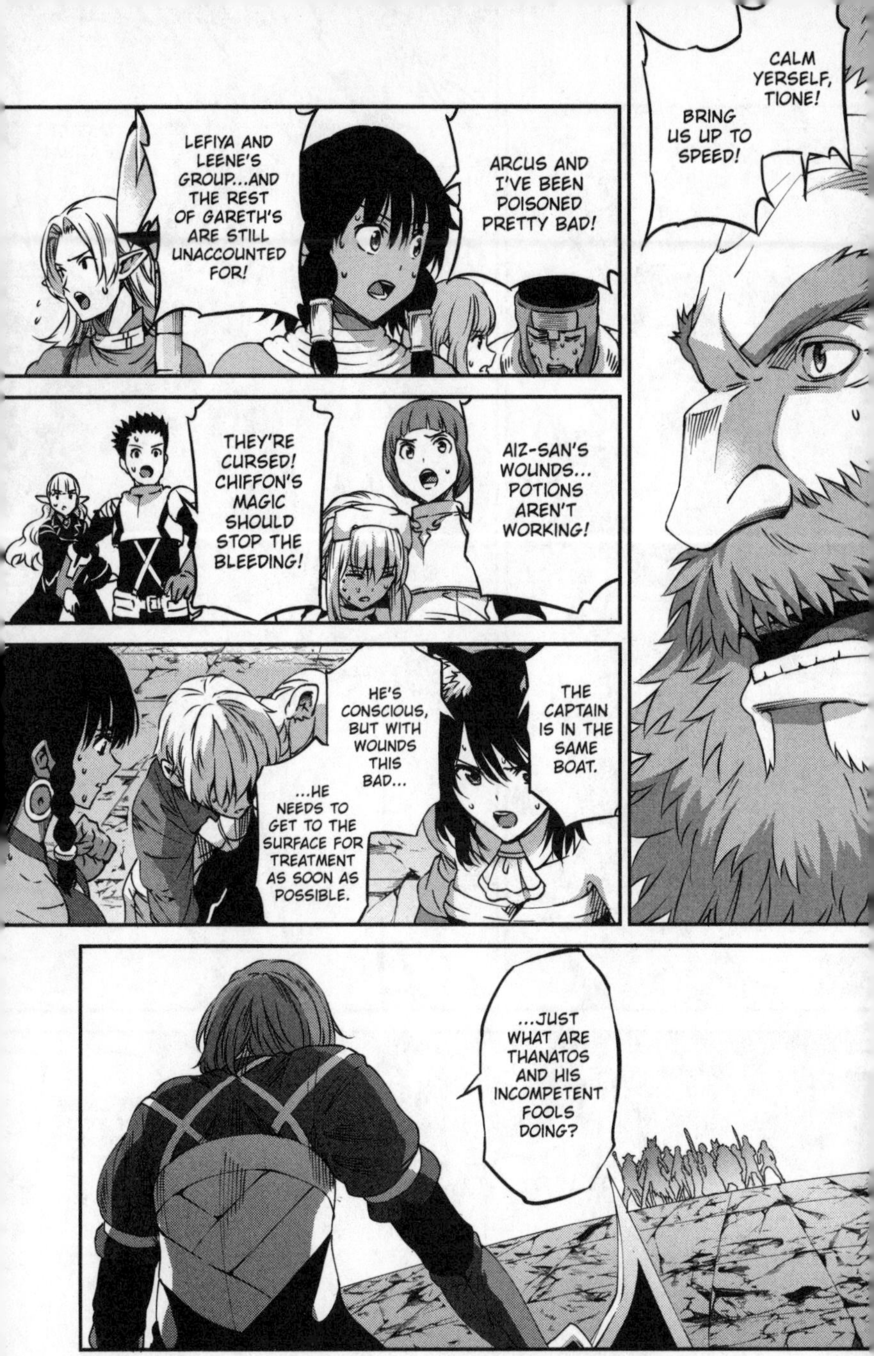
CALM YERSELF, TIONE!
BRING US UP TO SPEED!
ARCUS AND I'VE BEEN POISONED PRETTY BAD!
LEFIYA AND LEENE'S GROUP...AND THE REST OF GARETH'S ARE STILL UNACCOUNTED FOR!
AIZ-SAN'S WOUNDS... POTIONS AREN'T WORKING!
THEY'RE CURSED! CHIFFON'S MAGIC SHOULD STOP THE BLEEDING!
THE CAPTAIN IS IN THE SAME BOAT.
HE'S CONSCIOUS, BUT WITH WOUNDS THIS BAD...
...HE NEEDS TO GET TO THE SURFACE FOR TREATMENT AS SOON AS POSSIBLE.
...JUST WHAT ARE THANATOS AND HIS INCOMPETENT FOOLS DOING?

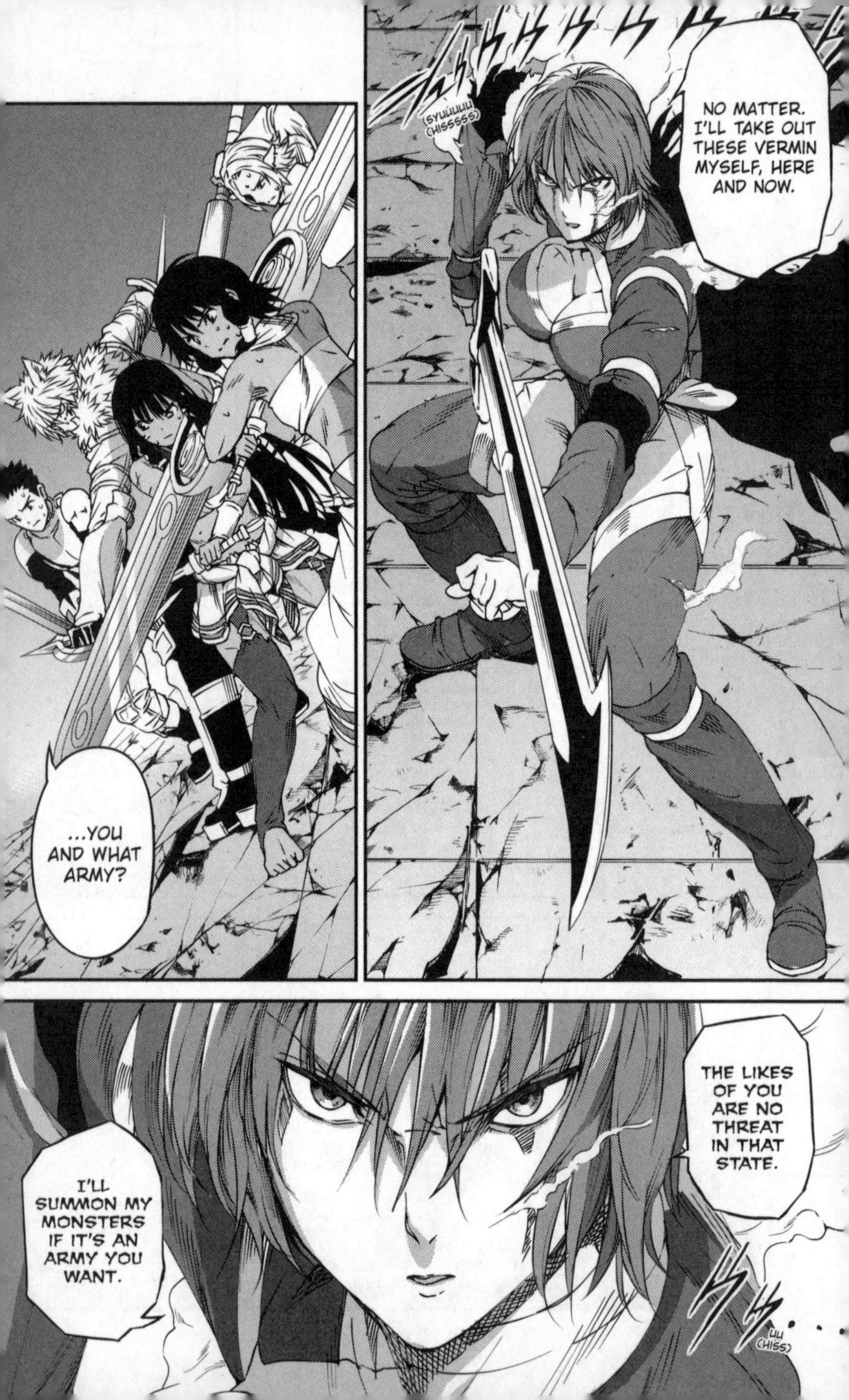
SYUUUUU (HISSSSS)
NO MATTER. I'LL TAKE OUT THESE VERMIN MYSELF, HERE AND NOW.
...YOU AND WHAT ARMY?
THE LIKES OF YOU ARE NO THREAT IN THAT STATE.
I'LL SUMMON MY MONSTERS IF IT'S AN ARMY YOU WANT.
UU (HISS)

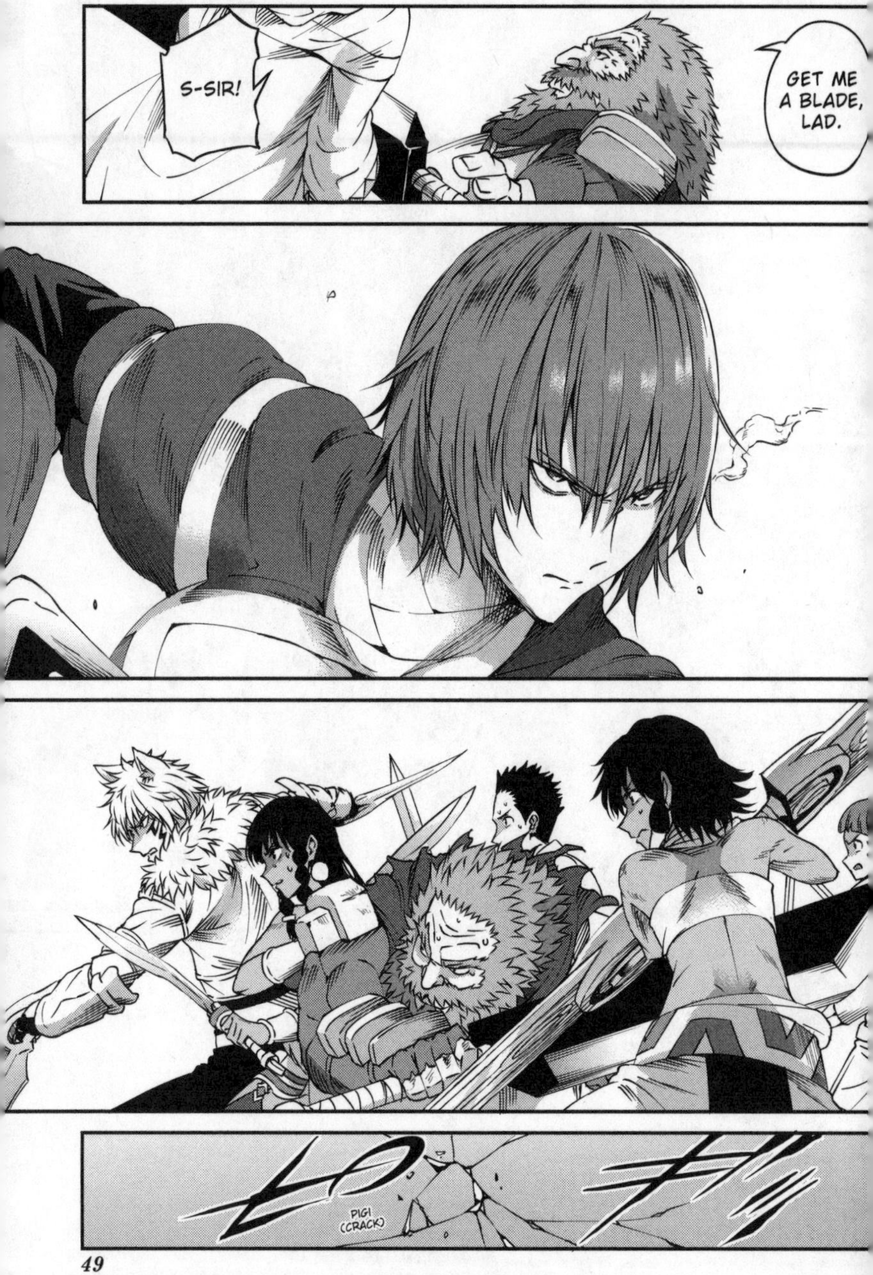
GET ME A BLADE, LAD.
S-SIR!
PIGI (CRACK)

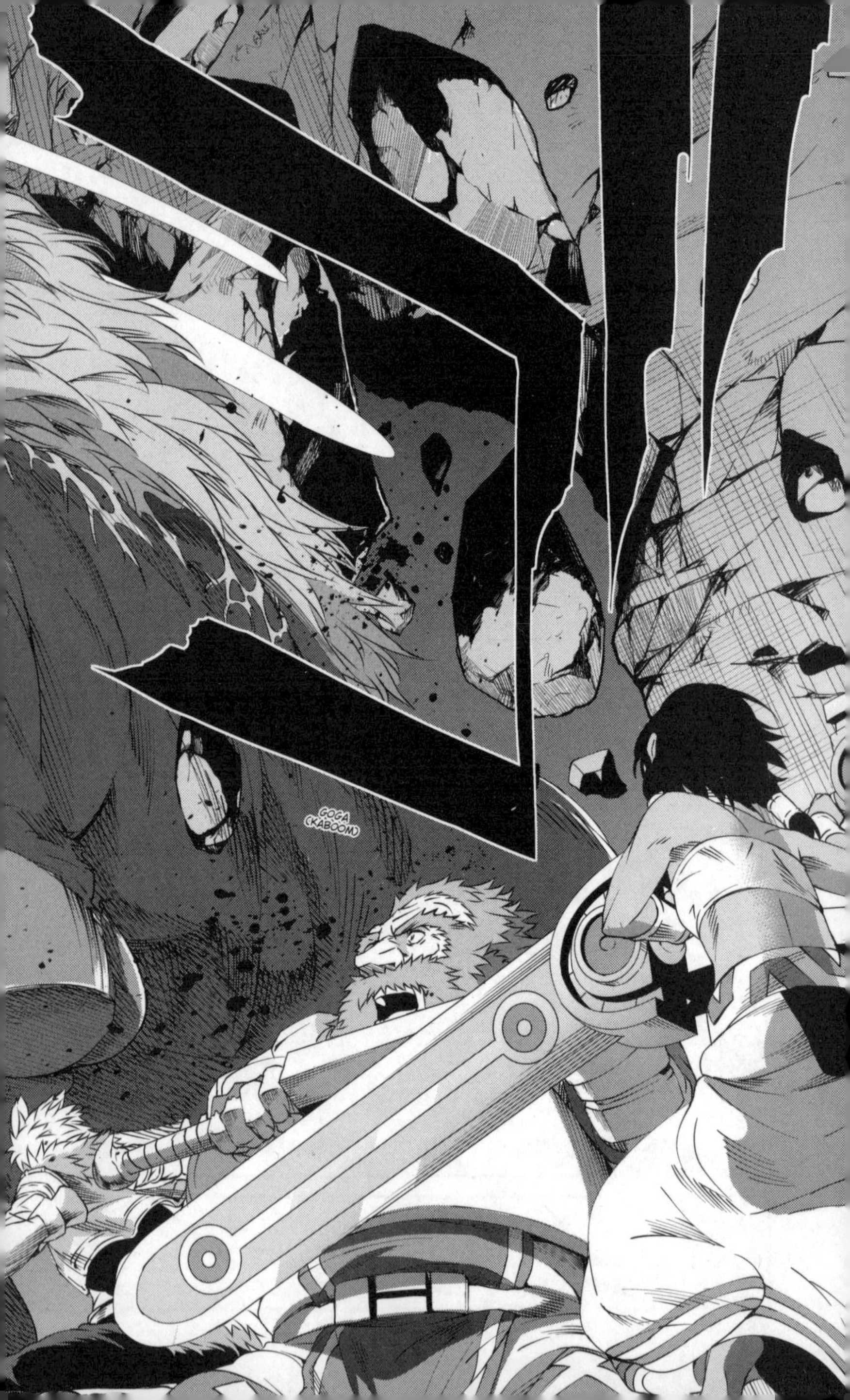
GOGA
(KABOOM)

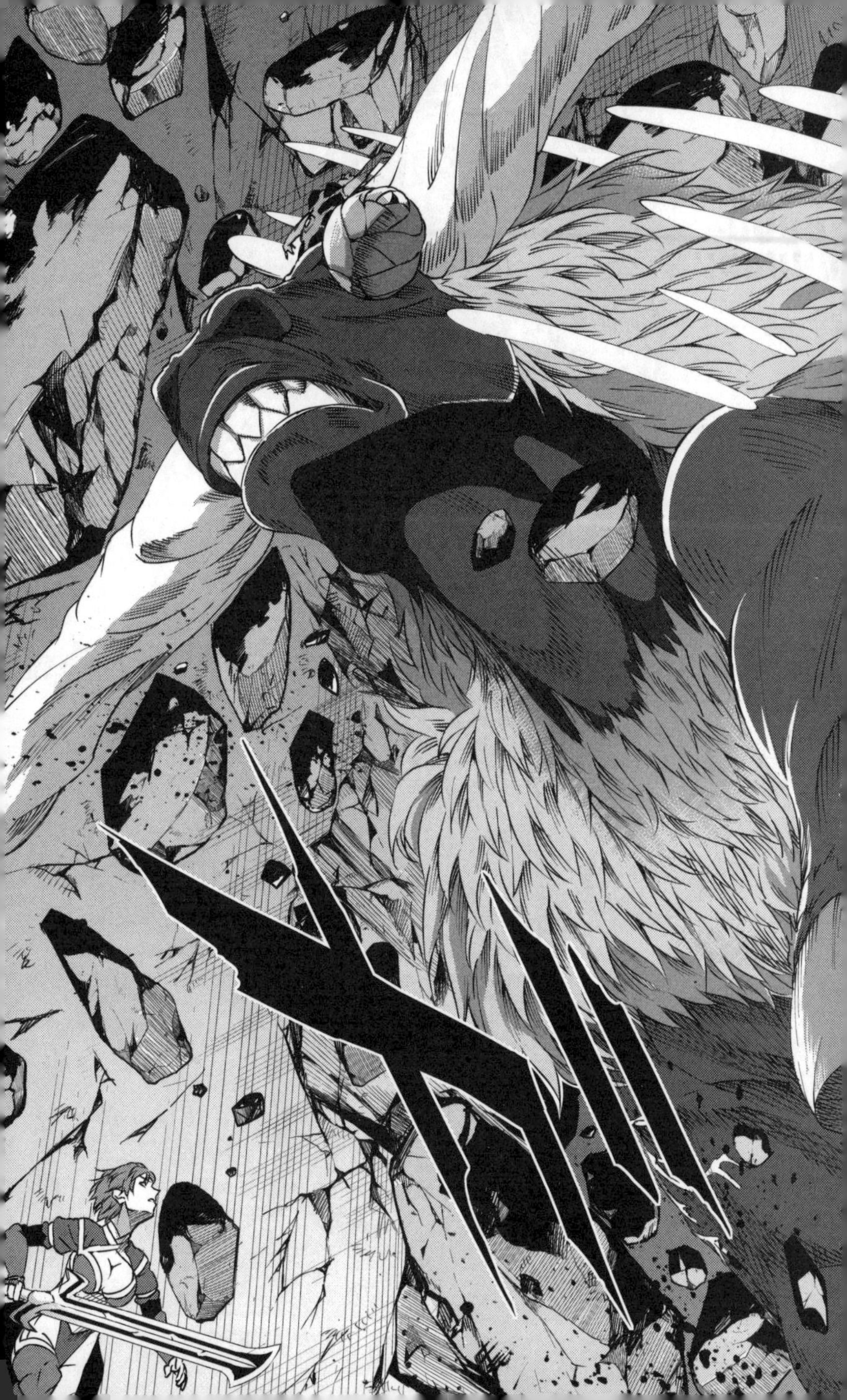

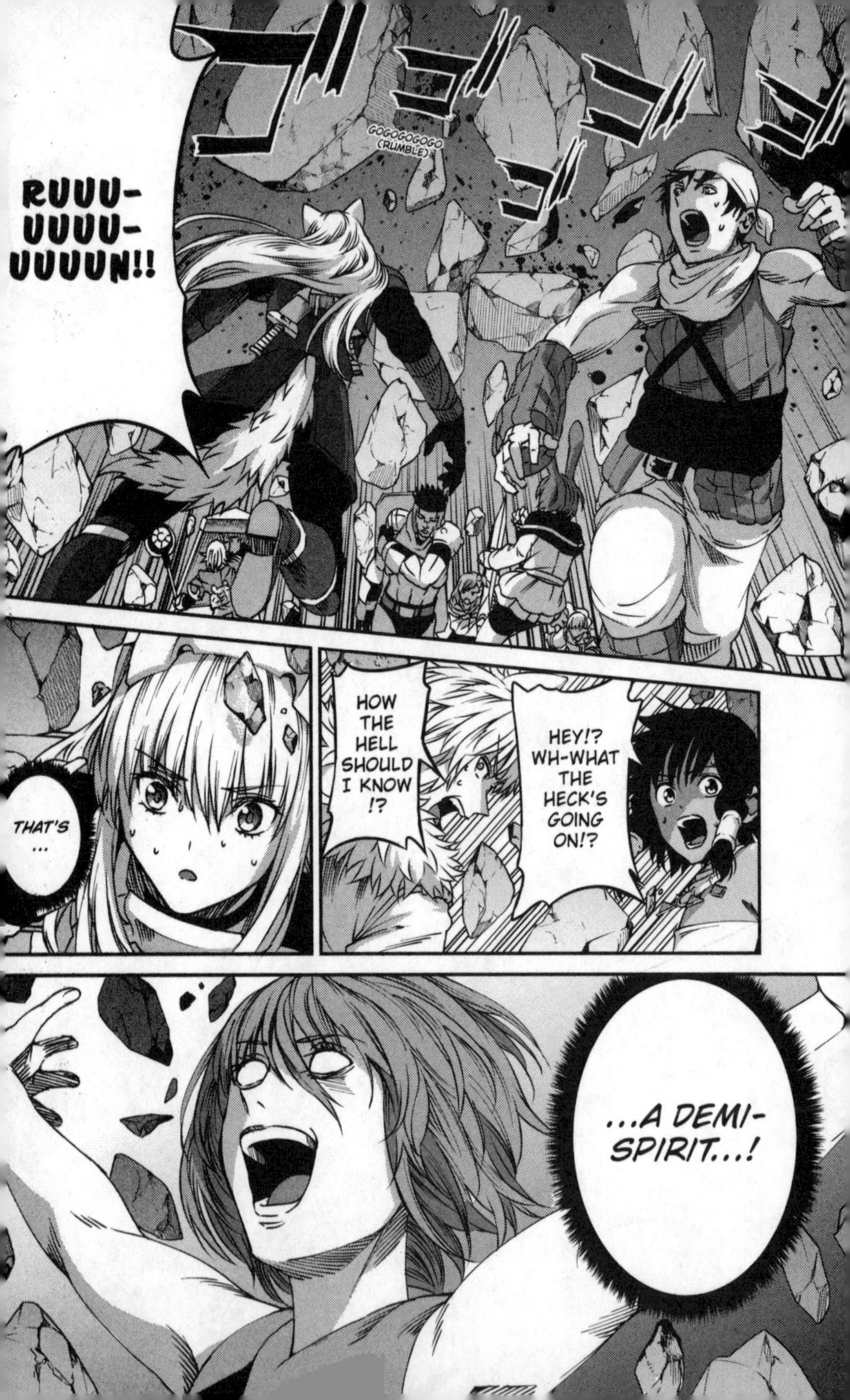
GOGOGOGOGO (RUMBLE)
RUUUU-UUUU-UUUUN!!
HEY!? WH-WHAT THE HECK'S GOING ON!?
HOW THE HELL SHOULD I KNOW!?
THAT'S ...
...A DEMI-SPIRIT...!

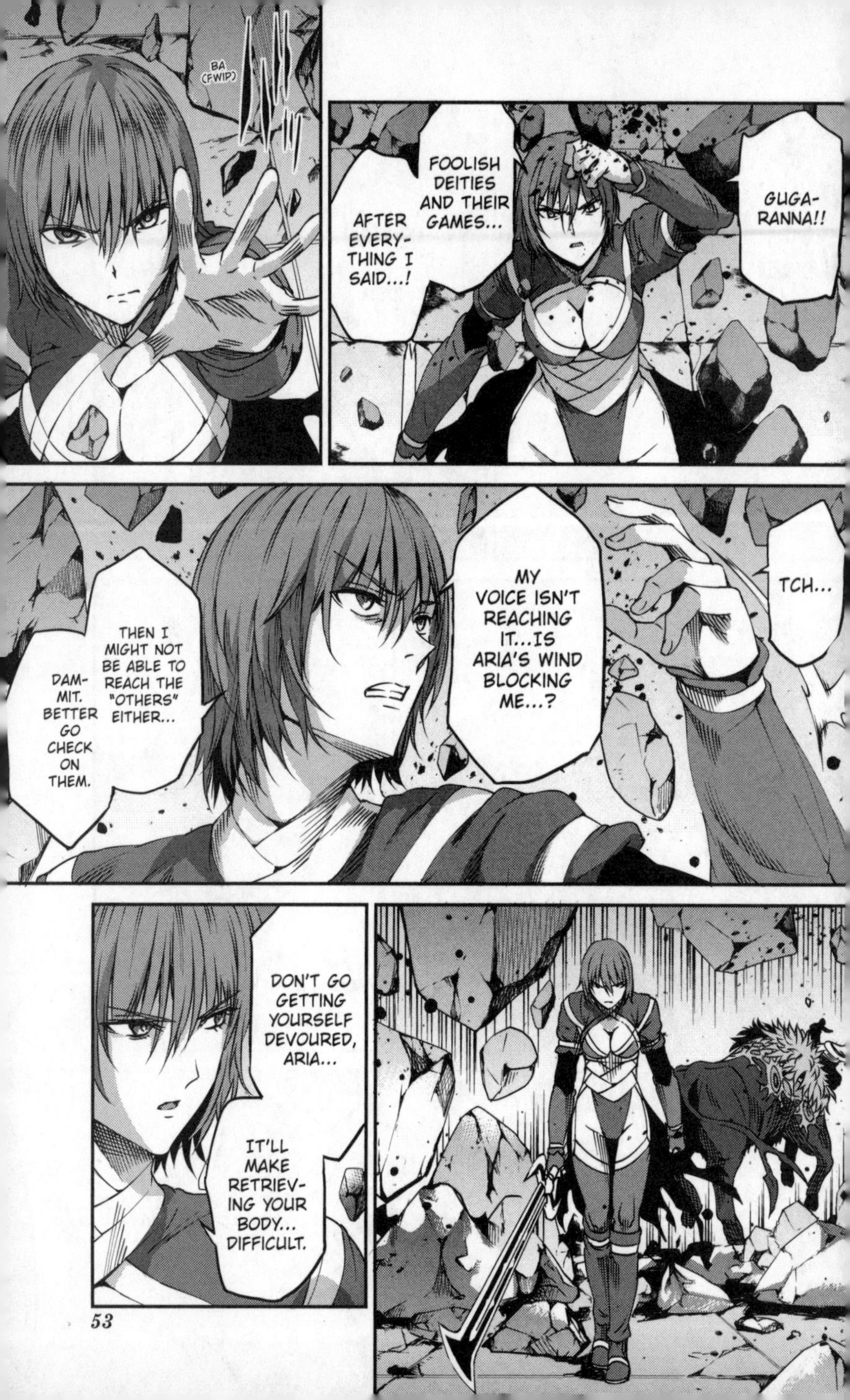
GUGA-RANNA!!
FOOLISH DEITIES AND THEIR GAMES...
AFTER EVERY-THING I SAID...!
BA (FWIP)
TCH...
MY VOICE ISN'T REACHING IT...IS ARIA'S WIND BLOCKING ME...?
THEN I MIGHT NOT BE ABLE TO REACH THE "OTHERS" EITHER...
DAM-MIT. BETTER GO CHECK ON THEM.
DON'T GO GETTING YOURSELF DEVOURED, ARIA...
IT'LL MAKE RETRIEV-ING YOUR BODY... DIFFICULT.

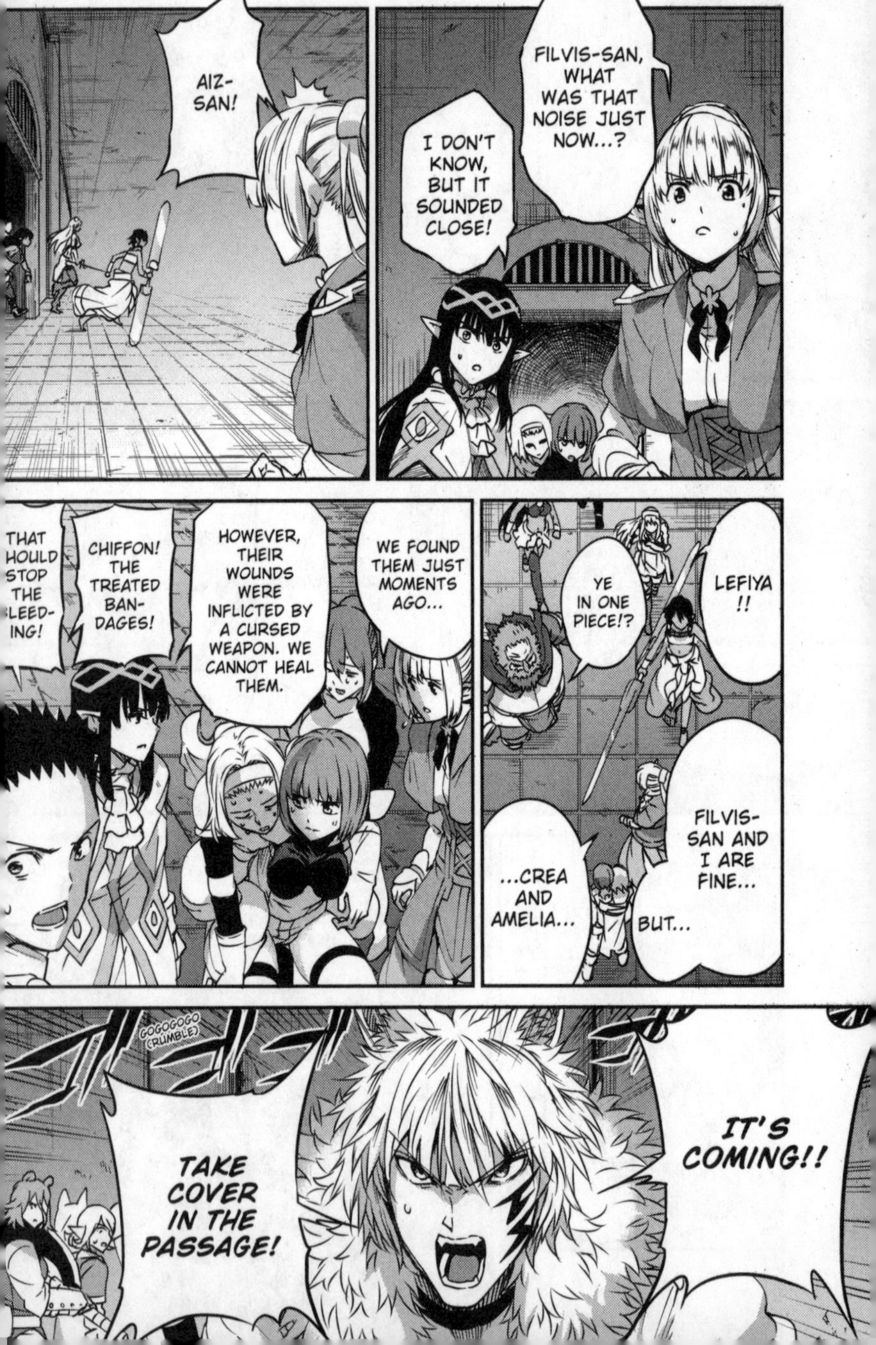
FILVIS-SAN, WHAT WAS THAT NOISE JUST NOW...?
I DON'T KNOW, BUT IT SOUNDED CLOSE!
AIZ-SAN!
LEFIYA!!
YE IN ONE PIECE!?
FILVIS-SAN AND I ARE FINE... BUT...
...CREA AND AMELIA...
WE FOUND THEM JUST MOMENTS AGO...
HOWEVER, THEIR WOUNDS WERE INFLICTED BY A CURSED WEAPON. WE CANNOT HEAL THEM.
CHIFFON! THE TREATED BAN-DAGES!
THAT HOULD STOP THE LEED-ING!
GOGOGOGO (RUMBLE)
IT'S COMING!!
TAKE COVER IN THE PASSAGE!

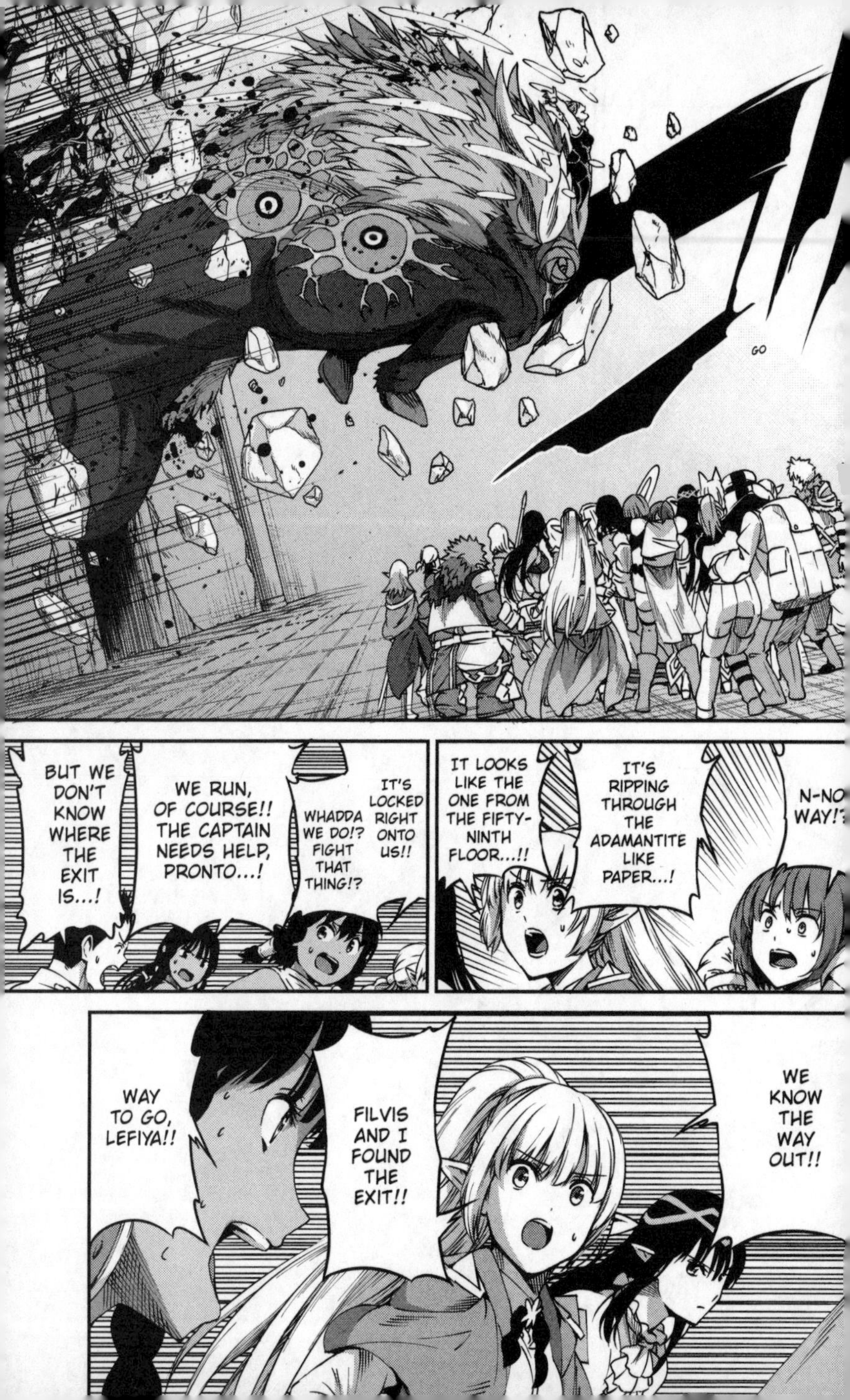
GO
N-NO WAY!?
IT'S RIPPING THROUGH THE ADAMANTITE LIKE PAPER...!
IT LOOKS LIKE THE ONE FROM THE FIFTY-NINTH FLOOR...!!
IT'S LOCKED RIGHT ONTO US!!
WHADDA WE DO!? FIGHT THAT THING!?
WE RUN, OF COURSE!! THE CAPTAIN NEEDS HELP, PRONTO...!
BUT WE DON'T KNOW WHERE THE EXIT IS...!
WE KNOW THE WAY OUT!!
FILVIS AND I FOUND THE EXIT!!
WAY TO GO, LEFIYA!!

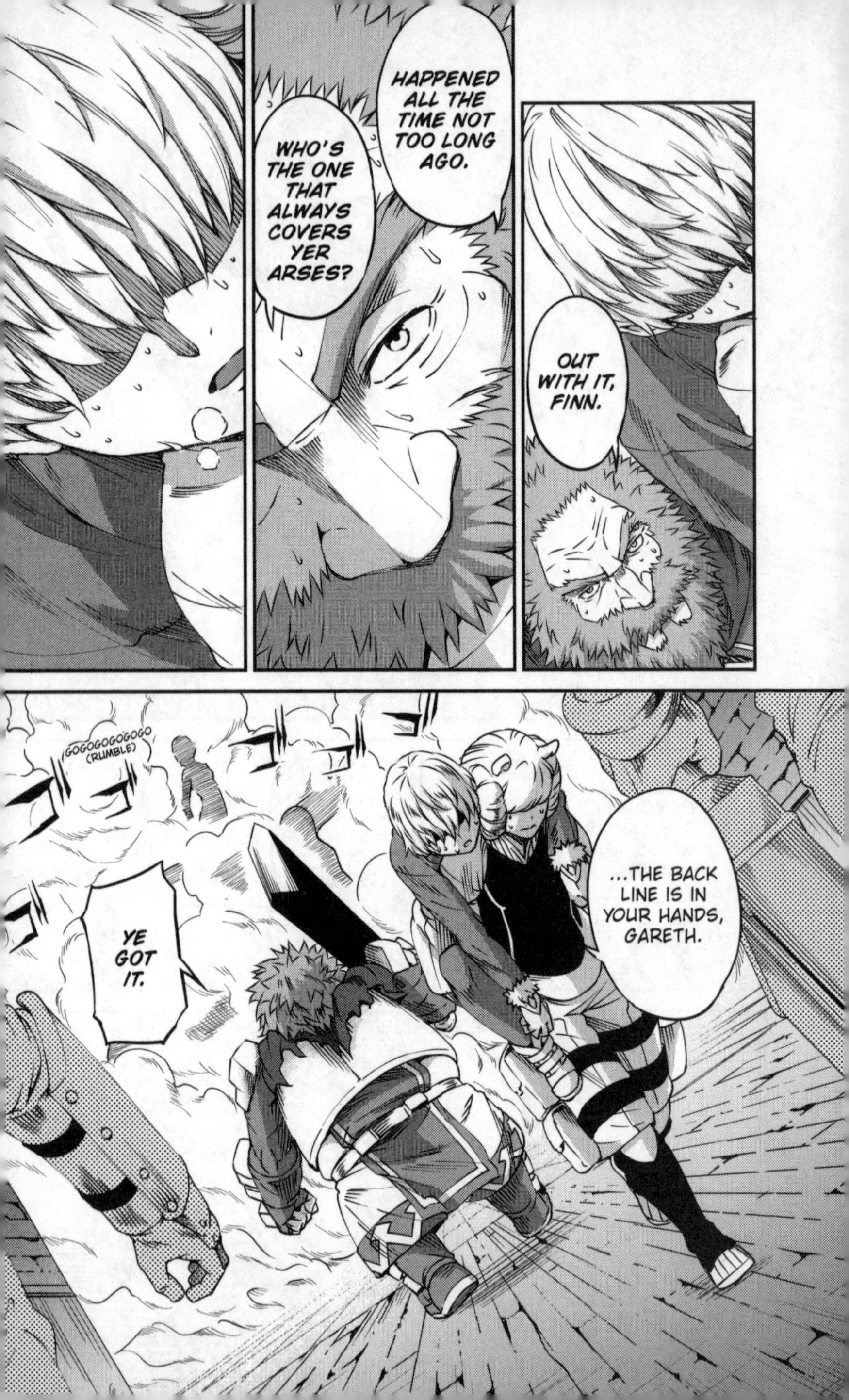
OUT WITH IT, FINN.
HAPPENED ALL THE TIME NOT TOO LONG AGO.
WHO'S THE ONE THAT ALWAYS COVERS YER ARSES?
...THE BACK LINE IS IN YOUR HANDS, GARETH.
GOGOGOGOGOGO (RUMBLE)
YE GOT IT.

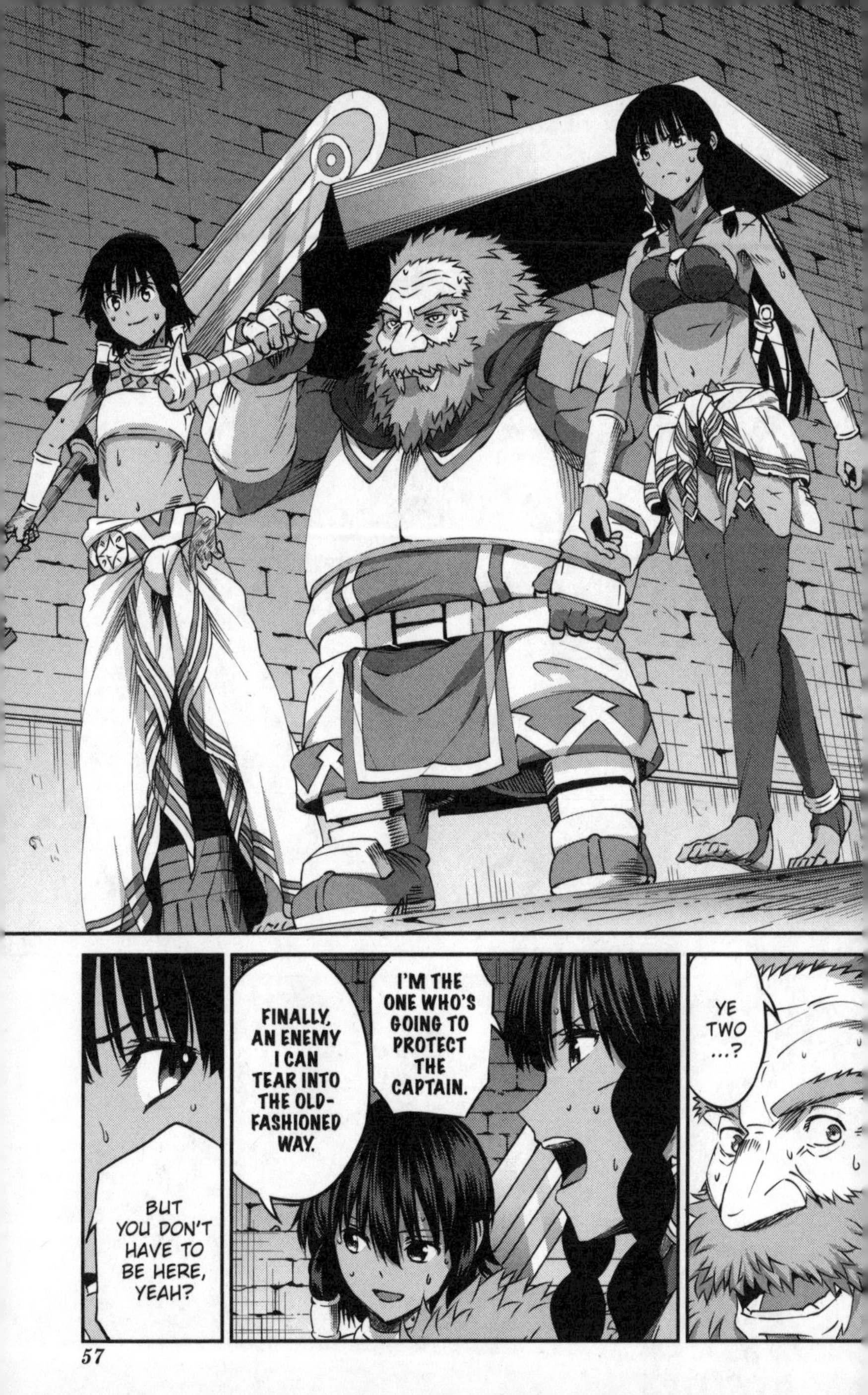
YE TWO ...?
I'M THE ONE WHO'S GOING TO PROTECT THE CAPTAIN.
FINALLY, AN ENEMY I CAN TEAR INTO THE OLD-FASHIONED WAY.
BUT YOU DON'T HAVE TO BE HERE, YEAH?

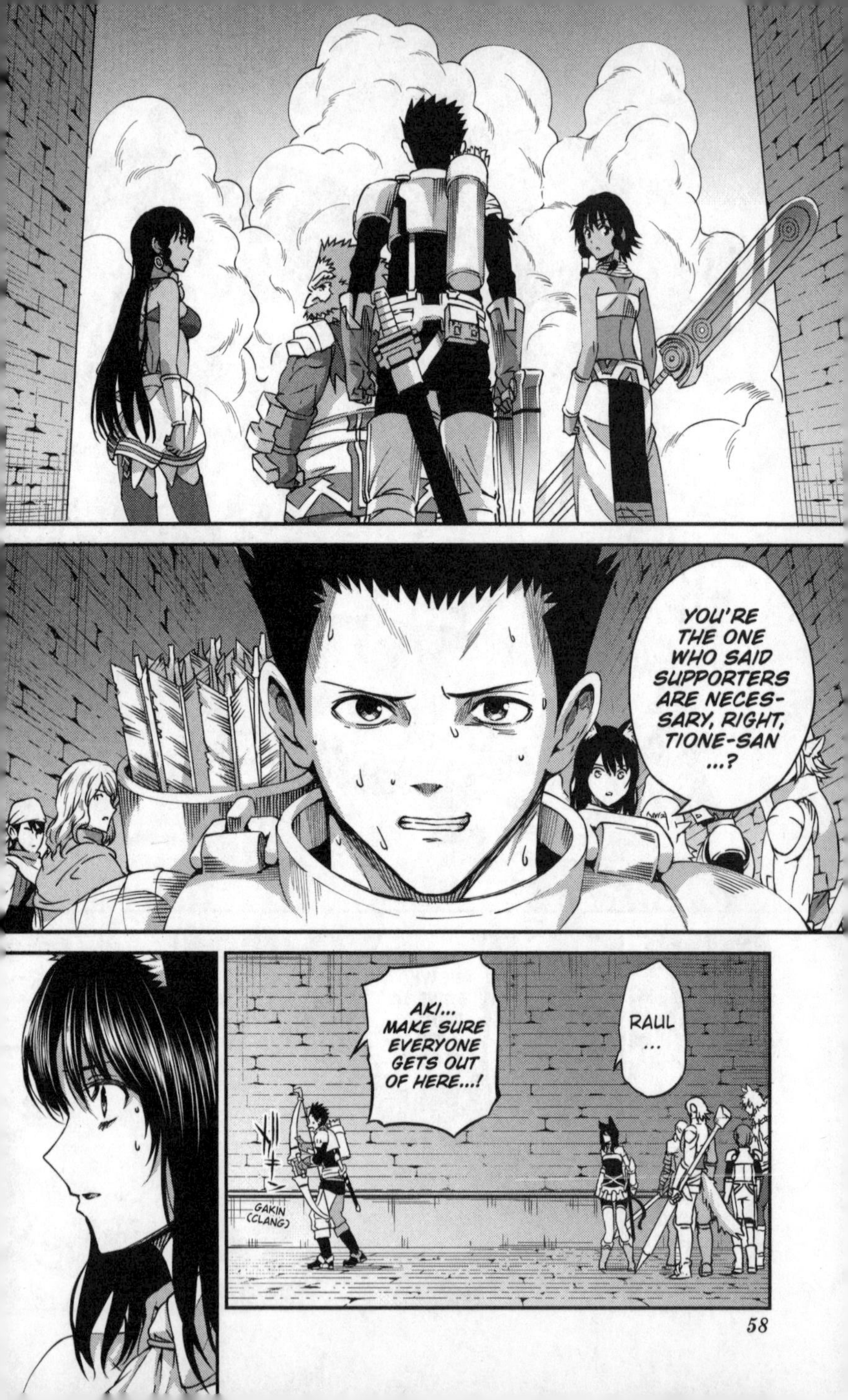
YOU'RE THE ONE WHO SAID SUPPORTERS ARE NECES-SARY, RIGHT, TIONE-SAN ...?
RAUL ...
AKI... MAKE SURE EVERYONE GETS OUT OF HERE...!
GAKIN (CLANG)

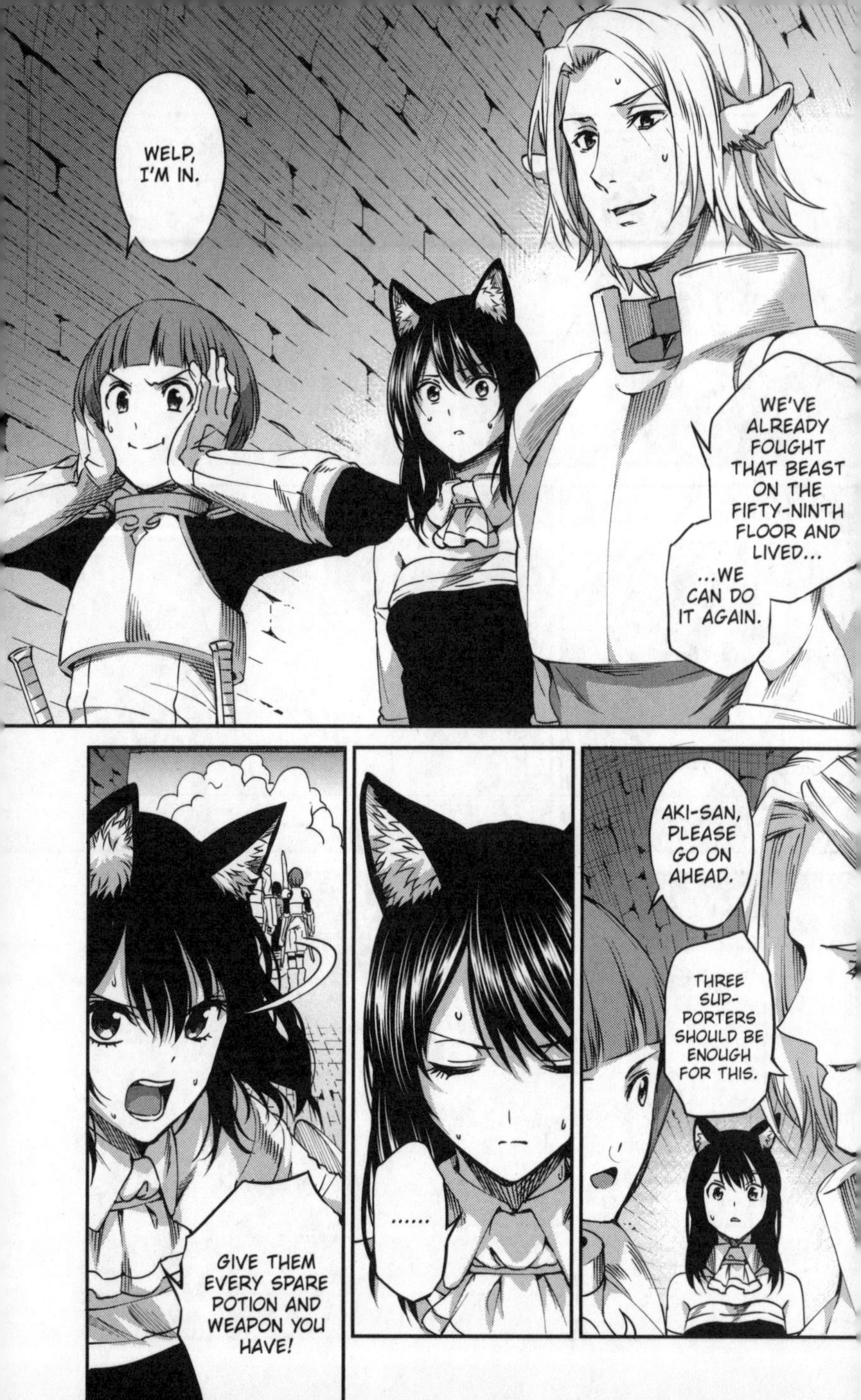
WE'VE ALREADY FOUGHT THAT BEAST ON THE FIFTY-NINTH FLOOR AND LIVED...
...WE CAN DO IT AGAIN.
WELP, I'M IN.
AKI-SAN, PLEASE GO ON AHEAD.
THREE SUP-PORTERS SHOULD BE ENOUGH FOR THIS.
......
GIVE THEM EVERY SPARE POTION AND WEAPON YOU HAVE!

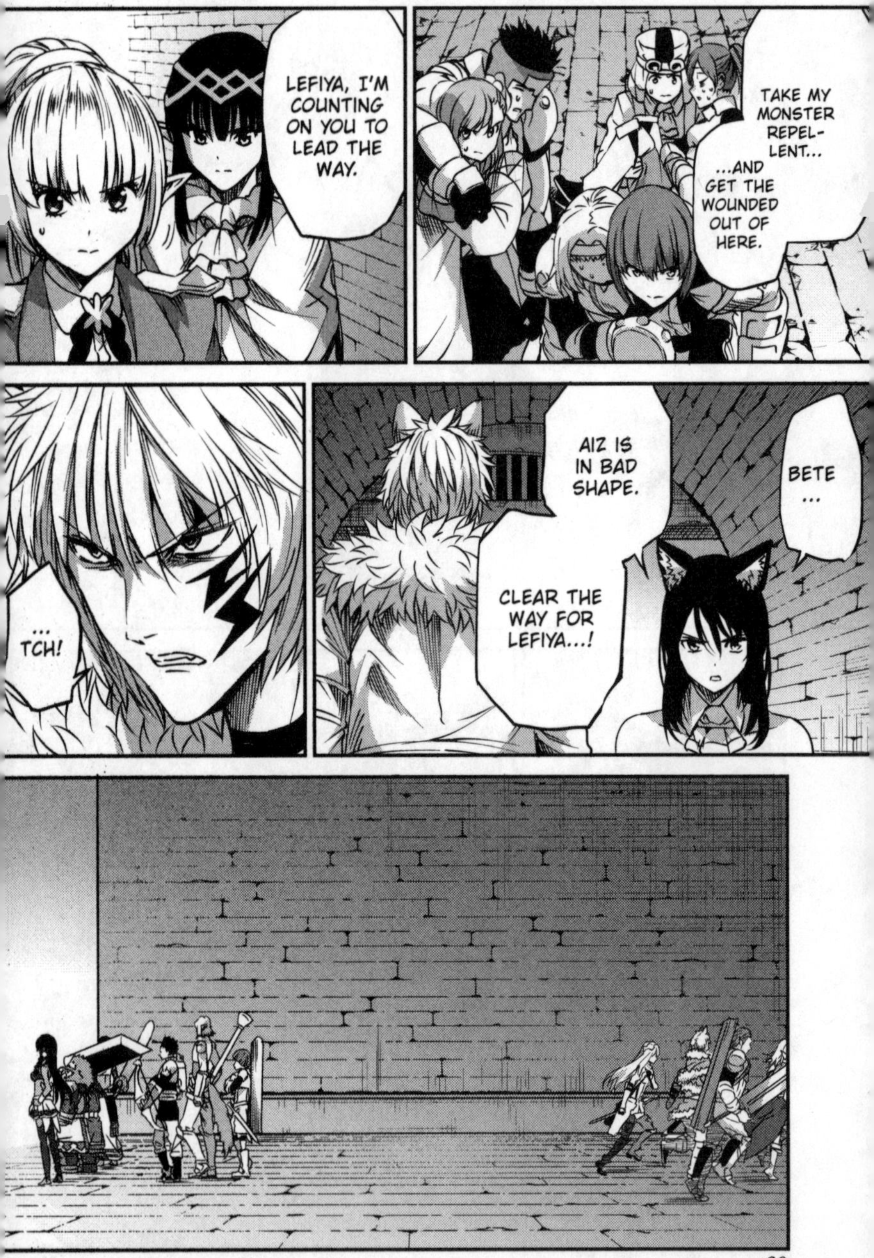
TAKE MY MONSTER REPEL-LENT...
...AND GET THE WOUNDED OUT OF HERE.
LEFIYA, I'M COUNTING ON YOU TO LEAD THE WAY.
BETE ...
AIZ IS IN BAD SHAPE.
CLEAR THE WAY FOR LEFIYA...!
... TCH!

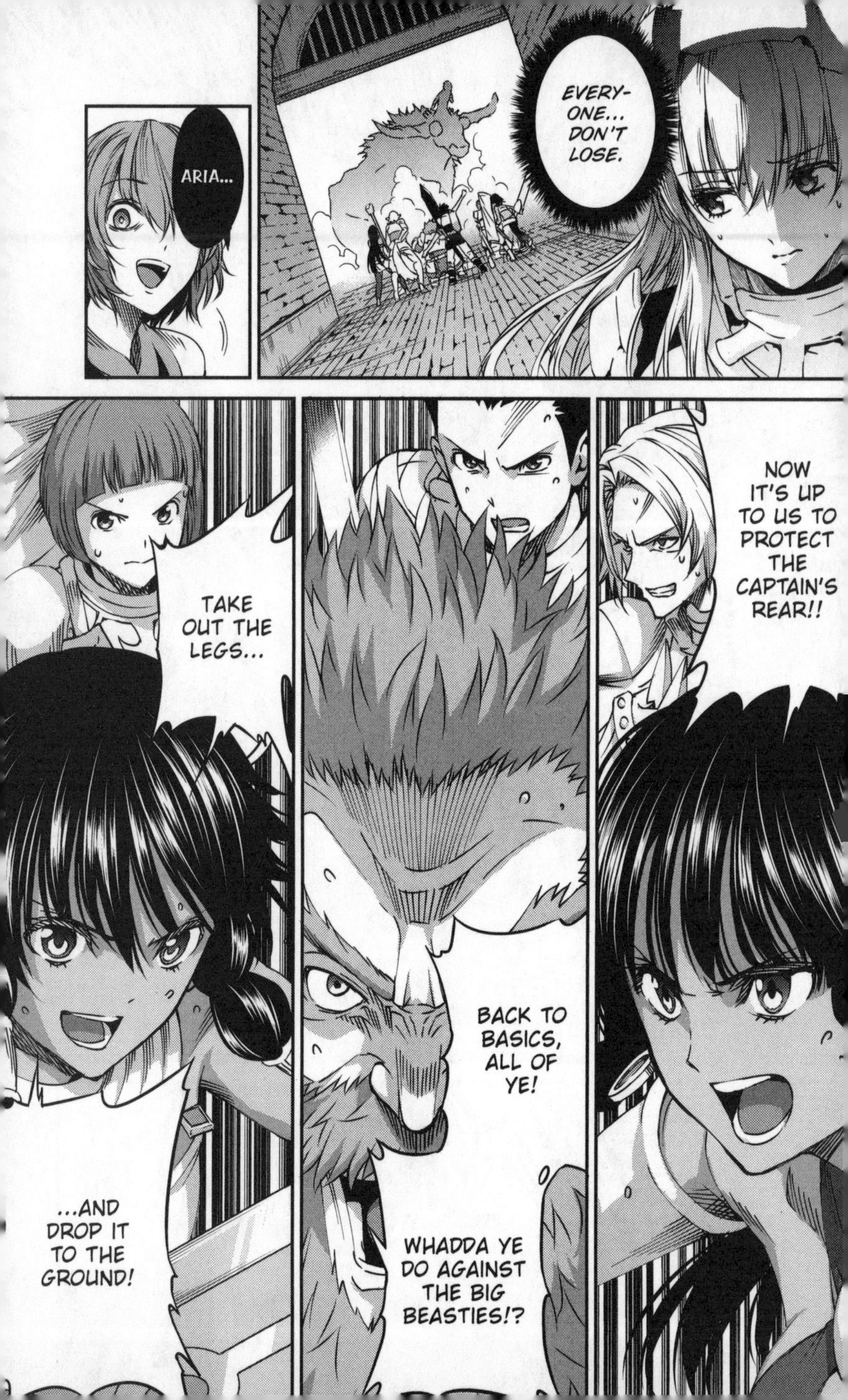
EVERY-ONE... DON'T LOSE.
ARIA...
NOW IT'S UP TO US TO PROTECT THE CAPTAIN'S REAR!!
BACK TO BASICS, ALL OF YE!
WHADDA YE DO AGAINST THE BIG BEASTIES!?
TAKE OUT THE LEGS...
...AND DROP IT TO THE GROUND!

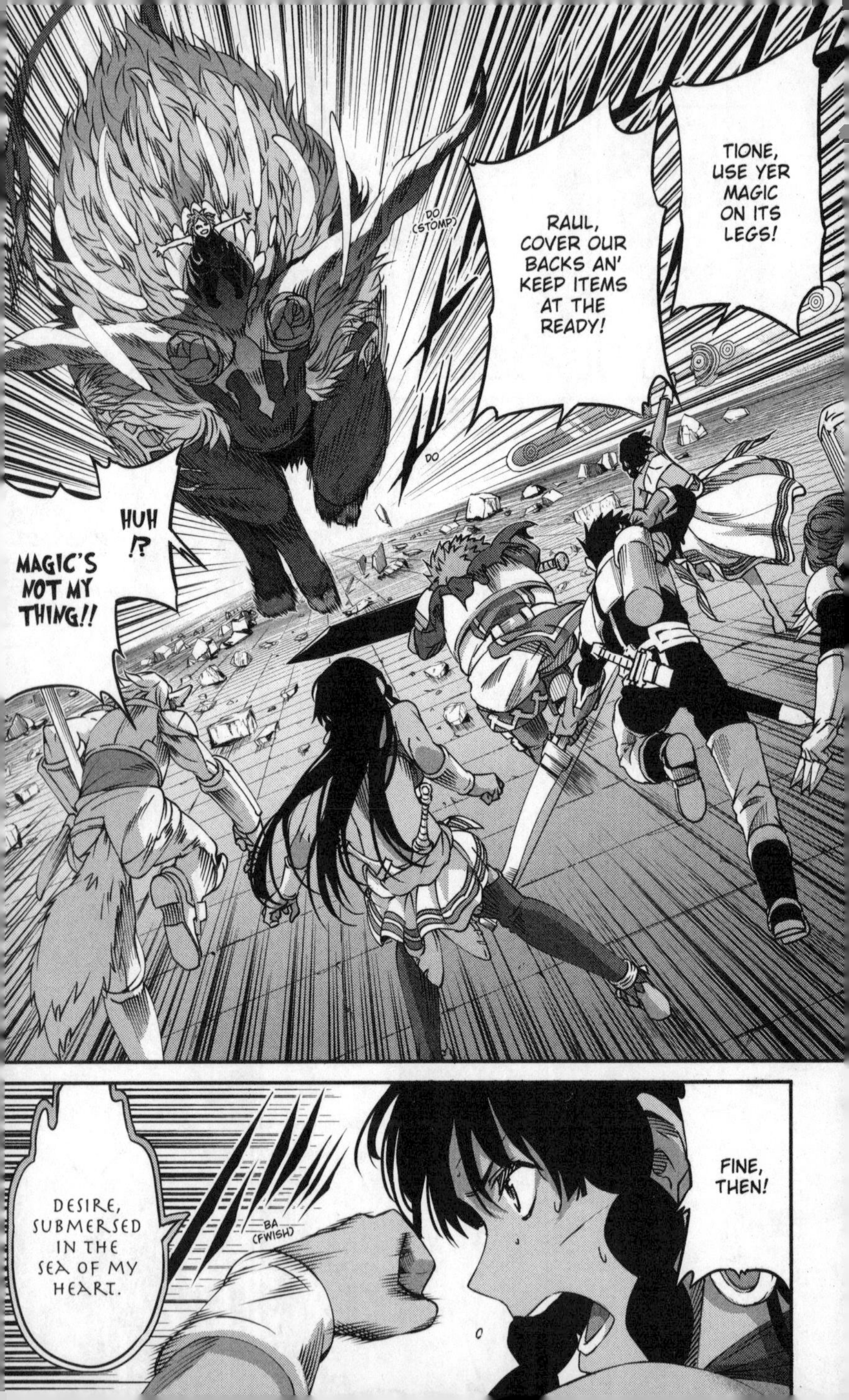
TIONE, USE YER MAGIC ON ITS LEGS!
RAUL, COVER OUR BACKS AN' KEEP ITEMS AT THE READY!
DO (STOMP)
DO
HUH !?
MAGIC'S NOT MY THING!!
FINE, THEN!
BA (FWISH)
DESIRE, SUBMERSED IN THE SEA OF MY HEART.

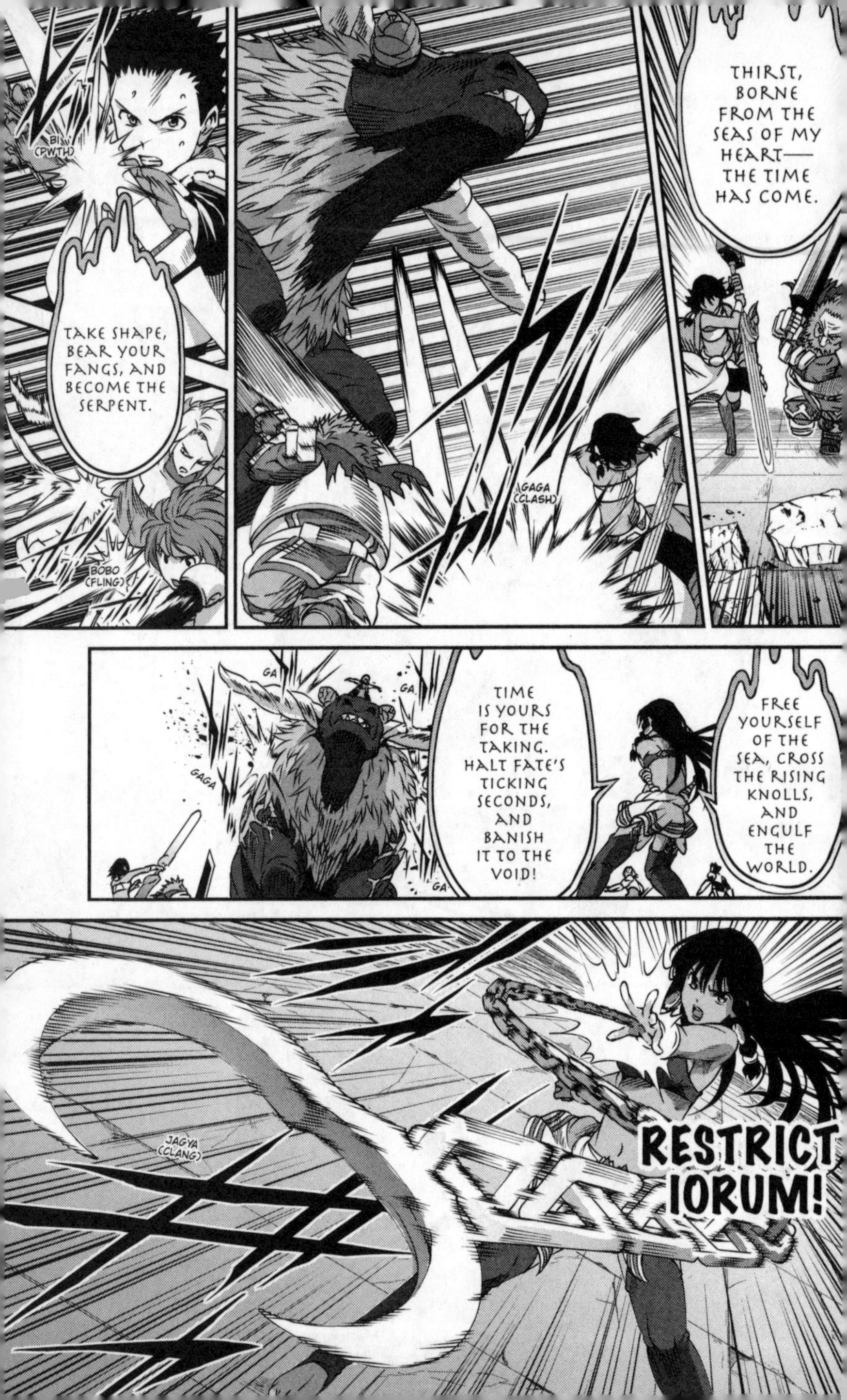
THIRST, BORNE FROM THE SEAS OF MY HEART—THE TIME HAS COME.
GAGA (CLASH)
BI (PWTH)
TAKE SHAPE, BEAR YOUR FANGS, AND BECOME THE SERPENT.
BOBO (FLING)
FREE YOURSELF OF THE SEA, CROSS THE RISING KNOLLS, AND ENGULF THE WORLD.
TIME IS YOURS FOR THE TAKING. HALT FATE'S TICKING SECONDS, AND BANISH IT TO THE VOID!
GA
GA
GAGA
GA
RESTRICT IORUM!
JAGYA (CLANG)

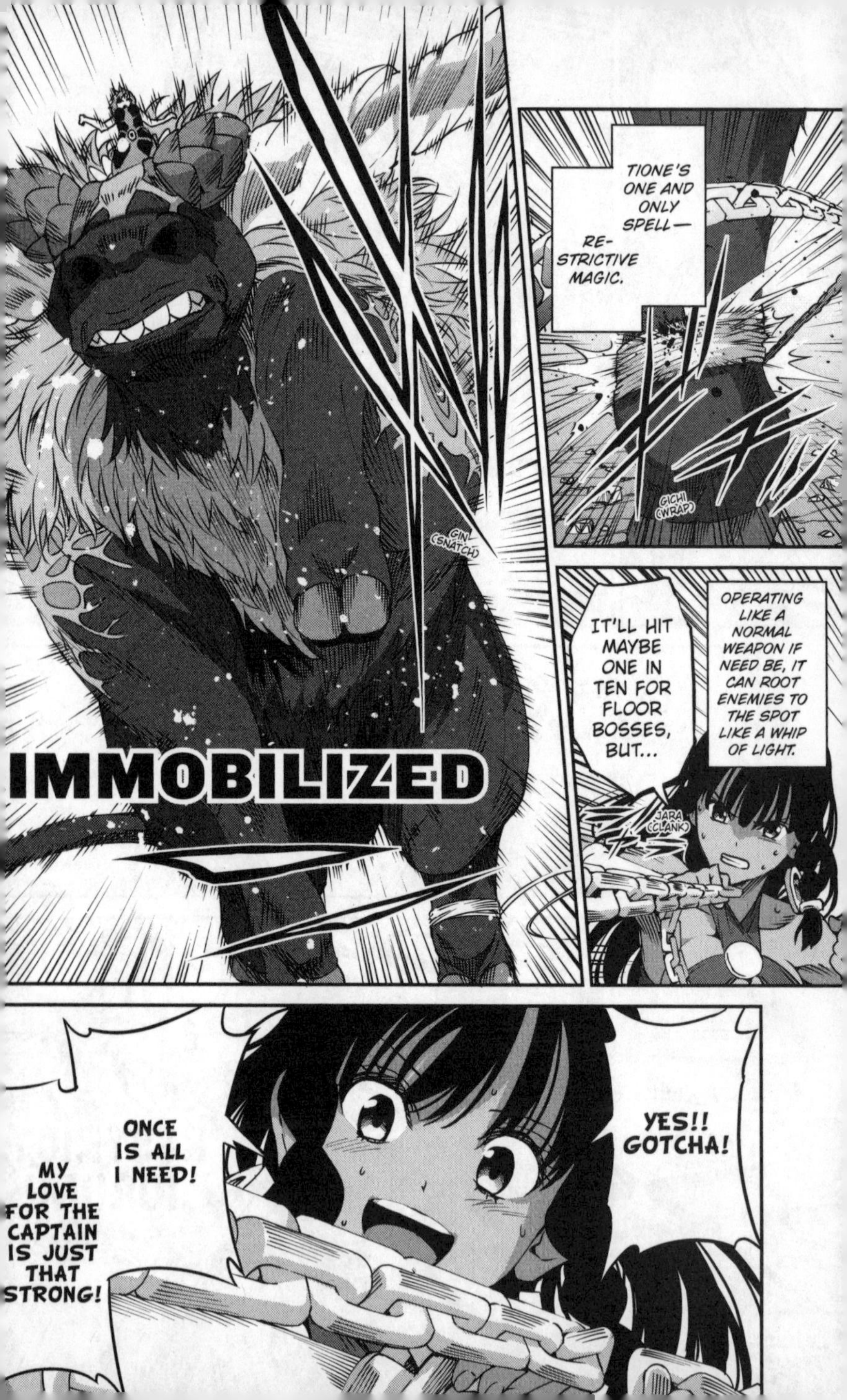
TIONE'S ONE AND ONLY SPELL—
RE-STRICTIVE MAGIC.
GICHI (WRAP)
OPERATING LIKE A NORMAL WEAPON IF NEED BE, IT CAN ROOT ENEMIES TO THE SPOT LIKE A WHIP OF LIGHT.
IT'LL HIT MAYBE ONE IN TEN FOR FLOOR BOSSES, BUT...
JARA (CLANK)
GIN (SNATCH)
IMMOBILIZED
YES!! GOTCHA!
ONCE IS ALL I NEED!
MY LOVE FOR THE CAPTAIN IS JUST THAT STRONG!

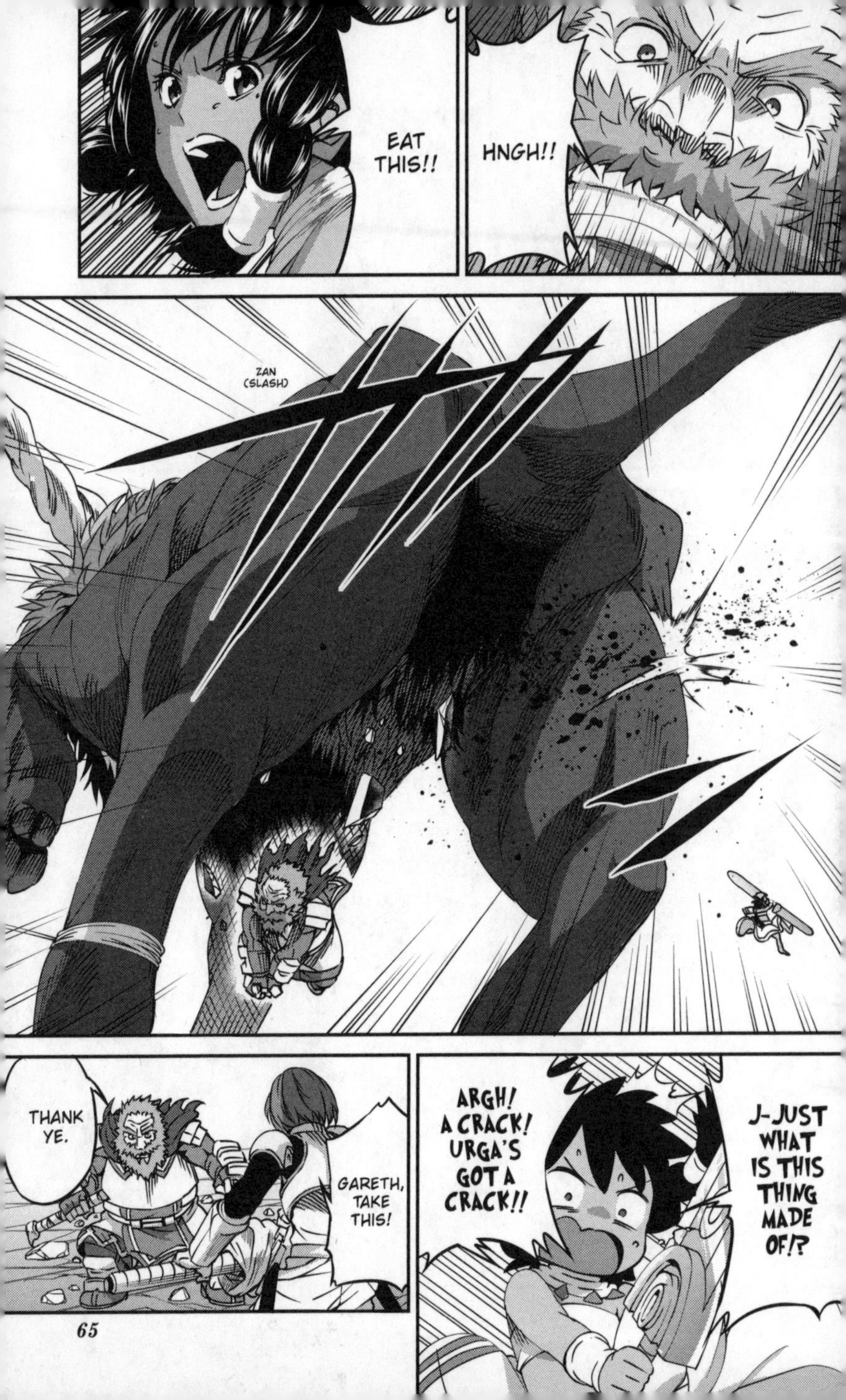
HNGH!!
EAT THIS!!
ZAN (SLASH)
J-JUST WHAT IS THIS THING MADE OF!?
ARGH! A CRACK! URGA'S GOT A CRACK!!
GARETH, TAKE THIS!
THANK YE.

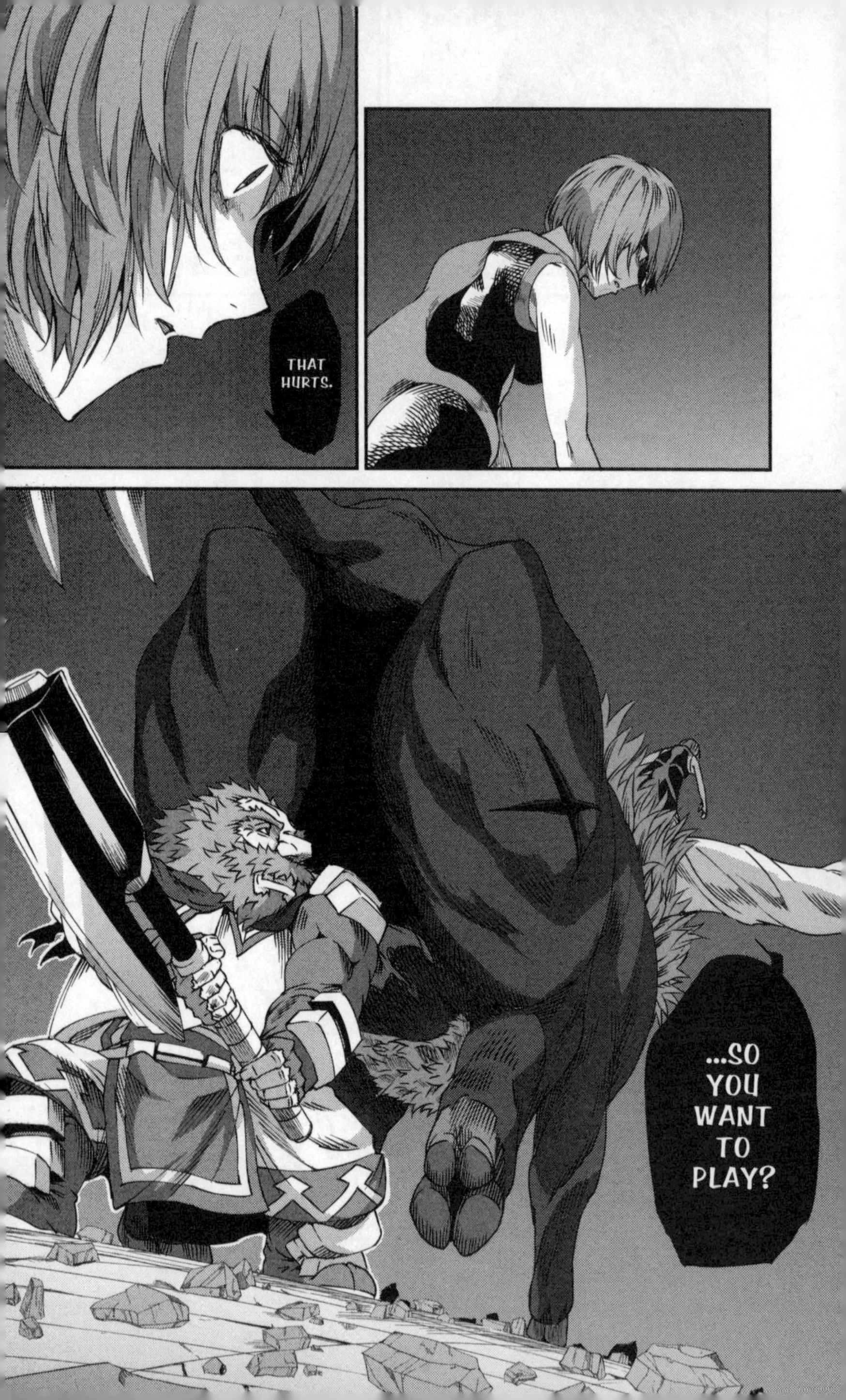
THAT HURTS.
...SO YOU WANT TO PLAY?

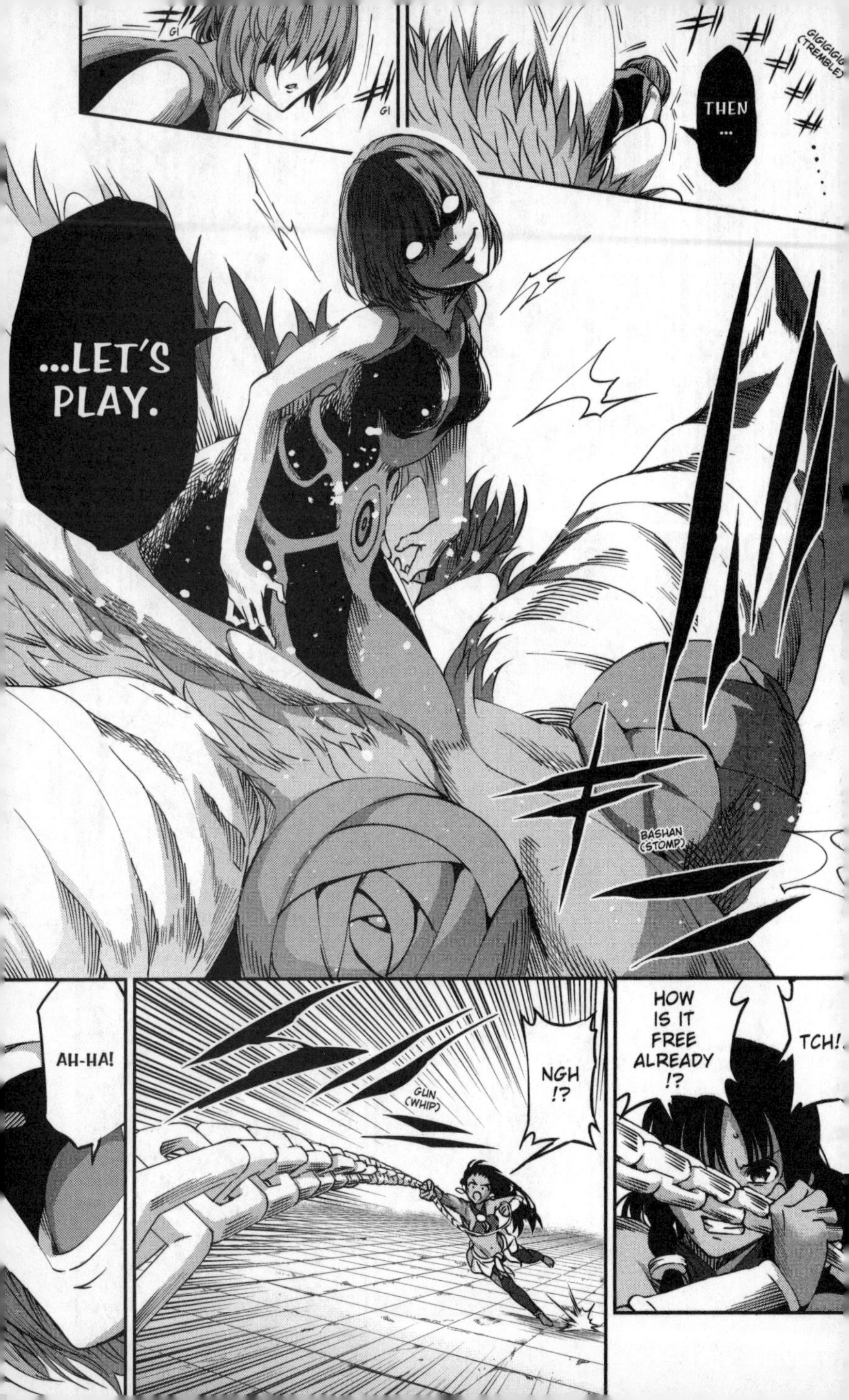
GIGIGIGI (TREMBLE)
THEN ...
GI
GI
...LET'S PLAY.
BASHAN (STOMP)
TCH!
HOW IS IT FREE ALREADY !?
NGH !?
GUN (WHIP)
AH-HA!

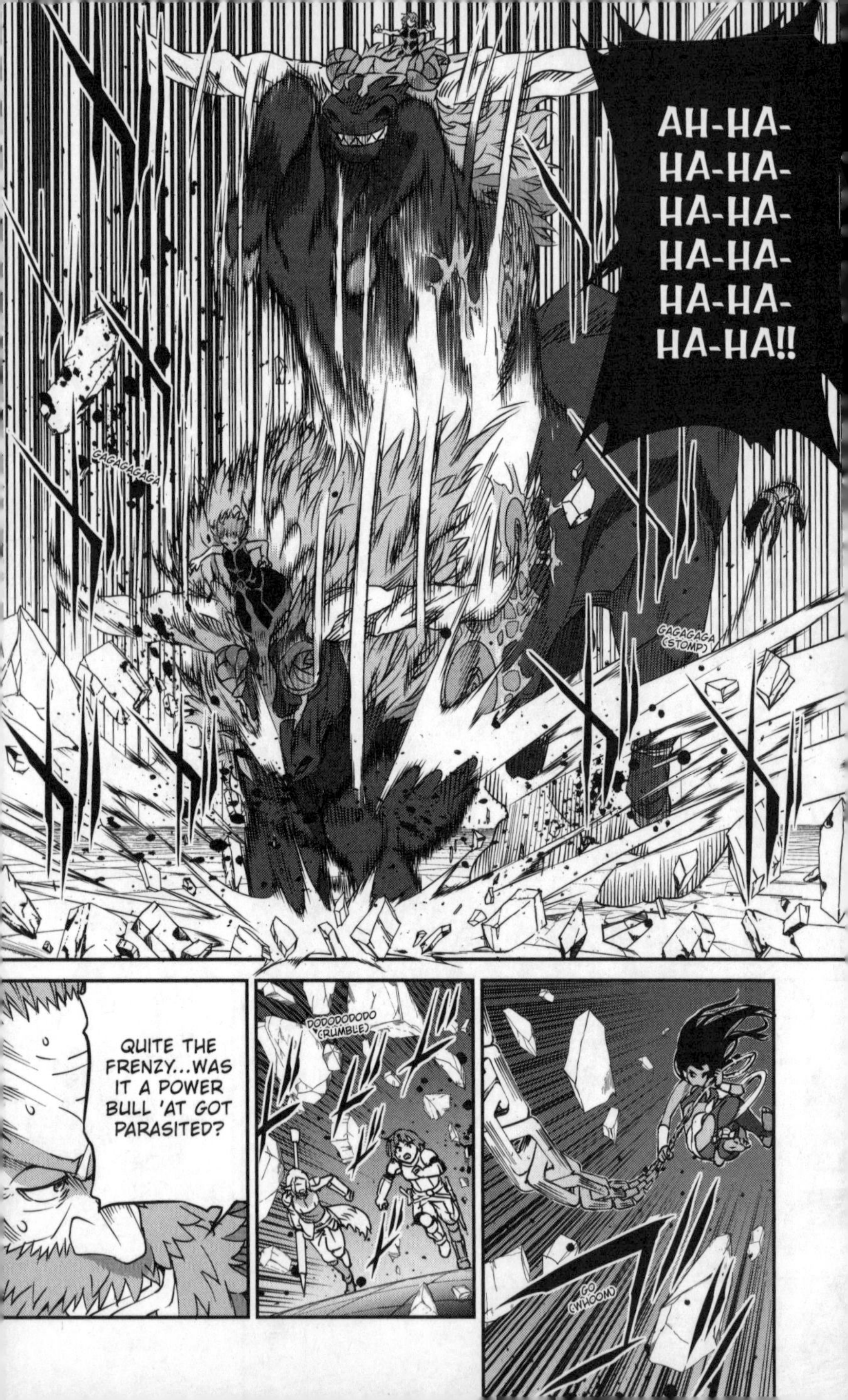
AH-HA-HA-HA-HA-HA-HA-HA-HA-HA-HA-HA!!
GAGAGAGA
GAGAGAGA (STOMP)
GO (WHOOM)
DODODODODO (RUMBLE)
QUITE THE FRENZY...WAS IT A POWER BULL 'AT GOT PARASITED?

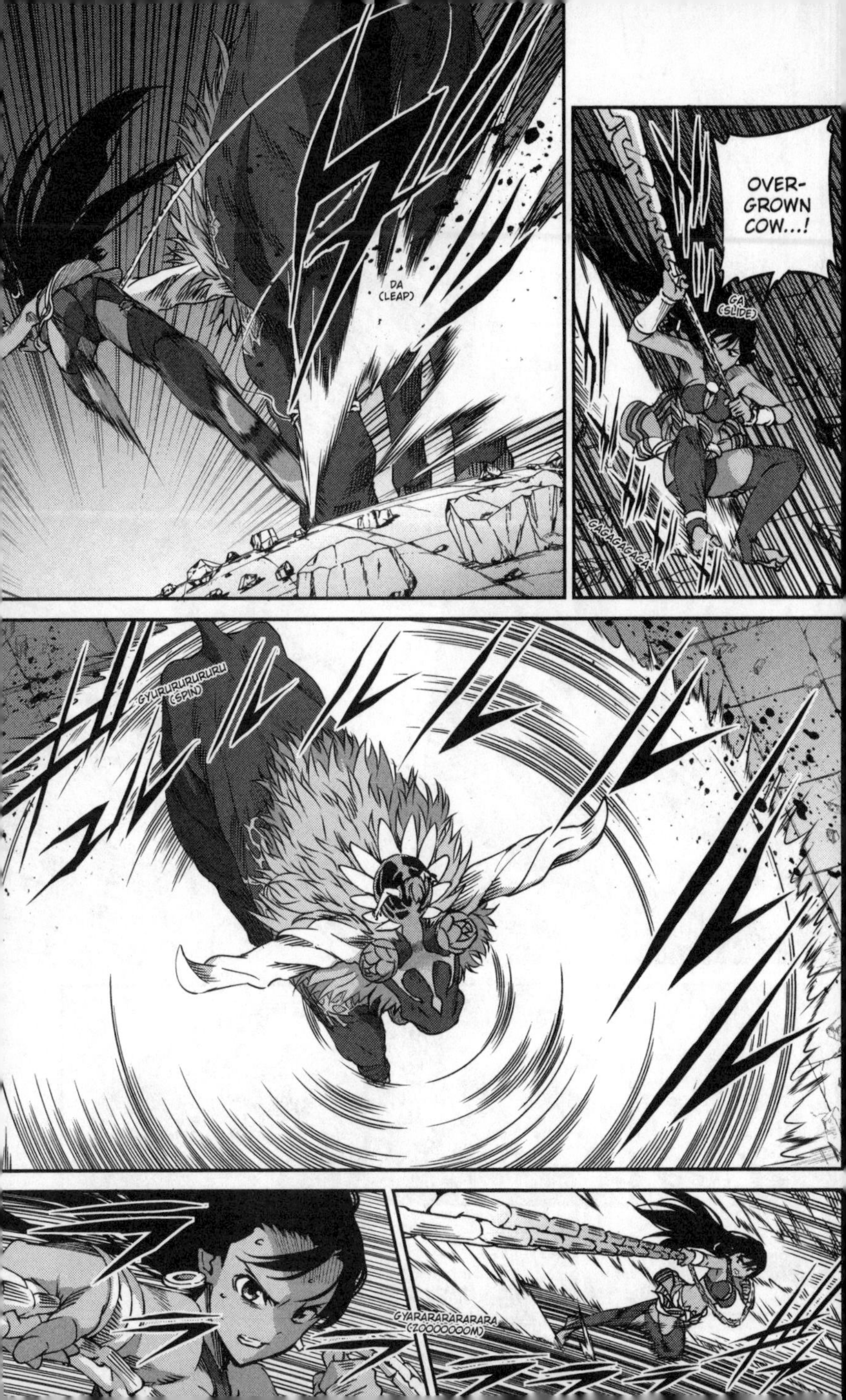
OVER-GROWN COW...!
GA (SLIDE)
GAGAGAGAGA
DA (LEAP)
GYURURURURURU (SPIN)
GYARARARARARARA (ZOOOOOOOM)

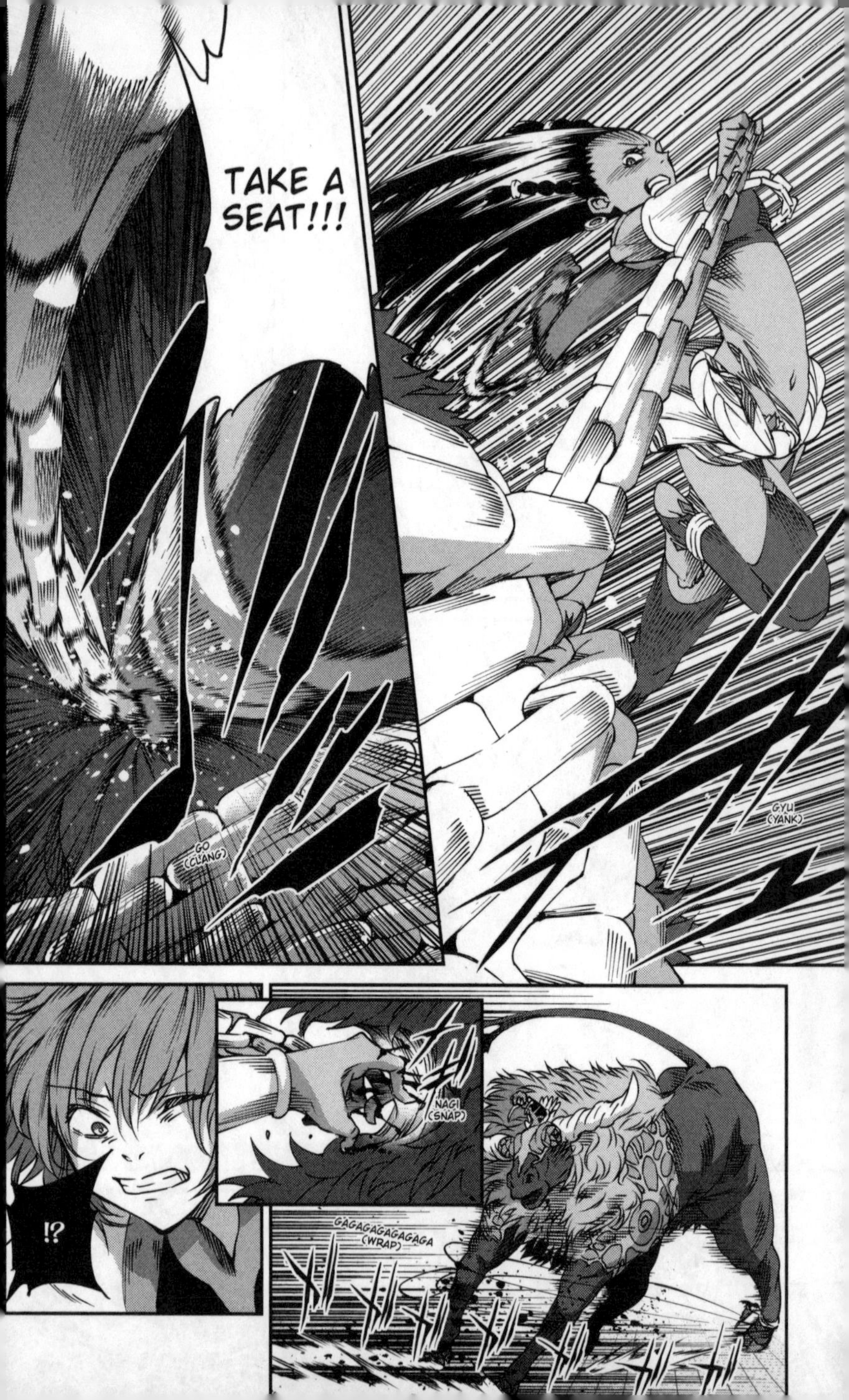
GYU
(YANK)
TAKE A SEAT!!!
GO
(CLANG)
NAGI
(SNAP)
GAGAGAGAGAGA
(WRAP)
!?

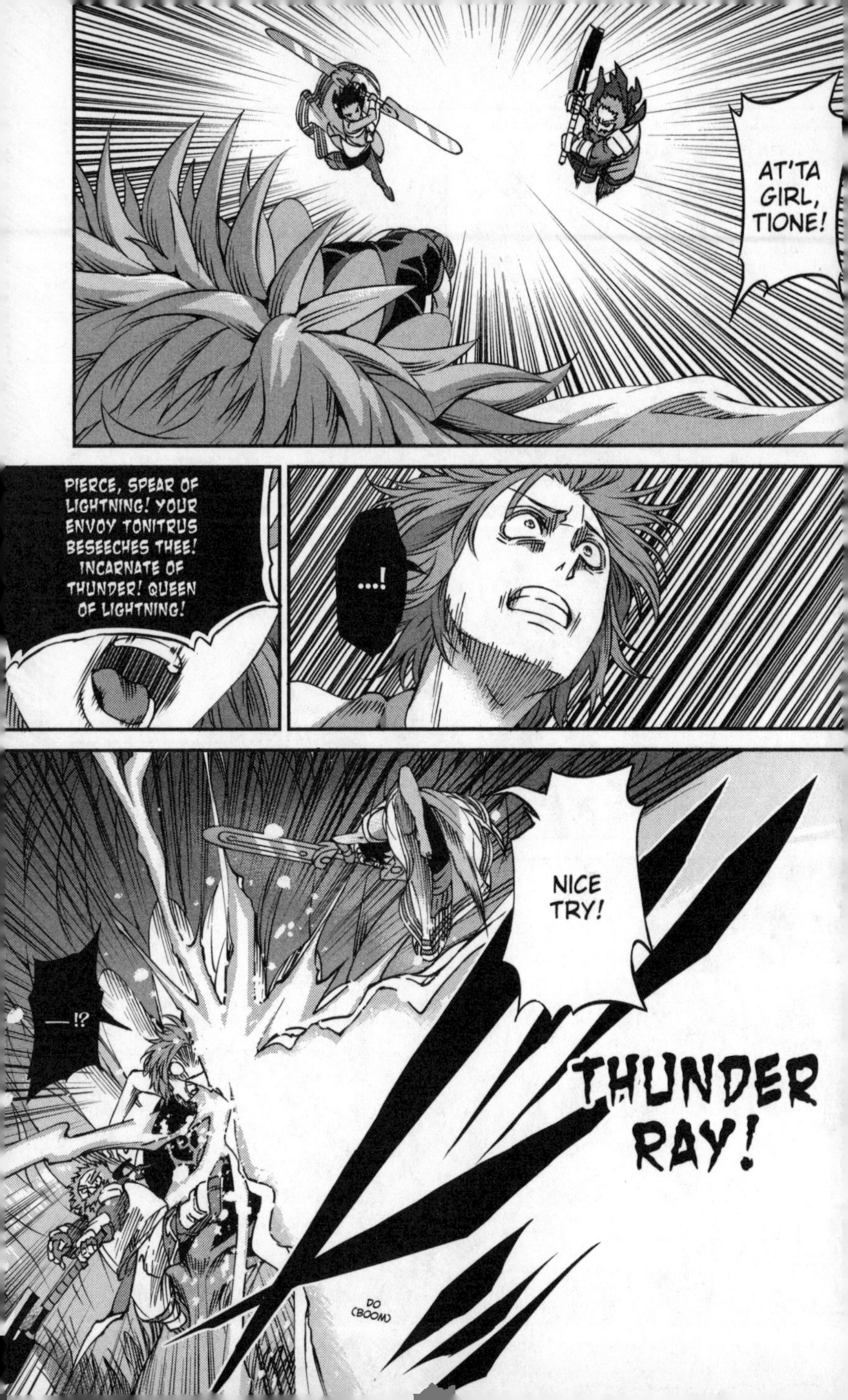
AT'TA GIRL, TIONE!
...!
PIERCE, SPEAR OF LIGHTNING! YOUR ENVOY TONITRUS BESEECHES THEE! INCARNATE OF THUNDER! QUEEN OF LIGHTNING!
NICE TRY!
THUNDER RAY!
—!?
DO (BOOM)

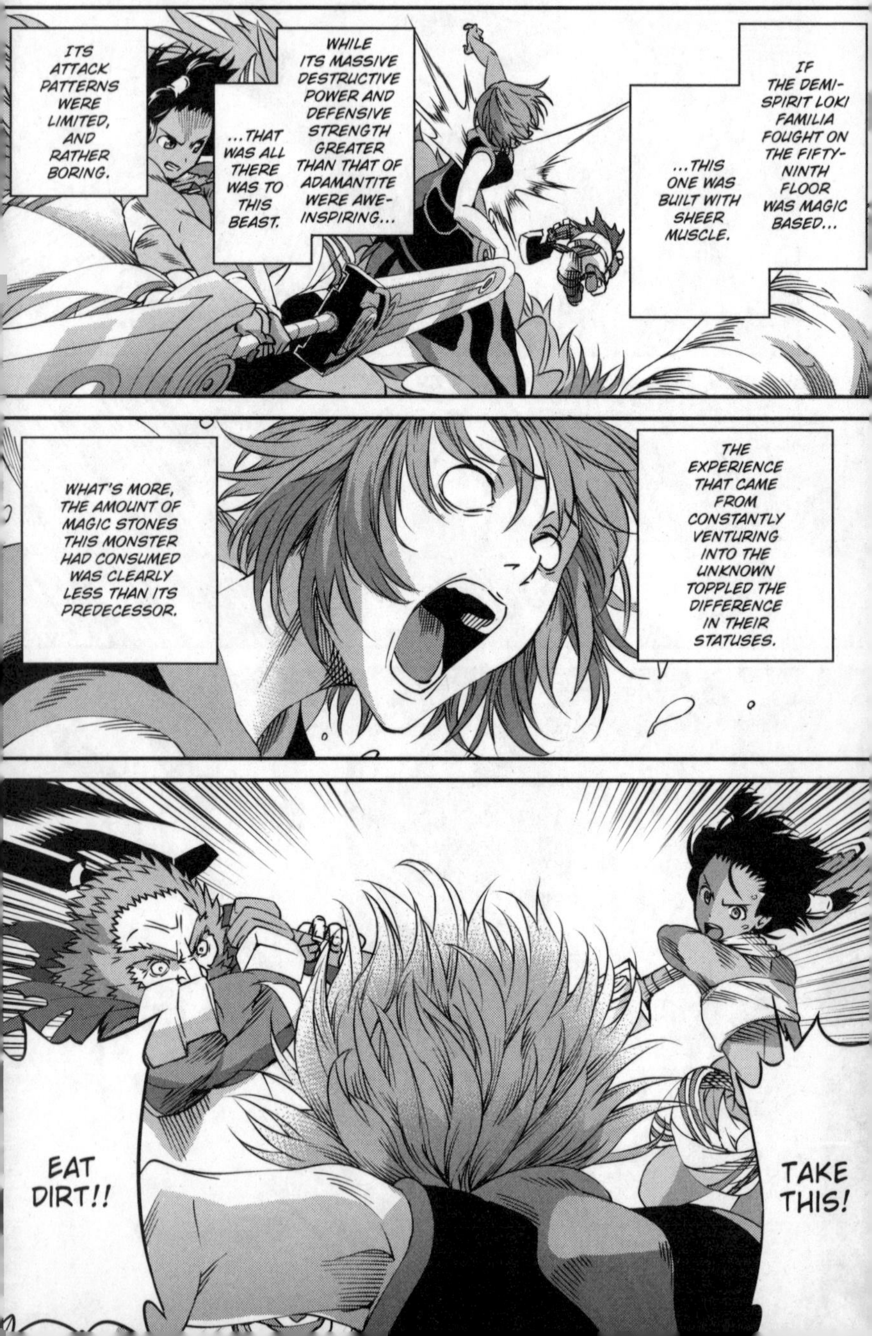
IF THE DEMI-SPIRIT LOKI FAMILIA FOUGHT ON THE FIFTY-NINTH FLOOR WAS MAGIC BASED...
...THIS ONE WAS BUILT WITH SHEER MUSCLE.
WHILE ITS MASSIVE DESTRUCTIVE POWER AND DEFENSIVE STRENGTH GREATER THAN THAT OF ADAMANTITE WERE AWE-INSPIRING...
...THAT WAS ALL THERE WAS TO THIS BEAST.
ITS ATTACK PATTERNS WERE LIMITED, AND RATHER BORING.
THE EXPERIENCE THAT CAME FROM CONSTANTLY VENTURING INTO THE UNKNOWN TOPPLED THE DIFFERENCE IN THEIR STATUSES.
WHAT'S MORE, THE AMOUNT OF MAGIC STONES THIS MONSTER HAD CONSUMED WAS CLEARLY LESS THAN ITS PREDECESSOR.
TAKE THIS!
EAT DIRT!!

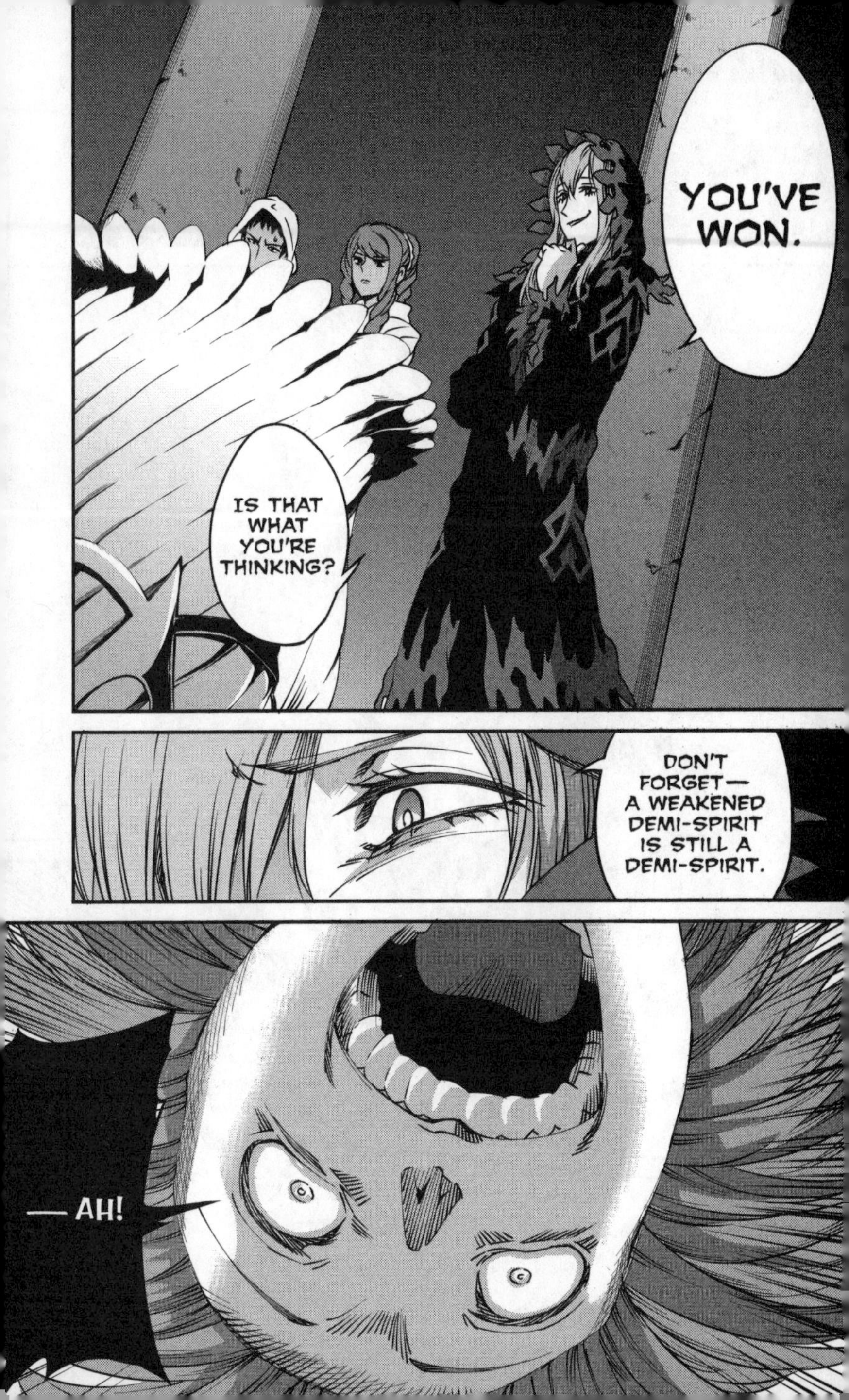
YOU'VE WON.
IS THAT WHAT YOU'RE THINKING?
DON'T FORGET— A WEAKENED DEMI-SPIRIT IS STILL A DEMI-SPIRIT.
—AH!

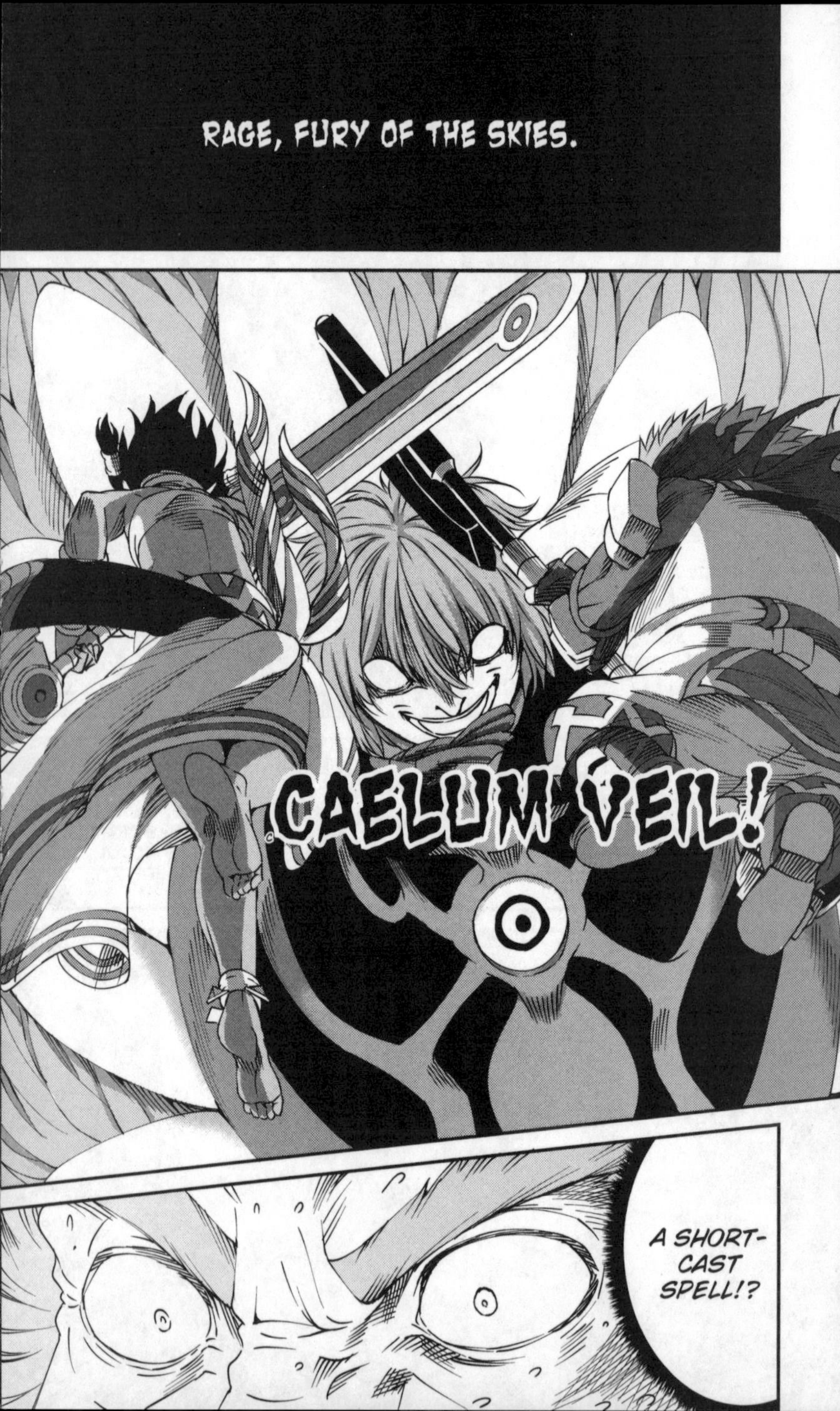
RAGE, FURY OF THE SKIES.
CAELUM VEIL!
A SHORT-CAST SPELL!?

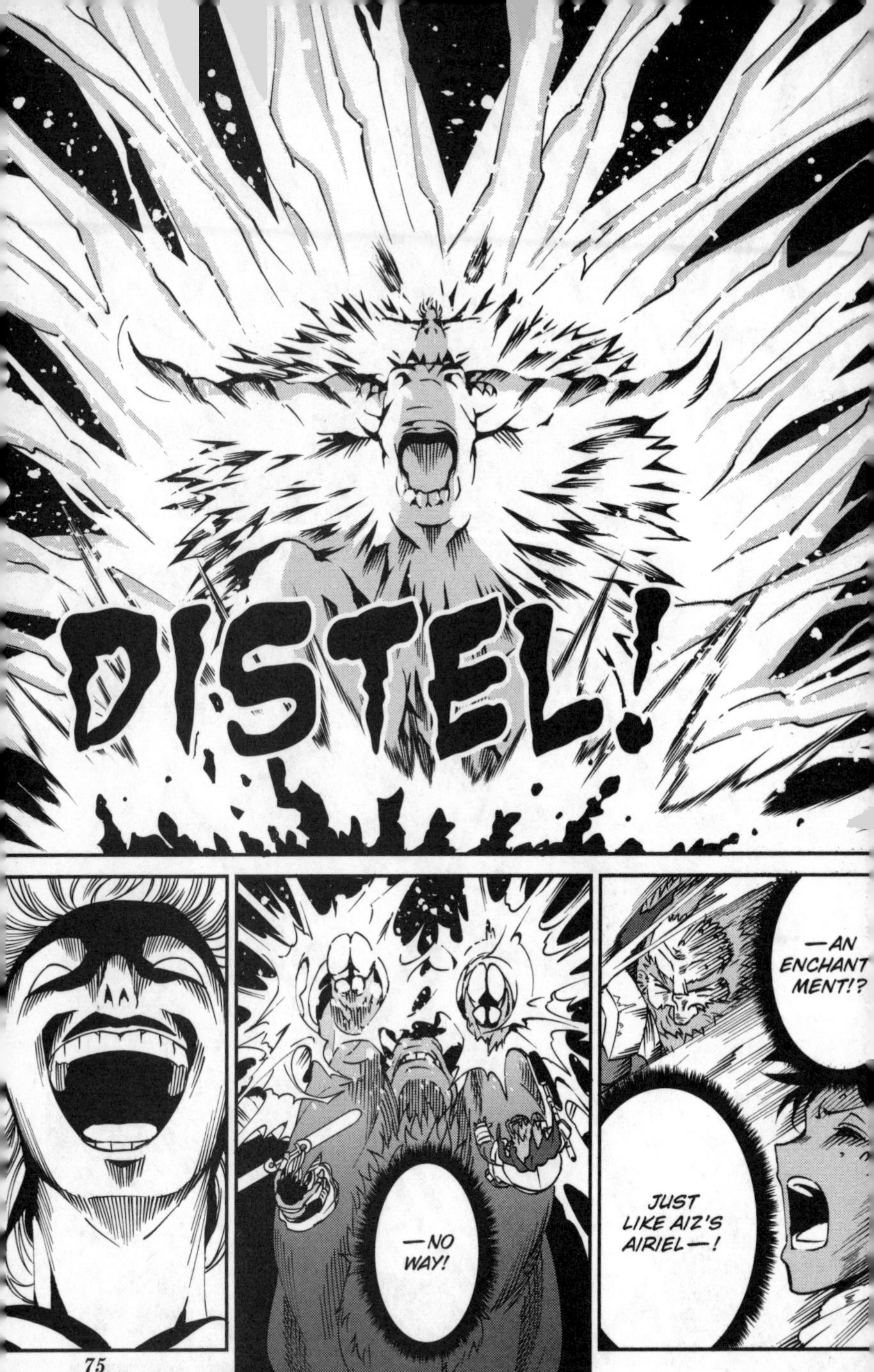
DISTEL!
—AN ENCHANTMENT!?
JUST LIKE AIZ'S AIRIEL—!
—NO WAY!

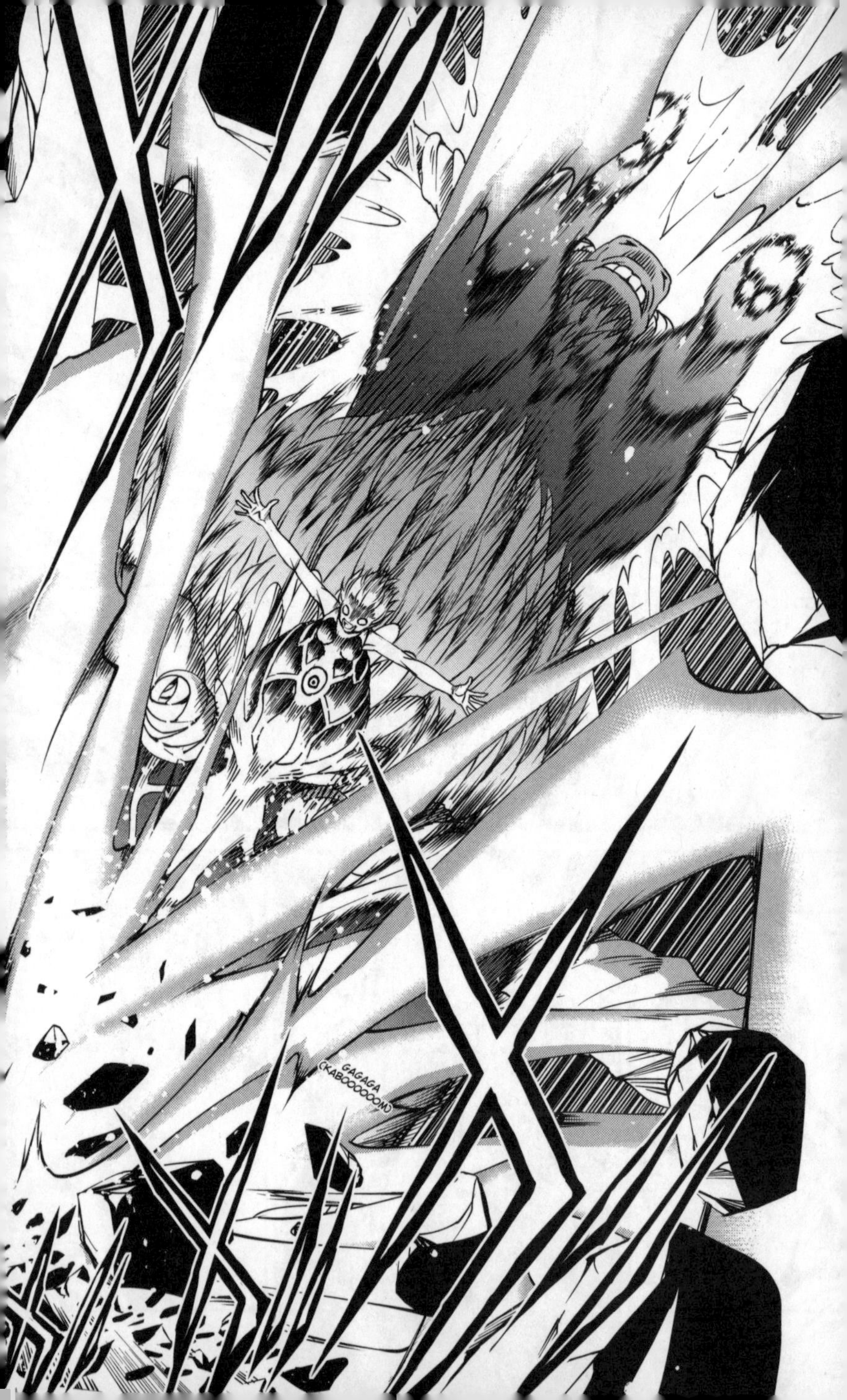
GAGAGA
(KABOOOOOOM)

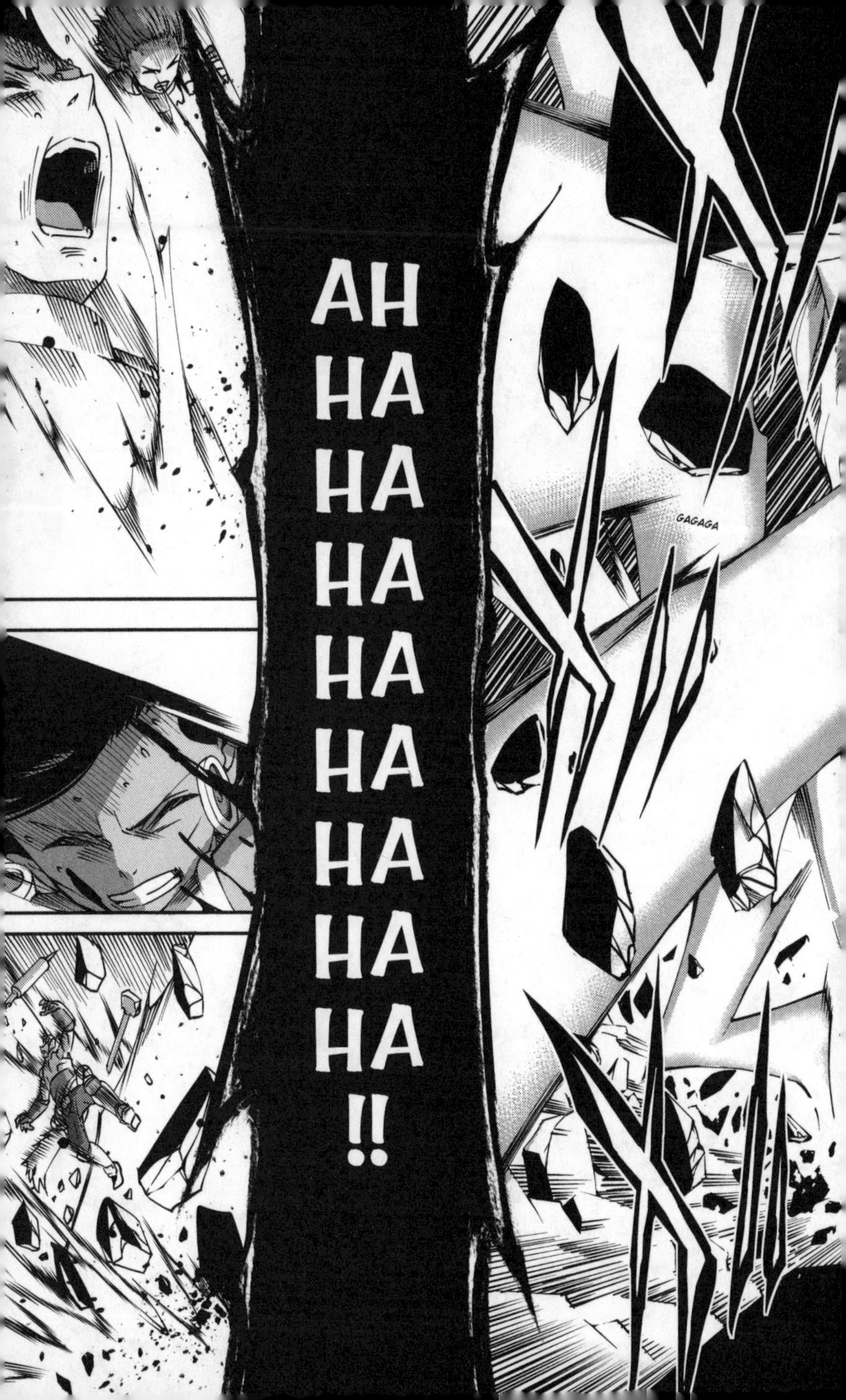
GAGAGA
AH HA HA HA HA HA HA HA HA HA!!

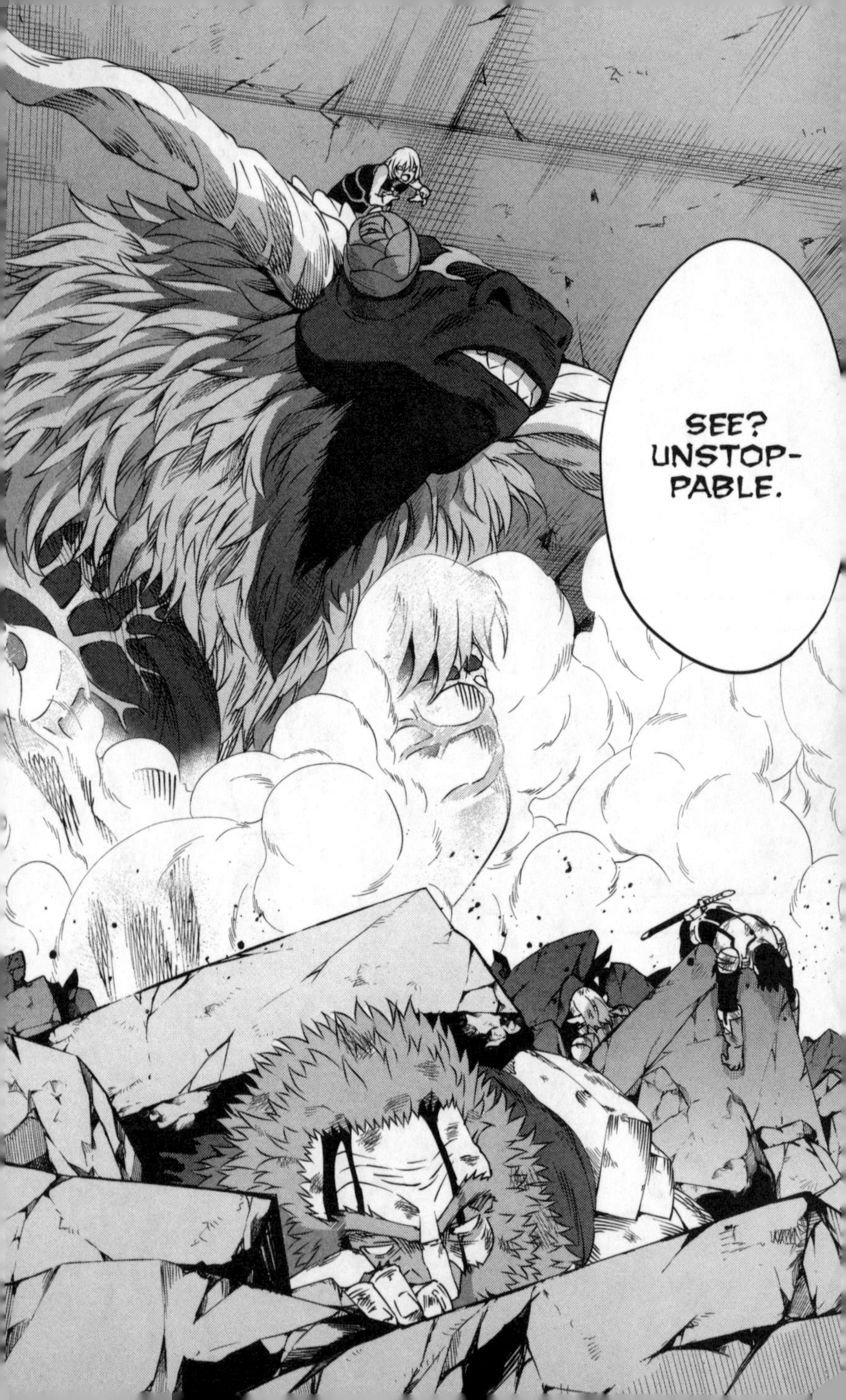
SEE? UNSTOP-PABLE.

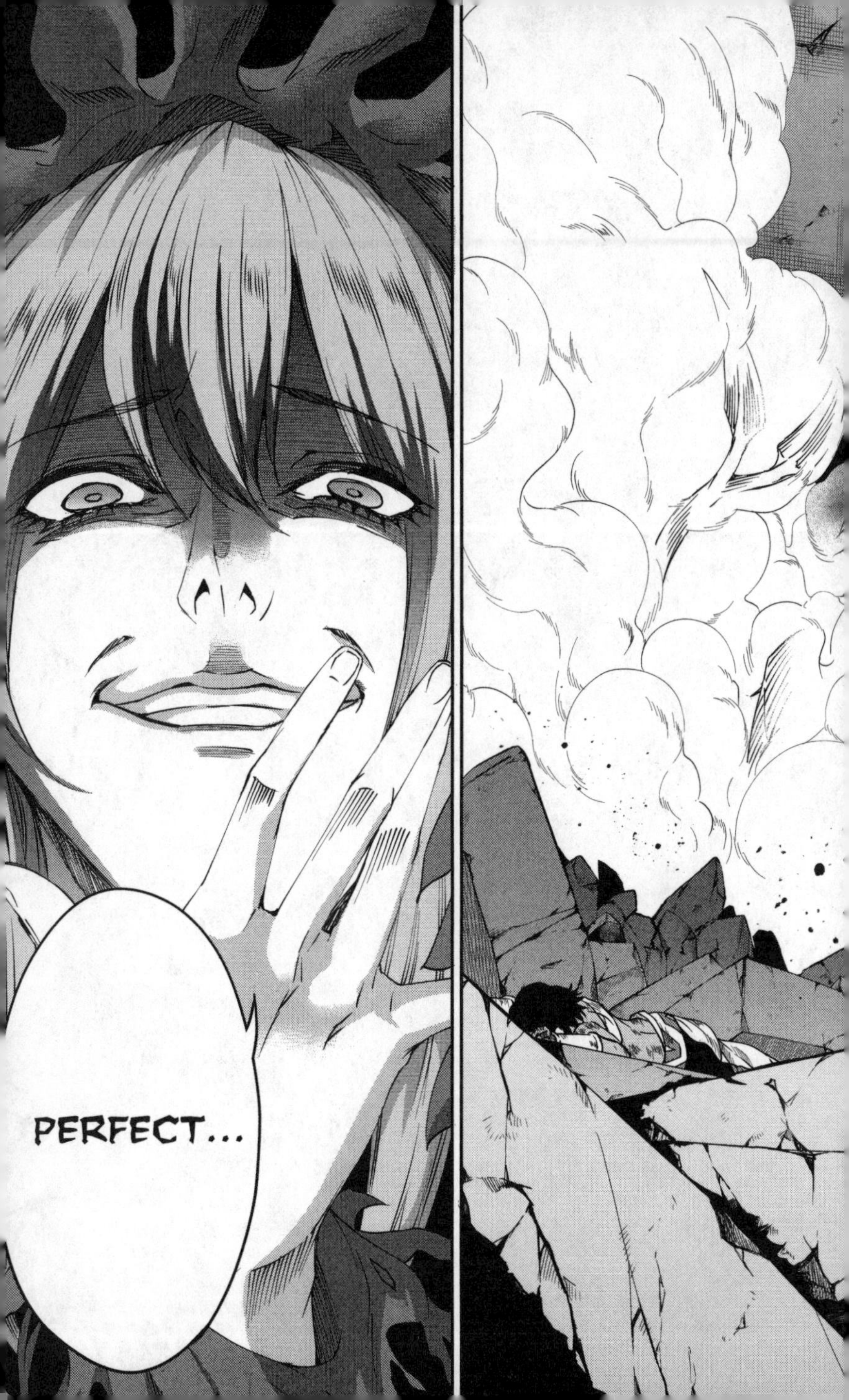
PERFECT...

Is it Wrong to Try to Pick Up Girls in a Dungeon? On the Side

Sword Oratoria

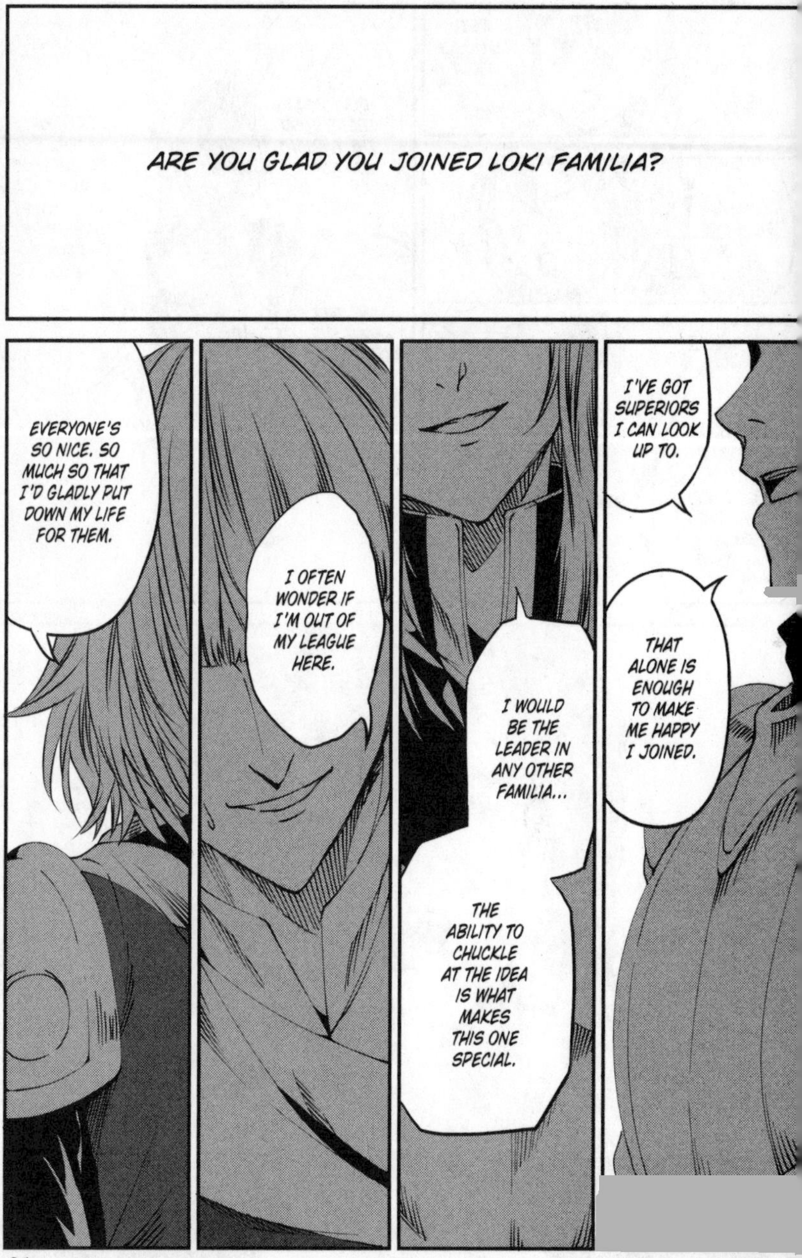
ARE YOU GLAD YOU JOINED LOKI FAMILIA?
I'VE GOT SUPERIORS I CAN LOOK UP TO.
THAT ALONE IS ENOUGH TO MAKE ME HAPPY I JOINED.
I WOULD BE THE LEADER IN ANY OTHER FAMILIA...
THE ABILITY TO CHUCKLE AT THE IDEA IS WHAT MAKES THIS ONE SPECIAL.
I OFTEN WONDER IF I'M OUT OF MY LEAGUE HERE.
EVERYONE'S SO NICE. SO MUCH SO THAT I'D GLADLY PUT DOWN MY LIFE FOR THEM.

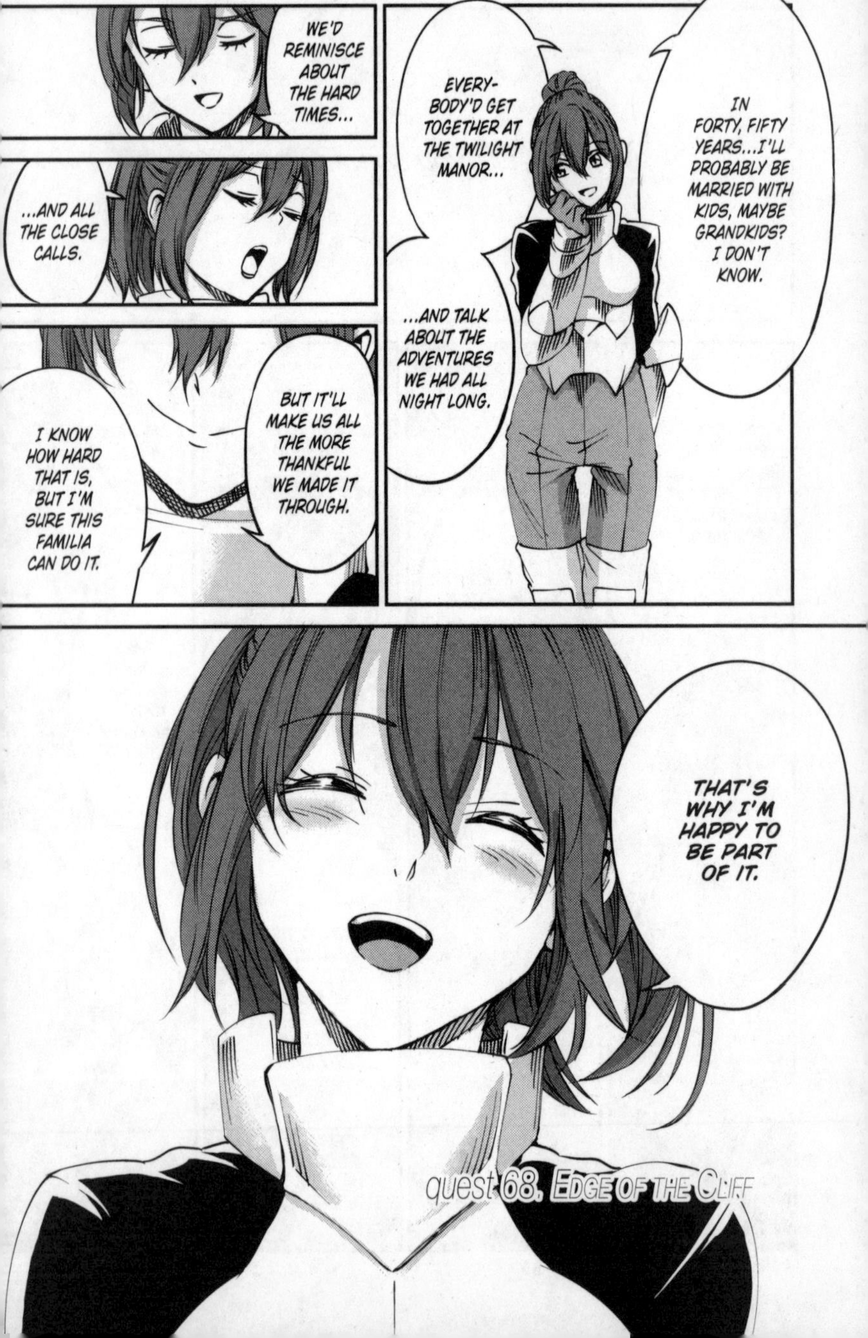
IN FORTY, FIFTY YEARS...I'LL PROBABLY BE MARRIED WITH KIDS, MAYBE GRANDKIDS? I DON'T KNOW.
EVERY-BODY'D GET TOGETHER AT THE TWILIGHT MANOR...
...AND TALK ABOUT THE ADVENTURES WE HAD ALL NIGHT LONG.
WE'D REMINISCE ABOUT THE HARD TIMES...
...AND ALL THE CLOSE CALLS.
BUT IT'LL MAKE US ALL THE MORE THANKFUL WE MADE IT THROUGH.
I KNOW HOW HARD THAT IS, BUT I'M SURE THIS FAMILIA CAN DO IT.
THAT'S WHY I'M HAPPY TO BE PART OF IT.
quest 68. Edge of the Cliff

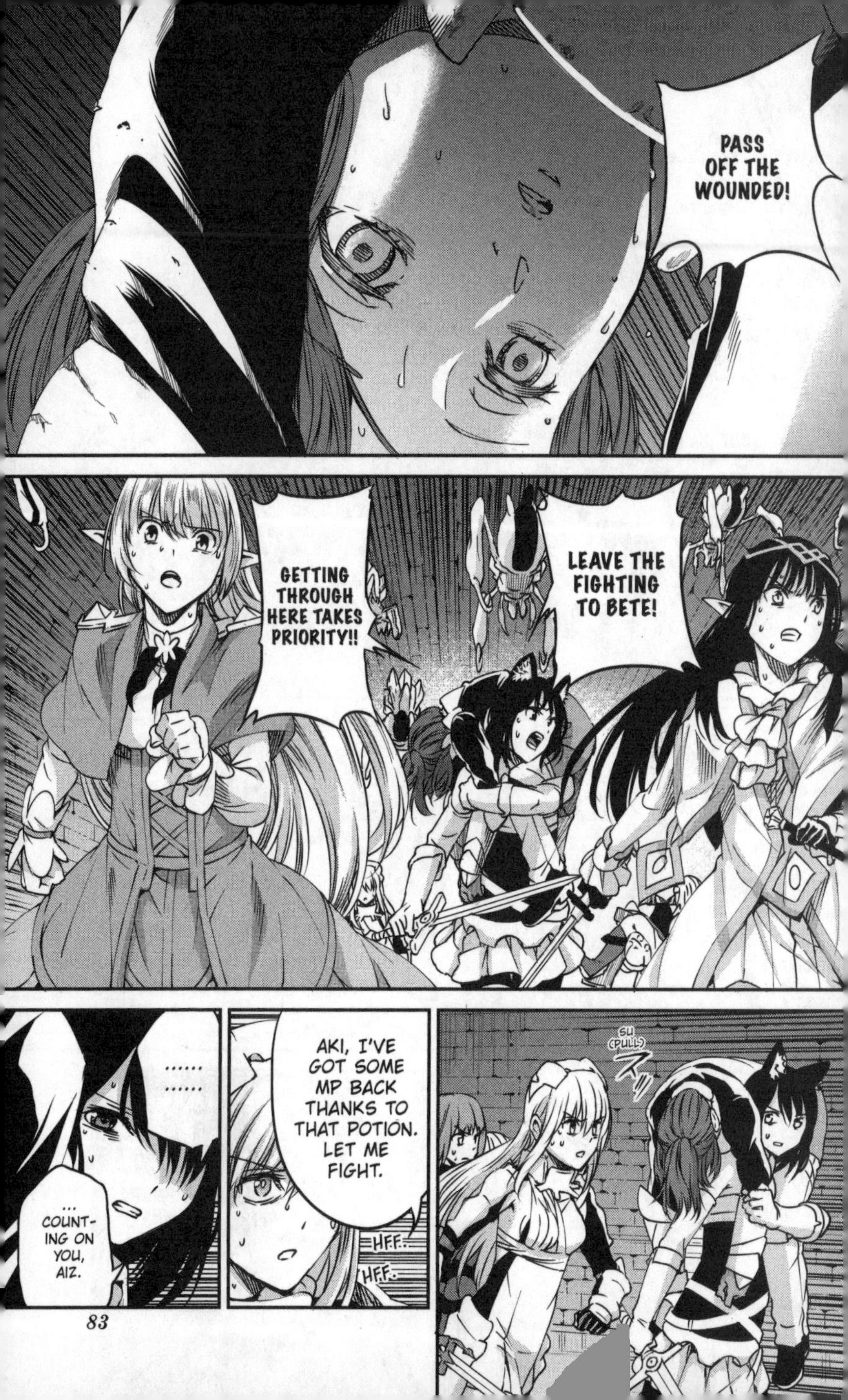
PASS OFF THE WOUNDED!
LEAVE THE FIGHTING TO BETE!
GETTING THROUGH HERE TAKES PRIORITY!!
SU (PULL)
AKI, I'VE GOT SOME MP BACK THANKS TO THAT POTION. LET ME FIGHT.
HFF..
HFF.
......
......
... COUNTING ON YOU, AIZ.

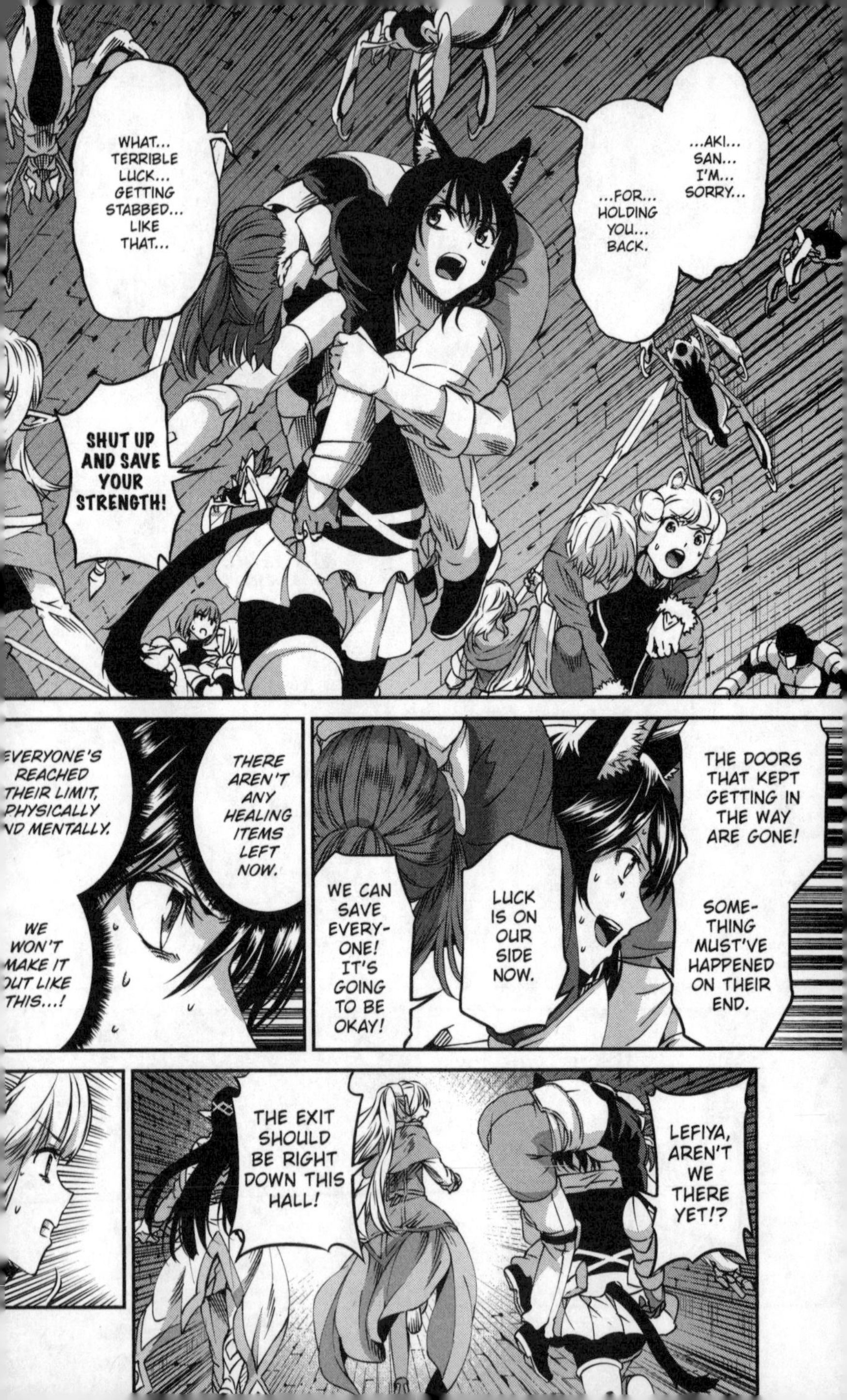
...AKI... SAN... I'M... SORRY... ...FOR... HOLDING YOU... BACK.
WHAT... TERRIBLE LUCK... GETTING STABBED... LIKE THAT...
SHUT UP AND SAVE YOUR STRENGTH!
THE DOORS THAT KEPT GETTING IN THE WAY ARE GONE!
SOME-THING MUST'VE HAPPENED ON THEIR END.
LUCK IS ON OUR SIDE NOW.
WE CAN SAVE EVERY-ONE! IT'S GOING TO BE OKAY!
THERE AREN'T ANY HEALING ITEMS LEFT NOW.
EVERYONE'S REACHED THEIR LIMIT, PHYSICALLY ND MENTALLY.
WE WON'T MAKE IT UT LIKE THIS...!
LEFIYA, AREN'T WE THERE YET!?
THE EXIT SHOULD BE RIGHT DOWN THIS HALL!

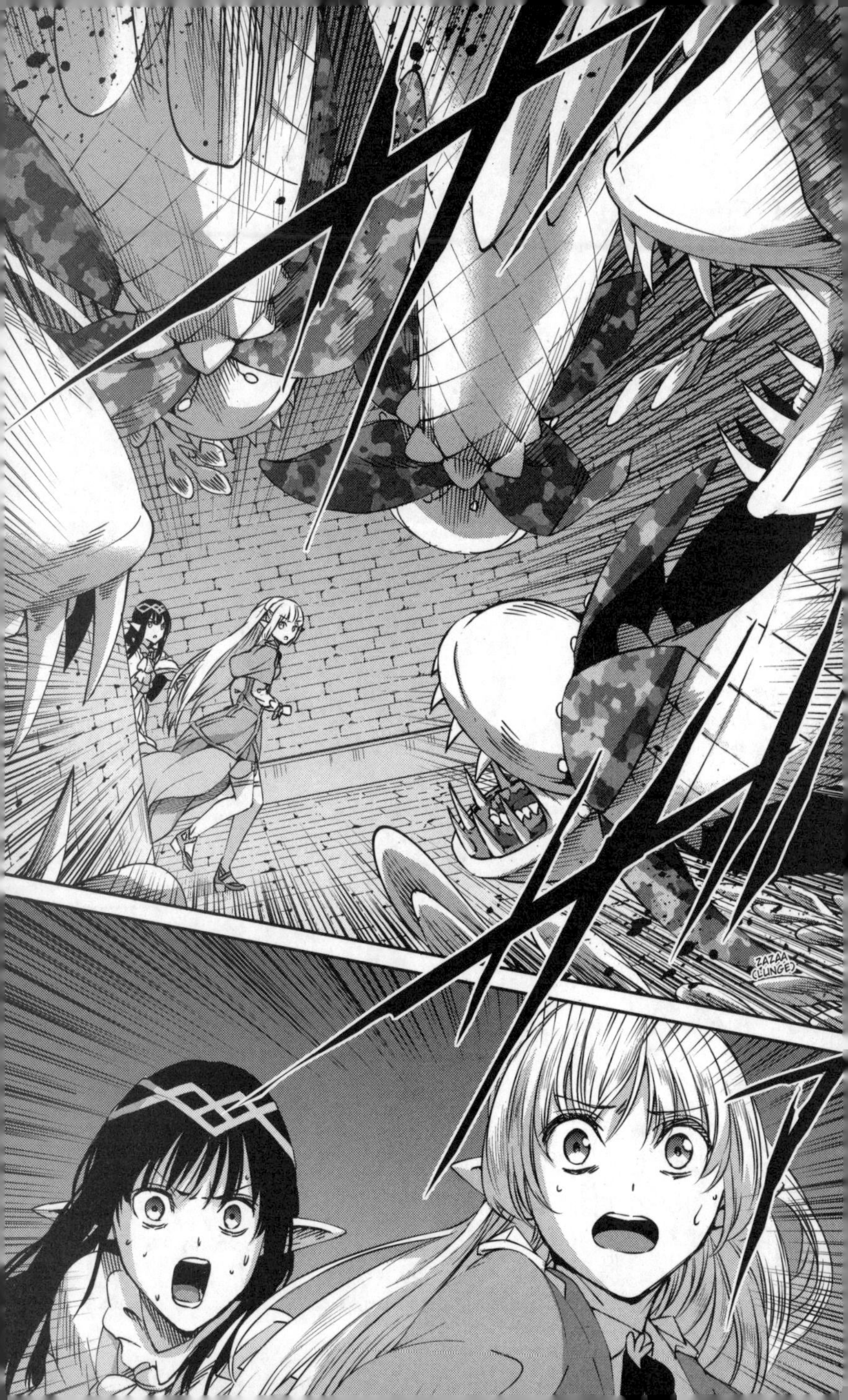
ZAZAA
(LUNGE)

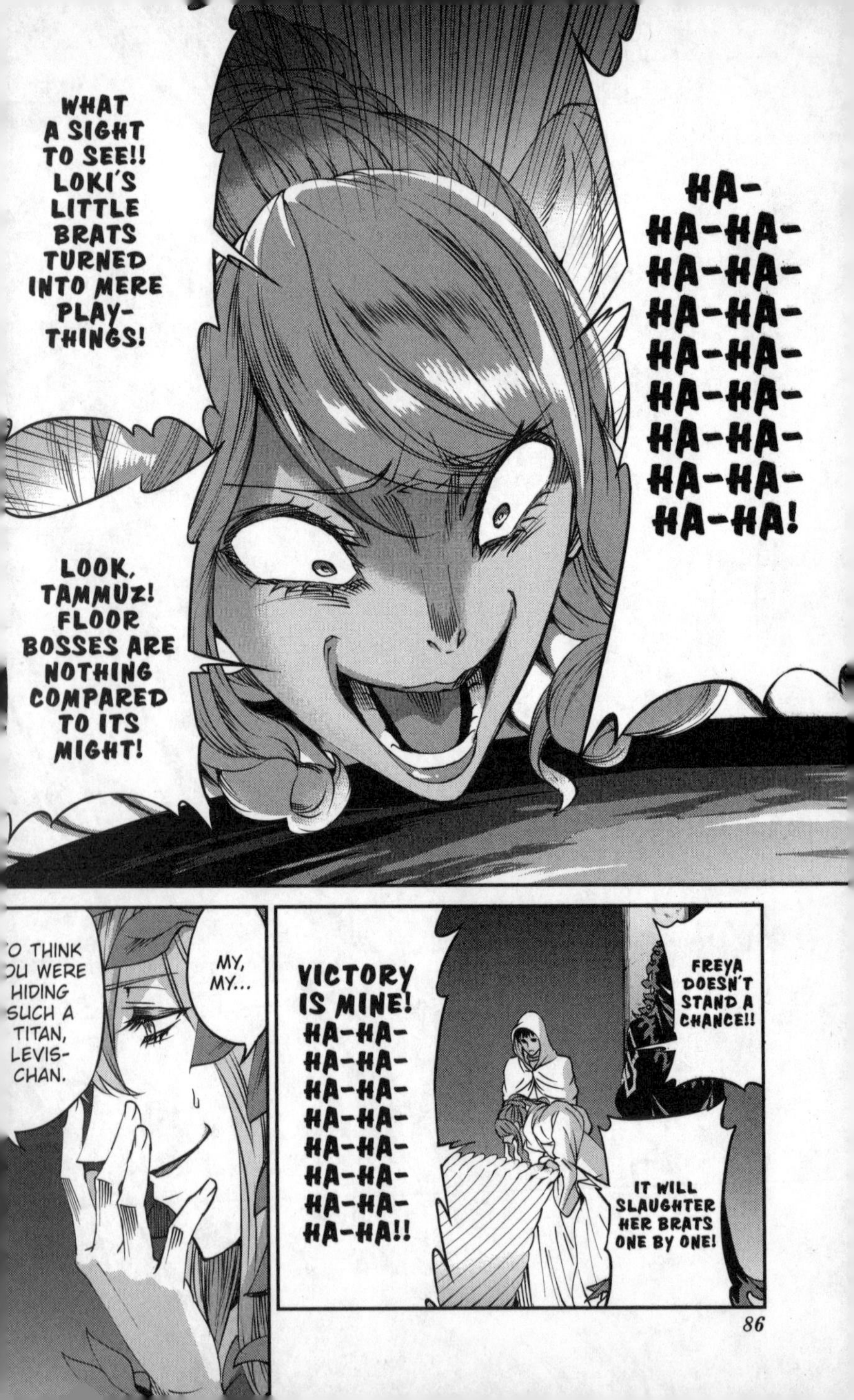
HA-HA-HA-HA-HA-HA-HA-HA-HA-HA-HA-HA-HA-HA-HA-HA-HA!
WHAT A SIGHT TO SEE!! LOKI'S LITTLE BRATS TURNED INTO MERE PLAY-THINGS!
LOOK, TAMMUZ! FLOOR BOSSES ARE NOTHING COMPARED TO ITS MIGHT!
FREYA DOESN'T STAND A CHANCE!!
VICTORY IS MINE! HA-HA-HA-HA-HA-HA-HA-HA-HA-HA-HA-HA-HA-HA-HA-HA!!
IT WILL SLAUGHTER HER BRATS ONE BY ONE!
MY, MY...
O THINK OU WERE HIDING SUCH A TITAN, LEVIS-CHAN.

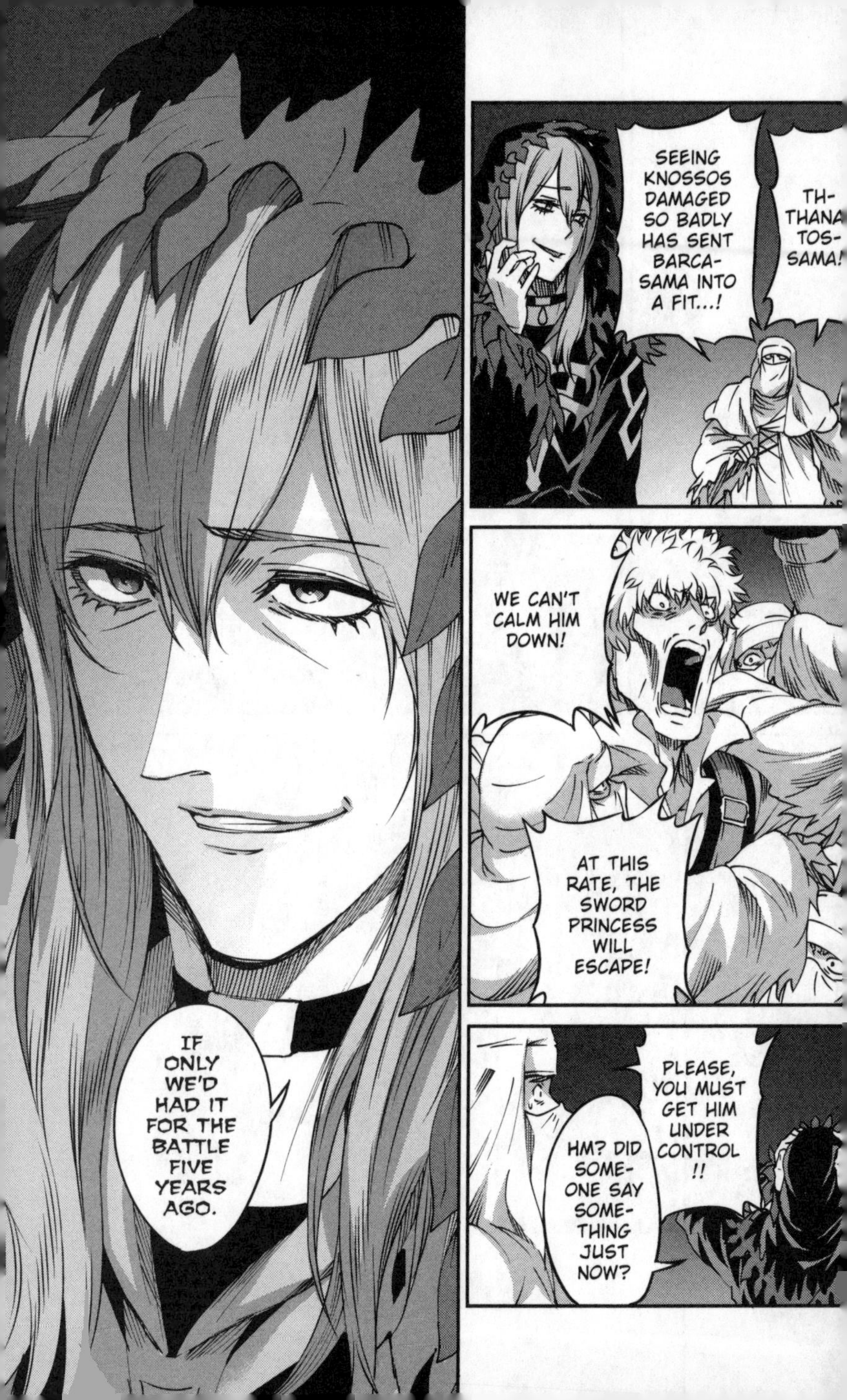
TH-THANATOS-SAMA!
SEEING KNOSSOS DAMAGED SO BADLY HAS SENT BARCA-SAMA INTO A FIT...!
WE CAN'T CALM HIM DOWN!
AT THIS RATE, THE SWORD PRINCESS WILL ESCAPE!
PLEASE, YOU MUST GET HIM UNDER CONTROL!!
HM? DID SOMEONE SAY SOMETHING JUST NOW?
IF ONLY WE'D HAD IT FOR THE BATTLE FIVE YEARS AGO.

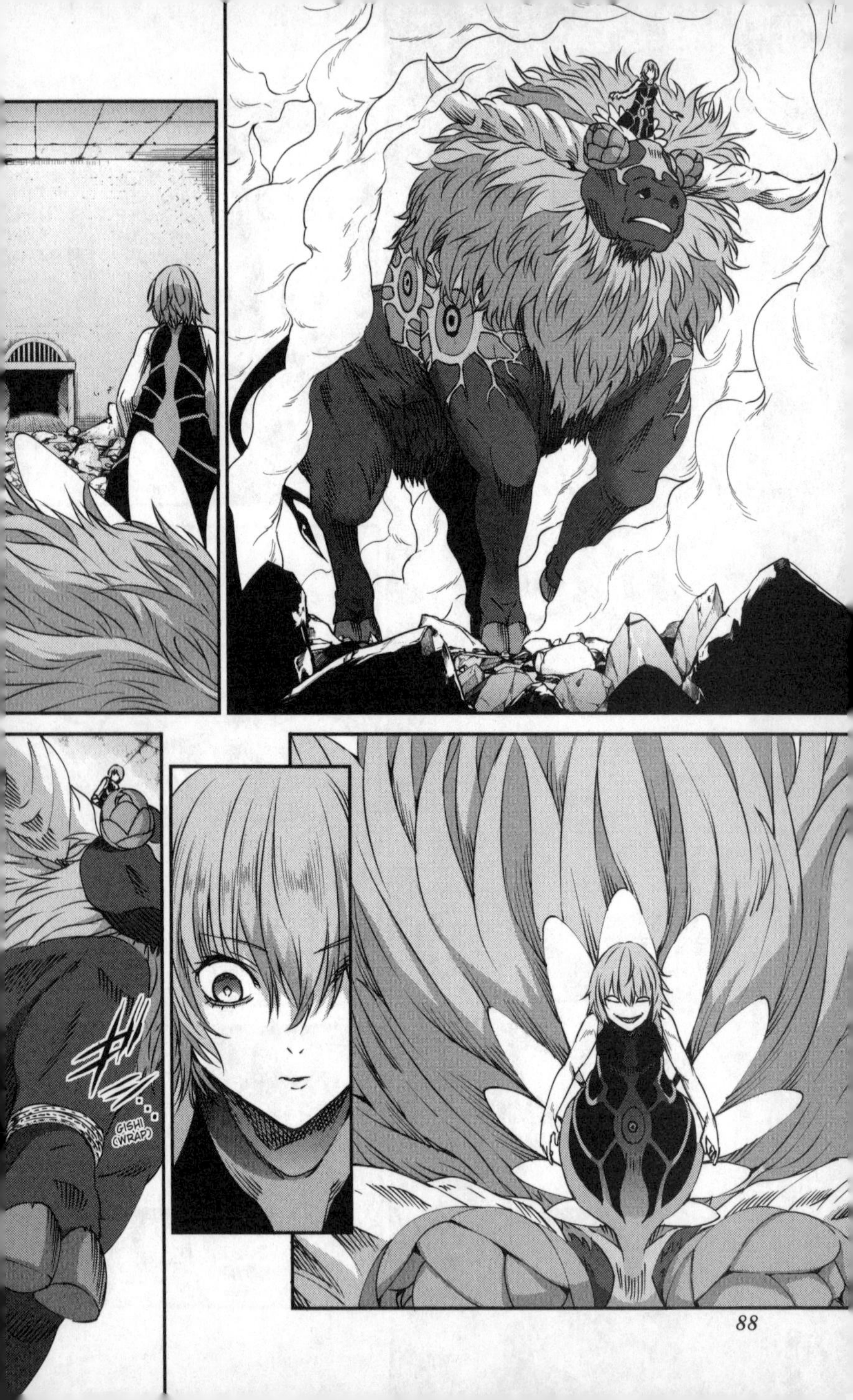
GISHI (WRAP)

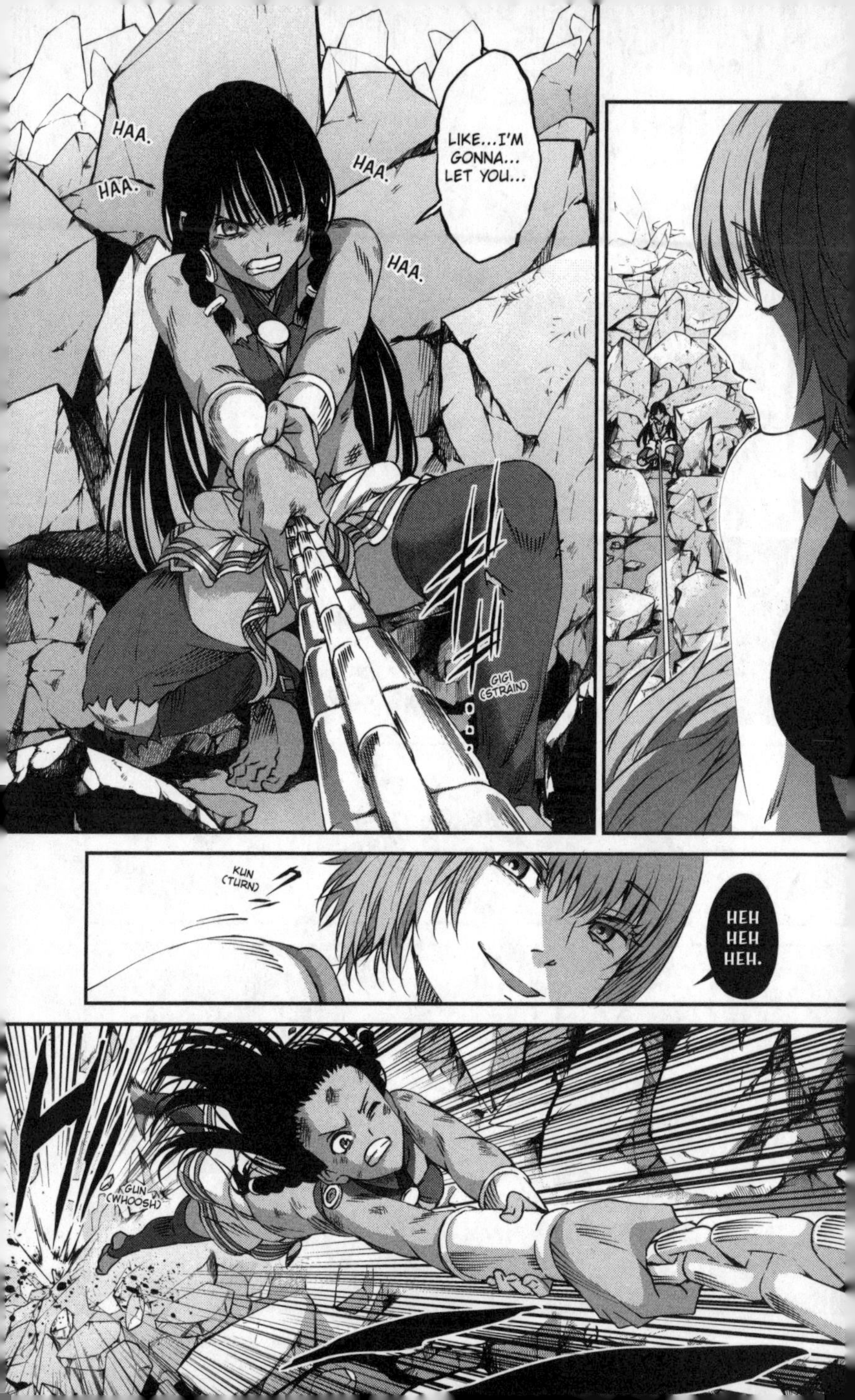
LIKE...I'M GONNA... LET YOU...
HAA.
HAA.
HAA.
HAA.
GIGI (STRAIN)
HEH HEH HEH.
KUN (TURN)
GUN (WHOOSH)

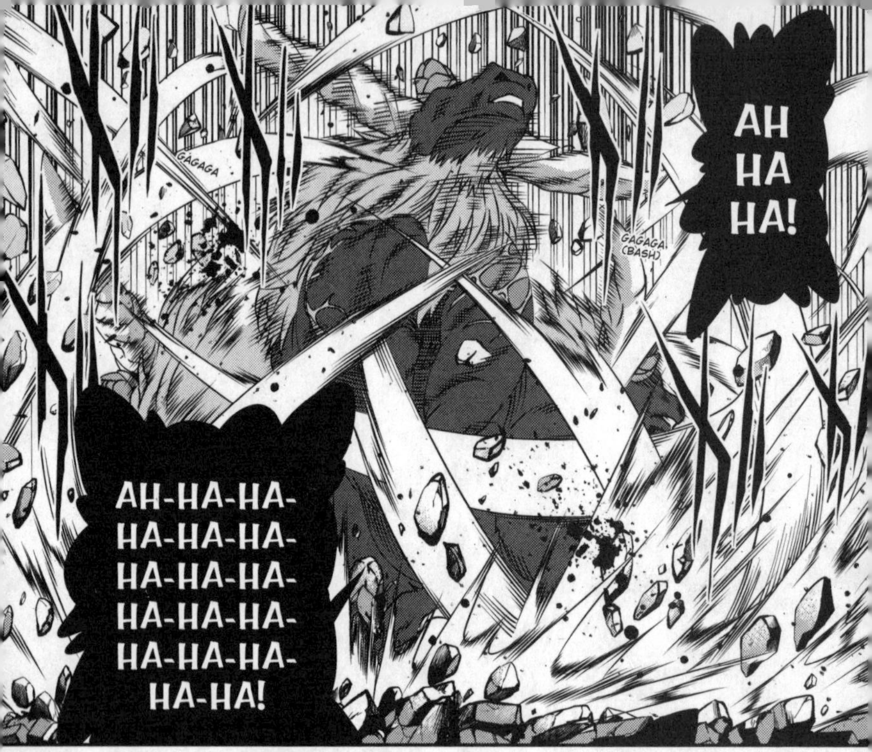
AH HA HA!
GAGAGA (BASH)
GAGAGA
AH-HA-HA-HA-HA-HA-HA-HA-HA-HA-HA-HA-HA-HA-HA-HA-HA!

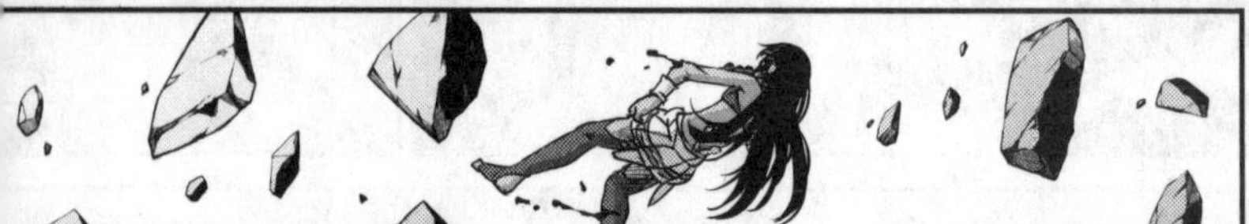

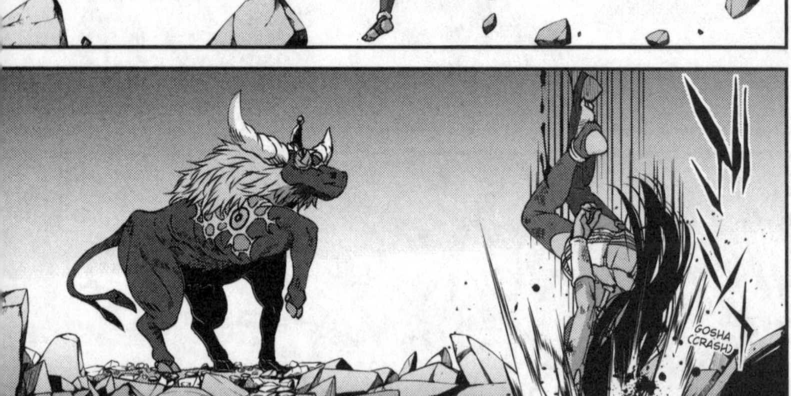
GOSHA (CRASH)

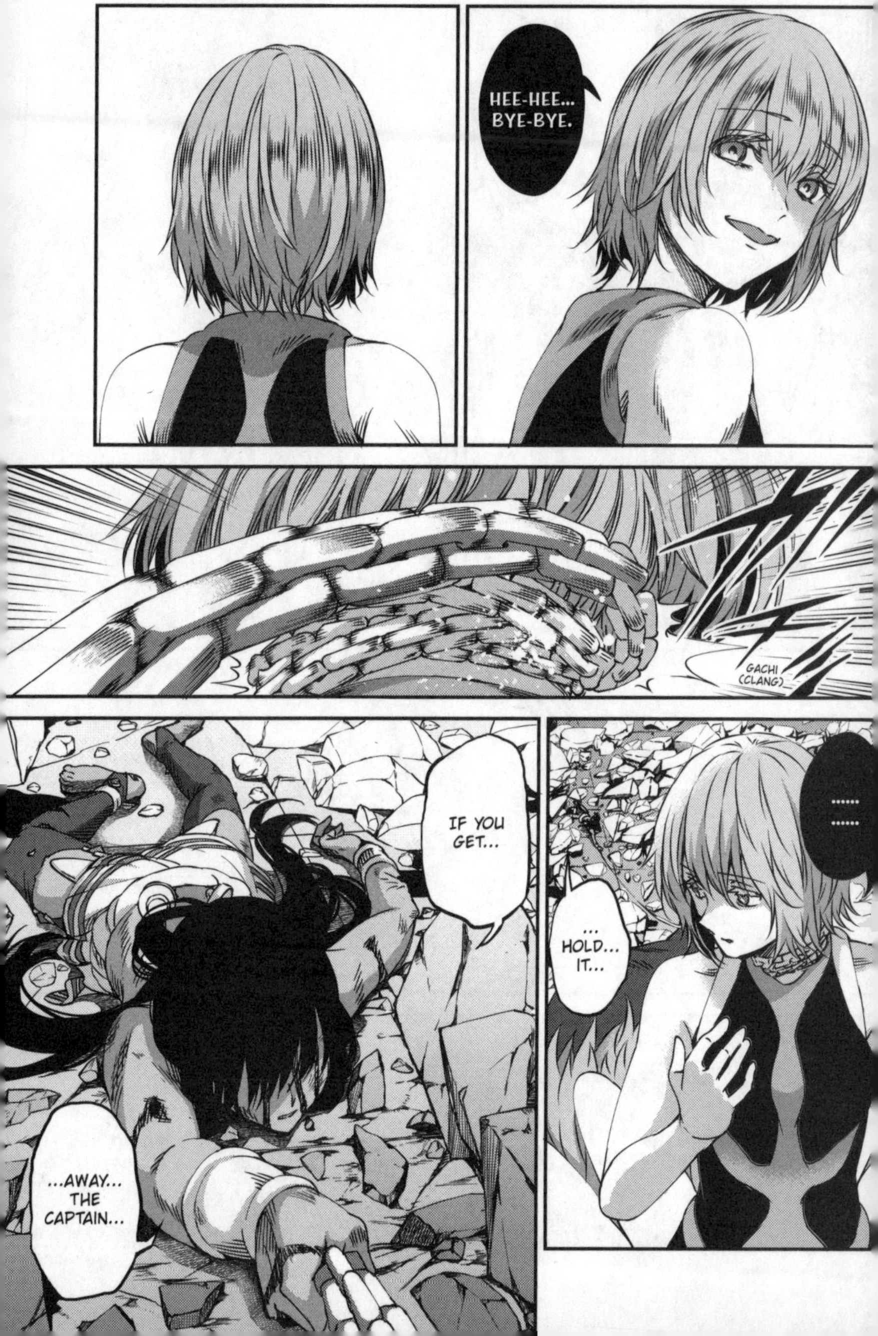
HEE-HEE... BYE-BYE.
GACHI (CLANG)
......
......
... HOLD... IT...
IF YOU GET...
...AWAY... THE CAPTAIN...

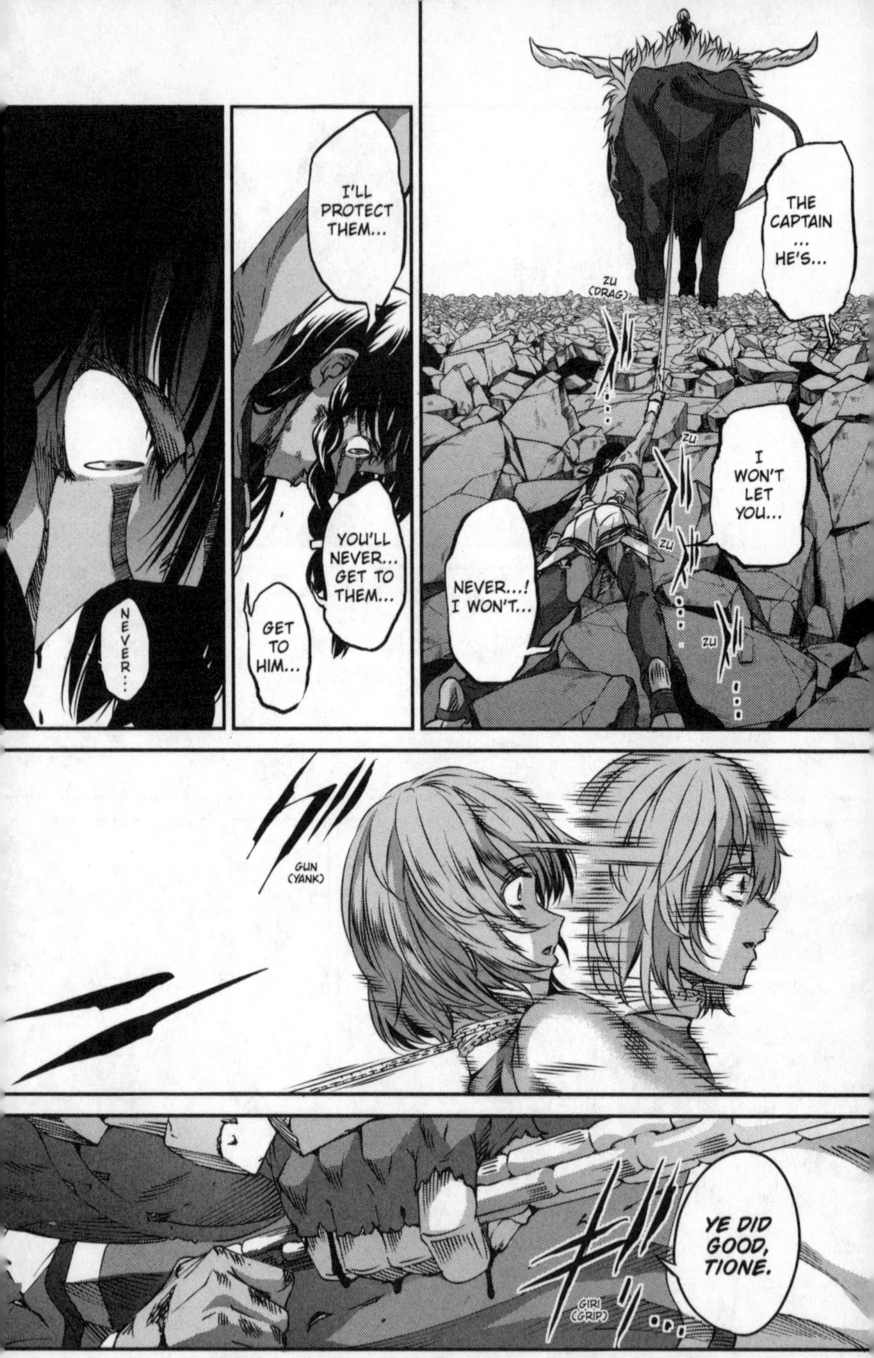
THE CAPTAIN ... HE'S...
ZU (DRAG)
I WON'T LET YOU...
ZU
ZU
NEVER...! I WON'T...
ZU
I'LL PROTECT THEM...
YOU'LL NEVER... GET TO THEM...
GET TO HIM...
NEVER...
GUN (YANK)
YE DID GOOD, TIONE.
GIRI (GRIP)

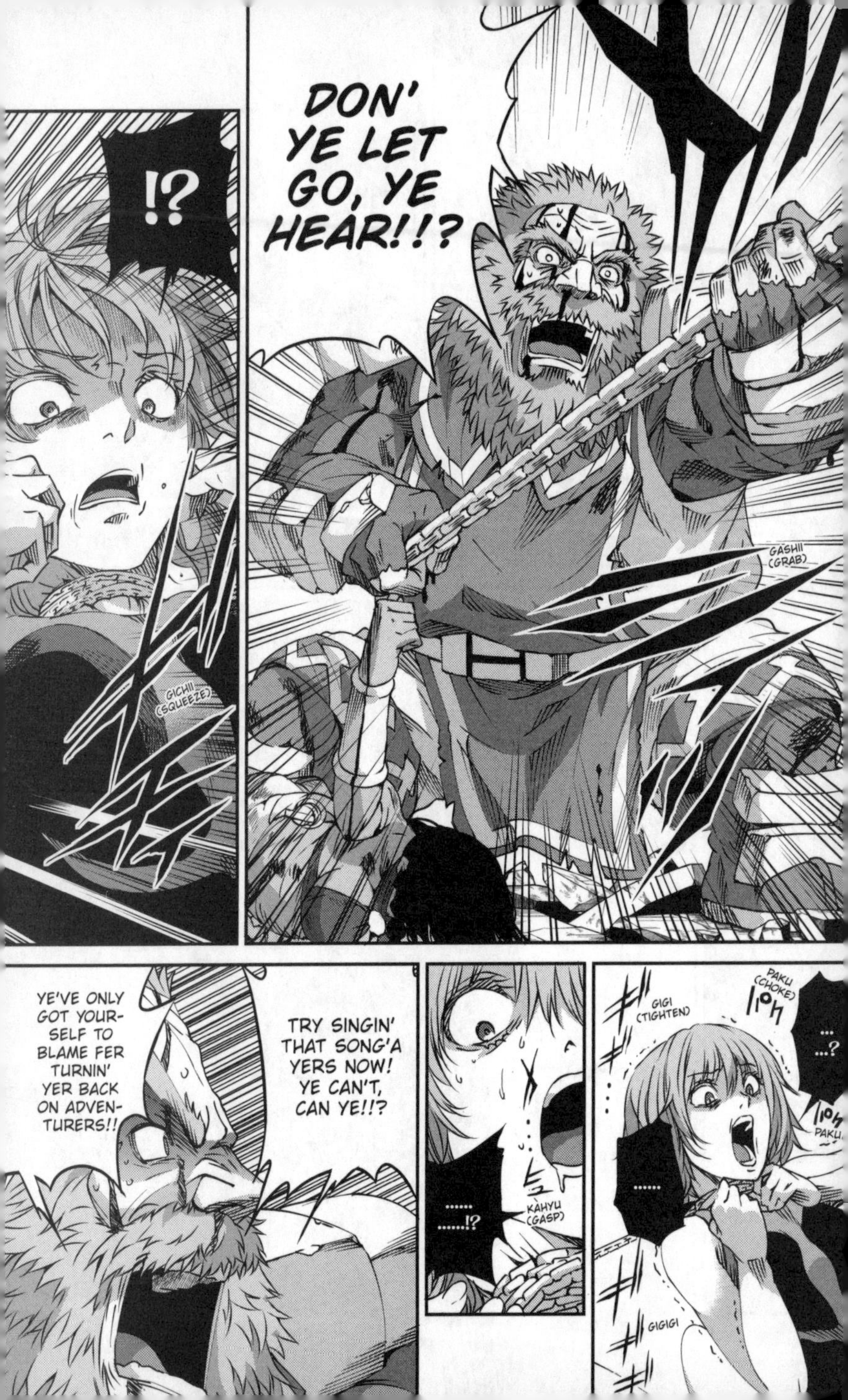
DON' YE LET GO, YE HEAR!!?
GASHII (GRAB)
!?
GICHII (SQUEEZE)
PAKU (CHOKE)
GIGI (TIGHTEN)
... ...?
......
PAKU
GIGIGI
KAHYU (GASP)
....!?
TRY SINGIN' THAT SONG'A YERS NOW! YE CAN'T, CAN YE!!?
YE'VE ONLY GOT YOURSELF TO BLAME FER TURNIN' YER BACK ON ADVENTURERS!!

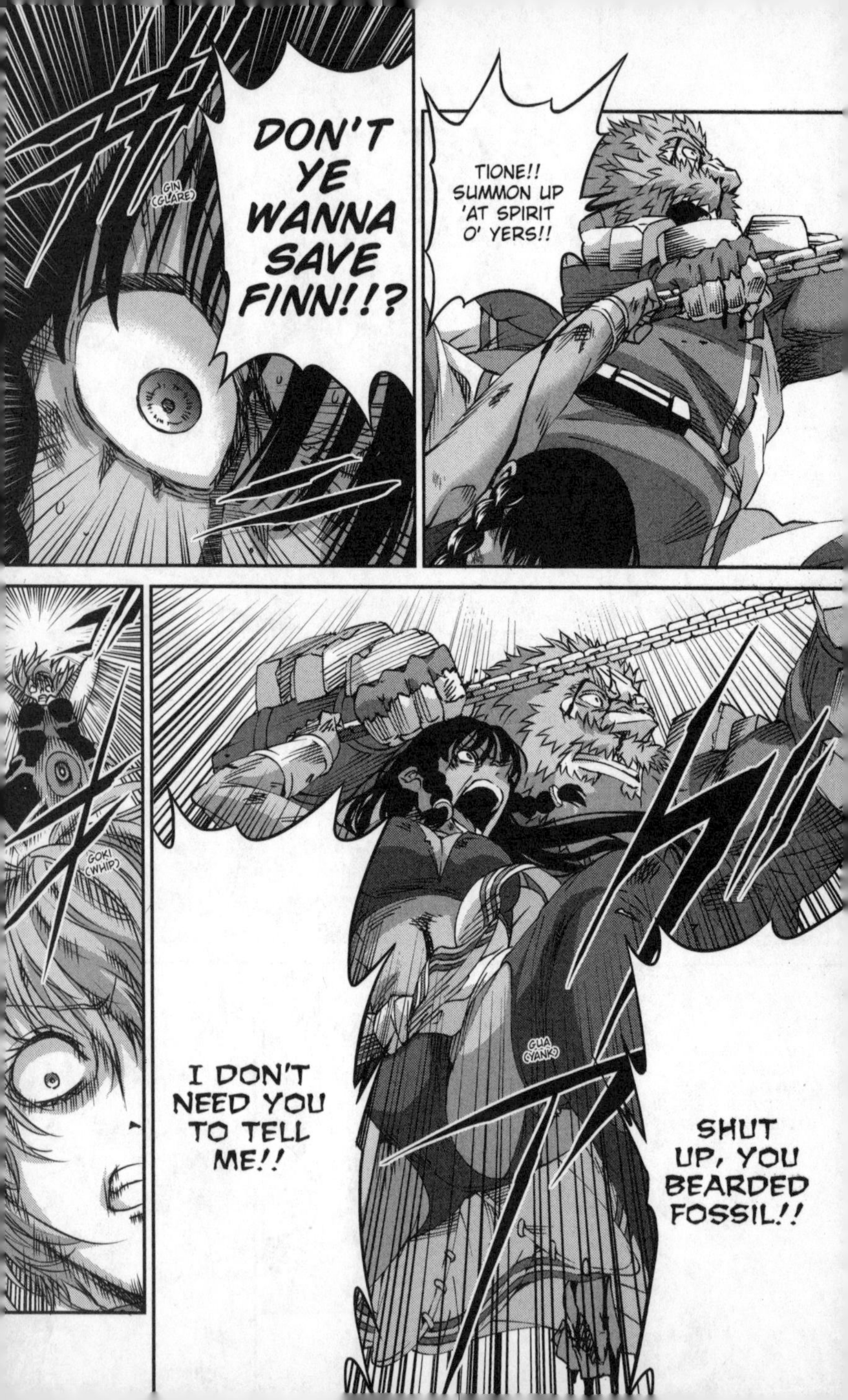
TIONE!! SUMMON UP 'AT SPIRIT O' YERS!!
DON'T YE WANNA SAVE FINN!!?
GIN (GLARE)
SHUT UP, YOU BEARDED FOSSIL!!
GUA (YANK)
I DON'T NEED YOU TO TELL ME!!
GOKI (WHIP)

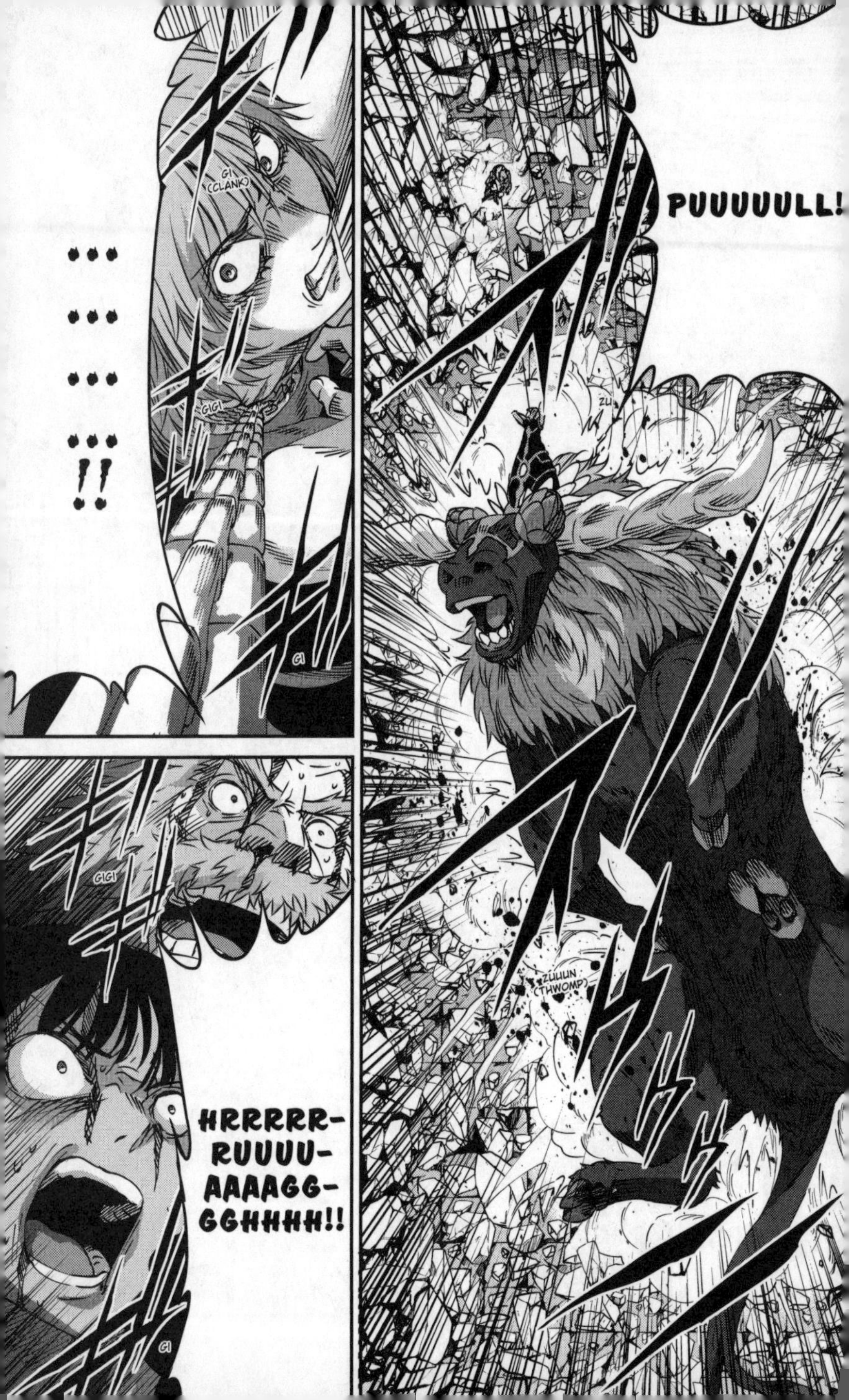
PUUUUULL!
ZU
ZUUUN (THWOMP)
GI (CLANK)
............!!
GIGI
GI
GIGI
HRRRRR-RUUUU-AAAAGG-GGHHHHH!!
GI

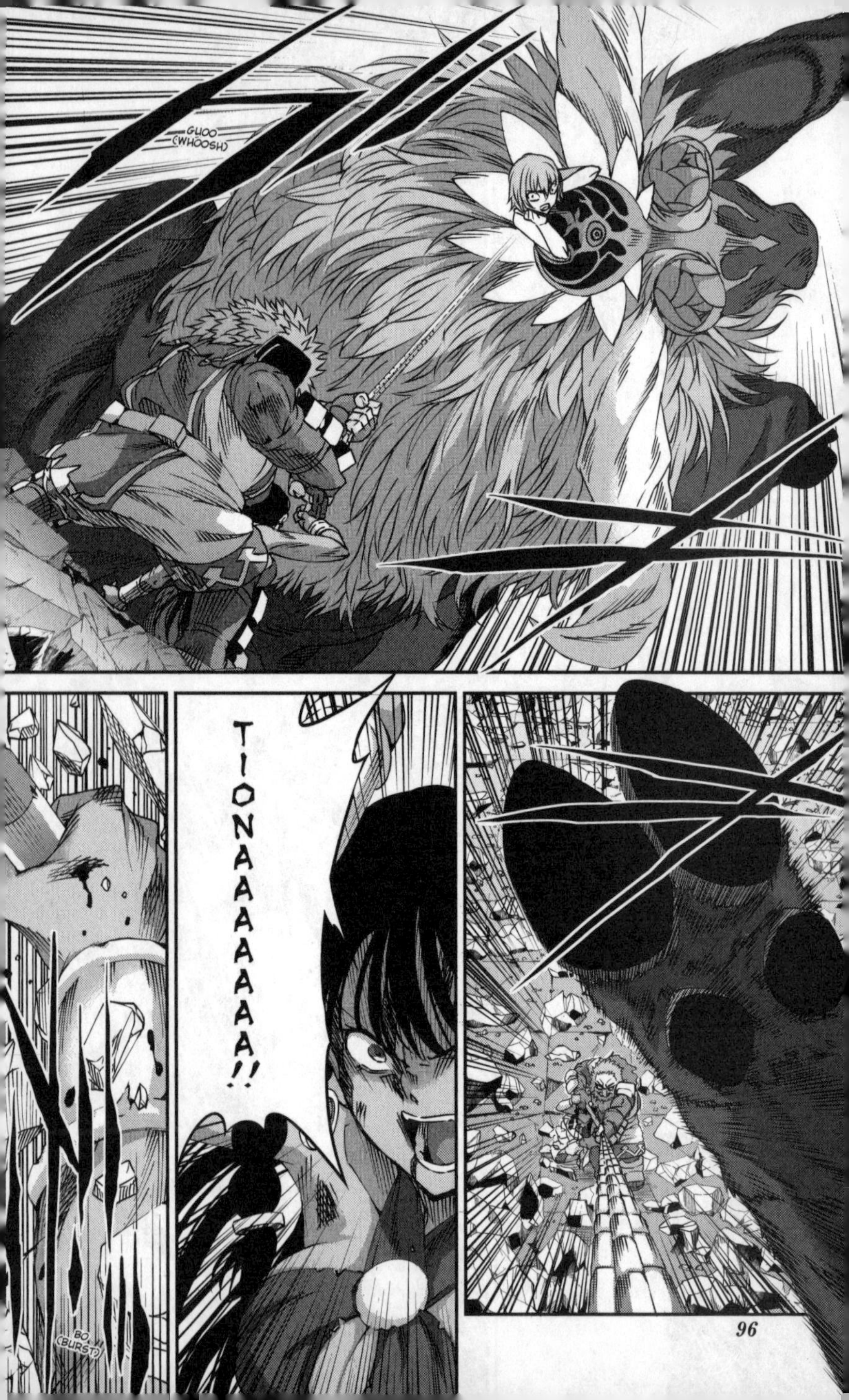
GUOO
(WHOOSH)
TIONAAAAAAA!!
BO
(BURST)

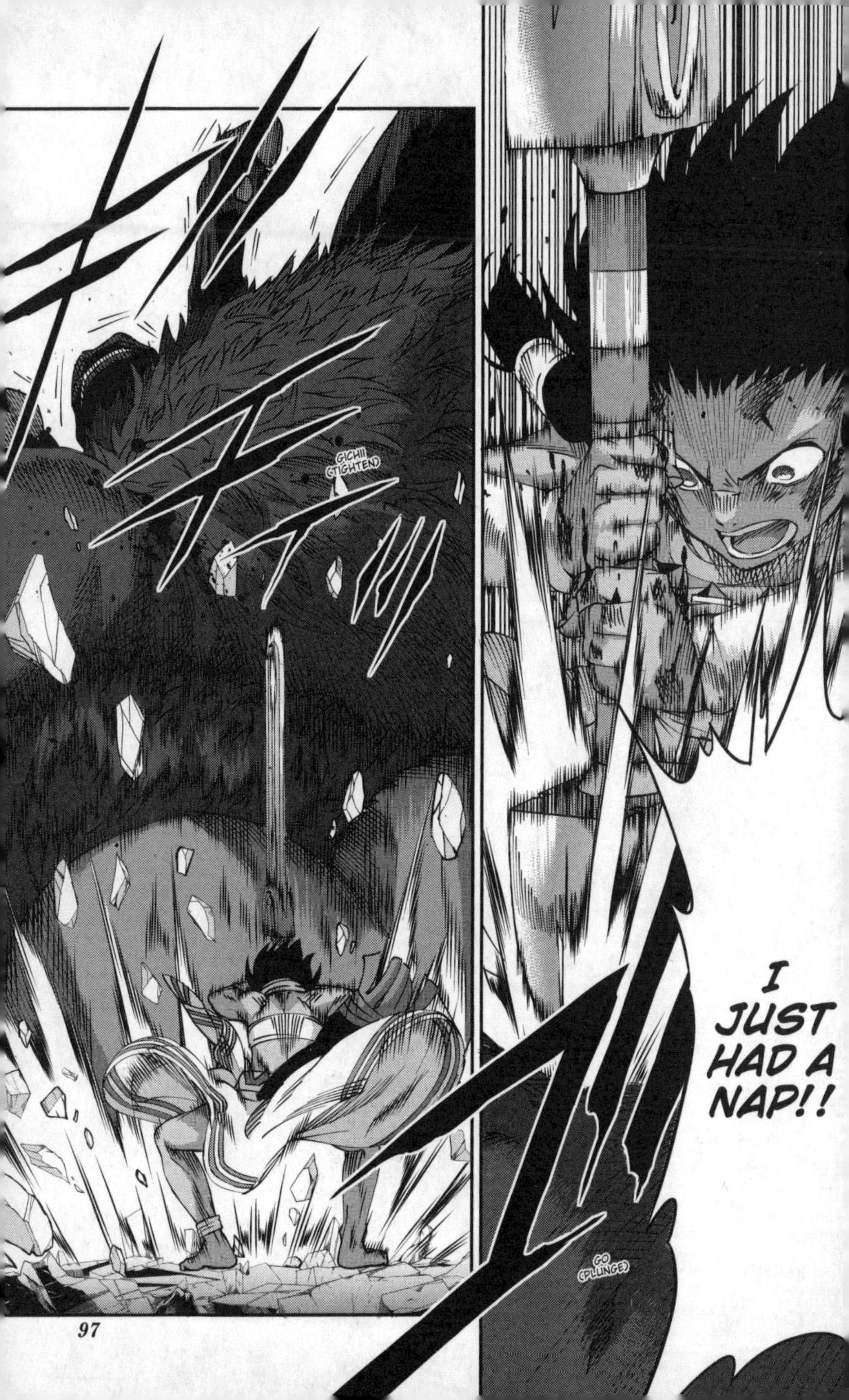
I JUST HAD A NAP!!
GO
(PLUNGE)
GICHII
(TIGHTEN)

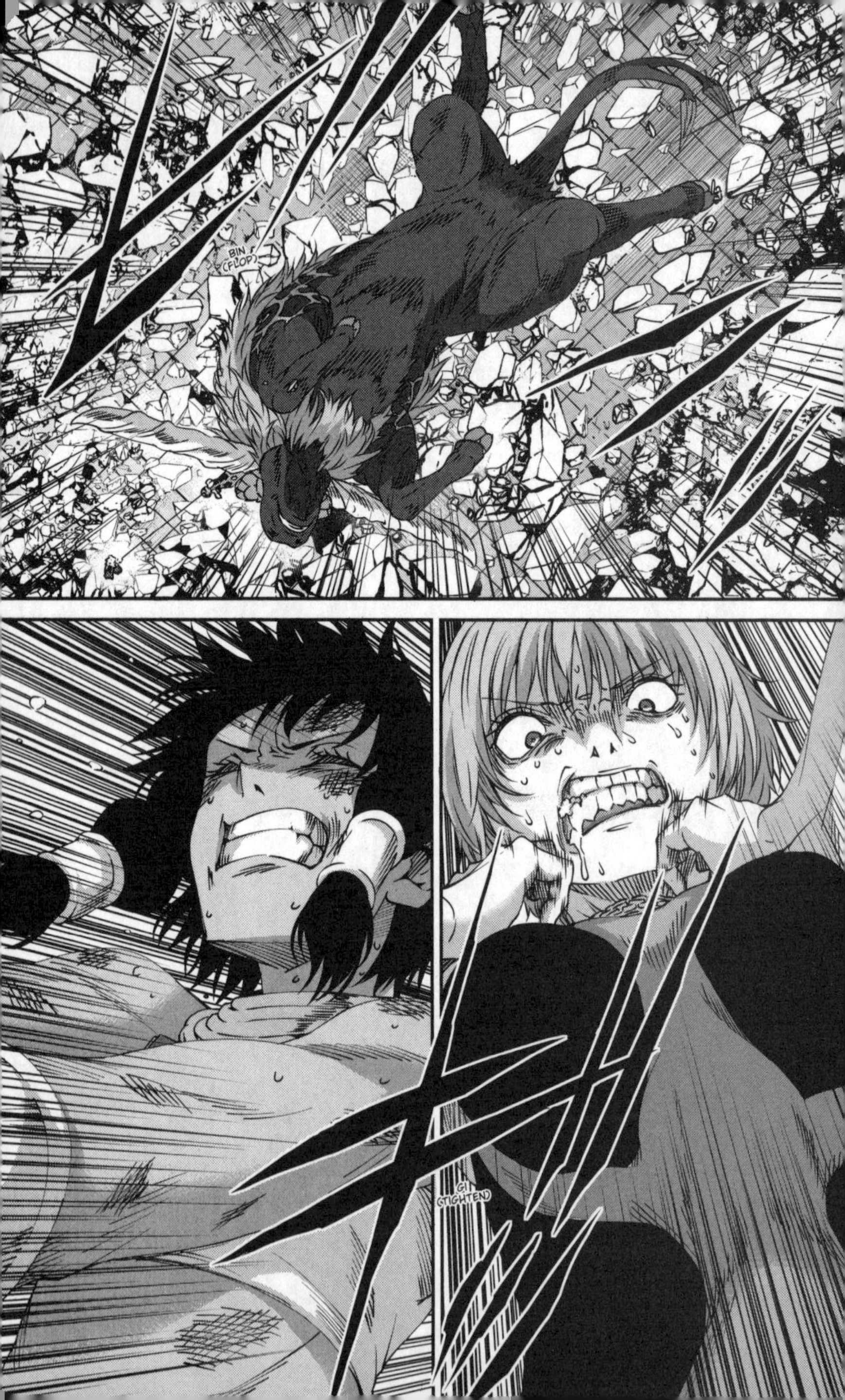
BIN
(FLOP)
GI
(TIGHTEN)

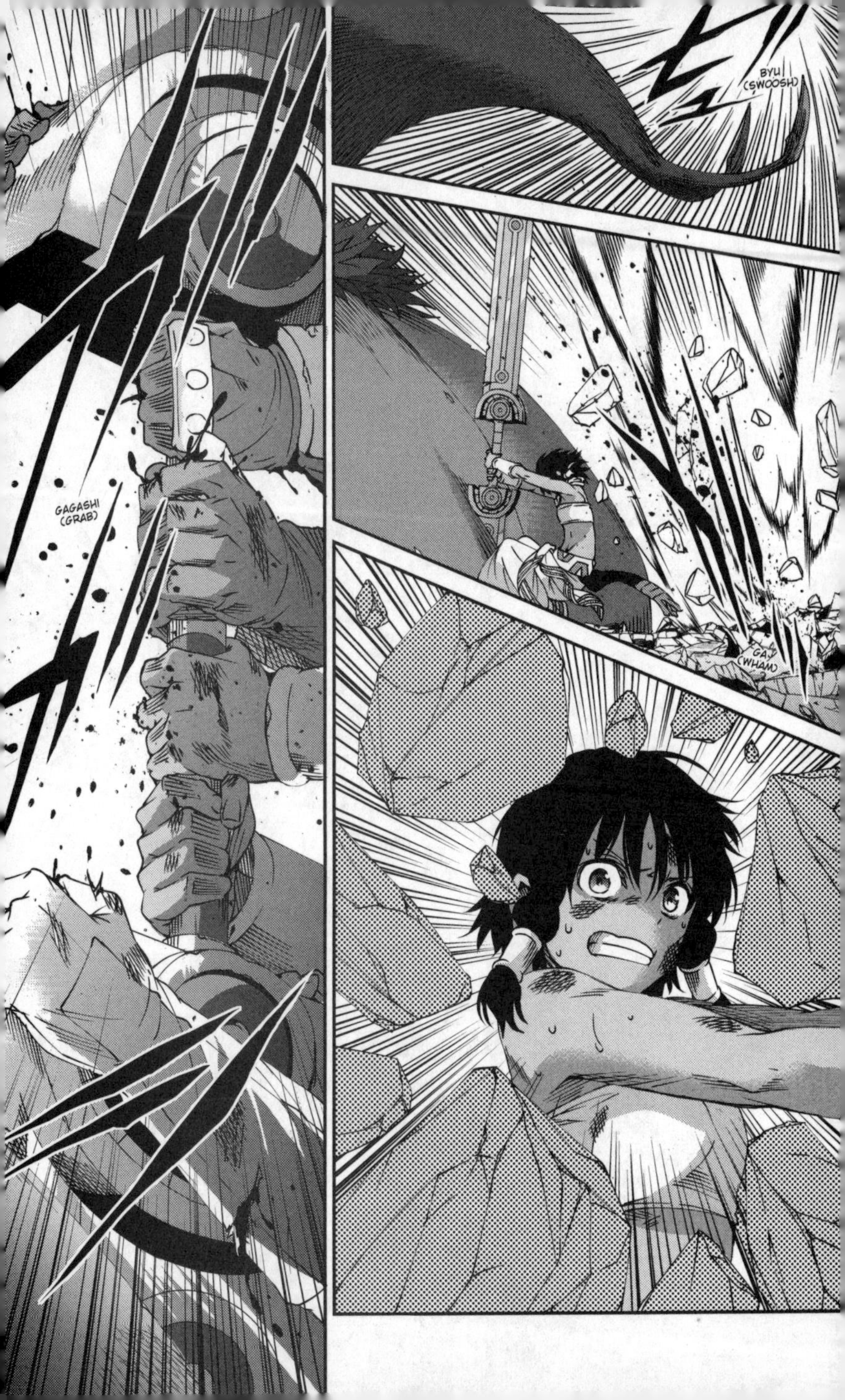
BYU (SWOOSH)
GAN (WHAM)
GAGASHI (GRAB)

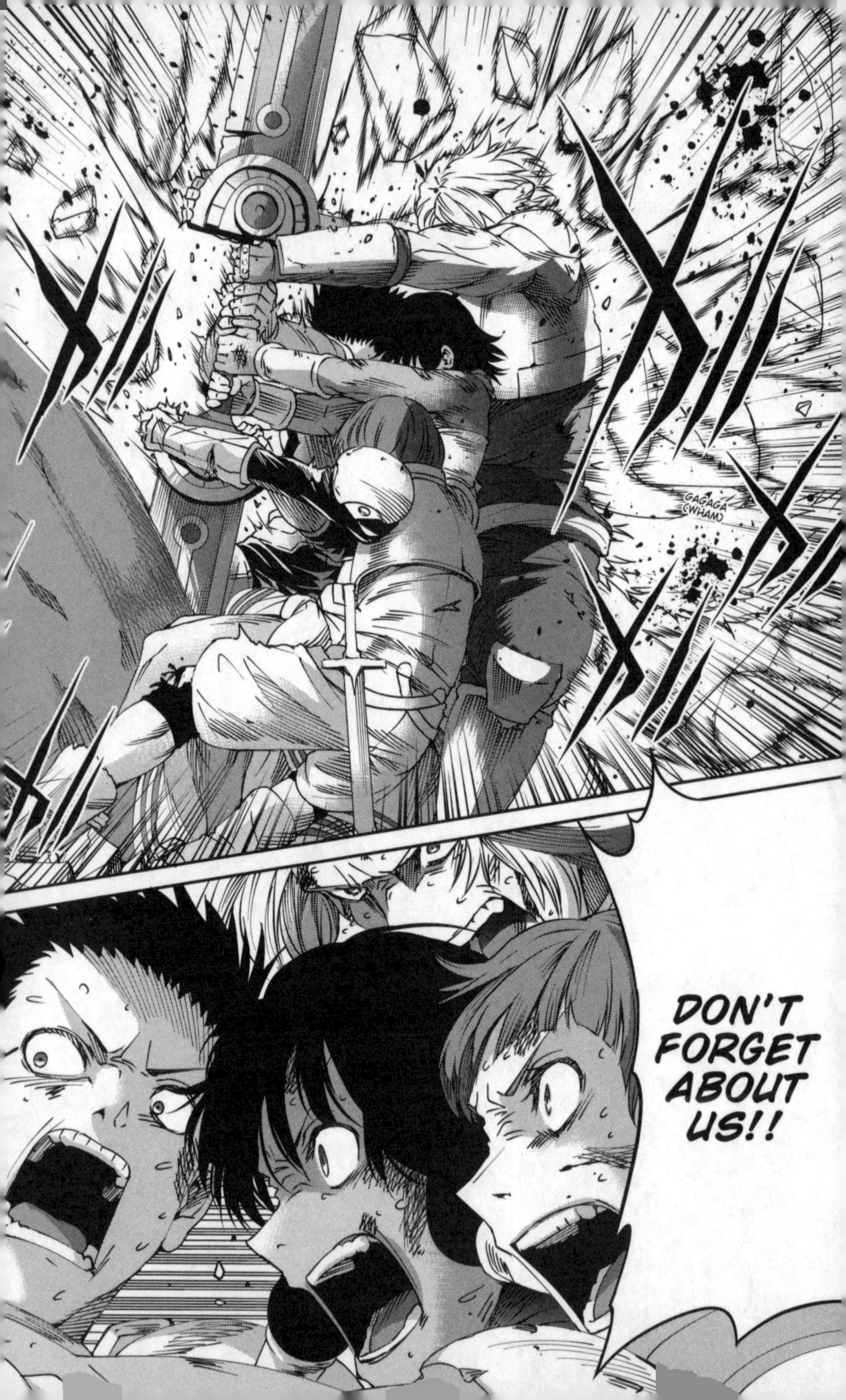
GAGAGA (WHAM)
DON'T FORGET ABOUT US!!

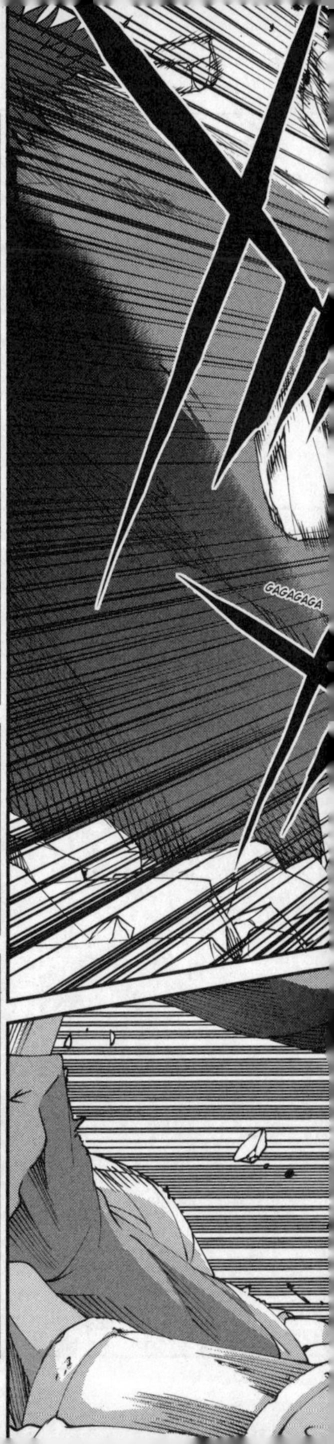
GAGAGAGA

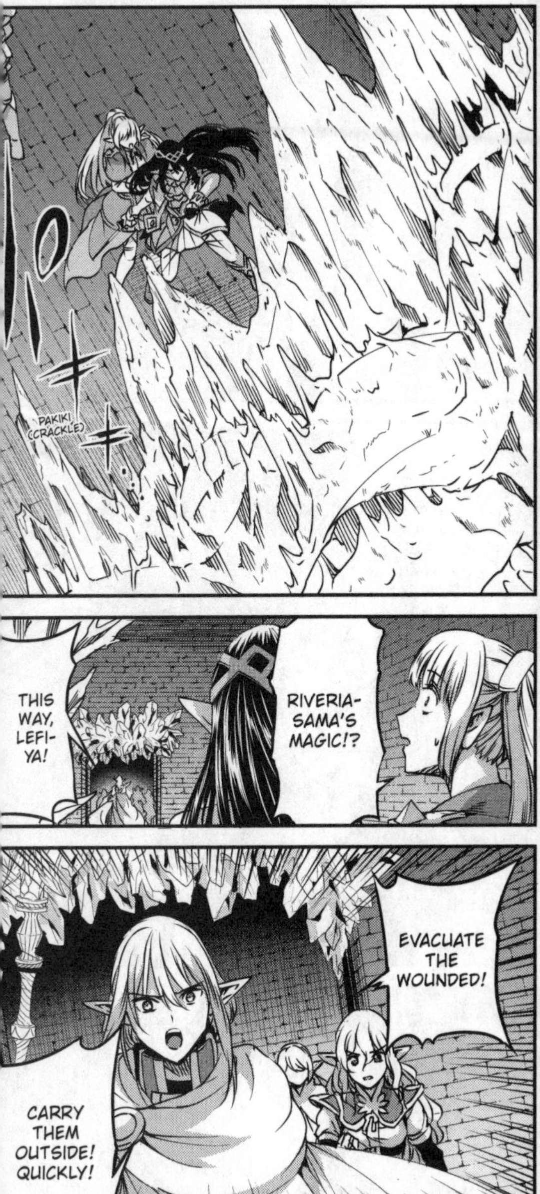
PAKIKI (CRACKLE)
RIVERIA-SAMA'S MAGIC!?
THIS WAY, LEFIYA!
EVACUATE THE WOUNDED!
CARRY THEM OUTSIDE! QUICKLY!

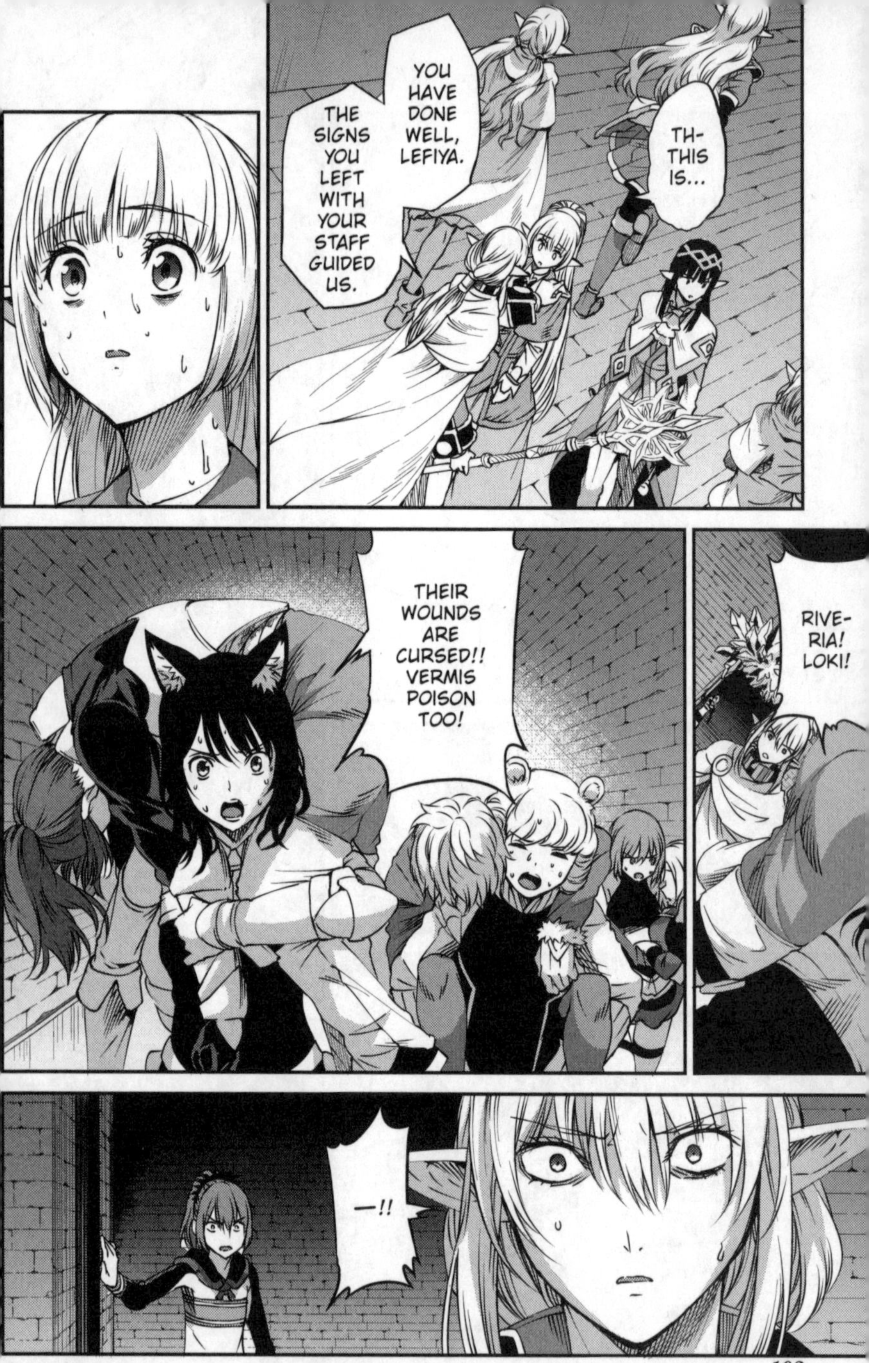
TH-THIS IS...
YOU HAVE DONE WELL, LEFIYA.
THE SIGNS YOU LEFT WITH YOUR STAFF GUIDED US.
RIVE-RIA! LOKI!
THEIR WOUNDS ARE CURSED!! VERMIS POISON TOO!
—!!

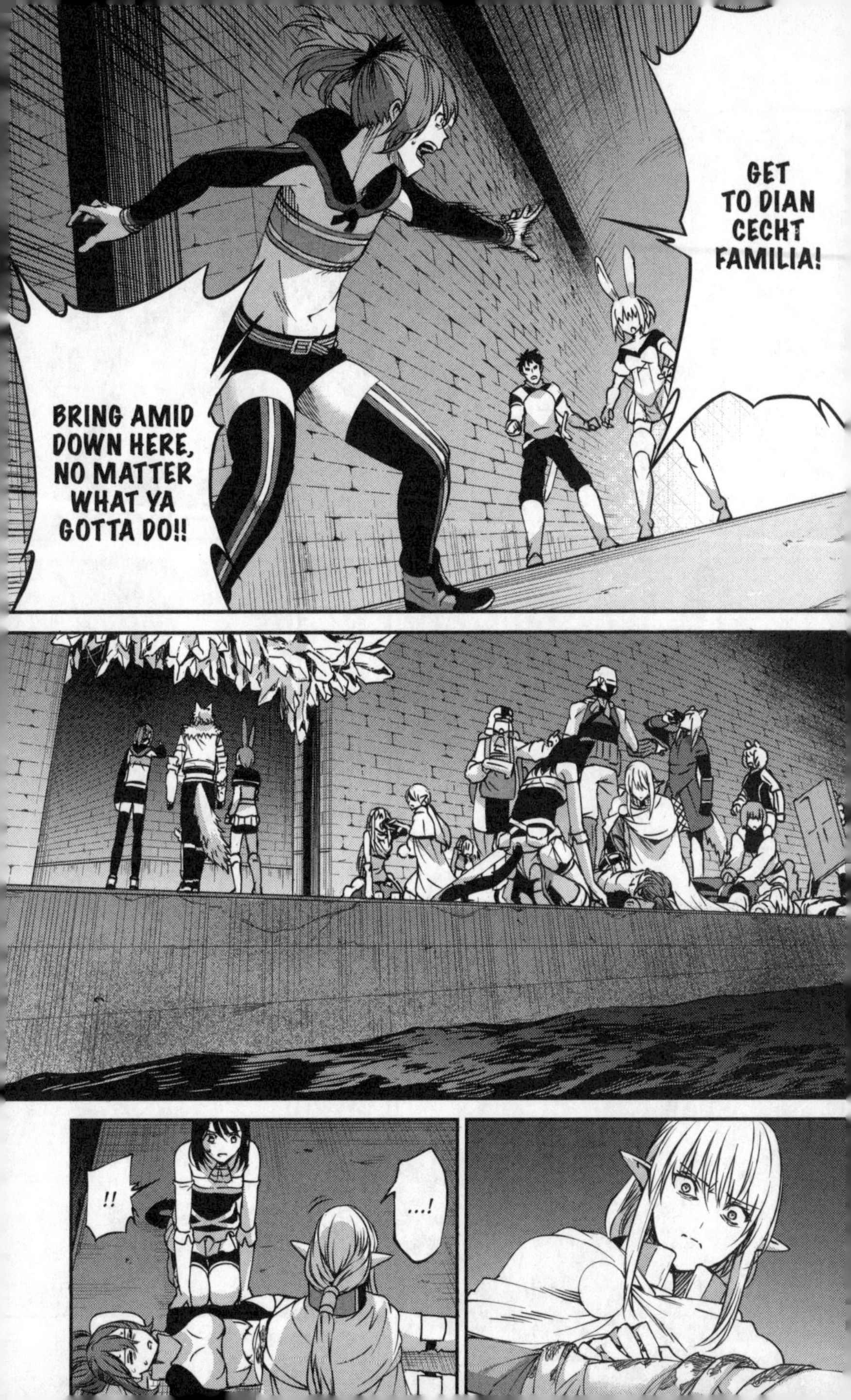
GET TO DIAN CECHT FAMILIA!
BRING AMID DOWN HERE, NO MATTER WHAT YA GOTTA DO!!
...!
!!

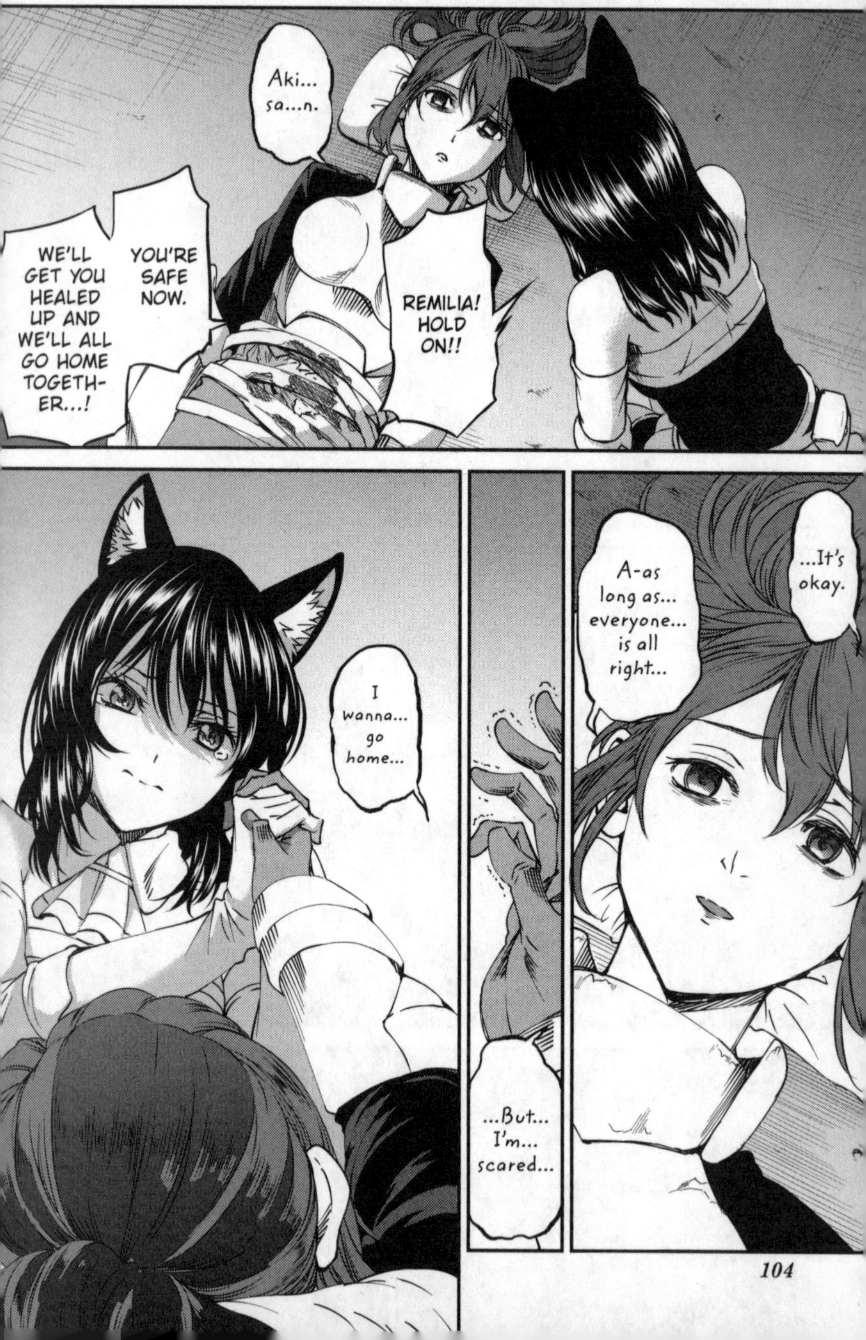

Aki... sa...n.
REMILIA! HOLD ON!!
YOU'RE SAFE NOW.
WE'LL GET YOU HEALED UP AND WE'LL ALL GO HOME TOGETH-ER...!
...It's okay.
A-as long as... everyone... is all right...
...But... I'm... scared...
I wanna... go home...

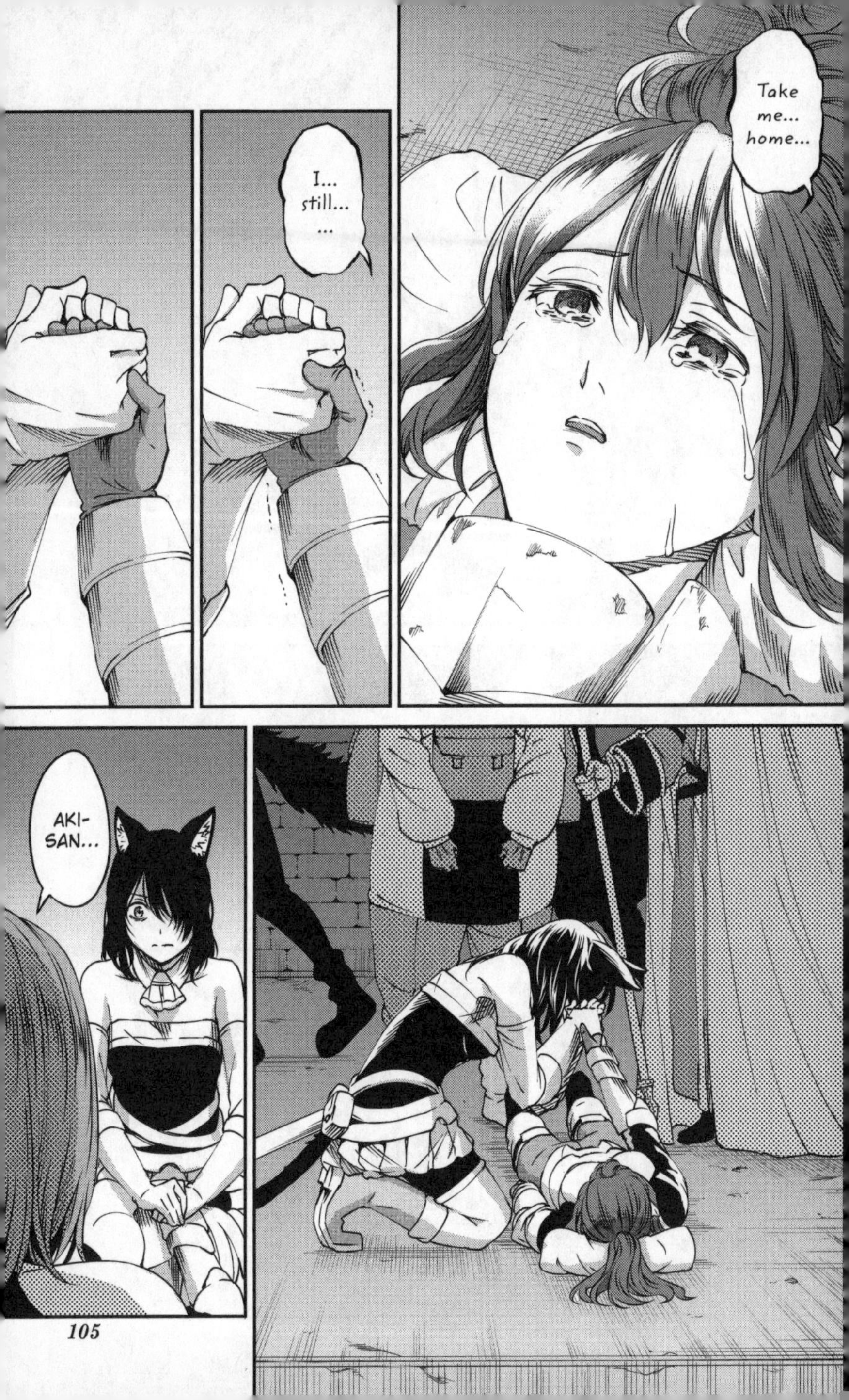
Take me... home...
I... still... ...
AKI-SAN...

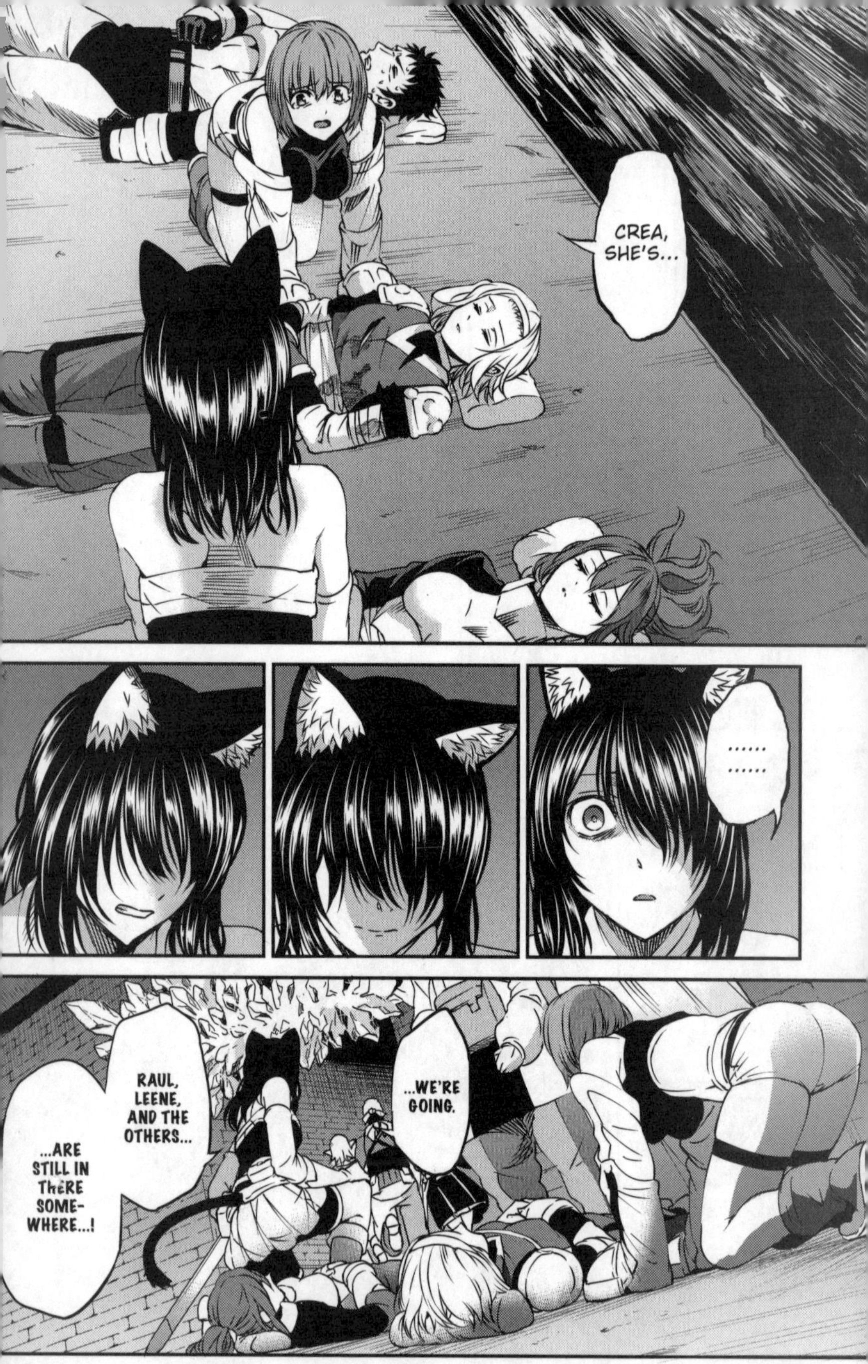
CREA, SHE'S...
......
......
...WE'RE GOING.
RAUL, LEENE, AND THE OTHERS...
...ARE STILL IN THERE SOME-WHERE...!

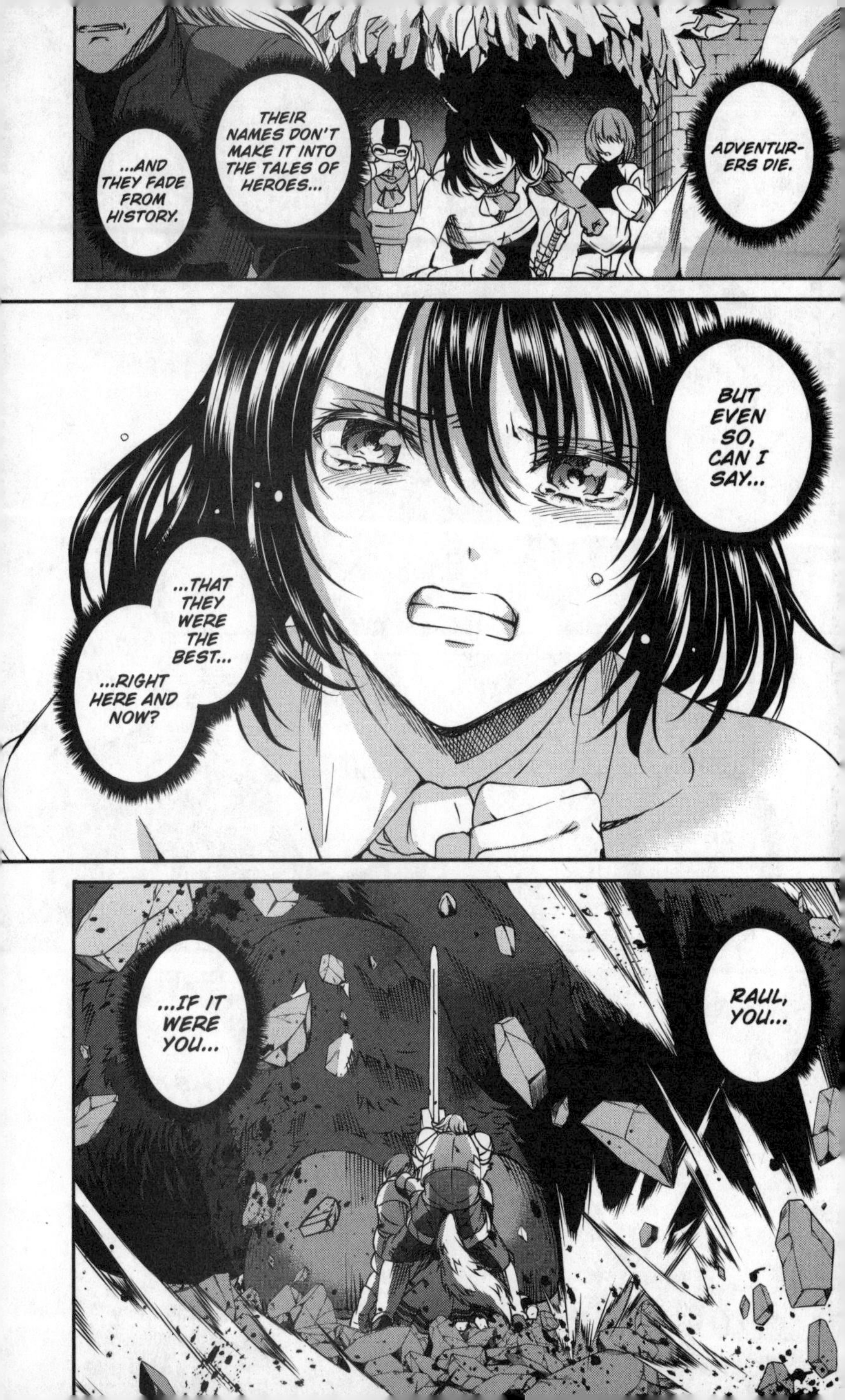
ADVENTUR-ERS DIE.
THEIR NAMES DON'T MAKE IT INTO THE TALES OF HEROES...
...AND THEY FADE FROM HISTORY.
BUT EVEN SO, CAN I SAY...
...THAT THEY WERE THE BEST...
...RIGHT HERE AND NOW?
RAUL, YOU...
...IF IT WERE YOU...

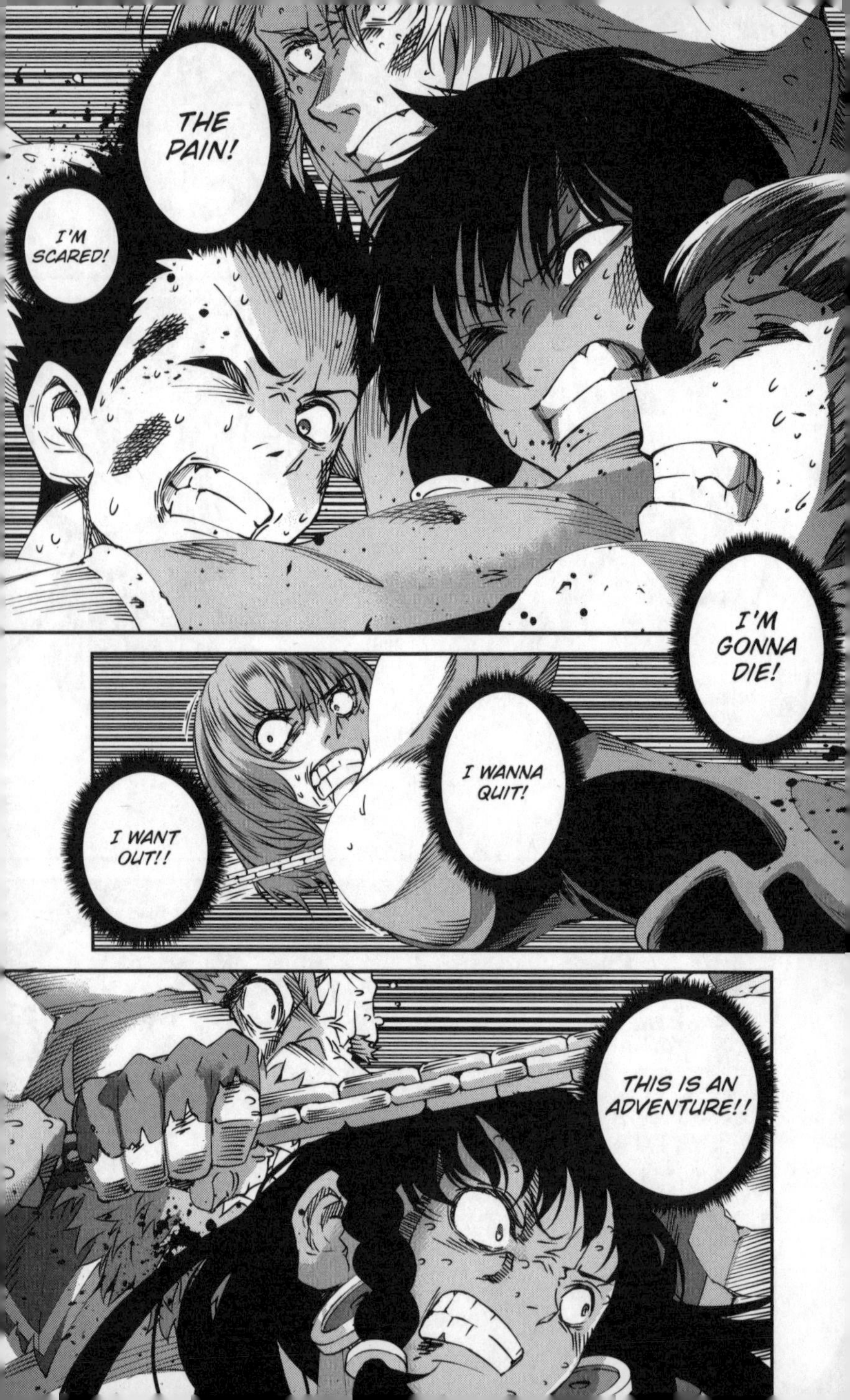
THE PAIN!
I'M SCARED!
I'M GONNA DIE!
I WANNA QUIT!
I WANT OUT!!
THIS IS AN ADVENTURE!!

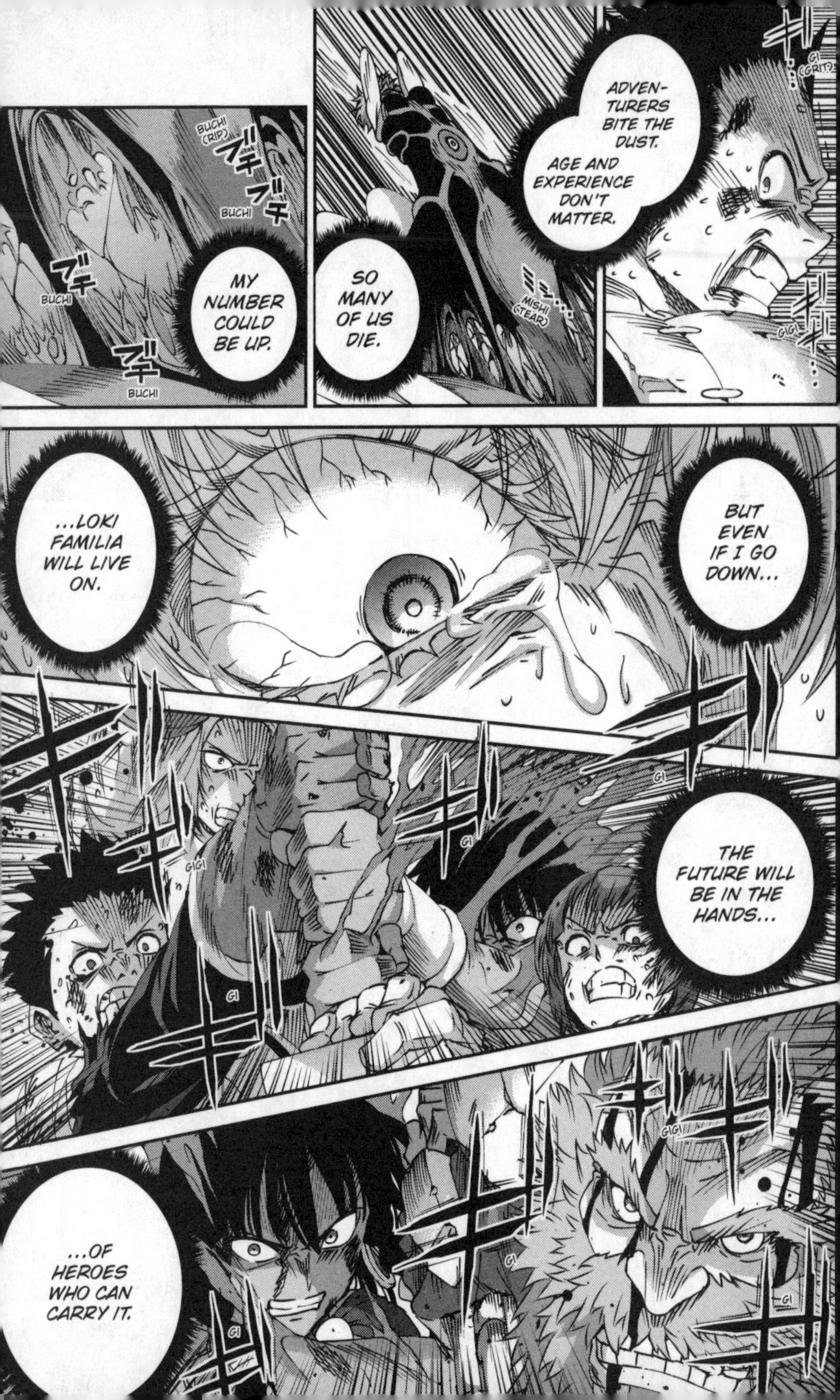
GI (GRIT)
ADVENTURERS BITE THE DUST.
AGE AND EXPERIENCE DON'T MATTER.
GIGI
SO MANY OF US DIE.
MISHI (TEAR)
BUCHI (RIP)
BUCHI
MY NUMBER COULD BE UP.
BUCHI
BUCHI
BUT EVEN IF I GO DOWN...
...LOKI FAMILIA WILL LIVE ON.
GI
THE FUTURE WILL BE IN THE HANDS...
GI
GIGI
GI
GIGI
GI
GI
...OF HEROES WHO CAN CARRY IT.
GI

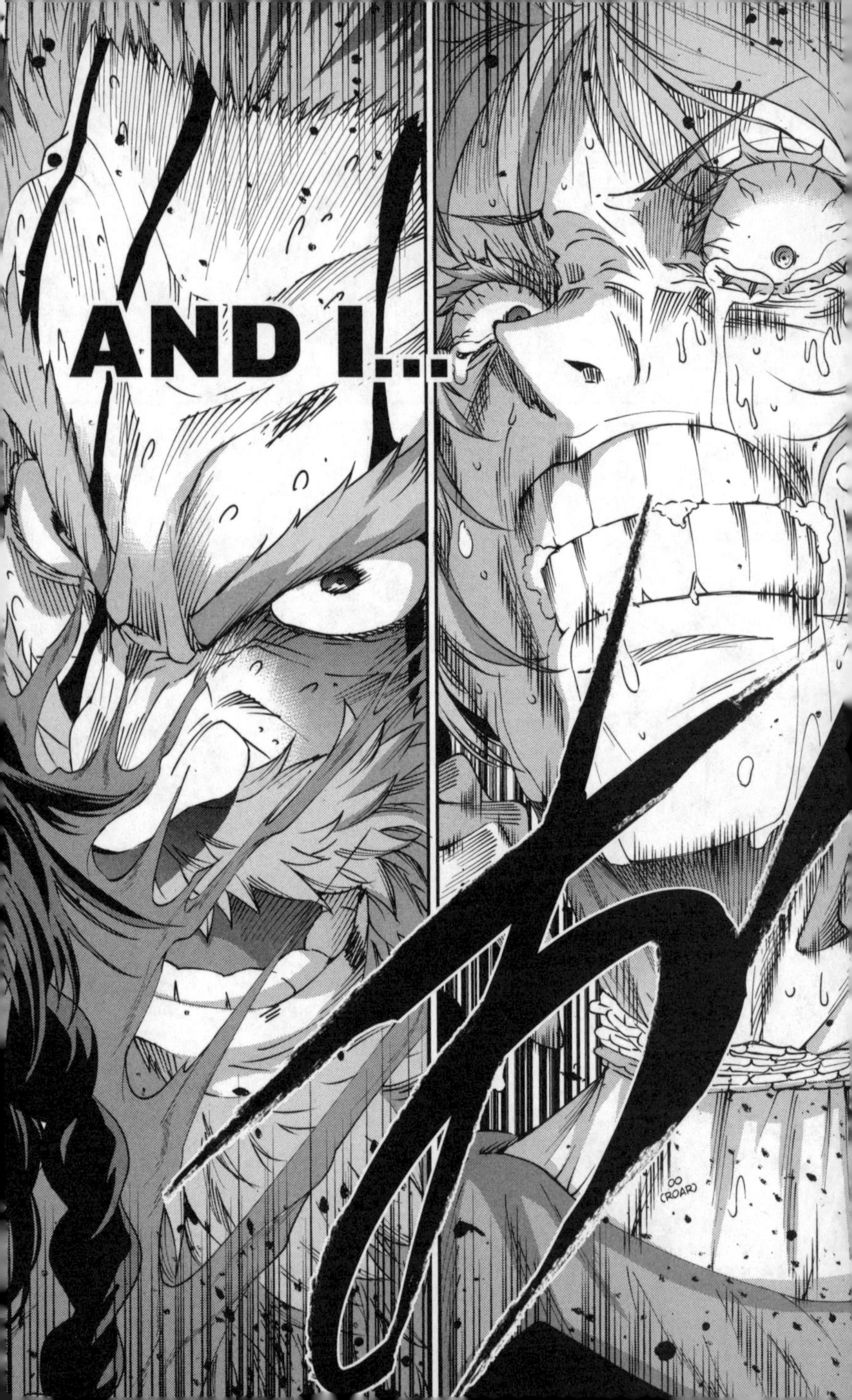
AND I...
OO
(ROAR)

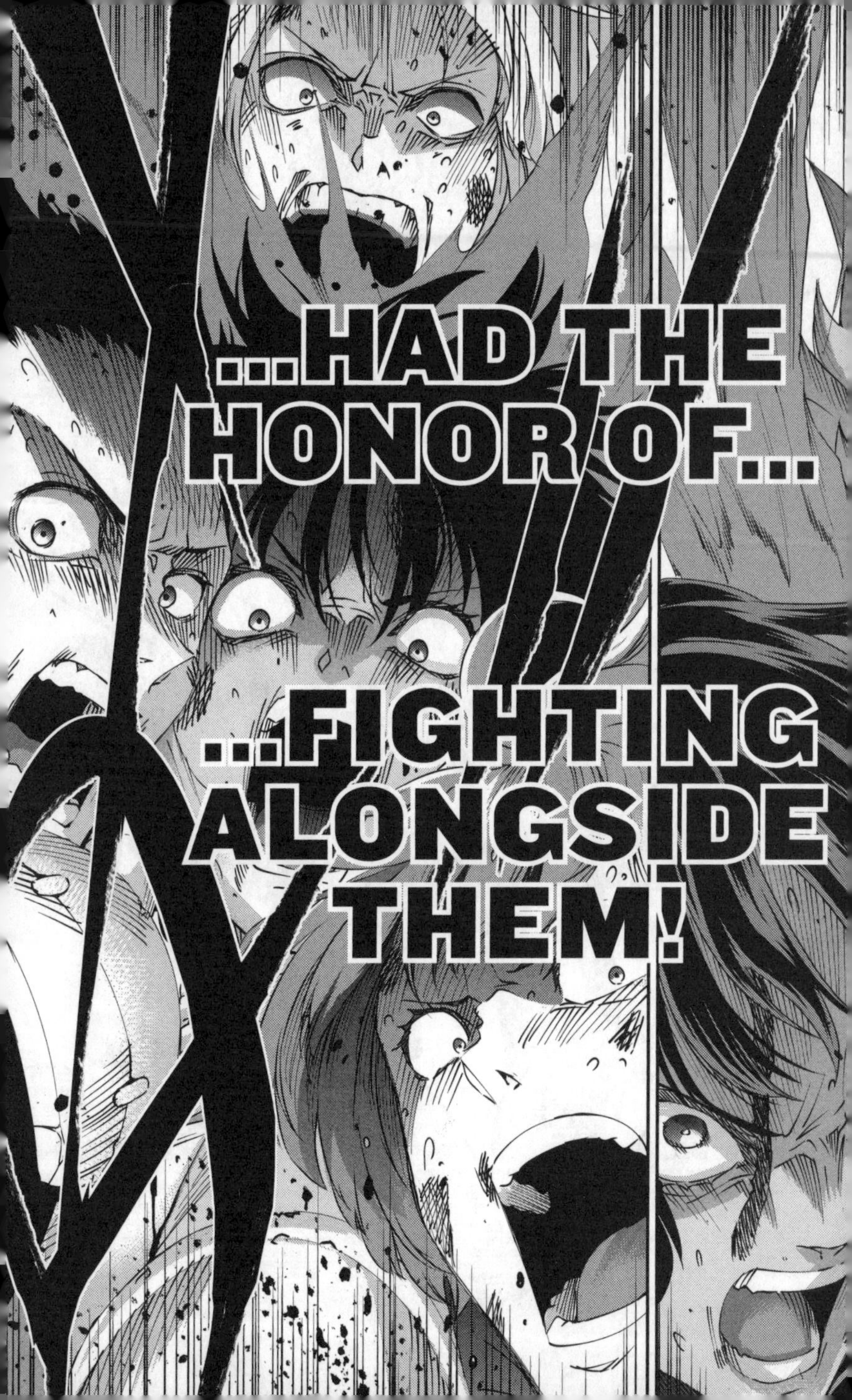
...HAD THE HONOR OF...
...FIGHTING ALONGSIDE THEM!

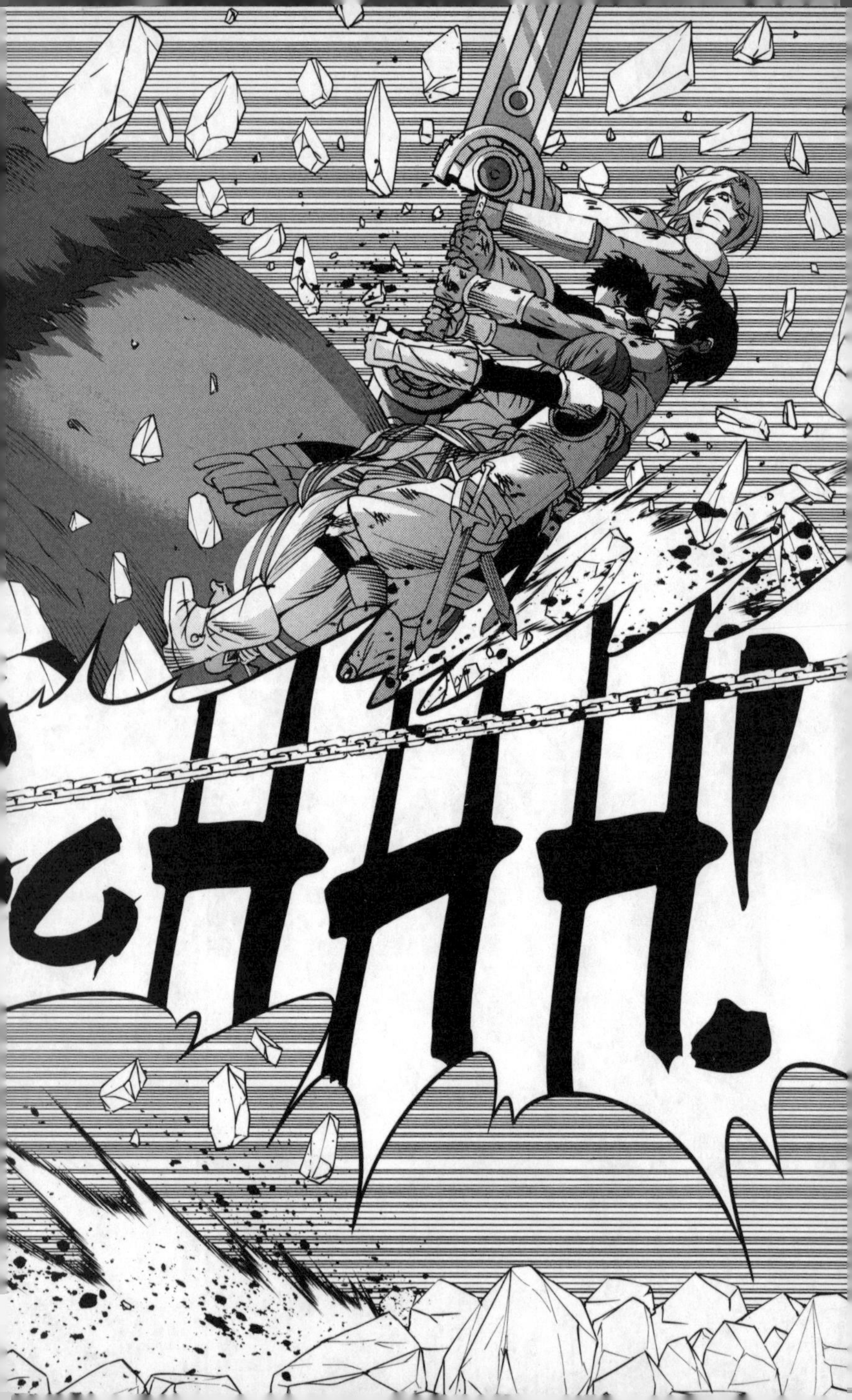
CHHH!

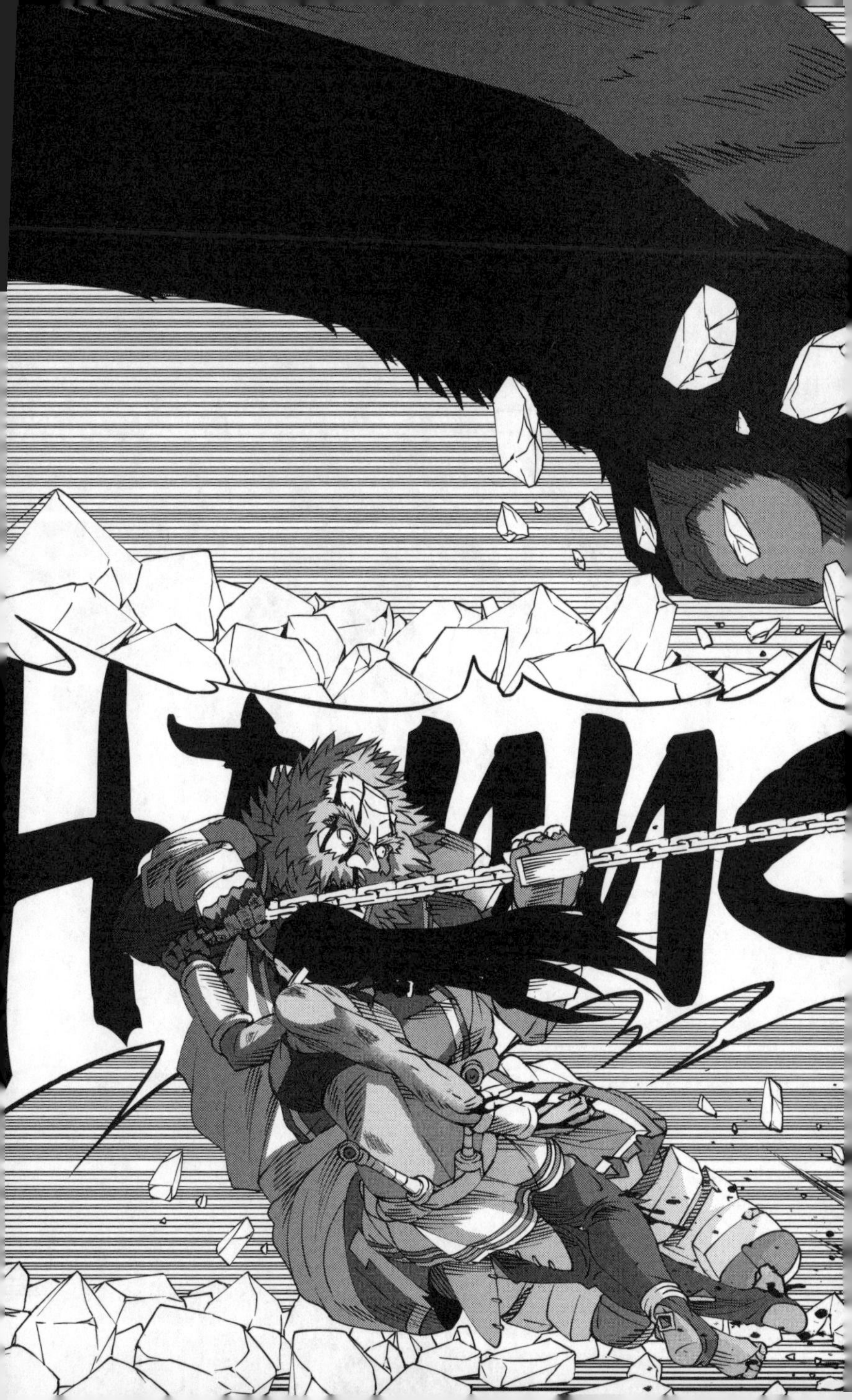

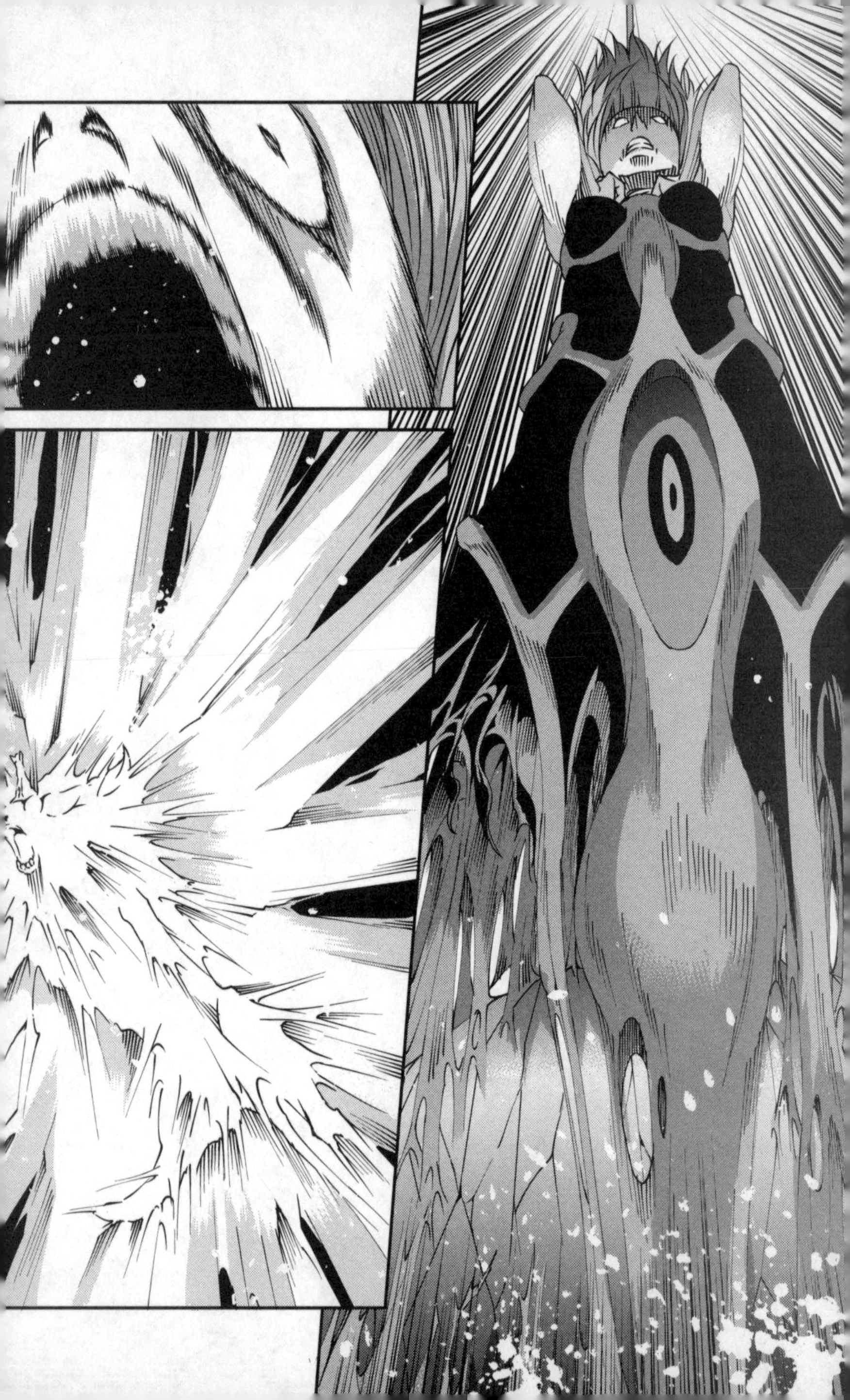

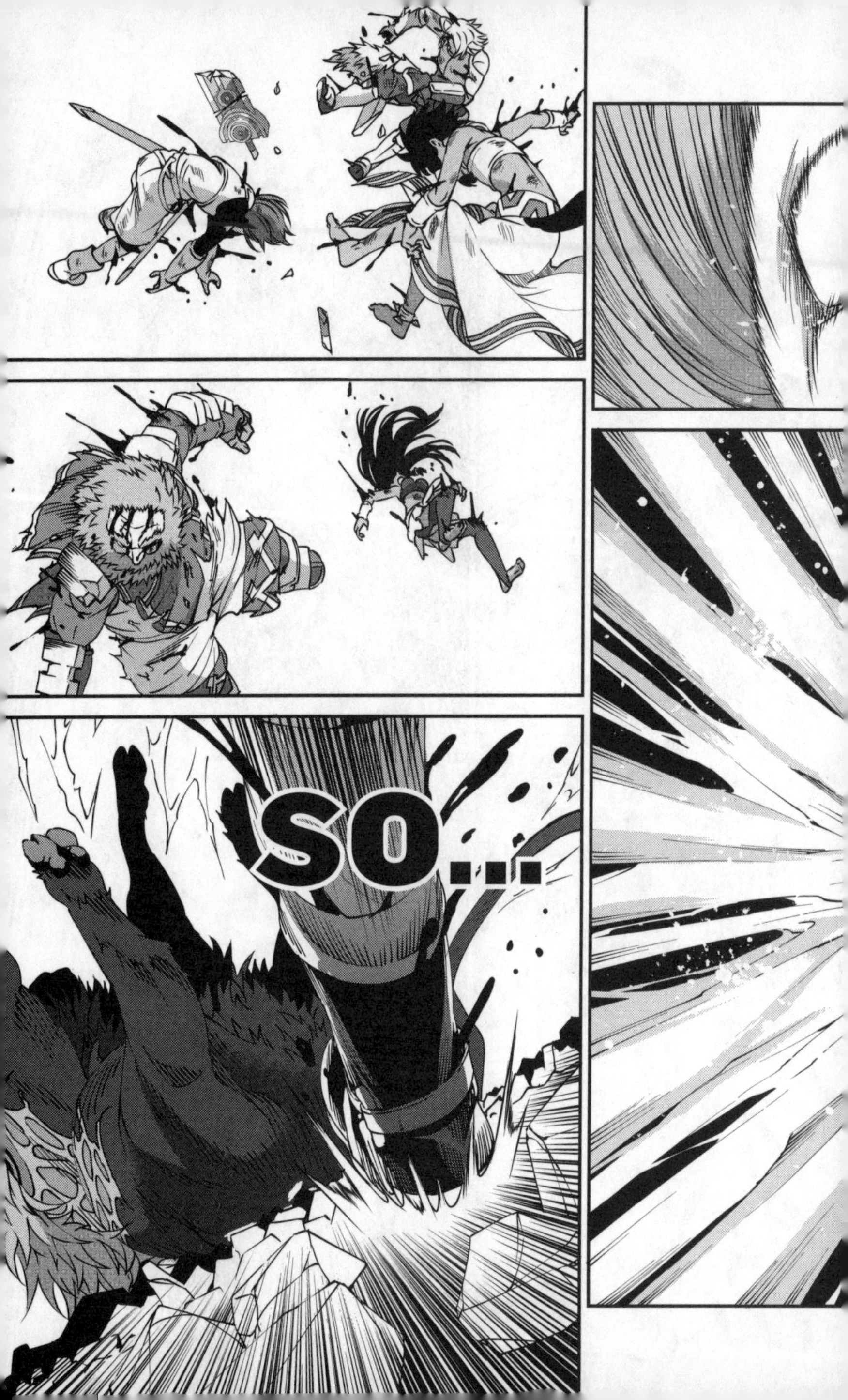
SO...

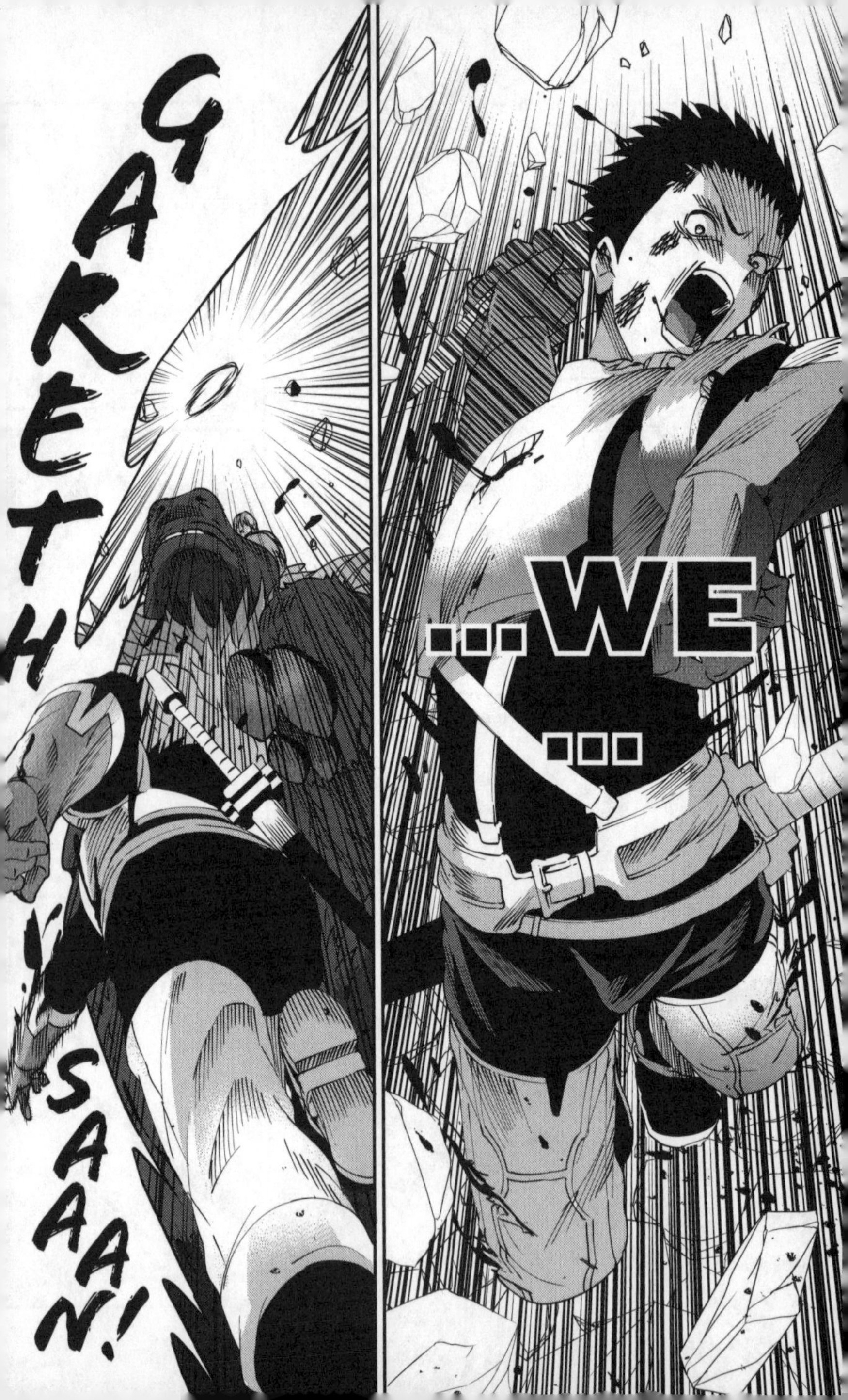
...WE
...
GARETH-SAAAN!

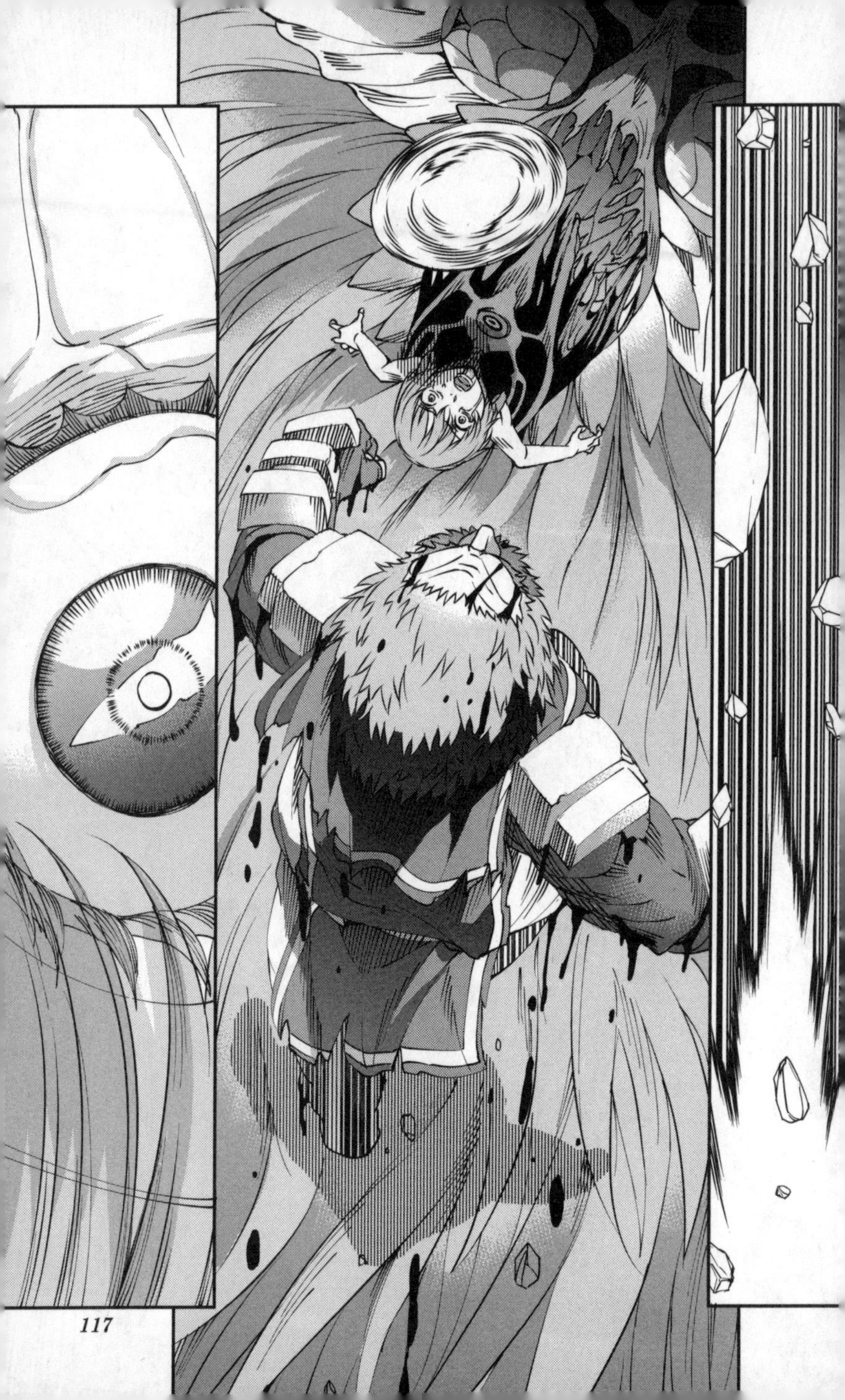

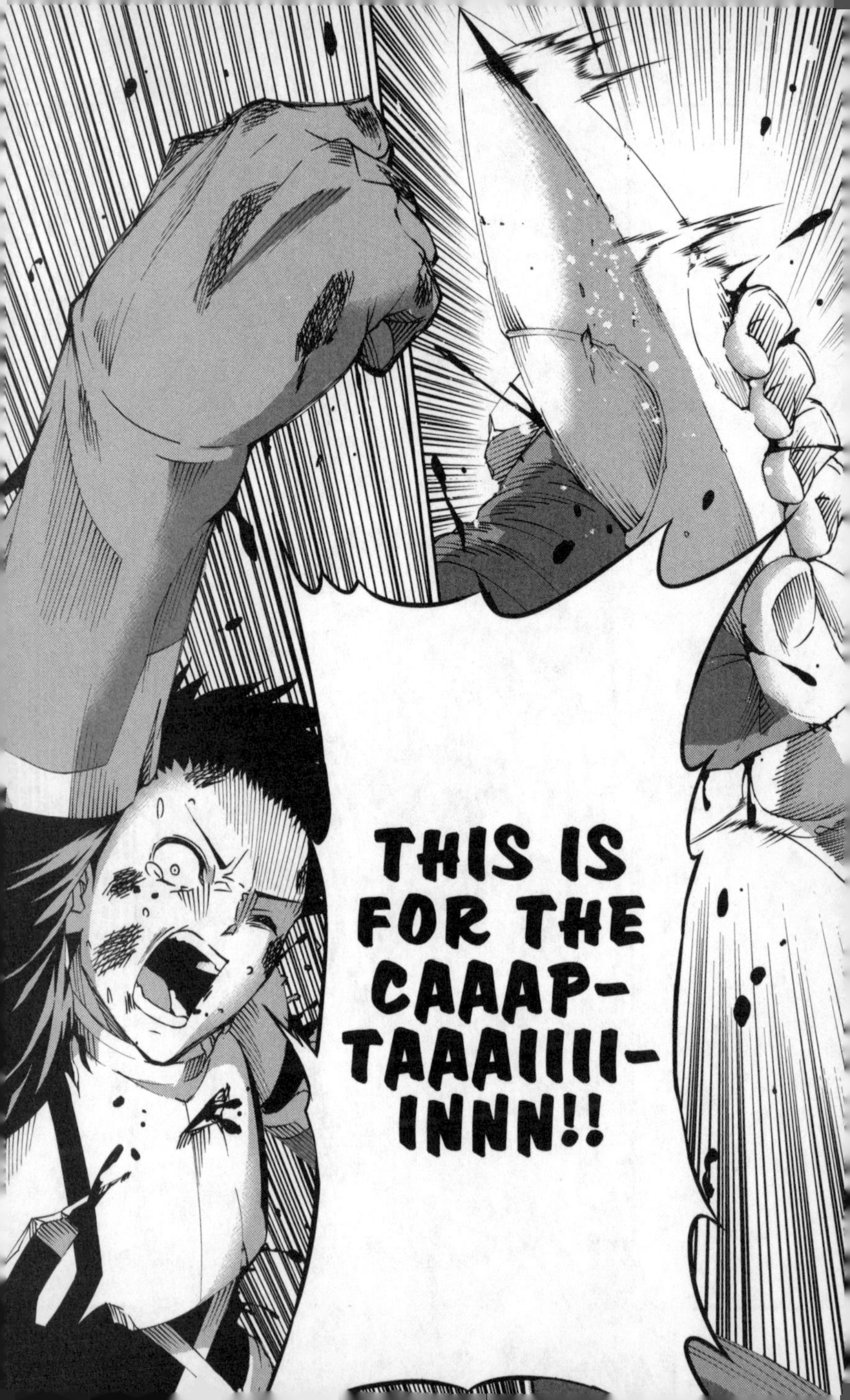
THIS IS FOR THE CAAAP-TAAAIIII-INNN!!

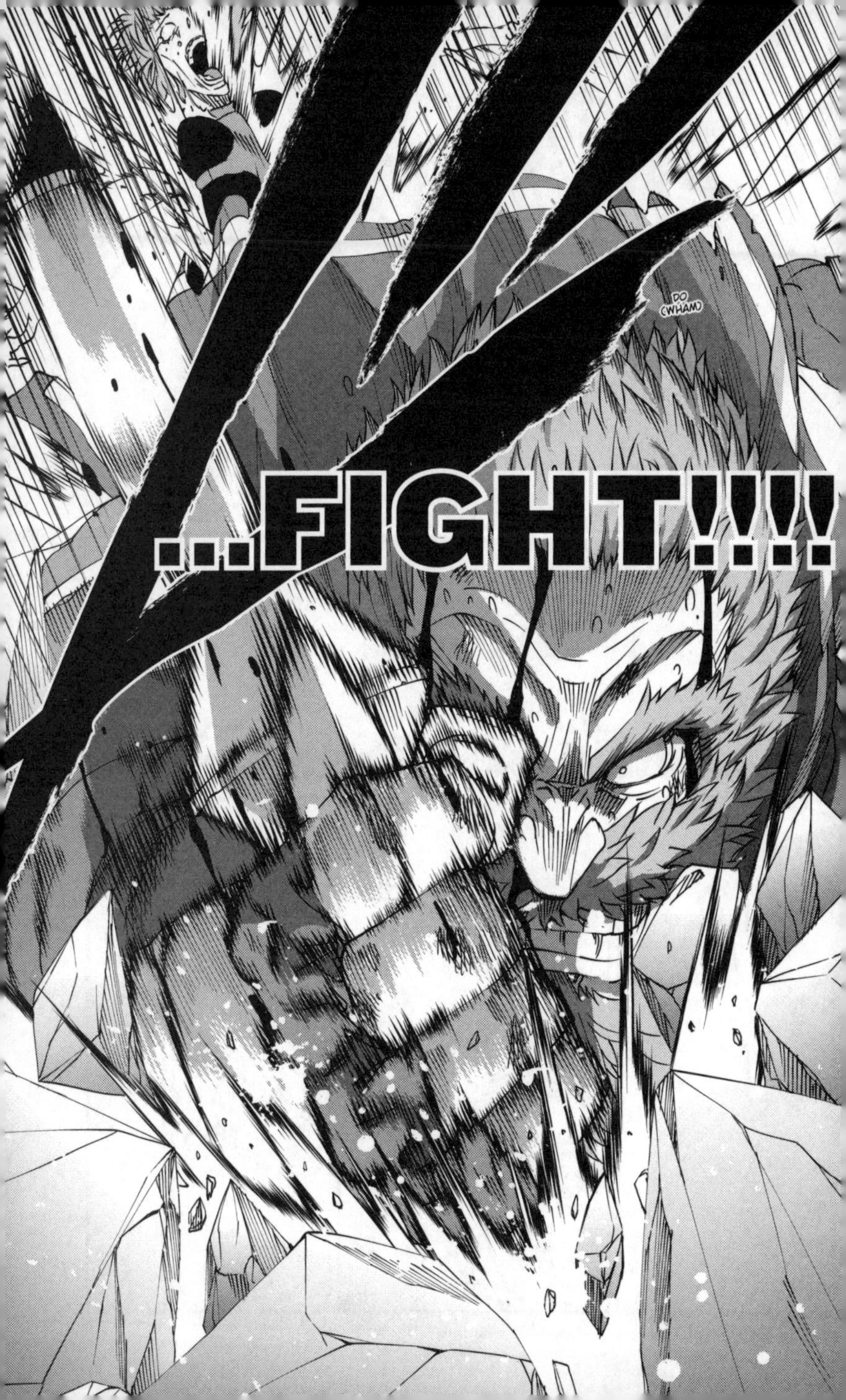
DO
(WHAM)
...FIGHT!!!!

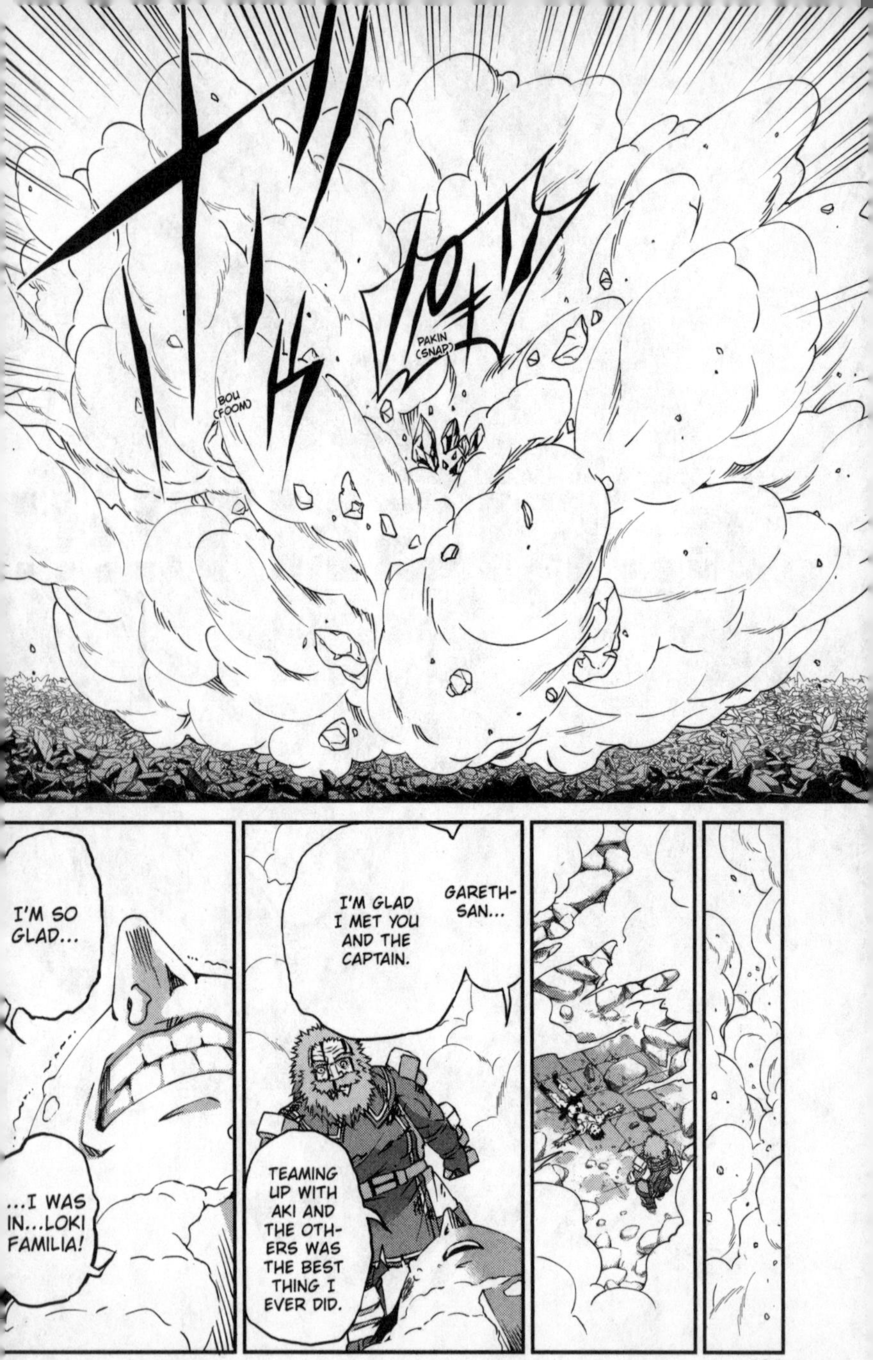
PAKIN (SNAP)
BOU (FOOM)
GARETH-SAN...
I'M GLAD I MET YOU AND THE CAPTAIN.
TEAMING UP WITH AKI AND THE OTHERS WAS THE BEST THING I EVER DID.
I'M SO GLAD...
...I WAS IN...LOKI FAMILIA!

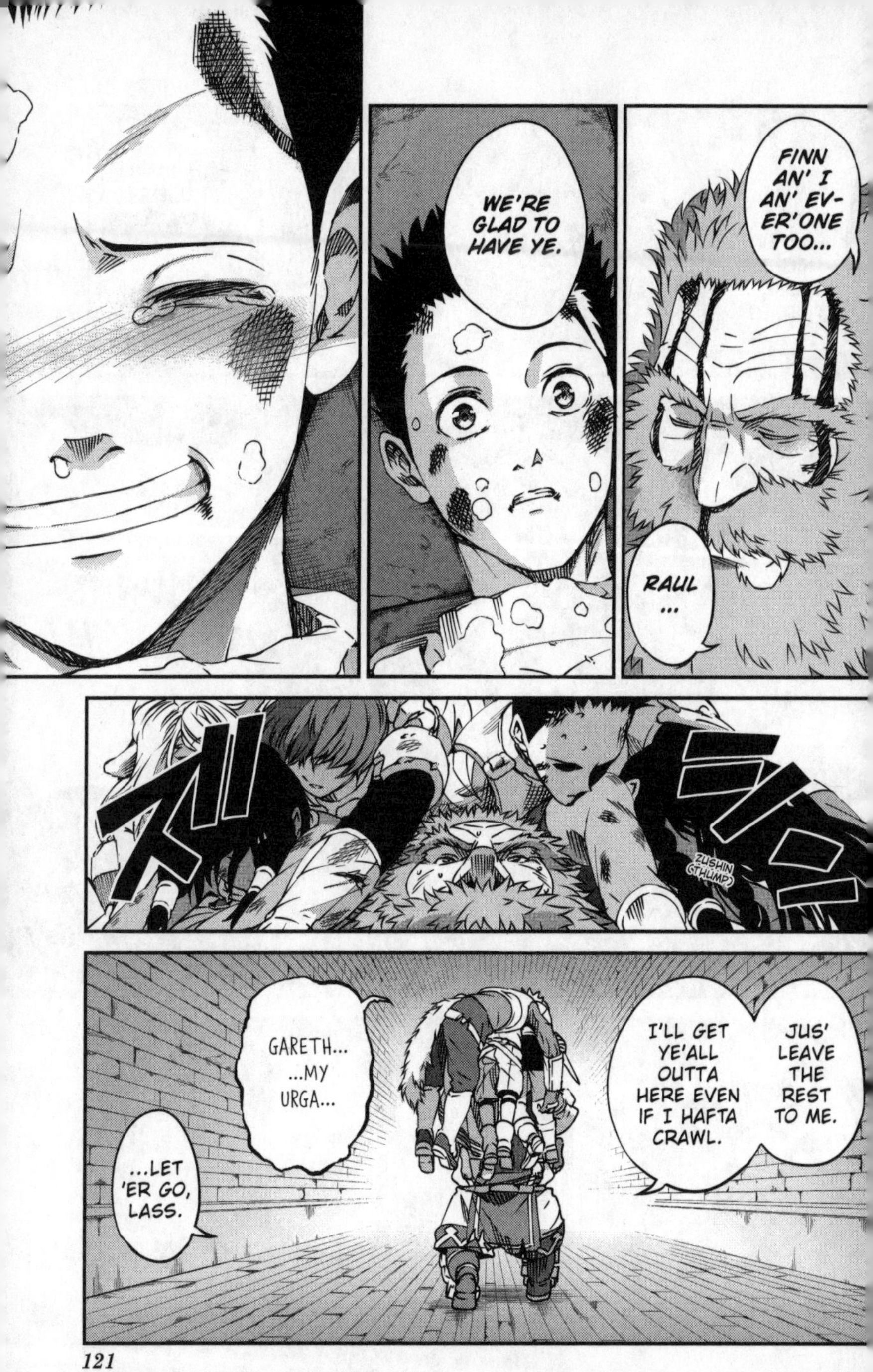
FINN AN' I AN' EV-ER'ONE TOO...
RAUL ...
WE'RE GLAD TO HAVE YE.
ZUSHIN (THUMP)
JUS' LEAVE THE REST TO ME.
I'LL GET YE'ALL OUTTA HERE EVEN IF I HAFTA CRAWL.
GARETH... ...MY URGA...
...LET 'ER GO, LASS.

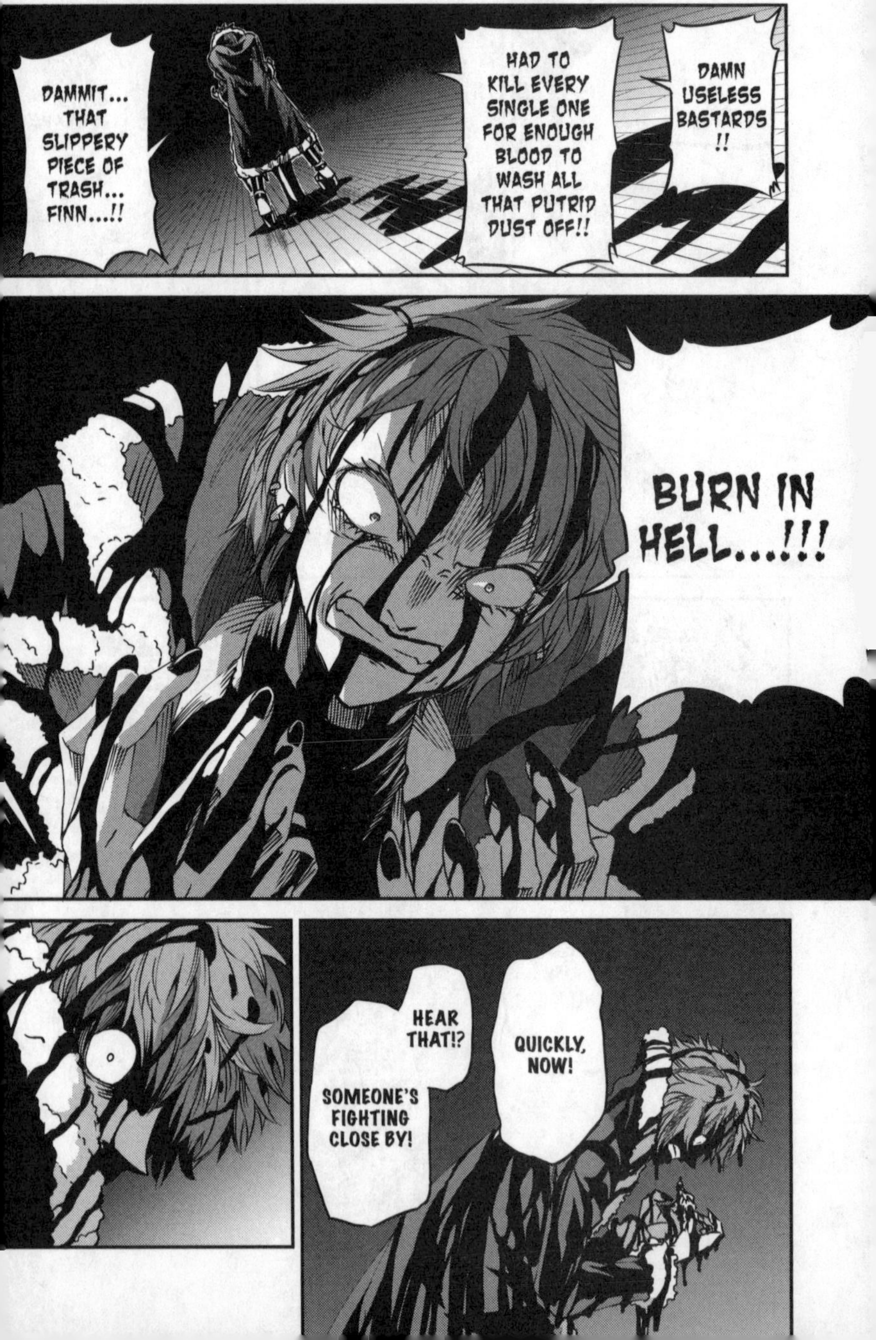
DAMN USELESS BASTARDS!!
HAD TO KILL EVERY SINGLE ONE FOR ENOUGH BLOOD TO WASH ALL THAT PUTRID DUST OFF!!
DAMMIT... THAT SLIPPERY PIECE OF TRASH... FINN...!!
BURN IN HELL...!!!
QUICKLY, NOW!
HEAR THAT!?
SOMEONE'S FIGHTING CLOSE BY!

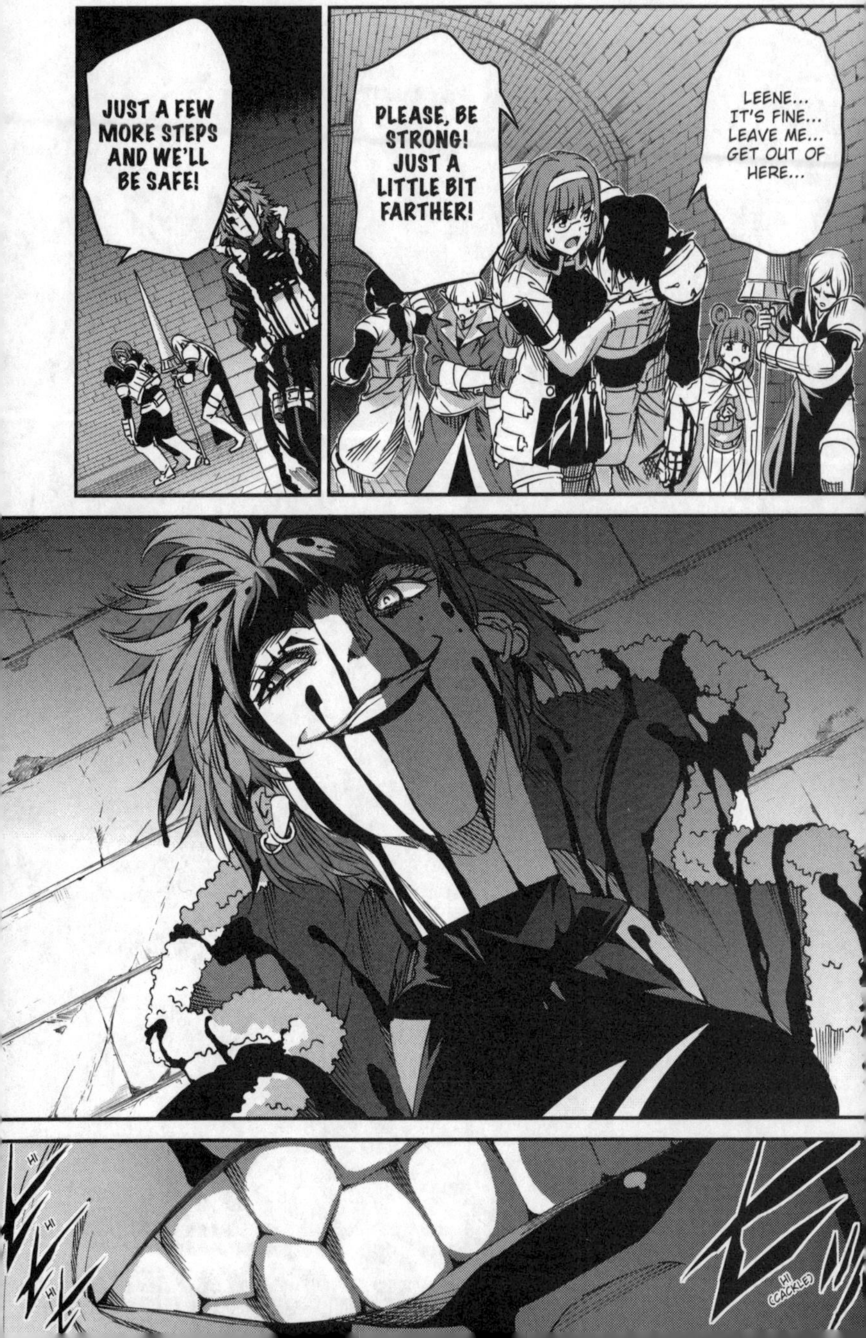
LEENE... IT'S FINE... LEAVE ME... GET OUT OF HERE...
PLEASE, BE STRONG! JUST A LITTLE BIT FARTHER!
JUST A FEW MORE STEPS AND WE'LL BE SAFE!
HI (CACKLE)
HI HI HI HI

Is it Wrong to Try to Pick Up Girls in a Dungeon? On the Side

Sword Oratoria

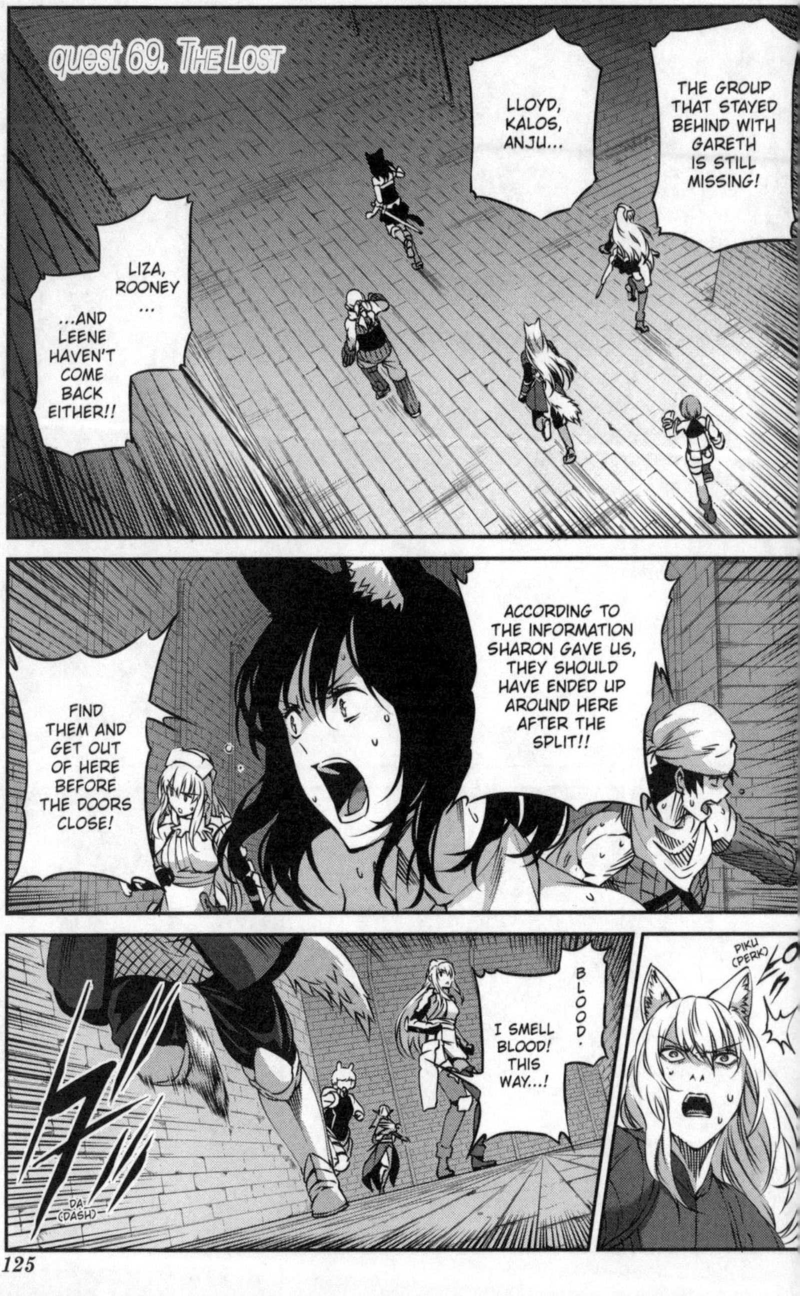
quest 69. The Lost
THE GROUP THAT STAYED BEHIND WITH GARETH IS STILL MISSING!
LLOYD, KALOS, ANJU...
LIZA, ROONEY ...
...AND LEENE HAVEN'T COME BACK EITHER!!
ACCORDING TO THE INFORMATION SHARON GAVE US, THEY SHOULD HAVE ENDED UP AROUND HERE AFTER THE SPLIT!!
FIND THEM AND GET OUT OF HERE BEFORE THE DOORS CLOSE!
PIKU (PERK)
BLOOD.
I SMELL BLOOD! THIS WAY...!
DA (DASH)

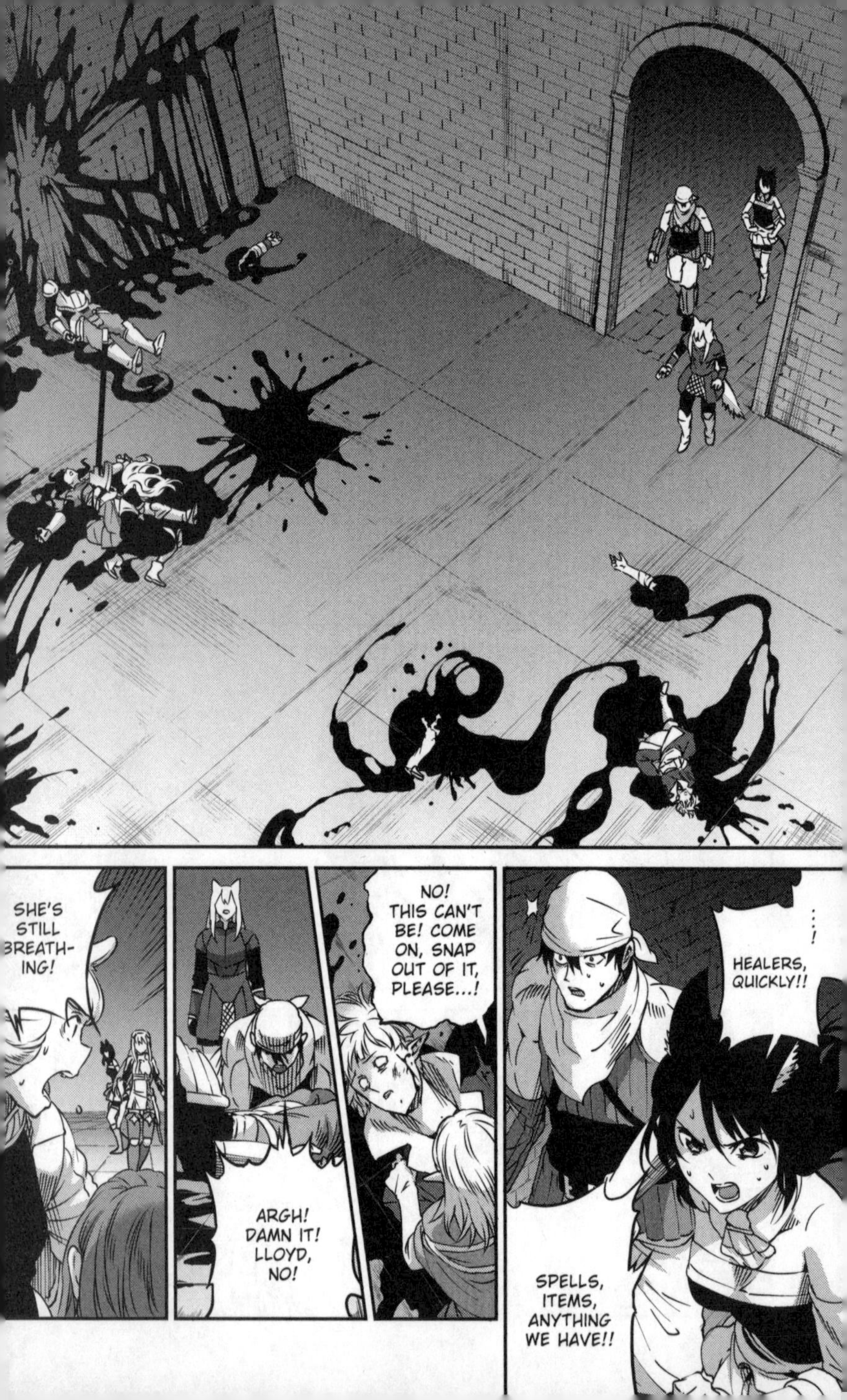
...!
HEALERS, QUICKLY!!
SPELLS, ITEMS, ANYTHING WE HAVE!!
NO! THIS CAN'T BE! COME ON, SNAP OUT OF IT, PLEASE...!
ARGH! DAMN IT! LLOYD, NO!
SHE'S STILL BREATHING!

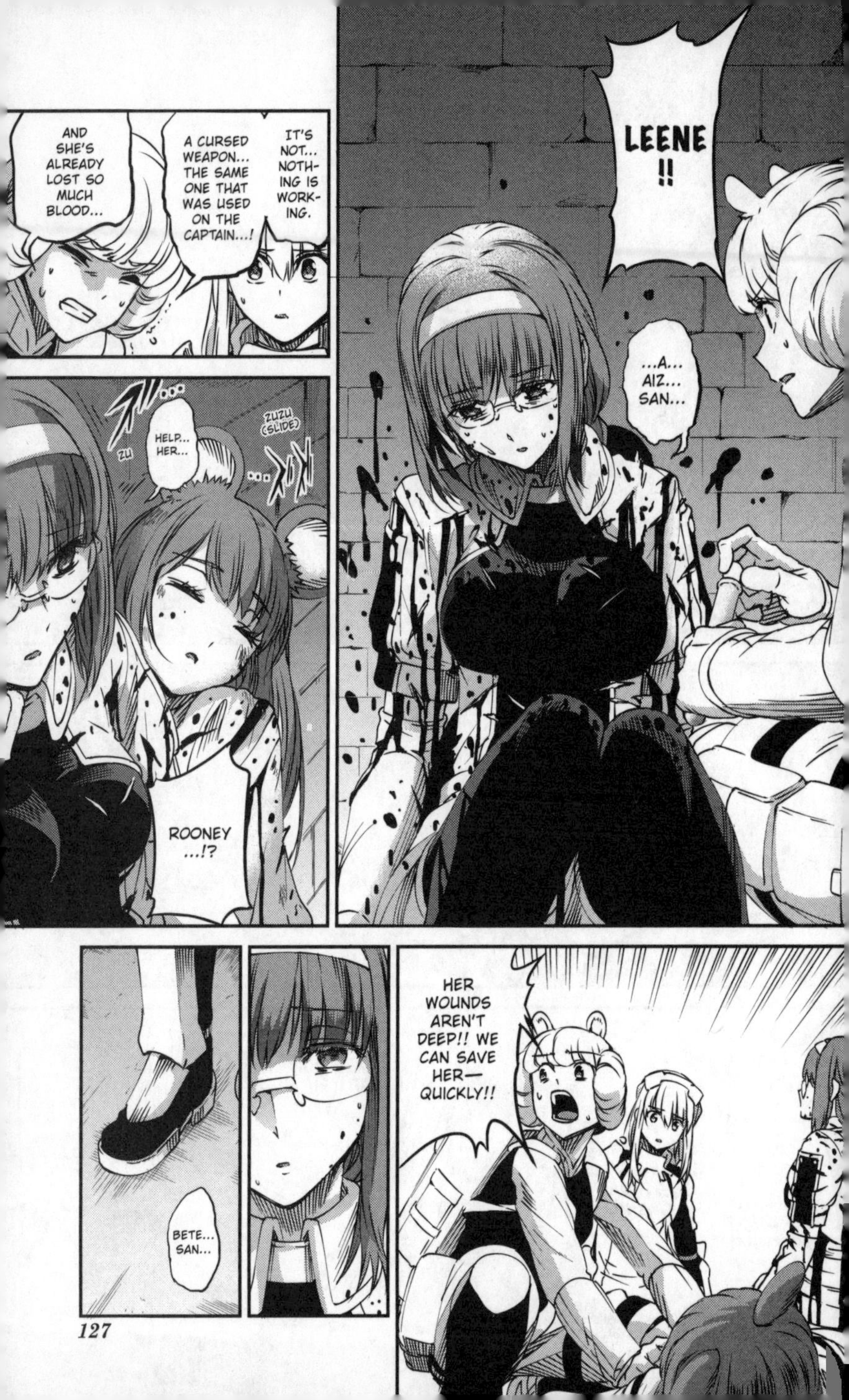
LEENE !!
...A... AIZ... SAN...
IT'S NOT... NOTHING IS WORKING.
A CURSED WEAPON... THE SAME ONE THAT WAS USED ON THE CAPTAIN...!
AND SHE'S ALREADY LOST SO MUCH BLOOD...
ZUZU (SLIDE)
HELP... HER...
ZU
ROONEY ...!?
HER WOUNDS AREN'T DEEP!! WE CAN SAVE HER— QUICKLY!!
BETE... SAN...

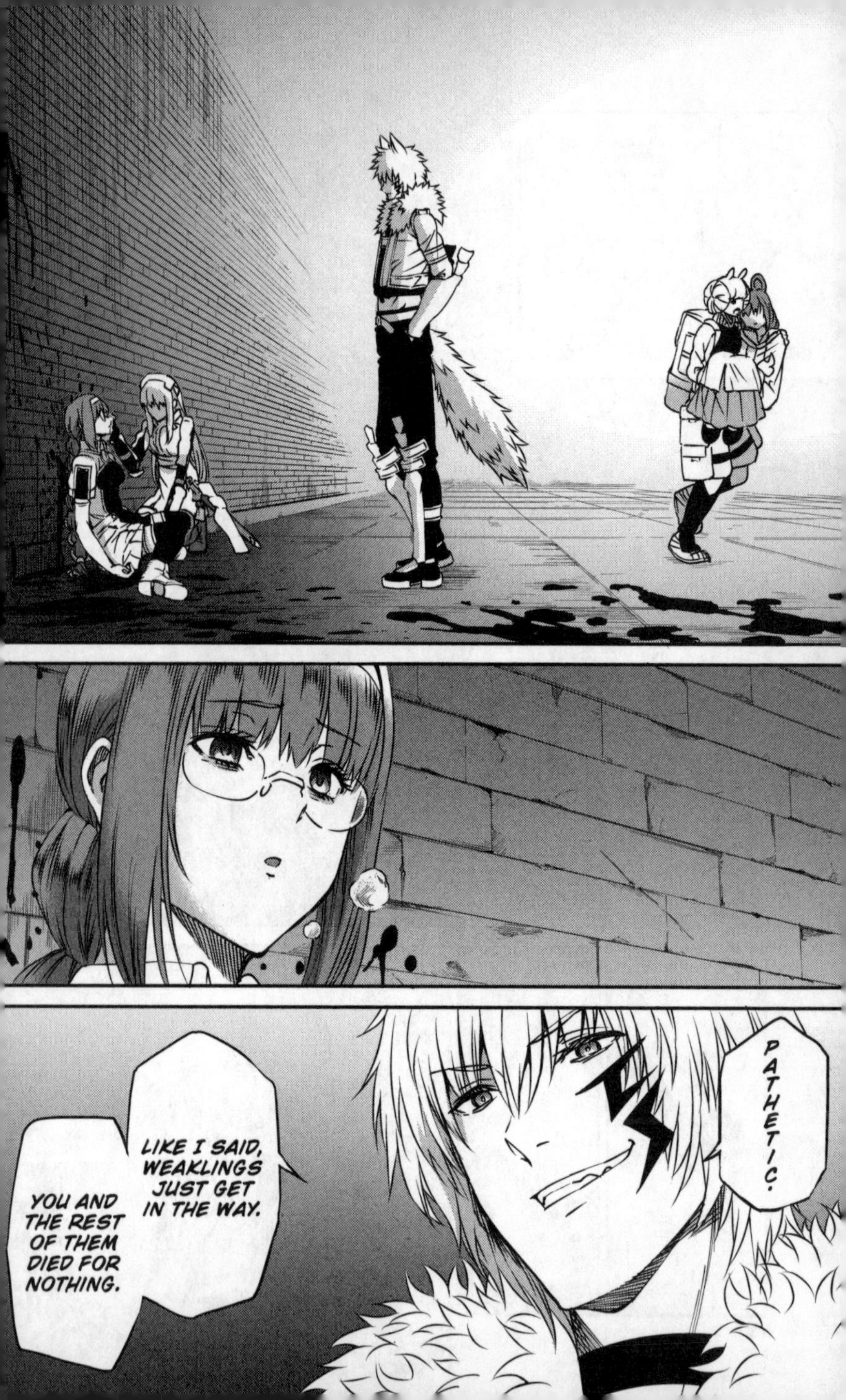
PATHETIC.
LIKE I SAID, WEAKLINGS JUST GET IN THE WAY.
YOU AND THE REST OF THEM DIED FOR NOTHING.

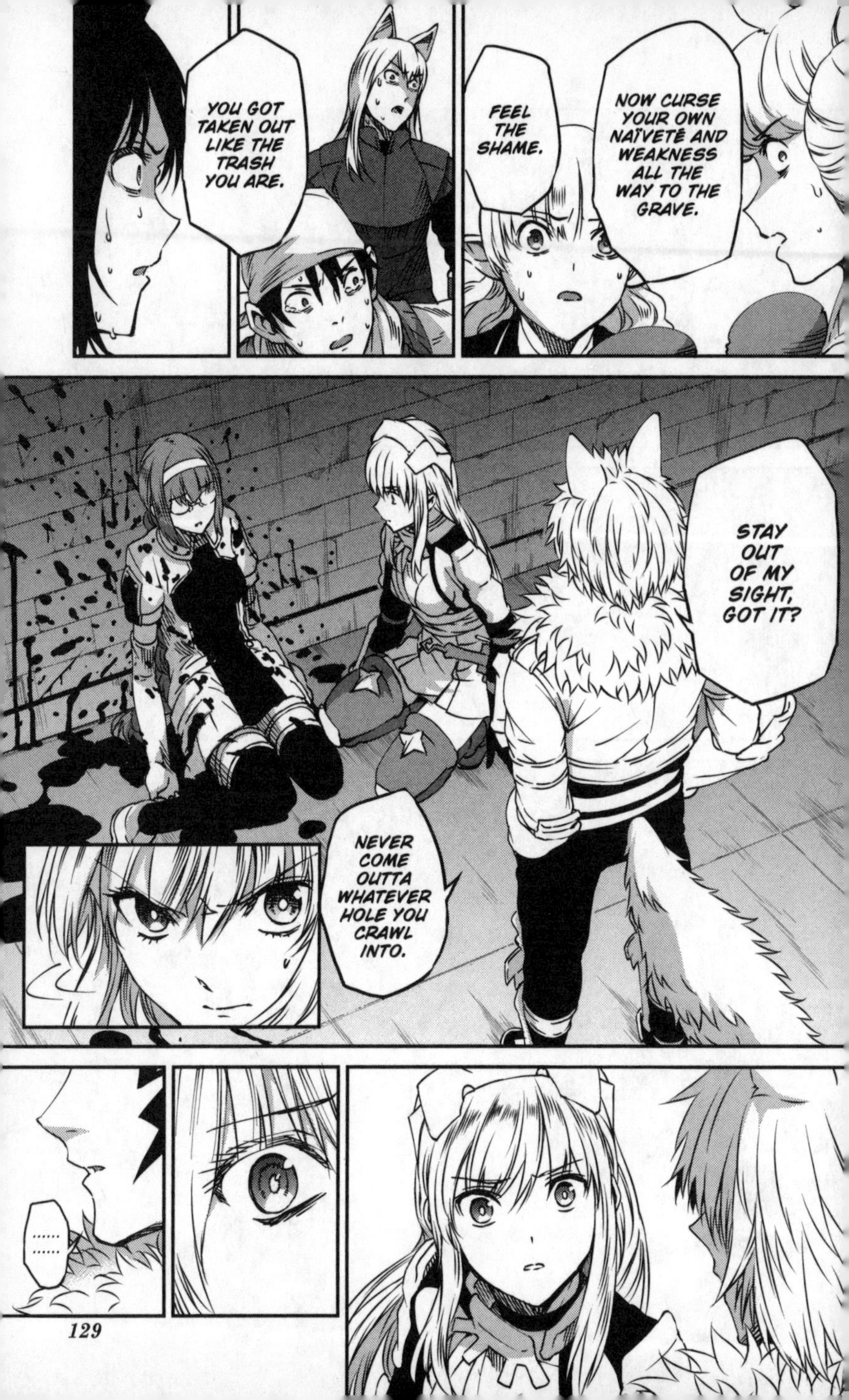
NOW CURSE YOUR OWN NAÏVETÉ AND WEAKNESS ALL THE WAY TO THE GRAVE.
FEEL THE SHAME.
YOU GOT TAKEN OUT LIKE THE TRASH YOU ARE.
STAY OUT OF MY SIGHT, GOT IT?
NEVER COME OUTTA WHATEVER HOLE YOU CRAWL INTO.
....

......AH.

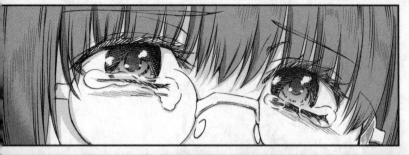

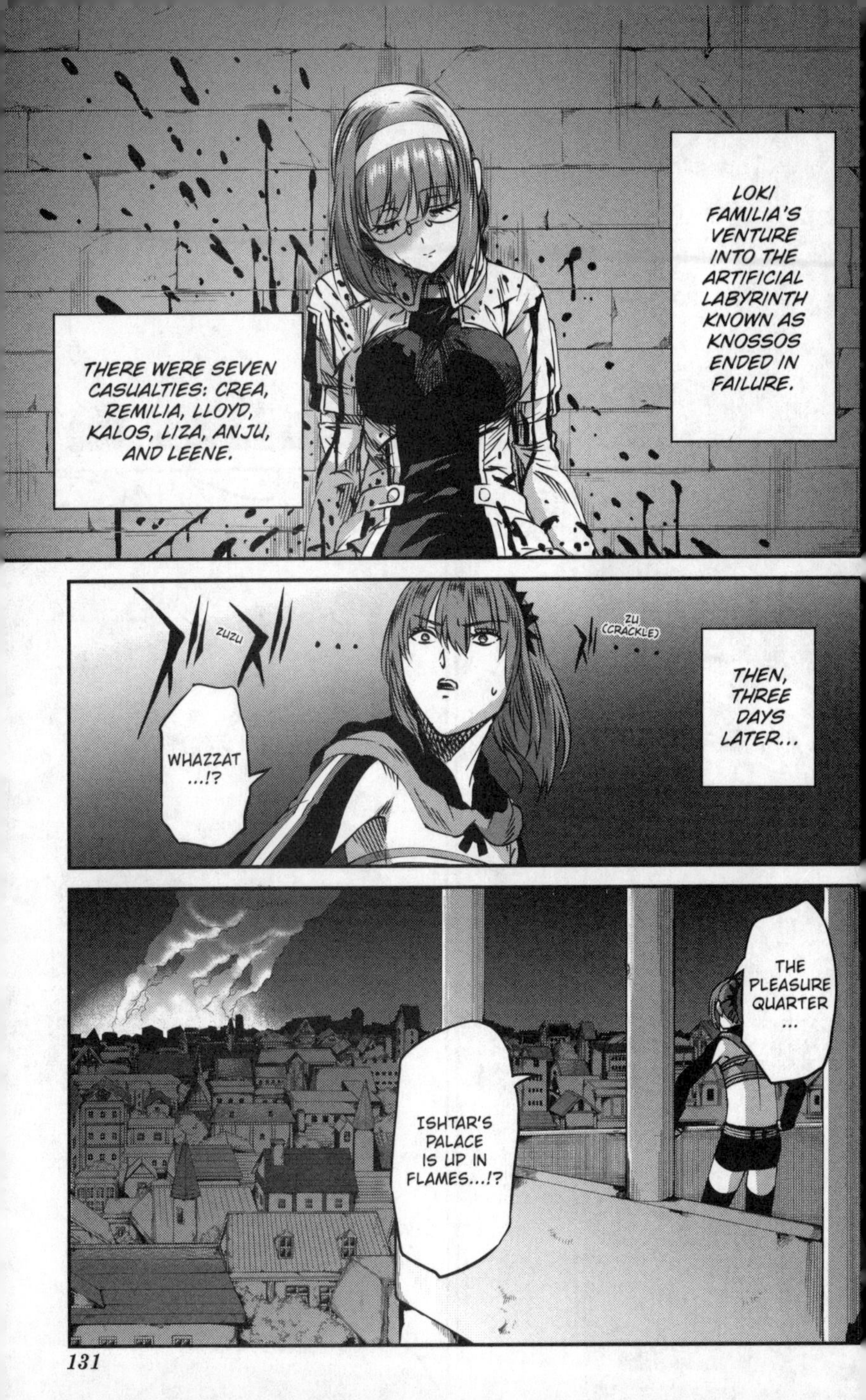
LOKI FAMILIA'S VENTURE INTO THE ARTIFICIAL LABYRINTH KNOWN AS KNOSSOS ENDED IN FAILURE.
THERE WERE SEVEN CASUALTIES: CREA, REMILIA, LLOYD, KALOS, LIZA, ANJU, AND LEENE.
THEN, THREE DAYS LATER...
ZU (CRACKLE)
...
ZUZU
WHAZZAT ...!?
THE PLEASURE QUARTER ...
ISHTAR'S PALACE IS UP IN FLAMES...!?

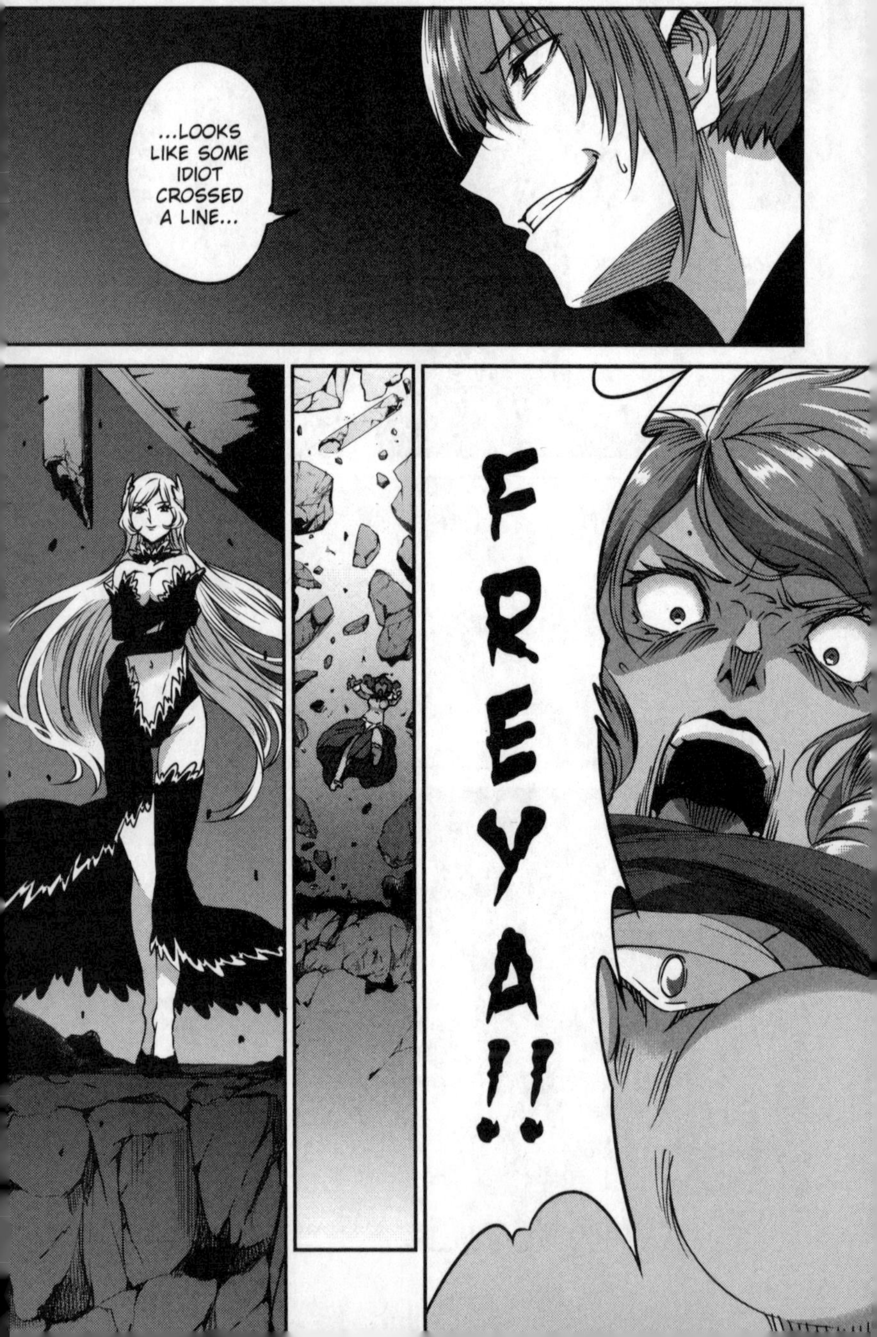
...LOOKS LIKE SOME IDIOT CROSSED A LINE...
FREYA!!

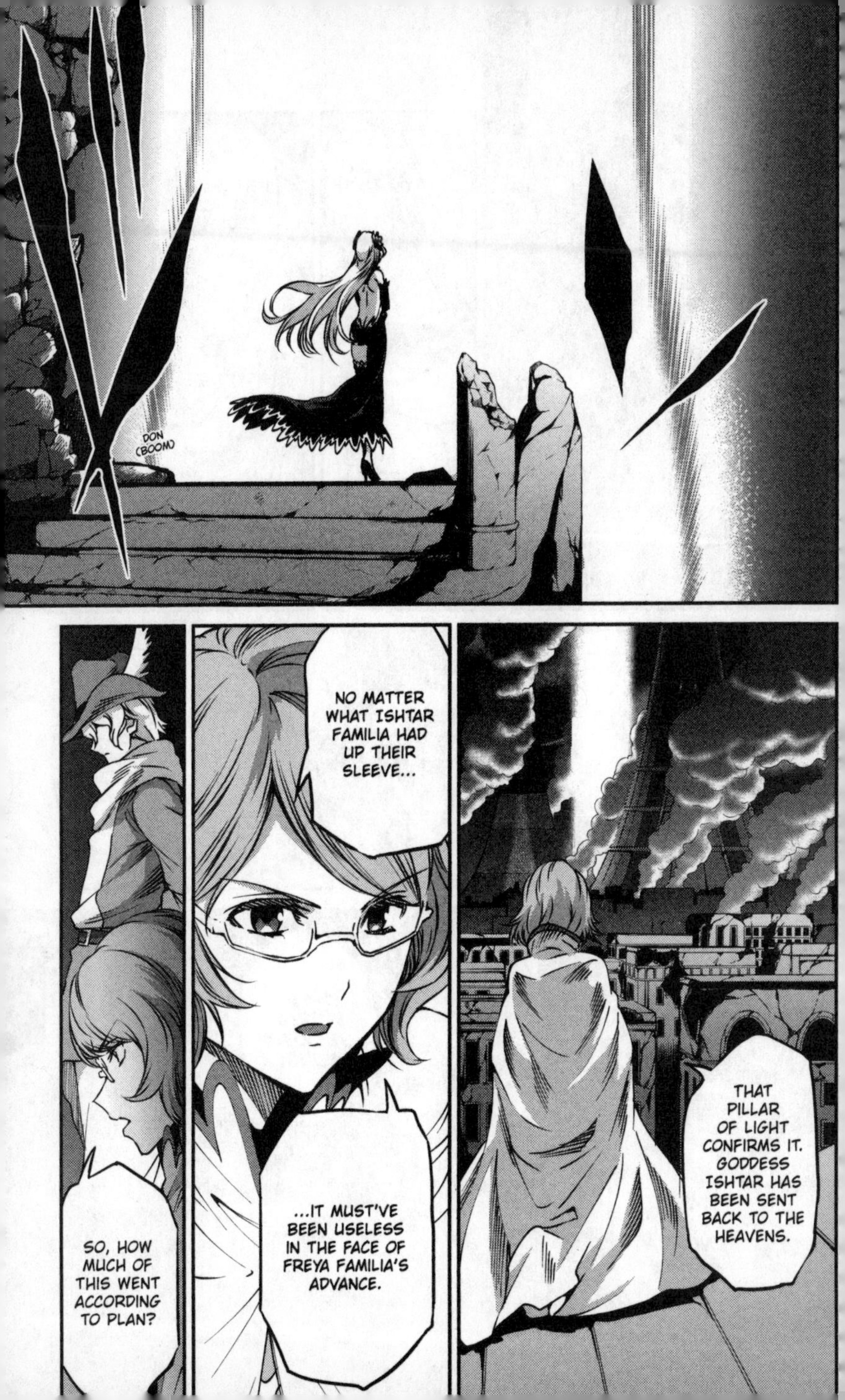
DON (BOOM)
THAT PILLAR OF LIGHT CONFIRMS IT. GODDESS ISHTAR HAS BEEN SENT BACK TO THE HEAVENS.
NO MATTER WHAT ISHTAR FAMILIA HAD UP THEIR SLEEVE...
...IT MUST'VE BEEN USELESS IN THE FACE OF FREYA FAMILIA'S ADVANCE.
SO, HOW MUCH OF THIS WENT ACCORDING TO PLAN?

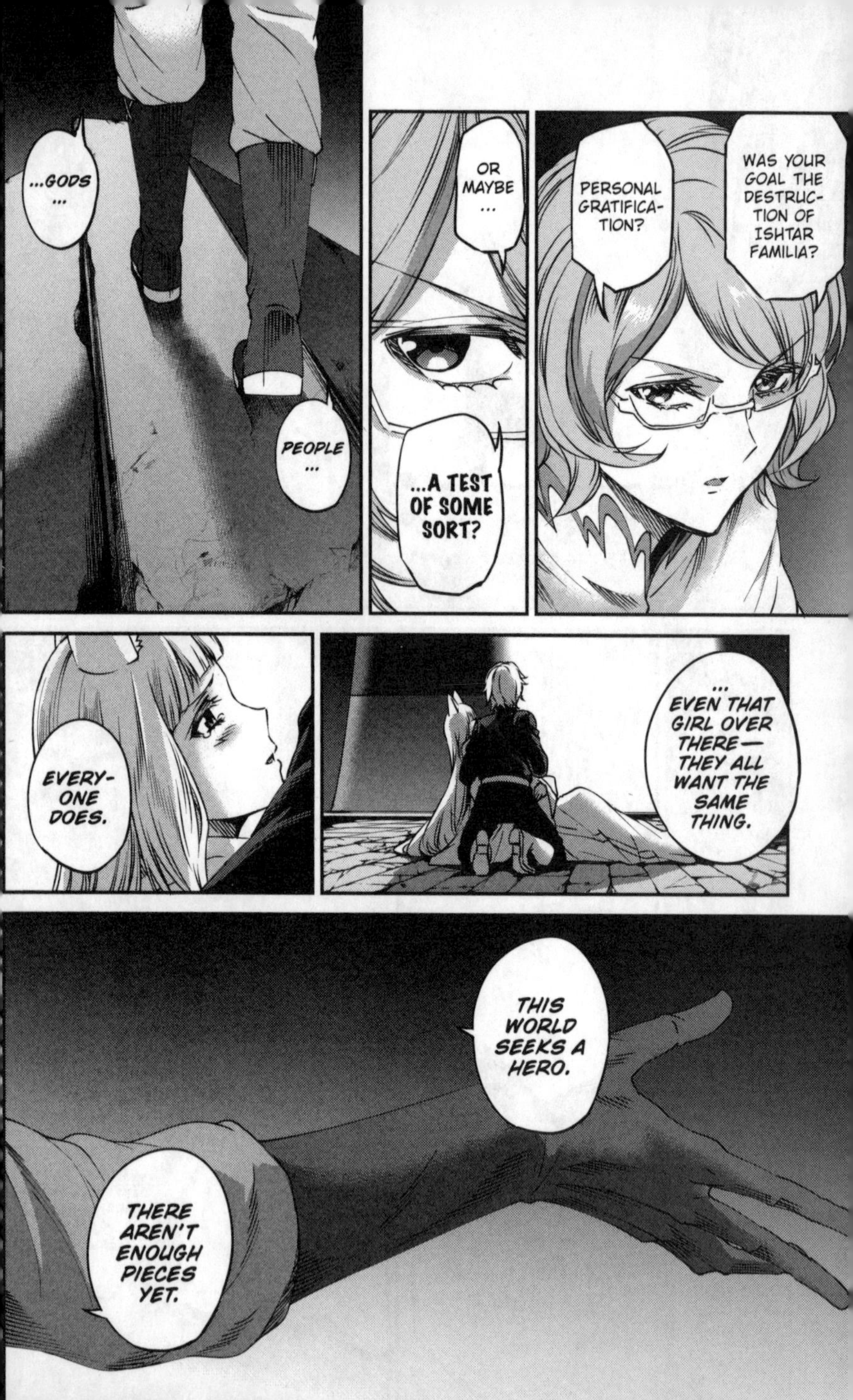
WAS YOUR GOAL THE DESTRUCTION OF ISHTAR FAMILIA?
PERSONAL GRATIFICATION?
OR MAYBE...
...A TEST OF SOME SORT?
...GODS...
PEOPLE...
...EVEN THAT GIRL OVER THERE—THEY ALL WANT THE SAME THING.
EVERYONE DOES.
THIS WORLD SEEKS A HERO.
THERE AREN'T ENOUGH PIECES YET.

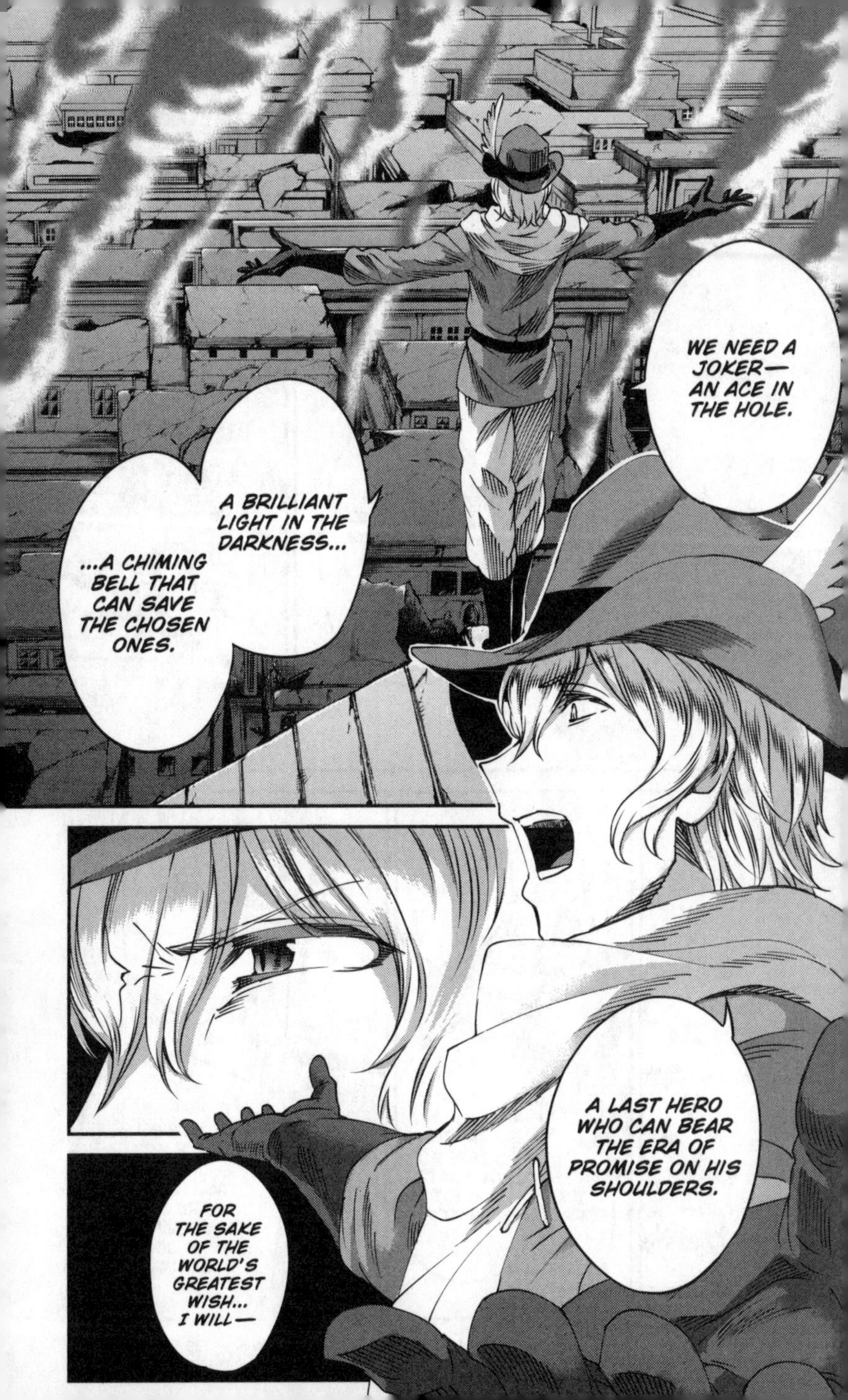
WE NEED A JOKER— AN ACE IN THE HOLE.
A BRILLIANT LIGHT IN THE DARKNESS...
...A CHIMING BELL THAT CAN SAVE THE CHOSEN ONES.
A LAST HERO WHO CAN BEAR THE ERA OF PROMISE ON HIS SHOULDERS.
FOR THE SAKE OF THE WORLD'S GREATEST WISH... I WILL—

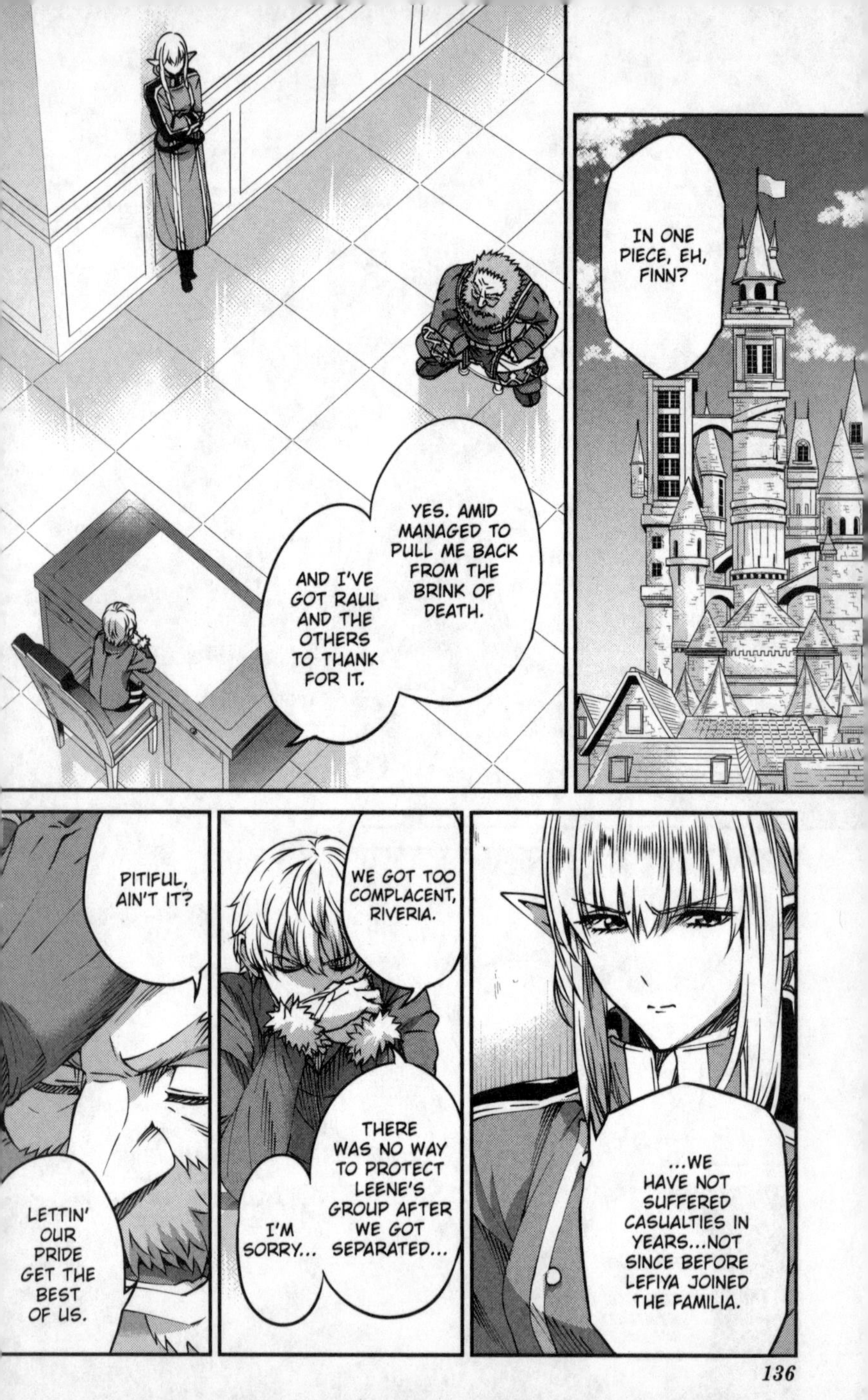
IN ONE PIECE, EH, FINN?
YES. AMID MANAGED TO PULL ME BACK FROM THE BRINK OF DEATH.
AND I'VE GOT RAUL AND THE OTHERS TO THANK FOR IT.
...WE HAVE NOT SUFFERED CASUALTIES IN YEARS...NOT SINCE BEFORE LEFIYA JOINED THE FAMILIA.
WE GOT TOO COMPLACENT, RIVERIA.
THERE WAS NO WAY TO PROTECT LEENE'S GROUP AFTER WE GOT SEPARATED...
I'M SORRY...
PITIFUL, AIN'T IT?
LETTIN' OUR PRIDE GET THE BEST OF US.

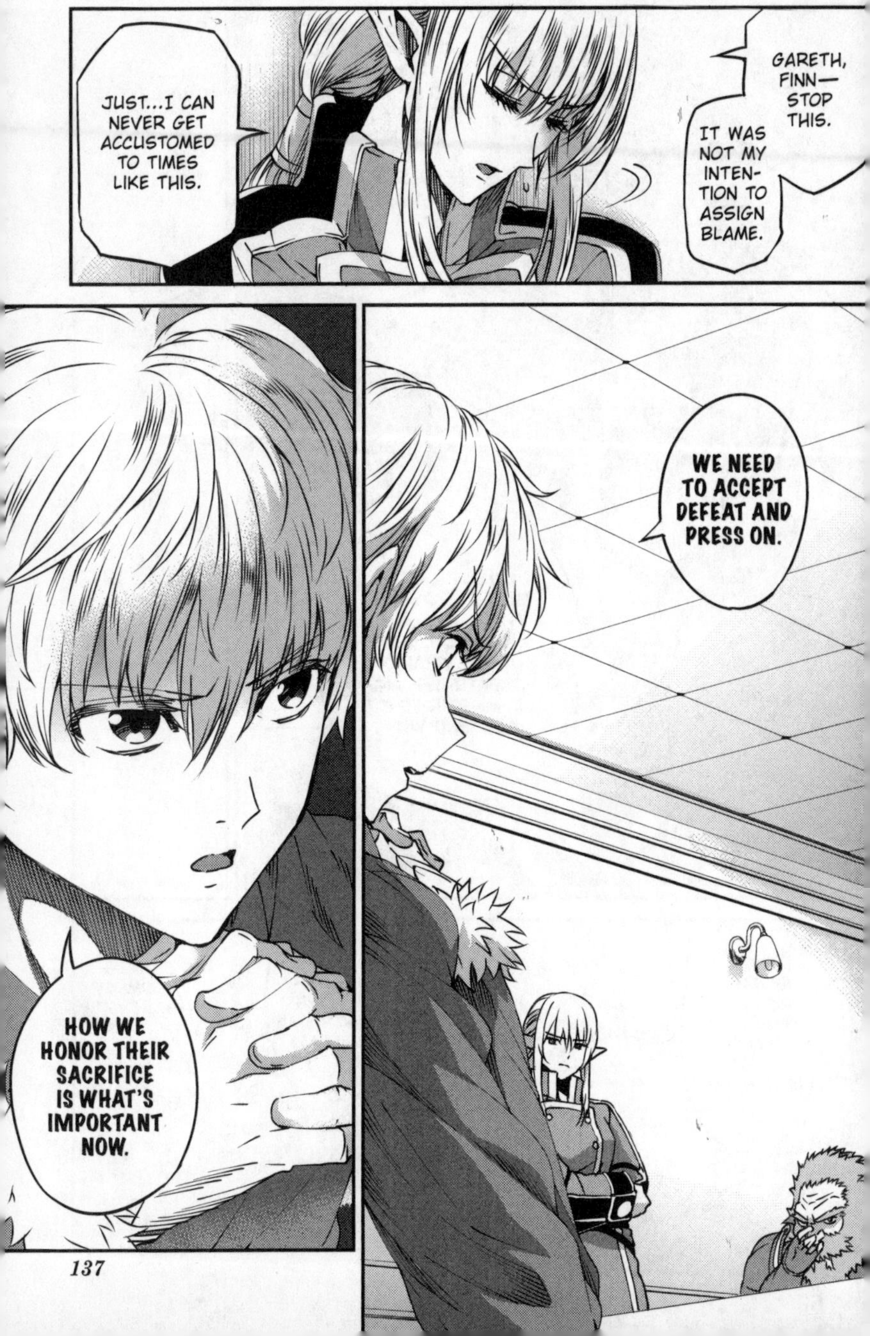
GARETH, FINN— STOP THIS.
IT WAS NOT MY INTEN-TION TO ASSIGN BLAME.
JUST...I CAN NEVER GET ACCUSTOMED TO TIMES LIKE THIS.
WE NEED TO ACCEPT DEFEAT AND PRESS ON.
HOW WE HONOR THEIR SACRIFICE IS WHAT'S IMPORTANT NOW.

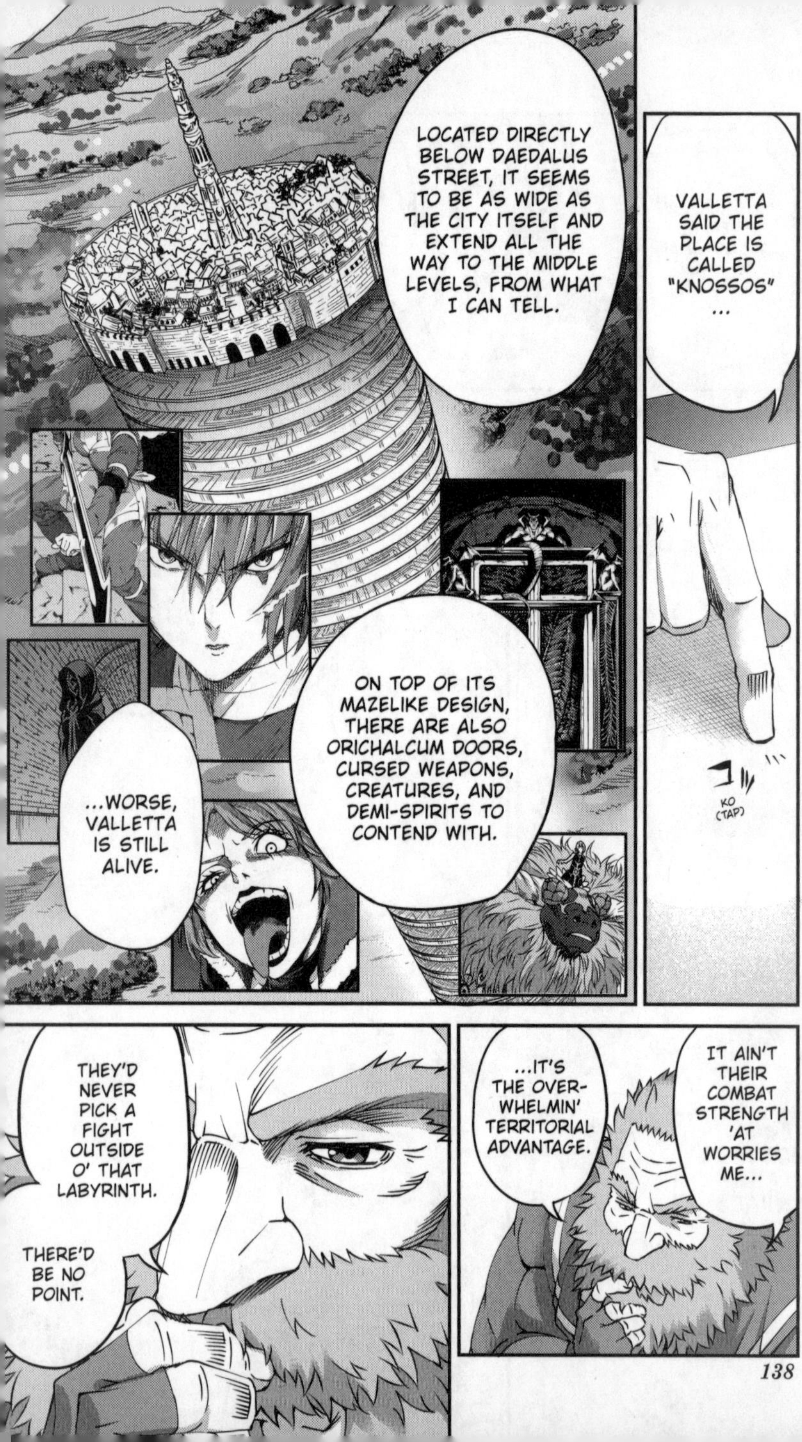

VALLETTA SAID THE PLACE IS CALLED "KNOSSOS" ...
KO (TAP)
LOCATED DIRECTLY BELOW DAEDALUS STREET, IT SEEMS TO BE AS WIDE AS THE CITY ITSELF AND EXTEND ALL THE WAY TO THE MIDDLE LEVELS, FROM WHAT I CAN TELL.
ON TOP OF ITS MAZELIKE DESIGN, THERE ARE ALSO ORICHALCUM DOORS, CURSED WEAPONS, CREATURES, AND DEMI-SPIRITS TO CONTEND WITH.
...WORSE, VALLETTA IS STILL ALIVE.
IT AIN'T THEIR COMBAT STRENGTH 'AT WORRIES ME...
...IT'S THE OVER-WHELMIN' TERRITORIAL ADVANTAGE.
THEY'D NEVER PICK A FIGHT OUTSIDE O' THAT LABYRINTH.
THERE'D BE NO POINT.

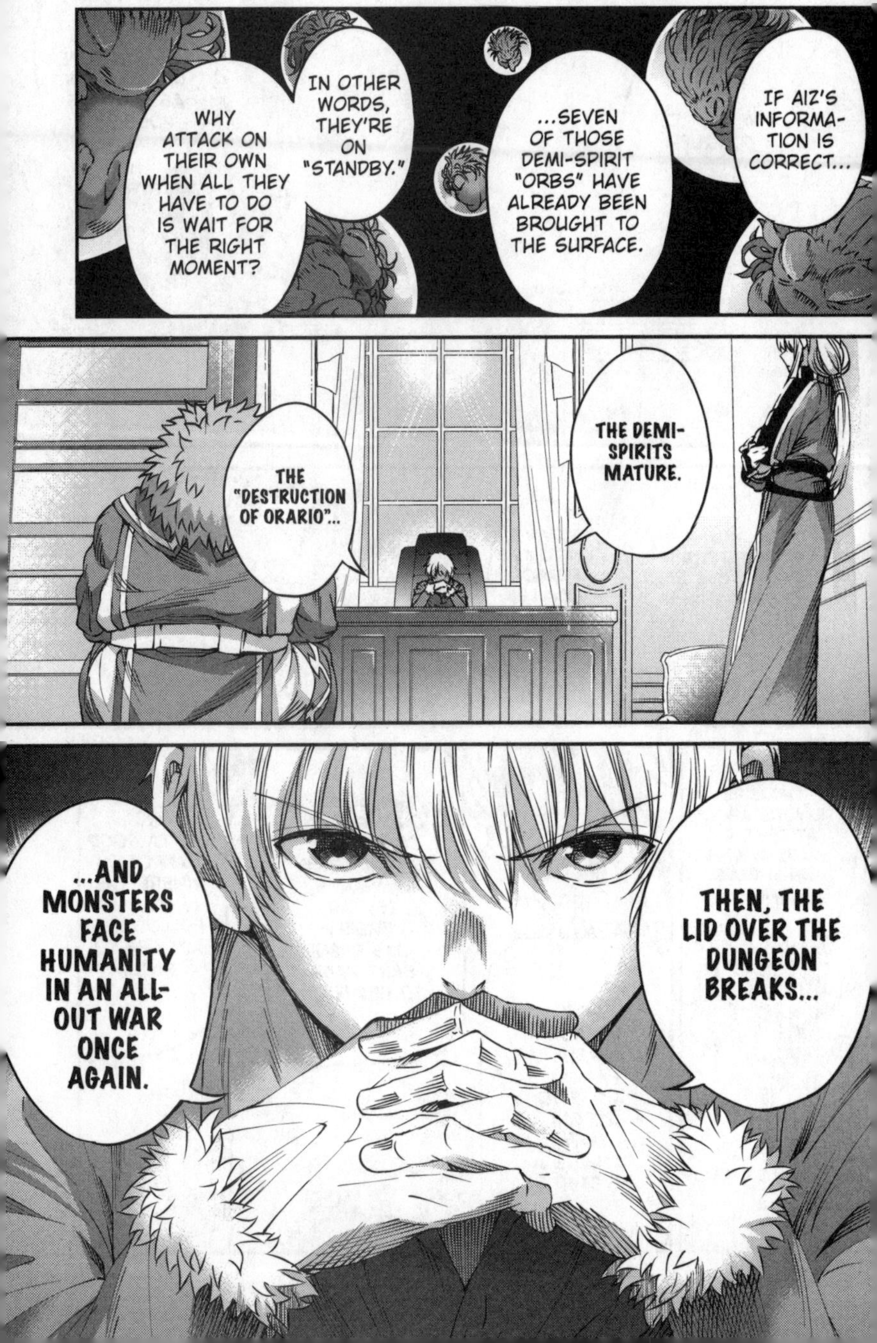
IF AIZ'S INFORMATION IS CORRECT...
...SEVEN OF THOSE DEMI-SPIRIT "ORBS" HAVE ALREADY BEEN BROUGHT TO THE SURFACE.
IN OTHER WORDS, THEY'RE ON "STANDBY."
WHY ATTACK ON THEIR OWN WHEN ALL THEY HAVE TO DO IS WAIT FOR THE RIGHT MOMENT?
THE DEMI-SPIRITS MATURE.
THE "DESTRUCTION OF ORARIO"...
THEN, THE LID OVER THE DUNGEON BREAKS...
...AND MONSTERS FACE HUMANITY IN AN ALL-OUT WAR ONCE AGAIN.

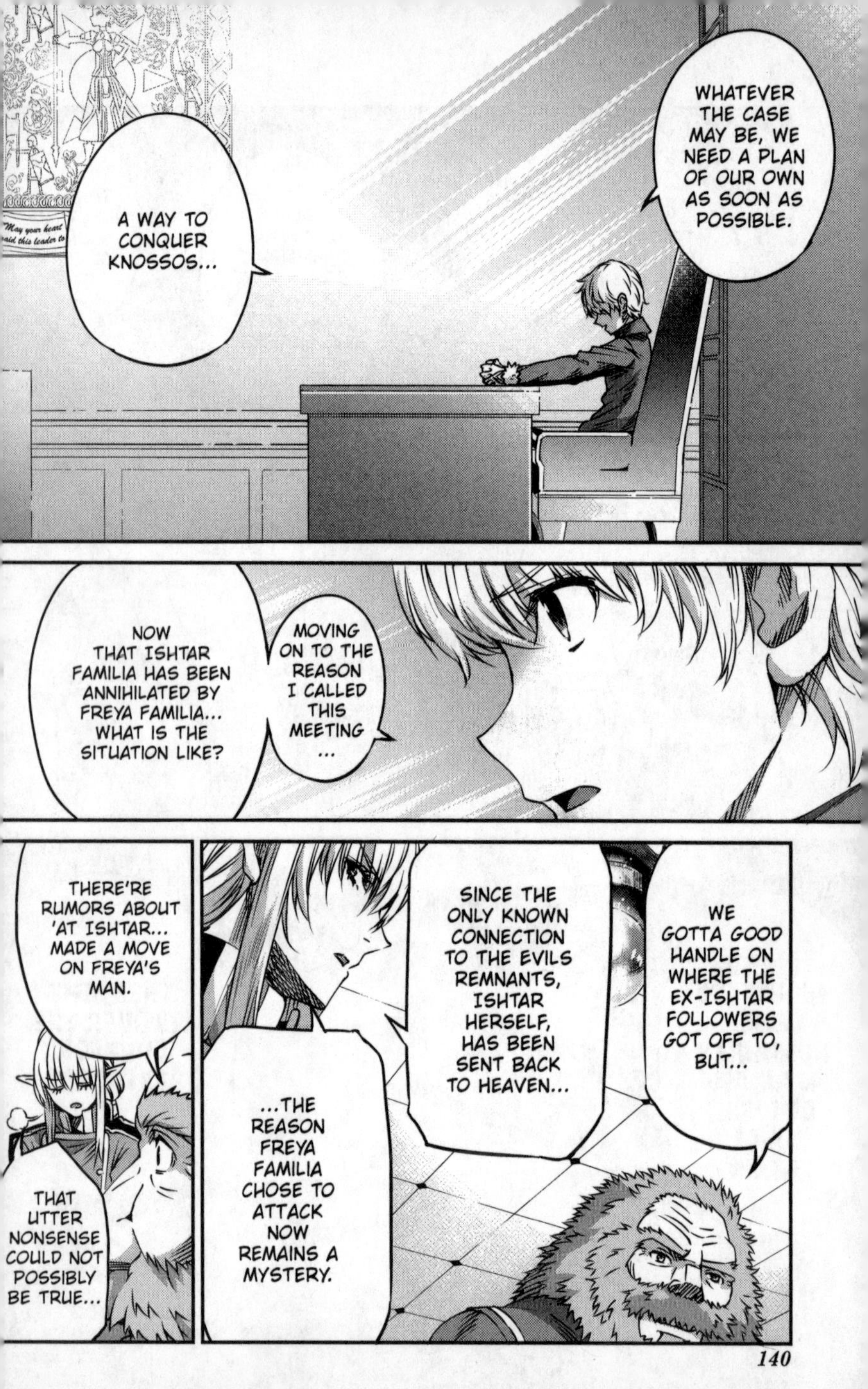
WHATEVER THE CASE MAY BE, WE NEED A PLAN OF OUR OWN AS SOON AS POSSIBLE.
A WAY TO CONQUER KNOSSOS...
MOVING ON TO THE REASON I CALLED THIS MEETING...
NOW THAT ISHTAR FAMILIA HAS BEEN ANNIHILATED BY FREYA FAMILIA... WHAT IS THE SITUATION LIKE?
WE GOTTA GOOD HANDLE ON WHERE THE EX-ISHTAR FOLLOWERS GOT OFF TO, BUT...
SINCE THE ONLY KNOWN CONNECTION TO THE EVILS REMNANTS, ISHTAR HERSELF, HAS BEEN SENT BACK TO HEAVEN...
...THE REASON FREYA FAMILIA CHOSE TO ATTACK NOW REMAINS A MYSTERY.
THERE'RE RUMORS ABOUT 'AT ISHTAR... MADE A MOVE ON FREYA'S MAN.
THAT UTTER NONSENSE COULD NOT POSSIBLY BE TRUE...

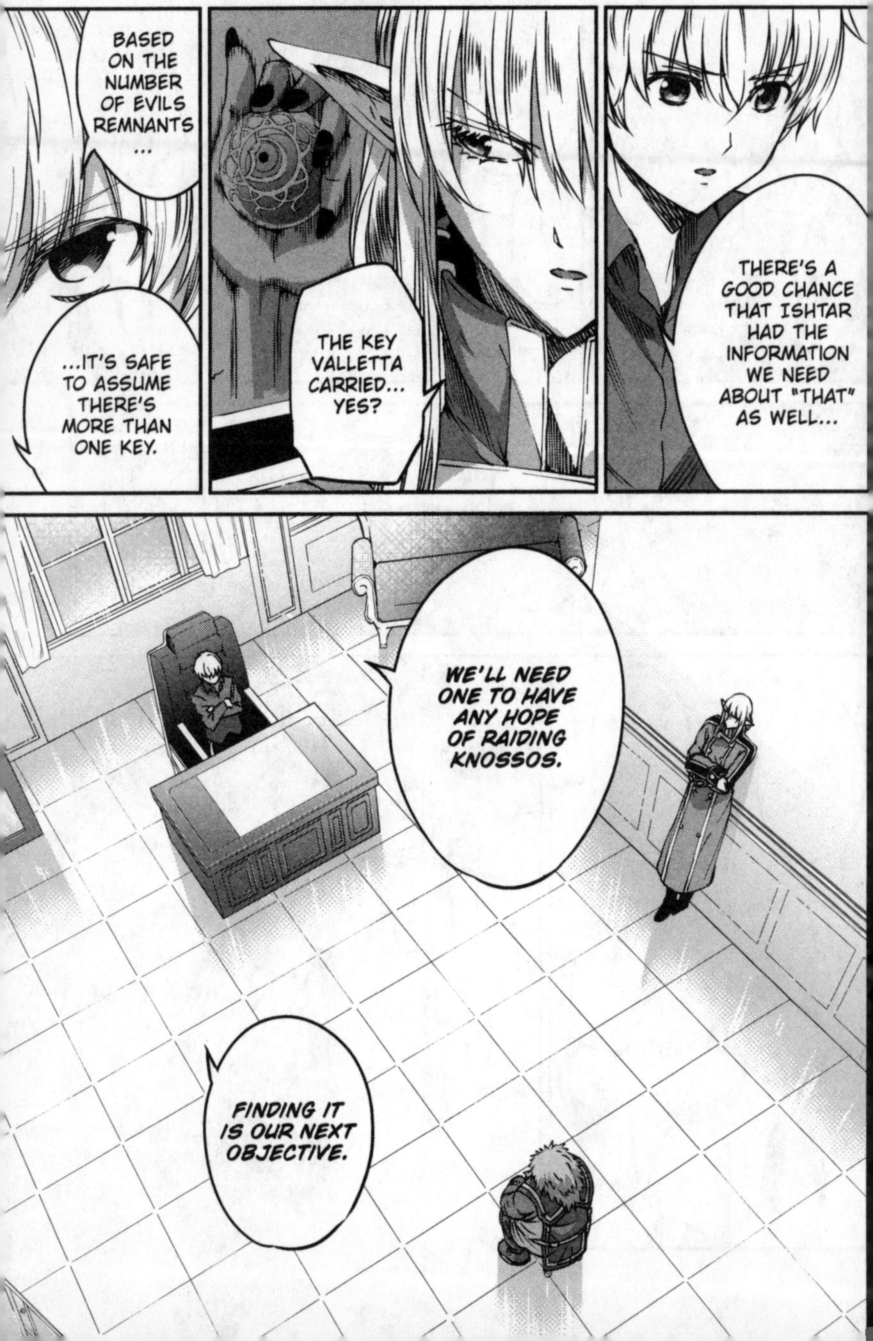
THERE'S A GOOD CHANCE THAT ISHTAR HAD THE INFORMATION WE NEED ABOUT "THAT" AS WELL...
THE KEY VALLETTA CARRIED... YES?
BASED ON THE NUMBER OF EVILS REMNANTS ...
...IT'S SAFE TO ASSUME THERE'S MORE THAN ONE KEY.
WE'LL NEED ONE TO HAVE ANY HOPE OF RAIDING KNOSSOS.
FINDING IT IS OUR NEXT OBJECTIVE.

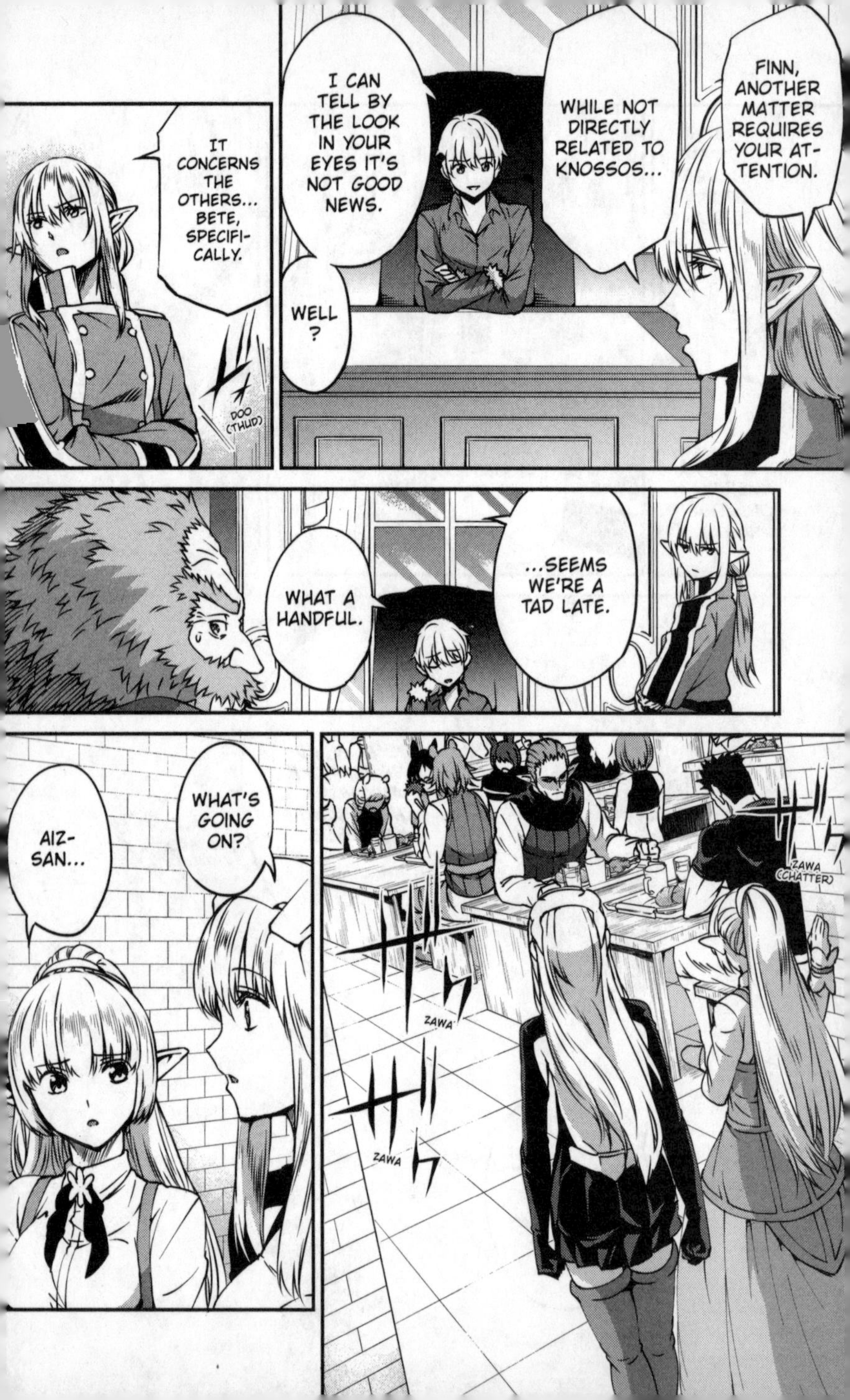
FINN, ANOTHER MATTER REQUIRES YOUR ATTENTION.
WHILE NOT DIRECTLY RELATED TO KNOSSOS...
I CAN TELL BY THE LOOK IN YOUR EYES IT'S NOT GOOD NEWS.
WELL?
IT CONCERNS THE OTHERS... BETE, SPECIFICALLY.
DOO (THUD)
...SEEMS WE'RE A TAD LATE.
WHAT A HANDFUL.
ZAWA (CHATTER)
ZAWA
ZAWA
WHAT'S GOING ON?
AIZ-SAN...

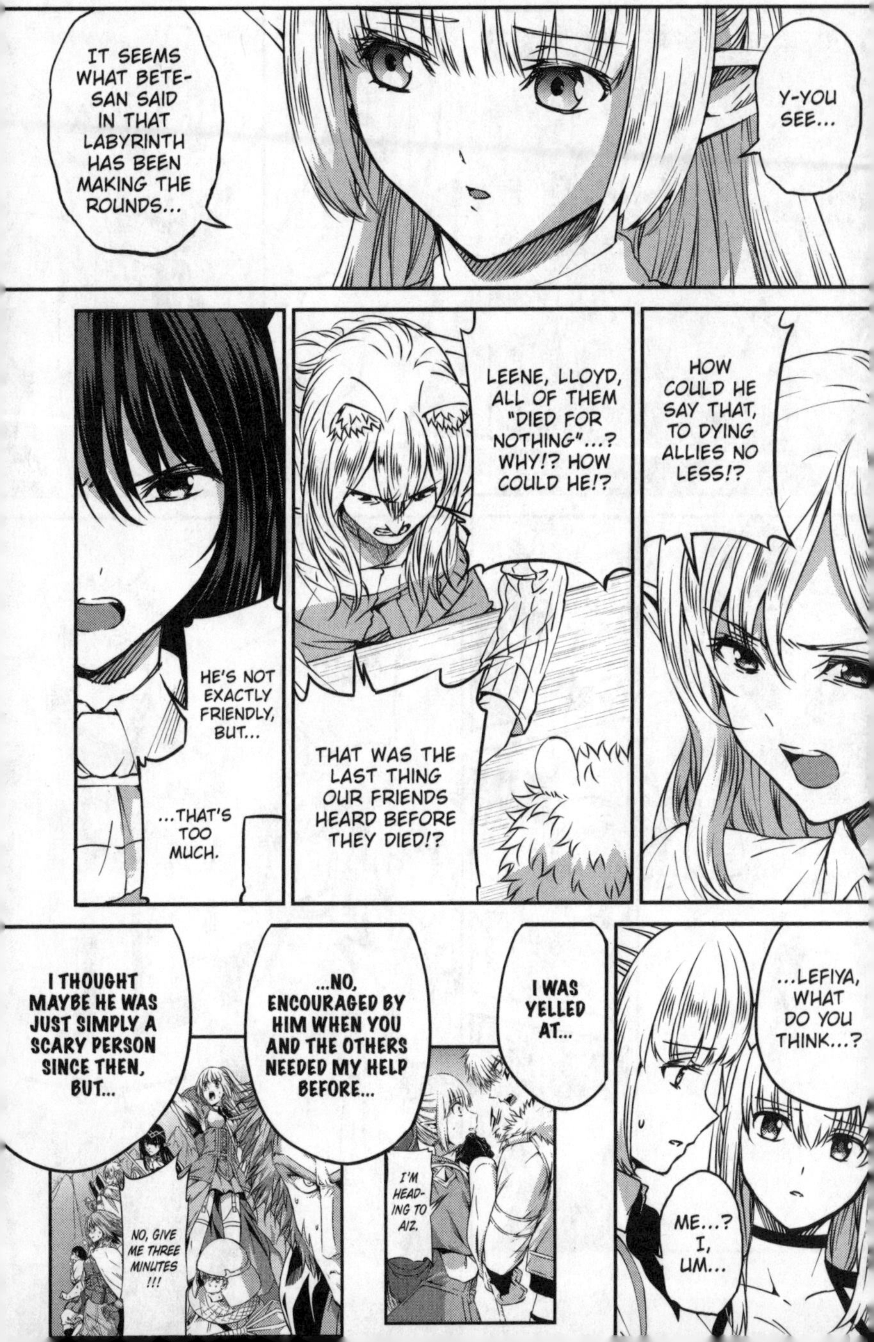
Y-YOU SEE...
IT SEEMS WHAT BETE-SAN SAID IN THAT LABYRINTH HAS BEEN MAKING THE ROUNDS...
HOW COULD HE SAY THAT, TO DYING ALLIES NO LESS!?
LEENE, LLOYD, ALL OF THEM "DIED FOR NOTHING"...? WHY!? HOW COULD HE!?
THAT WAS THE LAST THING OUR FRIENDS HEARD BEFORE THEY DIED!?
HE'S NOT EXACTLY FRIENDLY, BUT...
...THAT'S TOO MUCH.
...LEFIYA, WHAT DO YOU THINK...?
ME...? I, UM...
I WAS YELLED AT...
I'M HEADING TO AIZ.
...NO, ENCOURAGED BY HIM WHEN YOU AND THE OTHERS NEEDED MY HELP BEFORE...
NO, GIVE ME THREE MINUTES!!!
I THOUGHT MAYBE HE WAS JUST SIMPLY A SCARY PERSON SINCE THEN, BUT...

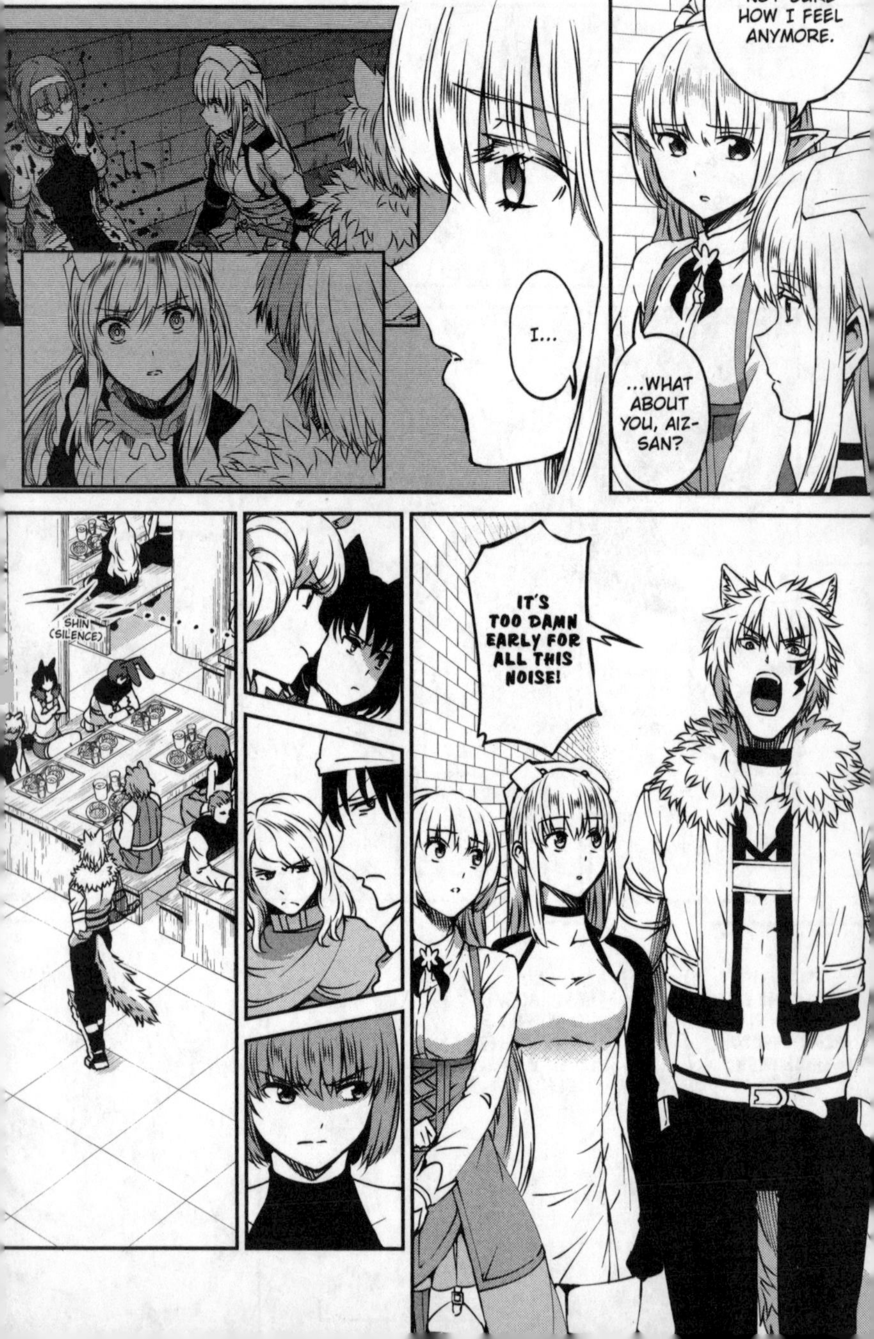
I'M... NOT SURE HOW I FEEL ANYMORE.
...WHAT ABOUT YOU, AIZ-SAN?
I...
IT'S TOO DAMN EARLY FOR ALL THIS NOISE!
SHIN (SILENCE)

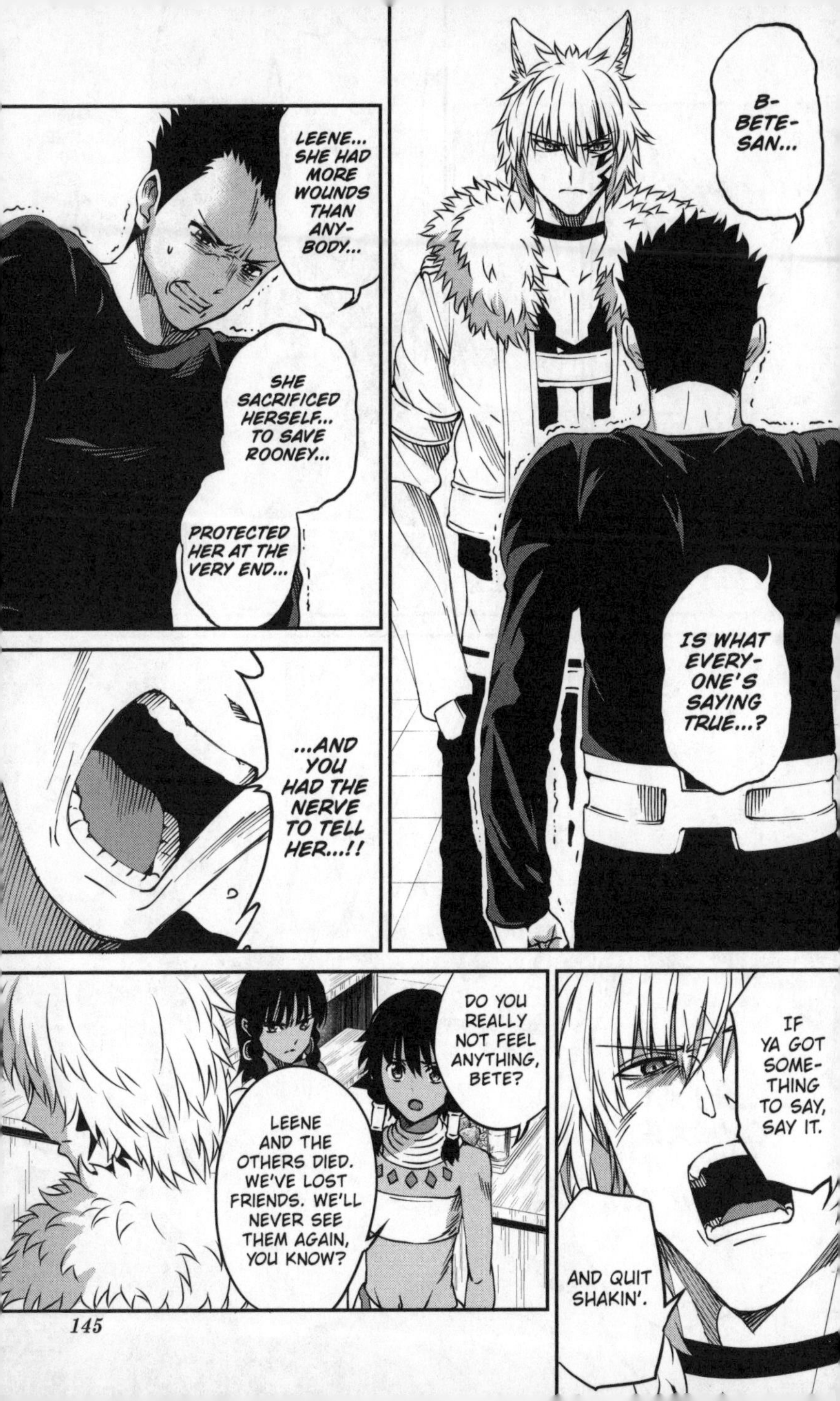
B-BETE-SAN...
IS WHAT EVERYONE'S SAYING TRUE...?
LEENE... SHE HAD MORE WOUNDS THAN ANYBODY...
SHE SACRIFICED HERSELF... TO SAVE ROONEY...
PROTECTED HER AT THE VERY END...
...AND YOU HAD THE NERVE TO TELL HER...!!
IF YA GOT SOMETHING TO SAY, SAY IT.
AND QUIT SHAKIN'.
DO YOU REALLY NOT FEEL ANYTHING, BETE?
LEENE AND THE OTHERS DIED. WE'VE LOST FRIENDS. WE'LL NEVER SEE THEM AGAIN, YOU KNOW?

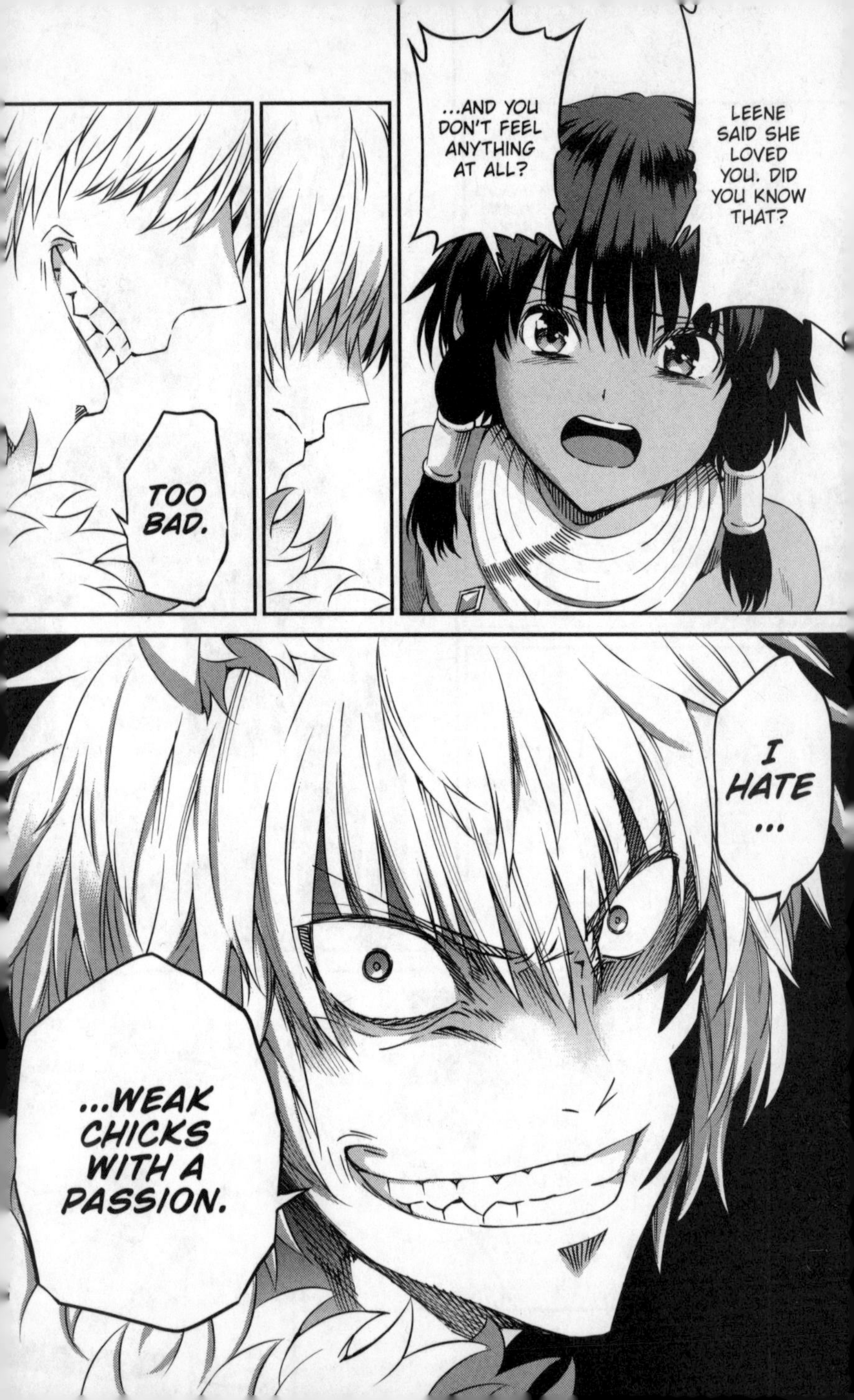
LEENE SAID SHE LOVED YOU. DID YOU KNOW THAT?
...AND YOU DON'T FEEL ANYTHING AT ALL?
TOO BAD.
I HATE...
...WEAK CHICKS WITH A PASSION.

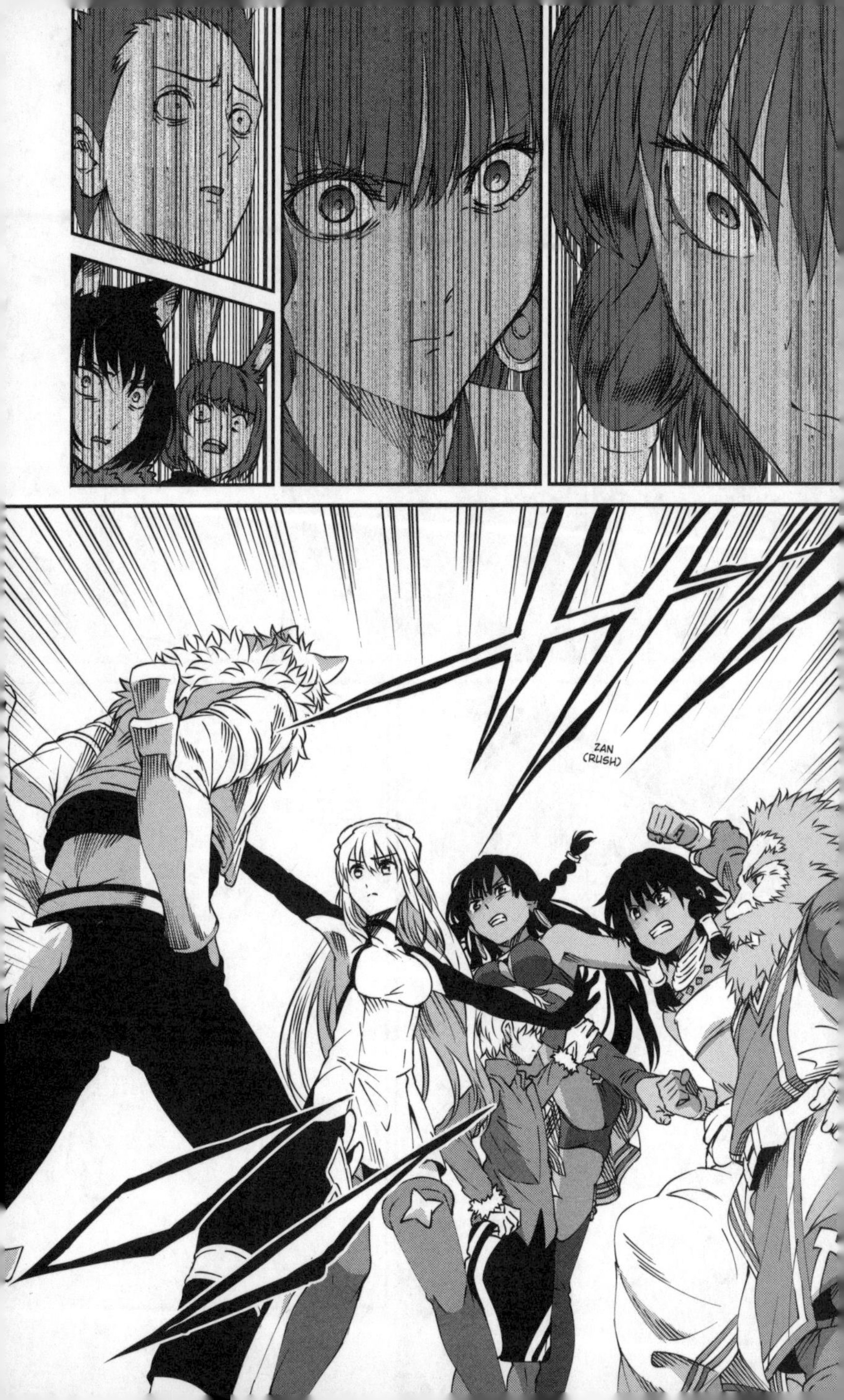
ZAN
(RUSH)

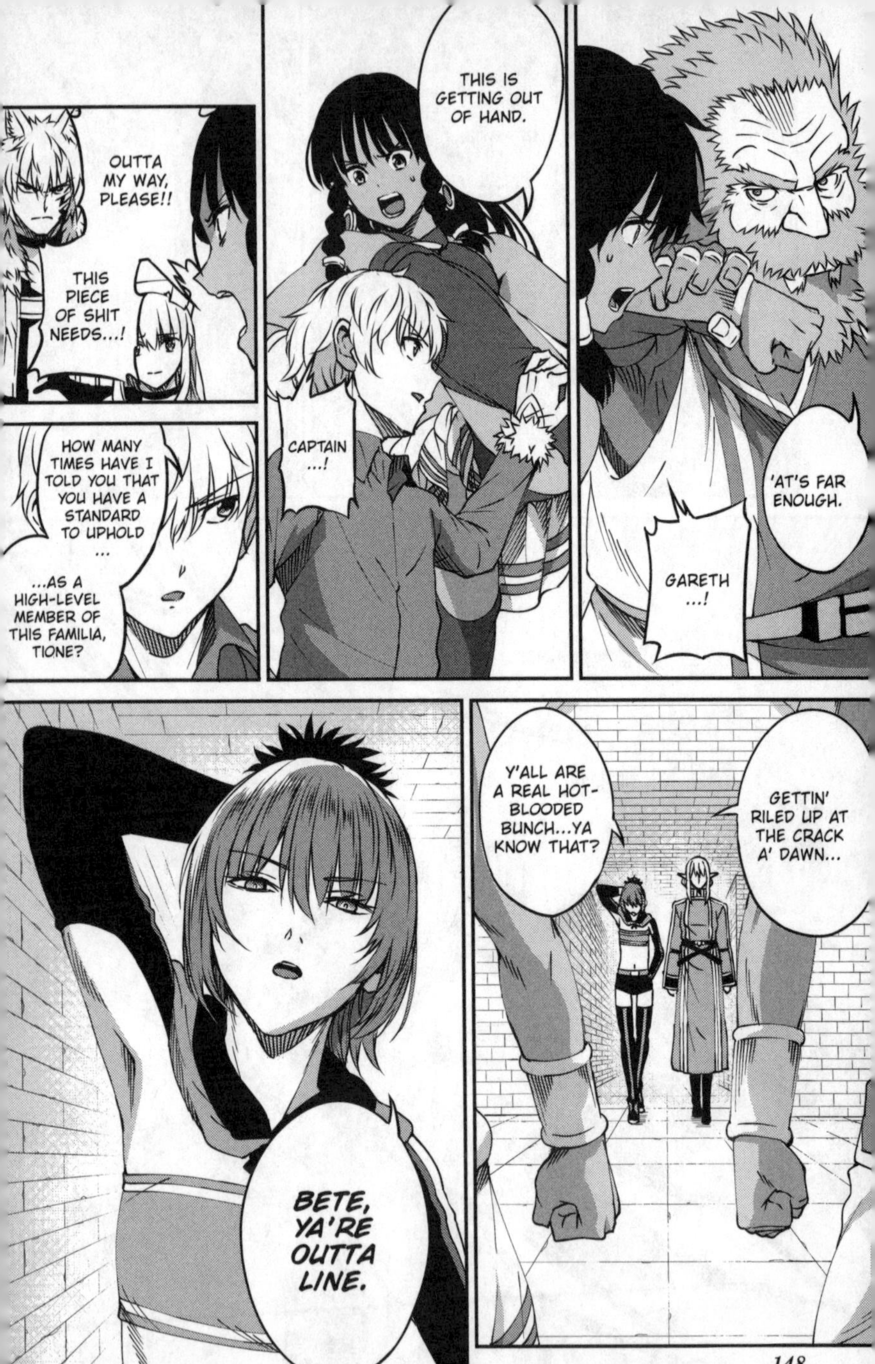
'AT'S FAR ENOUGH.
GARETH ...!
THIS IS GETTING OUT OF HAND.
CAPTAIN ...!
OUTTA MY WAY, PLEASE!!
THIS PIECE OF SHIT NEEDS...!
HOW MANY TIMES HAVE I TOLD YOU THAT YOU HAVE A STANDARD TO UPHOLD ...
...AS A HIGH-LEVEL MEMBER OF THIS FAMILIA, TIONE?
GETTIN' RILED UP AT THE CRACK A' DAWN...
Y'ALL ARE A REAL HOT-BLOODED BUNCH...YA KNOW THAT?
BETE, YA'RE OUTTA LINE.

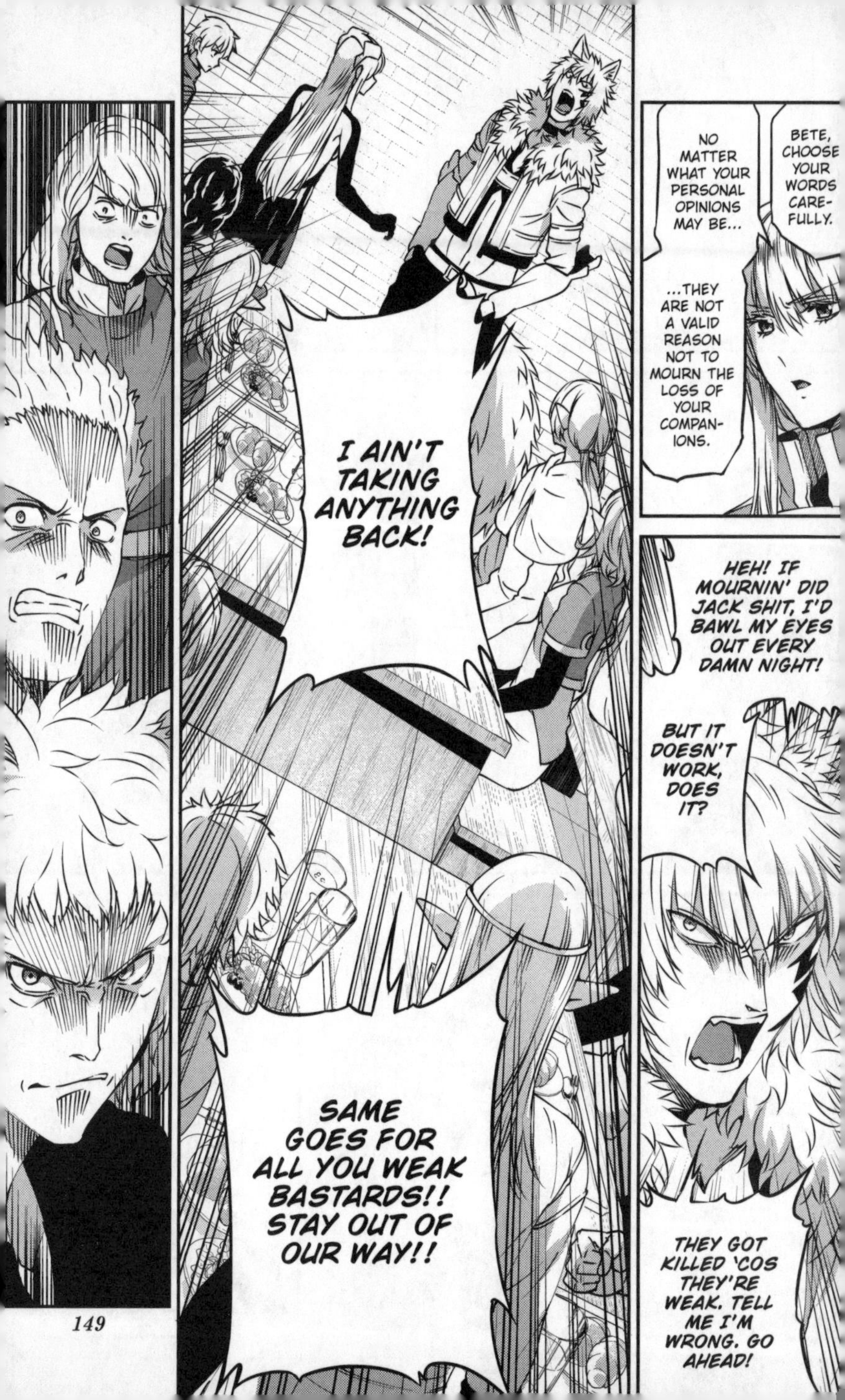
BETE, CHOOSE YOUR WORDS CARE-FULLY.
NO MATTER WHAT YOUR PERSONAL OPINIONS MAY BE...
...THEY ARE NOT A VALID REASON NOT TO MOURN THE LOSS OF YOUR COMPAN-IONS.
HEH! IF MOURNIN' DID JACK SHIT, I'D BAWL MY EYES OUT EVERY DAMN NIGHT!
BUT IT DOESN'T WORK, DOES IT?
THEY GOT KILLED 'COS THEY'RE WEAK. TELL ME I'M WRONG. GO AHEAD!
I AIN'T TAKING ANYTHING BACK!
SAME GOES FOR ALL YOU WEAK BASTARDS!! STAY OUT OF OUR WAY!!

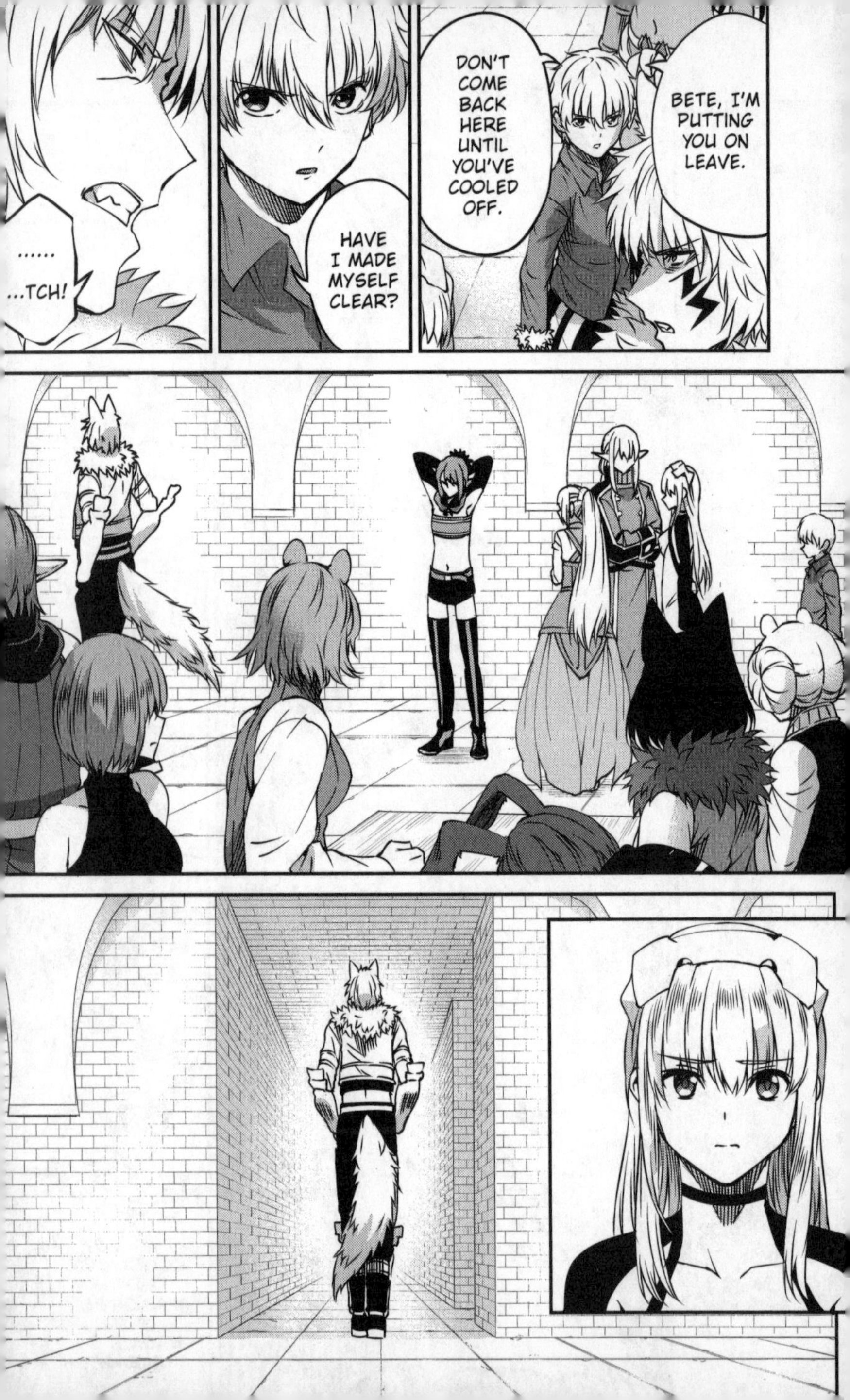
BETE, I'M PUTTING YOU ON LEAVE.
DON'T COME BACK HERE UNTIL YOU'VE COOLED OFF.
HAVE I MADE MYSELF CLEAR?
......
...TCH!

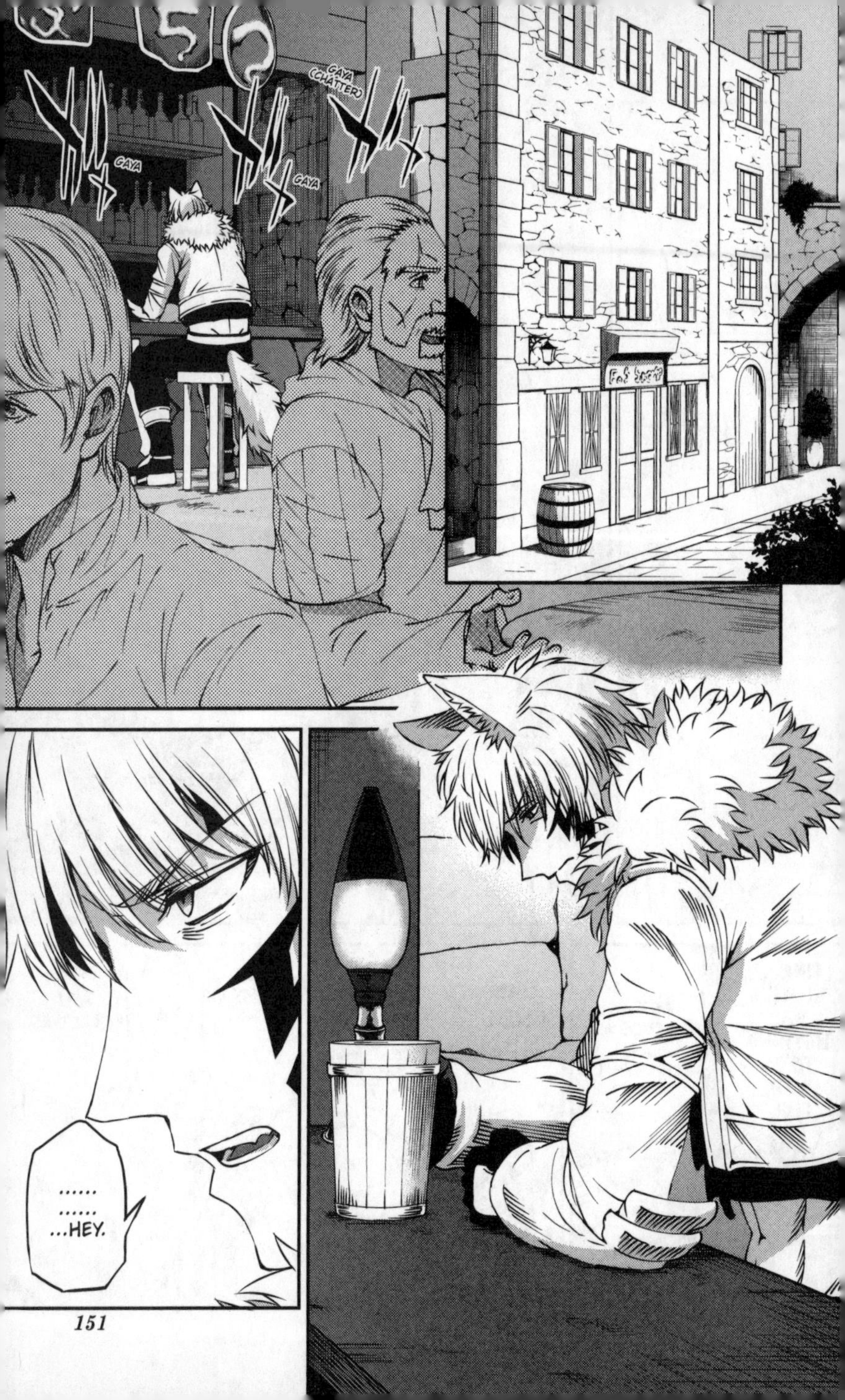
GAYA (CHATTER)
GAYA
GAYA
......
......
...HEY.

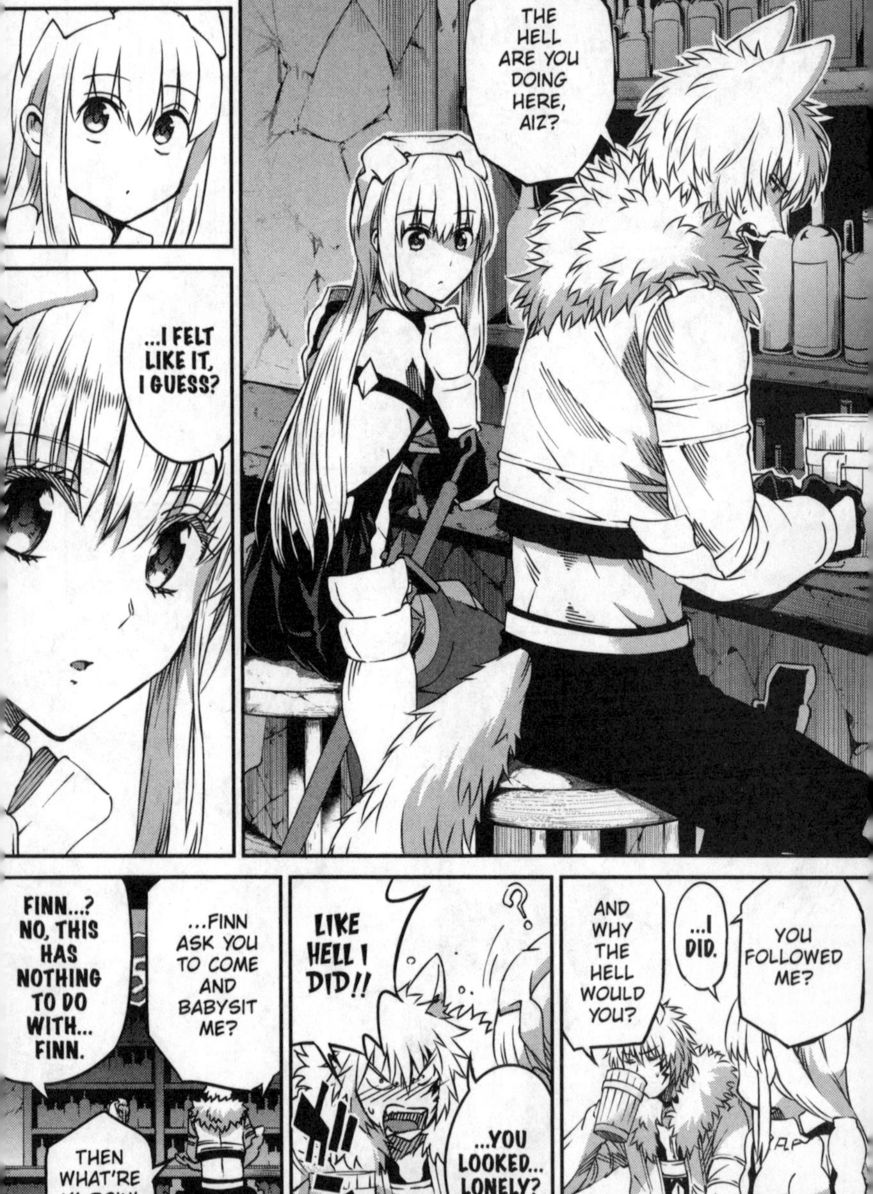
THE HELL ARE YOU DOING HERE, AIZ?
...I FELT LIKE IT, I GUESS?
YOU FOLLOWED ME?
...I DID.
AND WHY THE HELL WOULD YOU?
...YOU LOOKED... LONELY?
?
LIKE HELL I DID!!
GAN (SLAM)
...FINN ASK YOU TO COME AND BABYSIT ME?
FINN...? NO, THIS HAS NOTHING TO DO WITH... FINN.
THEN WHAT'RE YA DOIN' HERE?

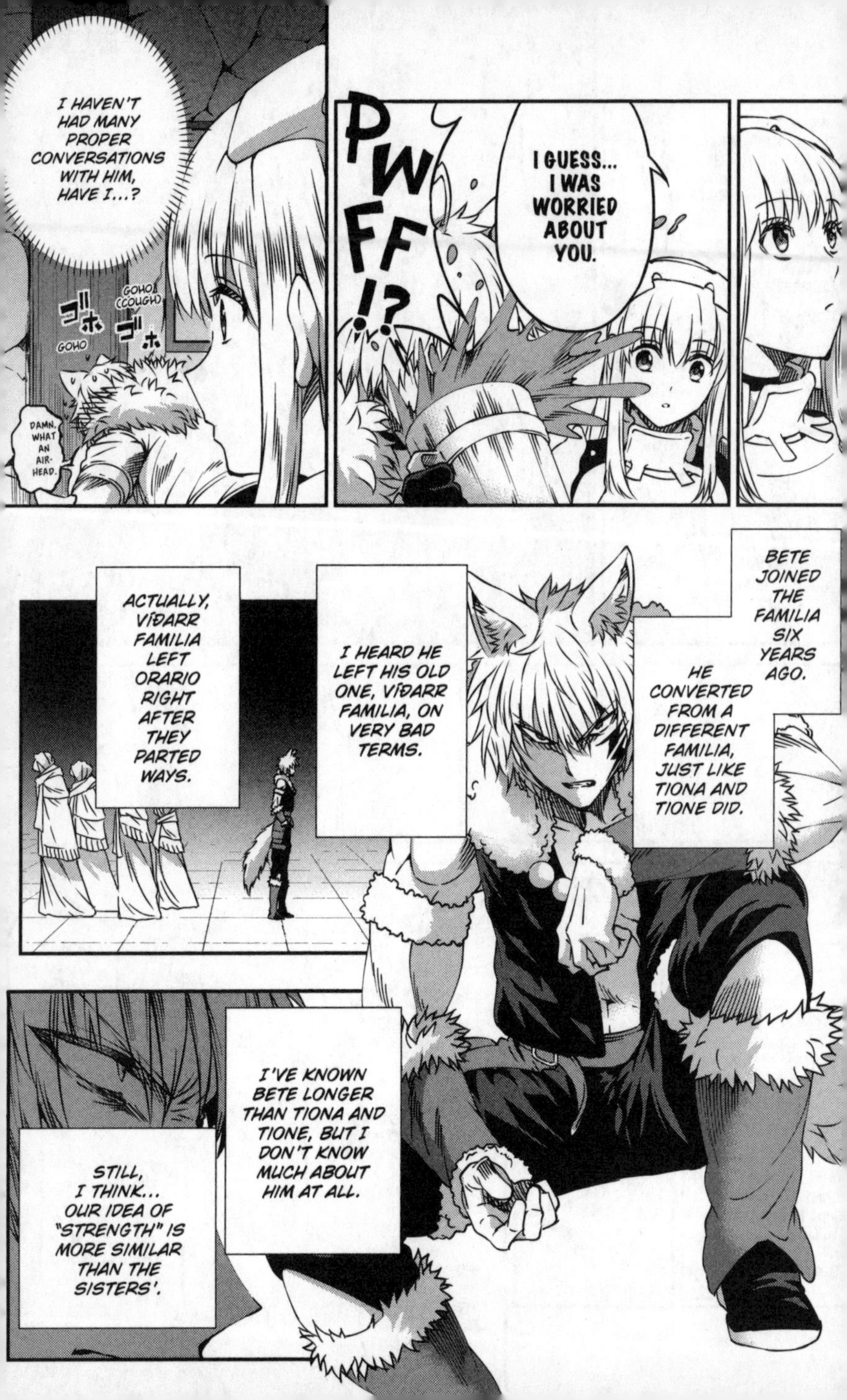
I GUESS... I WAS WORRIED ABOUT YOU.
PWFF!?
I HAVEN'T HAD MANY PROPER CONVERSATIONS WITH HIM, HAVE I...?
ゴホ
GOHO (COUGH)
ゴホ
GOHO
DAMN, WHAT AN AIR-HEAD.
BETE JOINED THE FAMILIA SIX YEARS AGO.
HE CONVERTED FROM A DIFFERENT FAMILIA, JUST LIKE TIONA AND TIONE DID.
I HEARD HE LEFT HIS OLD ONE, VÍÐARR FAMILIA, ON VERY BAD TERMS.
ACTUALLY, VÍÐARR FAMILIA LEFT ORARIO RIGHT AFTER THEY PARTED WAYS.
I'VE KNOWN BETE LONGER THAN TIONA AND TIONE, BUT I DON'T KNOW MUCH ABOUT HIM AT ALL.
STILL, I THINK... OUR IDEA OF "STRENGTH" IS MORE SIMILAR THAN THE SISTERS'.

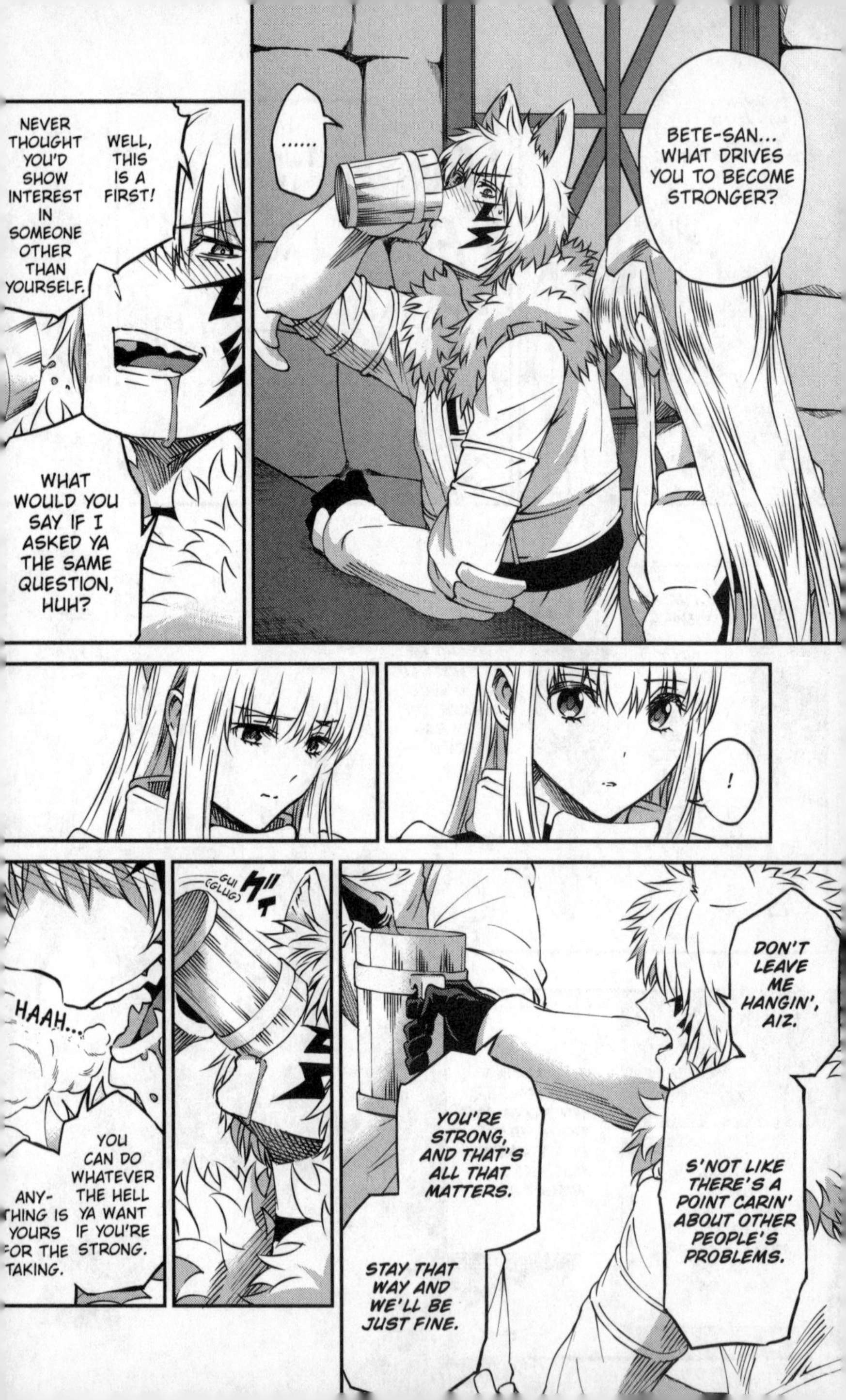
BETE-SAN... WHAT DRIVES YOU TO BECOME STRONGER?
......
WELL, THIS IS A FIRST!
NEVER THOUGHT YOU'D SHOW INTEREST IN SOMEONE OTHER THAN YOURSELF.
WHAT WOULD YOU SAY IF I ASKED YA THE SAME QUESTION, HUH?
!
DON'T LEAVE ME HANGIN', AIZ.
S'NOT LIKE THERE'S A POINT CARIN' ABOUT OTHER PEOPLE'S PROBLEMS.
YOU'RE STRONG, AND THAT'S ALL THAT MATTERS.
STAY THAT WAY AND WE'LL BE JUST FINE.
GUI (GLUG)
HAAH...
YOU CAN DO WHATEVER THE HELL YA WANT IF YOU'RE STRONG.
ANY-THING IS YOURS FOR THE TAKING.

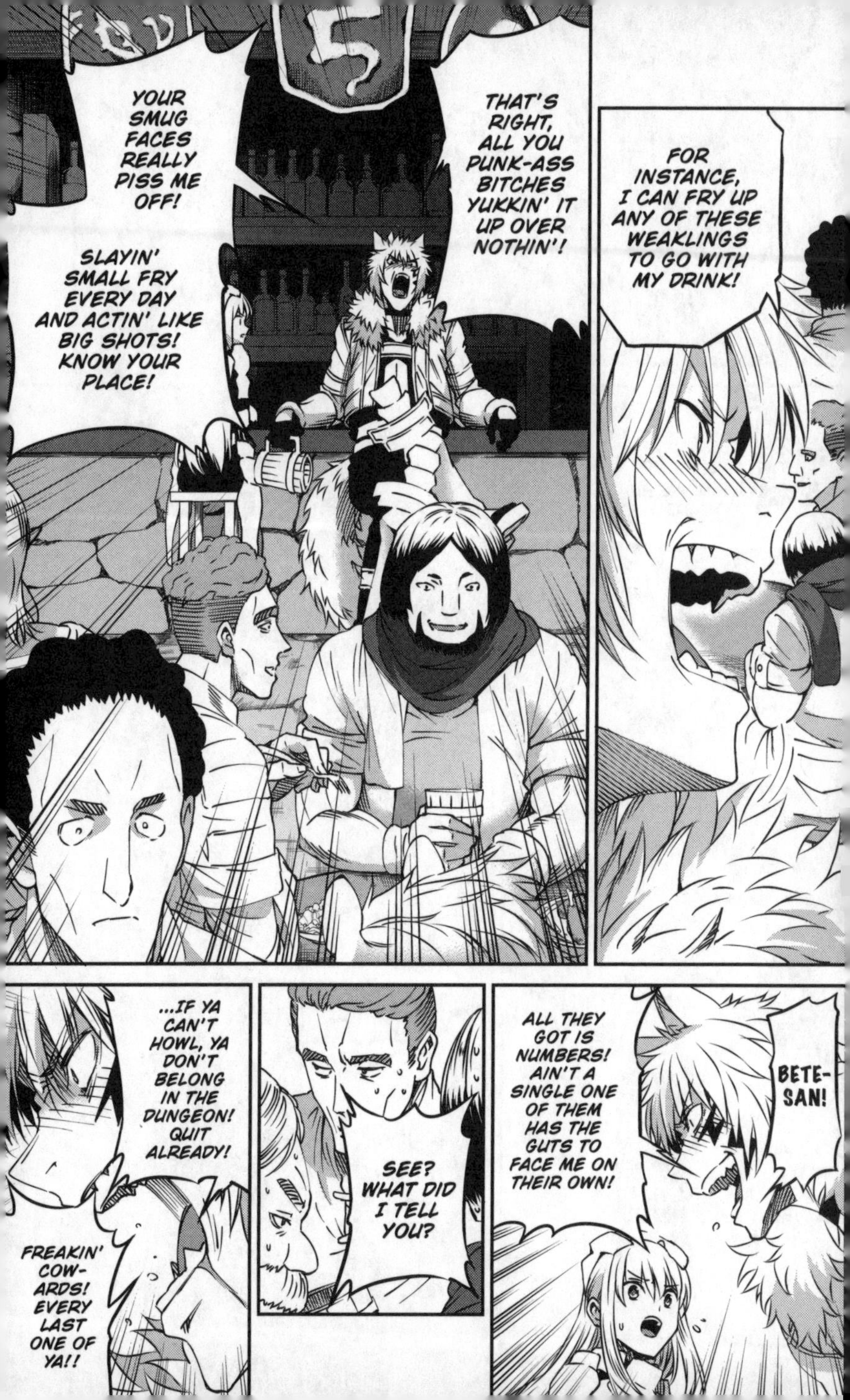
FOR INSTANCE, I CAN FRY UP ANY OF THESE WEAKLINGS TO GO WITH MY DRINK!
THAT'S RIGHT, ALL YOU PUNK-ASS BITCHES YUKKIN' IT UP OVER NOTHIN'!
YOUR SMUG FACES REALLY PISS ME OFF!
SLAYIN' SMALL FRY EVERY DAY AND ACTIN' LIKE BIG SHOTS! KNOW YOUR PLACE!
ALL THEY GOT IS NUMBERS! AIN'T A SINGLE ONE OF THEM HAS THE GUTS TO FACE ME ON THEIR OWN!
BETE-SAN!
SEE? WHAT DID I TELL YOU?
...IF YA CAN'T HOWL, YA DON'T BELONG IN THE DUNGEON! QUIT ALREADY!
FREAKIN' COW-ARDS! EVERY LAST ONE OF YA!!

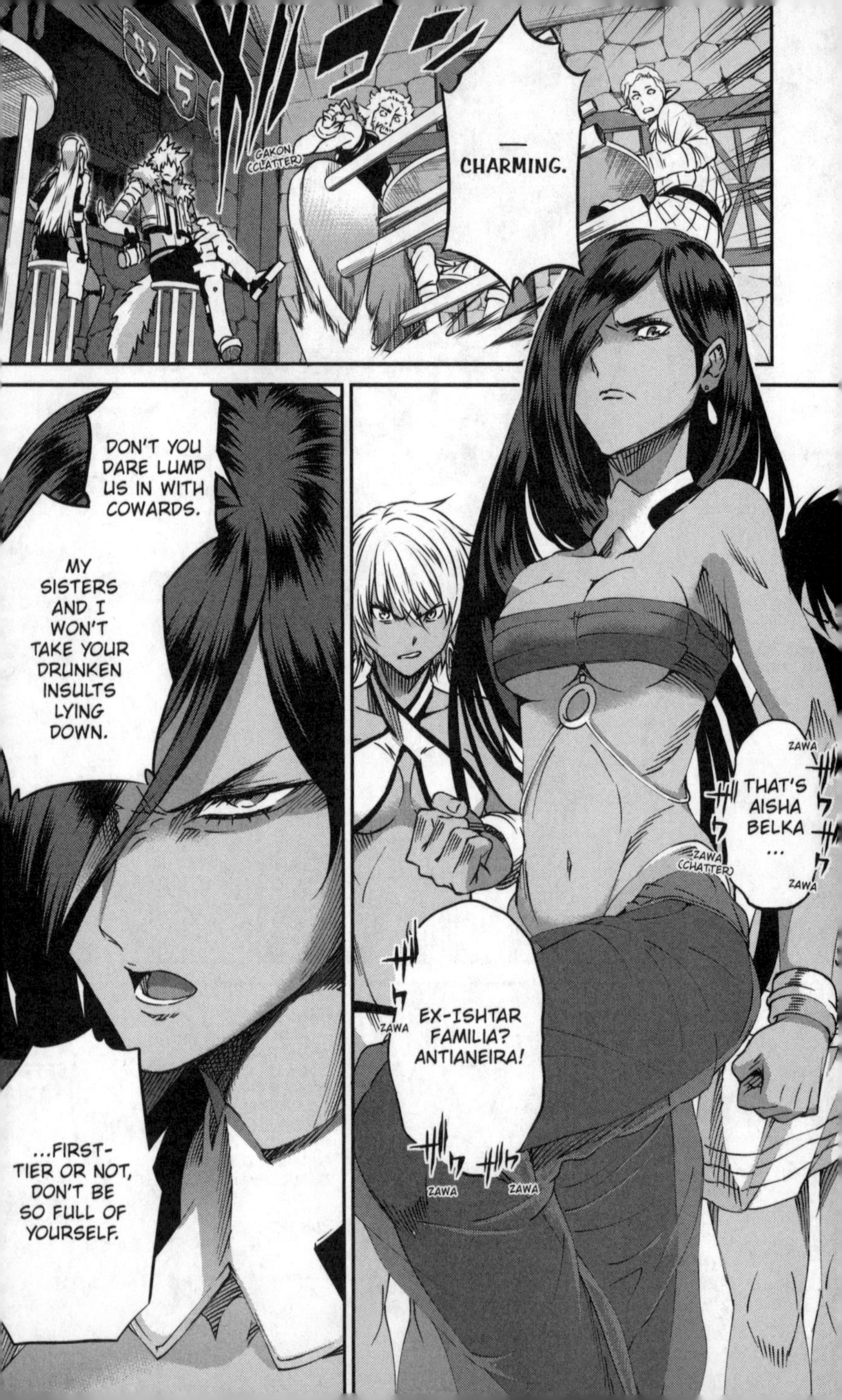

—CHARMING.
GAKON (CLATTER)
ZAWA
THAT'S AISHA BELKA ...
ZAWA (CHATTER)
ZAWA
ZAWA
EX-ISHTAR FAMILIA? ANTIANEIRA!
ZAWA
ZAWA
DON'T YOU DARE LUMP US IN WITH COWARDS.
MY SISTERS AND I WON'T TAKE YOUR DRUNKEN INSULTS LYING DOWN.
...FIRST-TIER OR NOT, DON'T BE SO FULL OF YOURSELF.

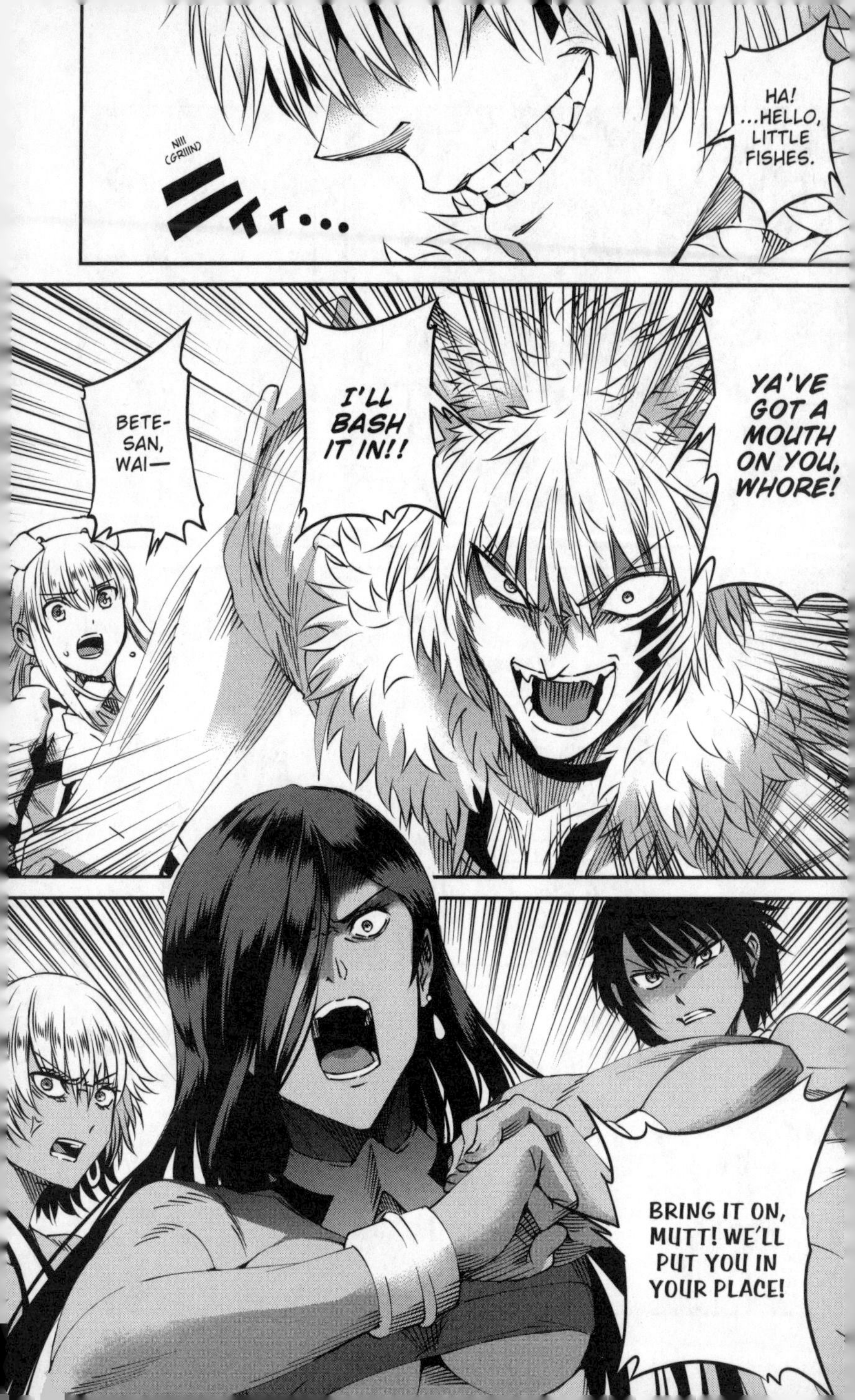
HA! ...HELLO, LITTLE FISHES.
NIII (GRIIIN)
YA'VE GOT A MOUTH ON YOU, WHORE!
I'LL BASH IT IN!!
BETE-SAN, WAI—
BRING IT ON, MUTT! WE'LL PUT YOU IN YOUR PLACE!

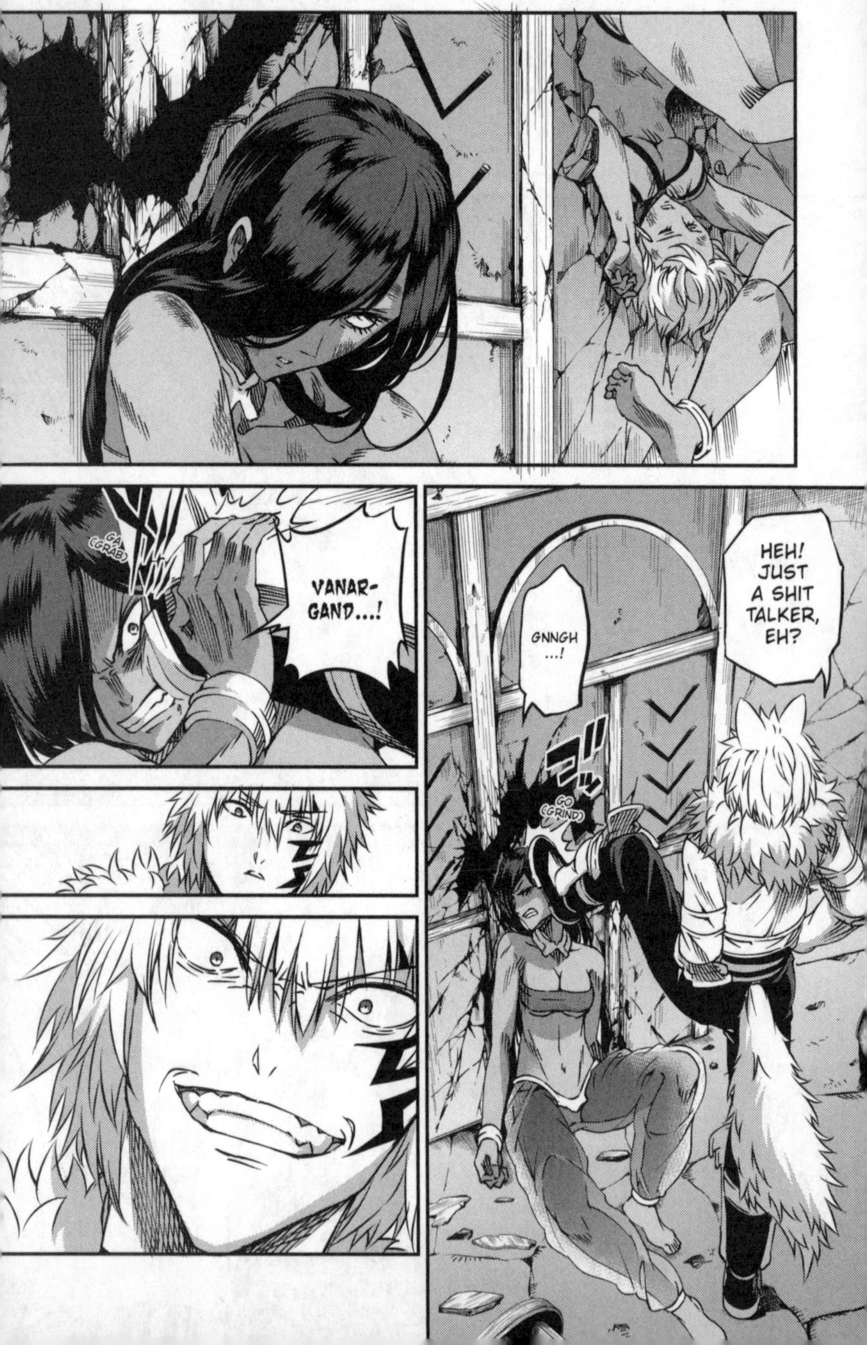
HEH! JUST A SHIT TALKER, EH?
GNNGH ...!
GO (GRIND)
GA (GRAB)
VANAR-GAND...!

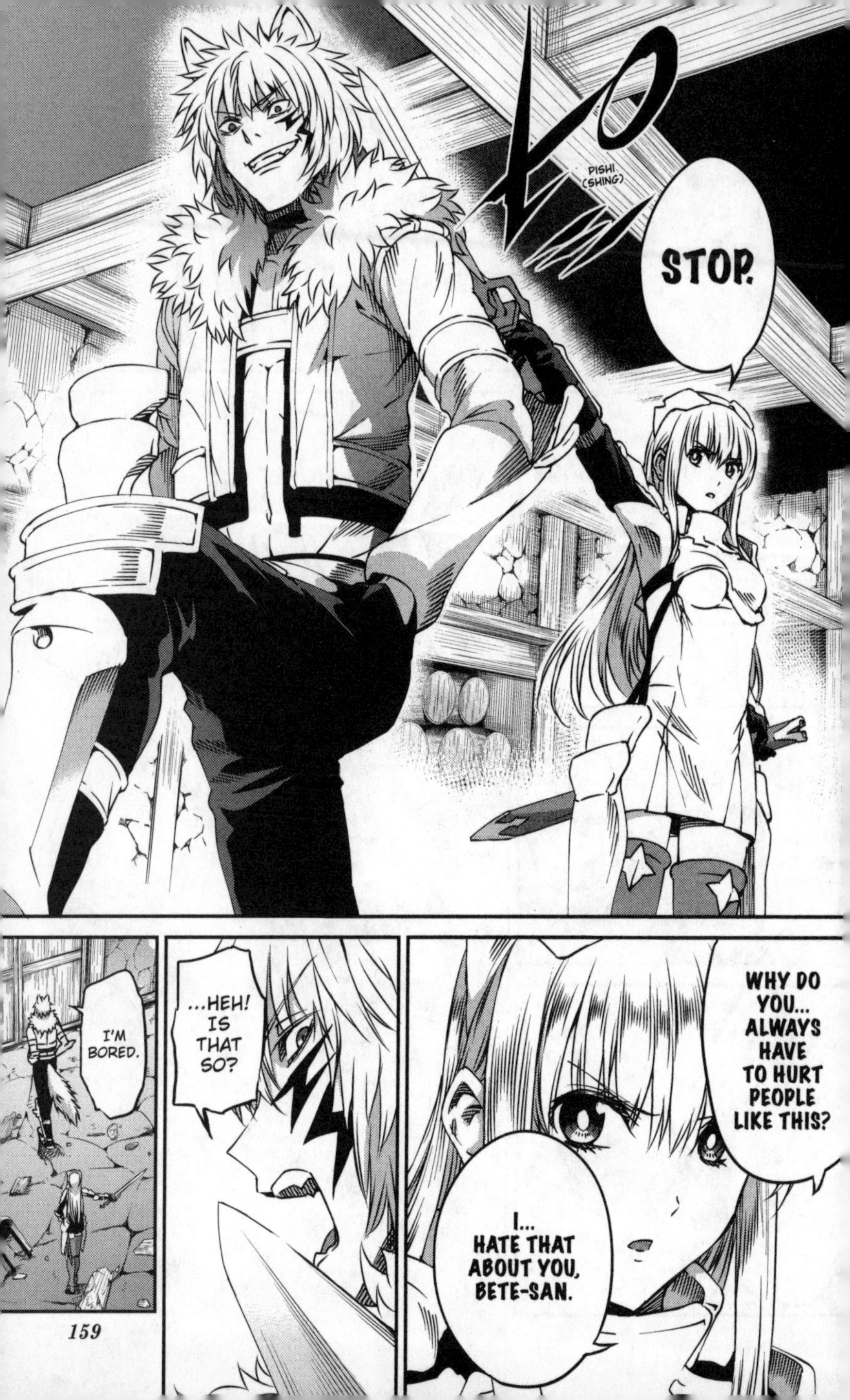
PISHI (SHING)
STOP.
WHY DO YOU... ALWAYS HAVE TO HURT PEOPLE LIKE THIS?
I... HATE THAT ABOUT YOU, BETE-SAN.
...HEH! IS THAT SO?
I'M BORED.

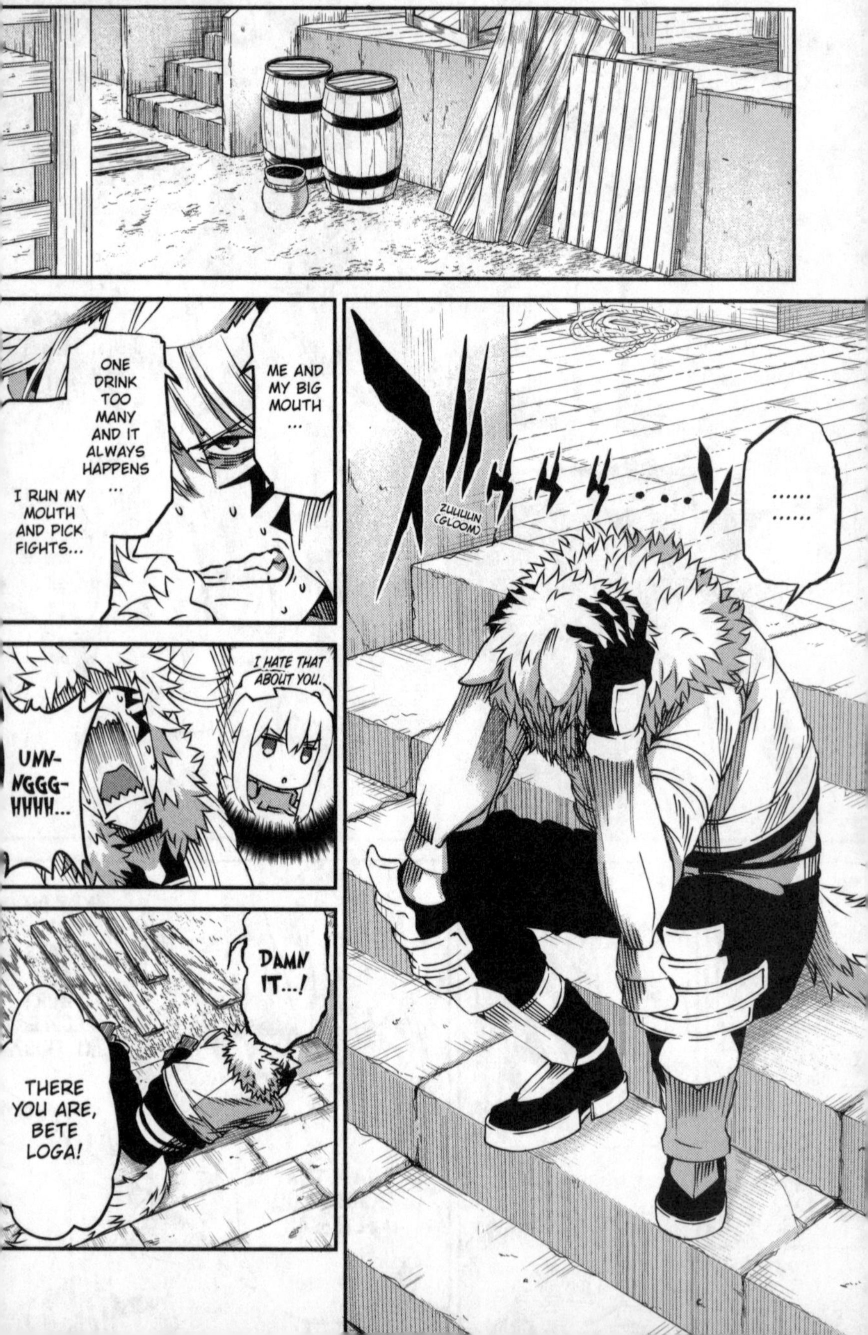
ZUUUUUN (GLOOM)
....
ME AND MY BIG MOUTH ...
ONE DRINK TOO MANY AND IT ALWAYS HAPPENS ...
I RUN MY MOUTH AND PICK FIGHTS...
I HATE THAT ABOUT YOU.
UNN-NGGG-HHHH...
DAMN IT...!
THERE YOU ARE, BETE LOGA!

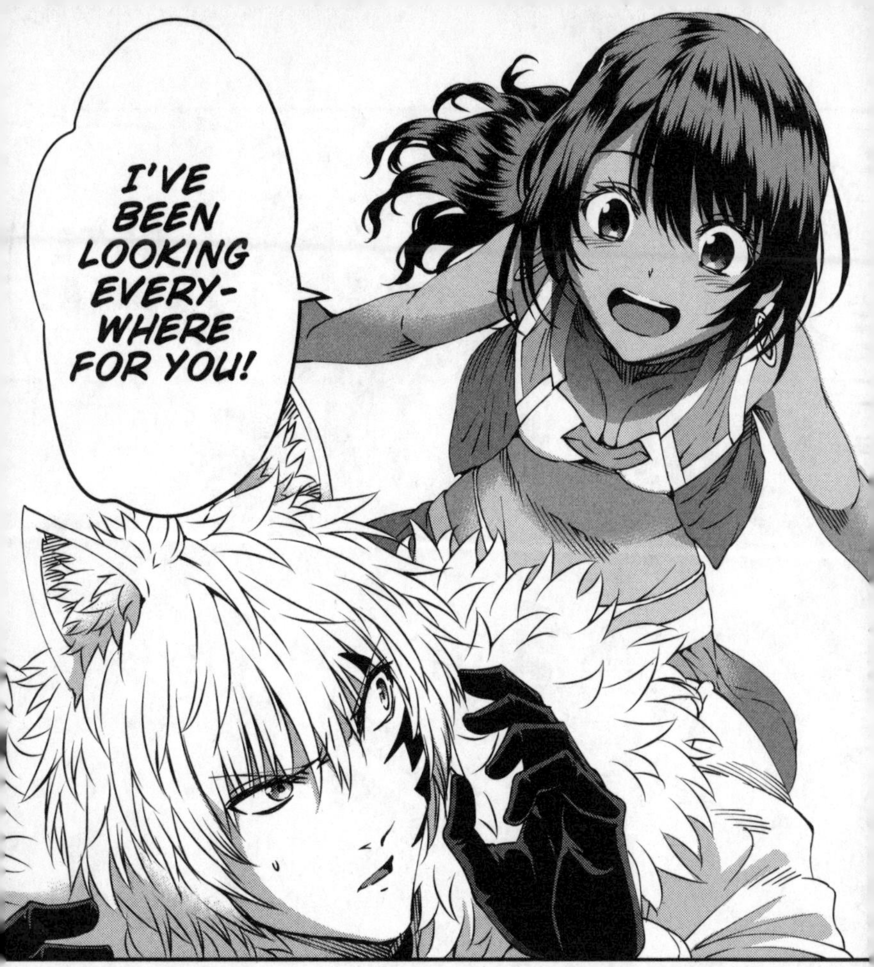
I'VE BEEN LOOKING EVERY-WHERE FOR YOU!

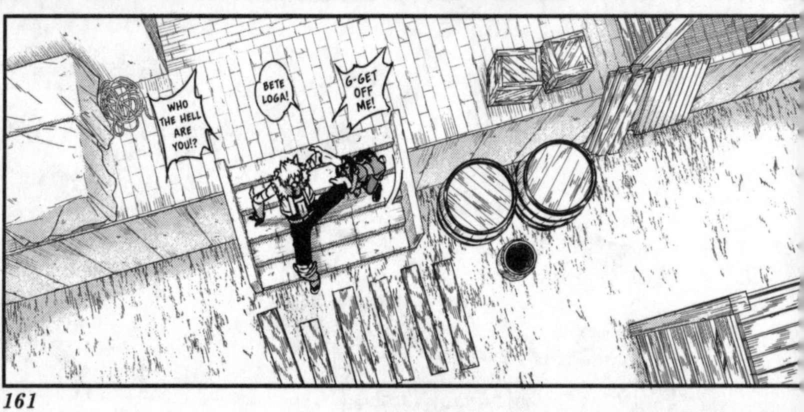
G-GET OFF ME!
BETE LOGA!
WHO THE HELL ARE YOU!?

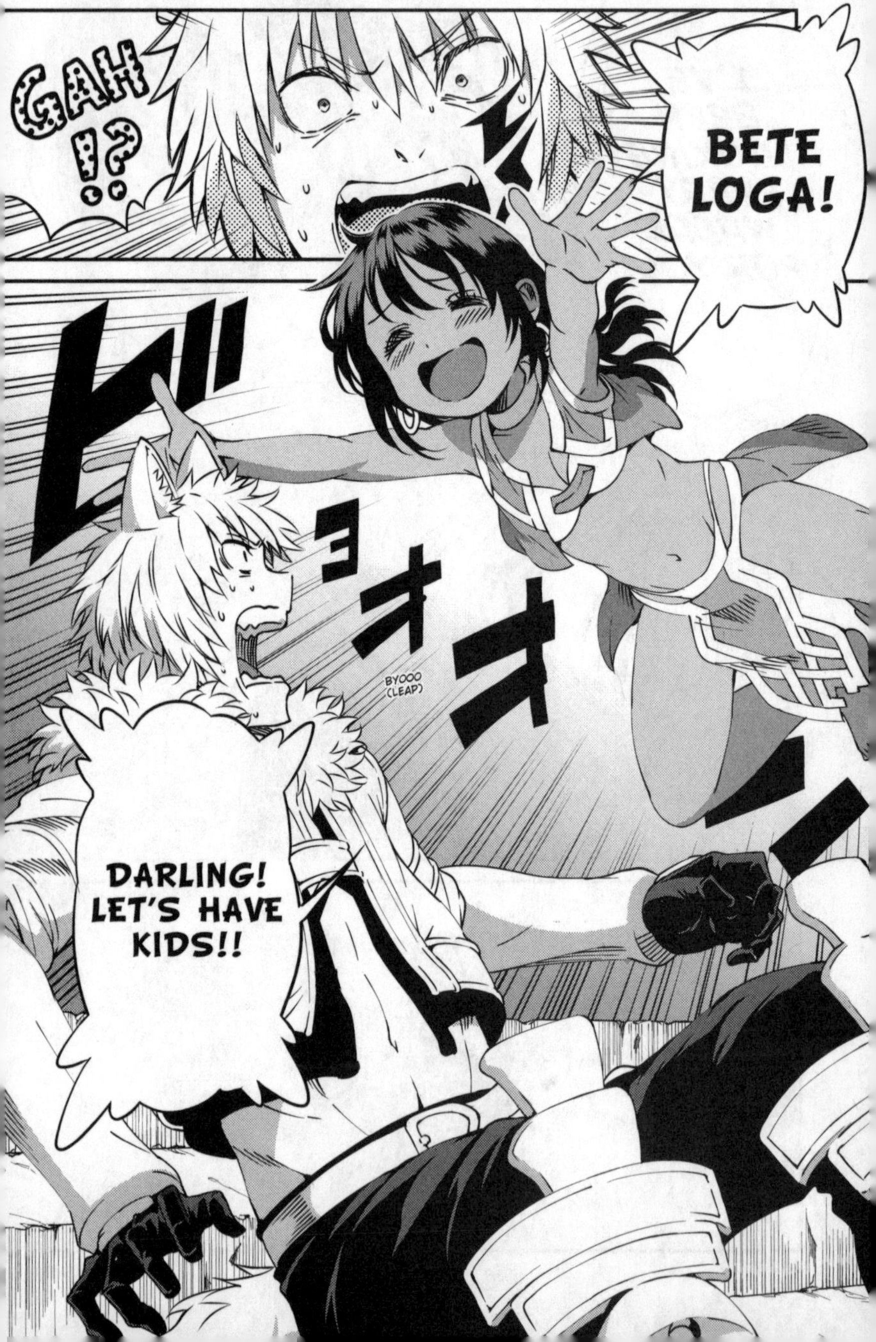
BETE LOGA!
GAH!?
BYOOO (LEAP)
DARLING! LET'S HAVE KIDS!!

Is it WRONG to TRY to PICK UP GIRLS IN A DUNGEON? ON THE SIDE

Sword Oratoria

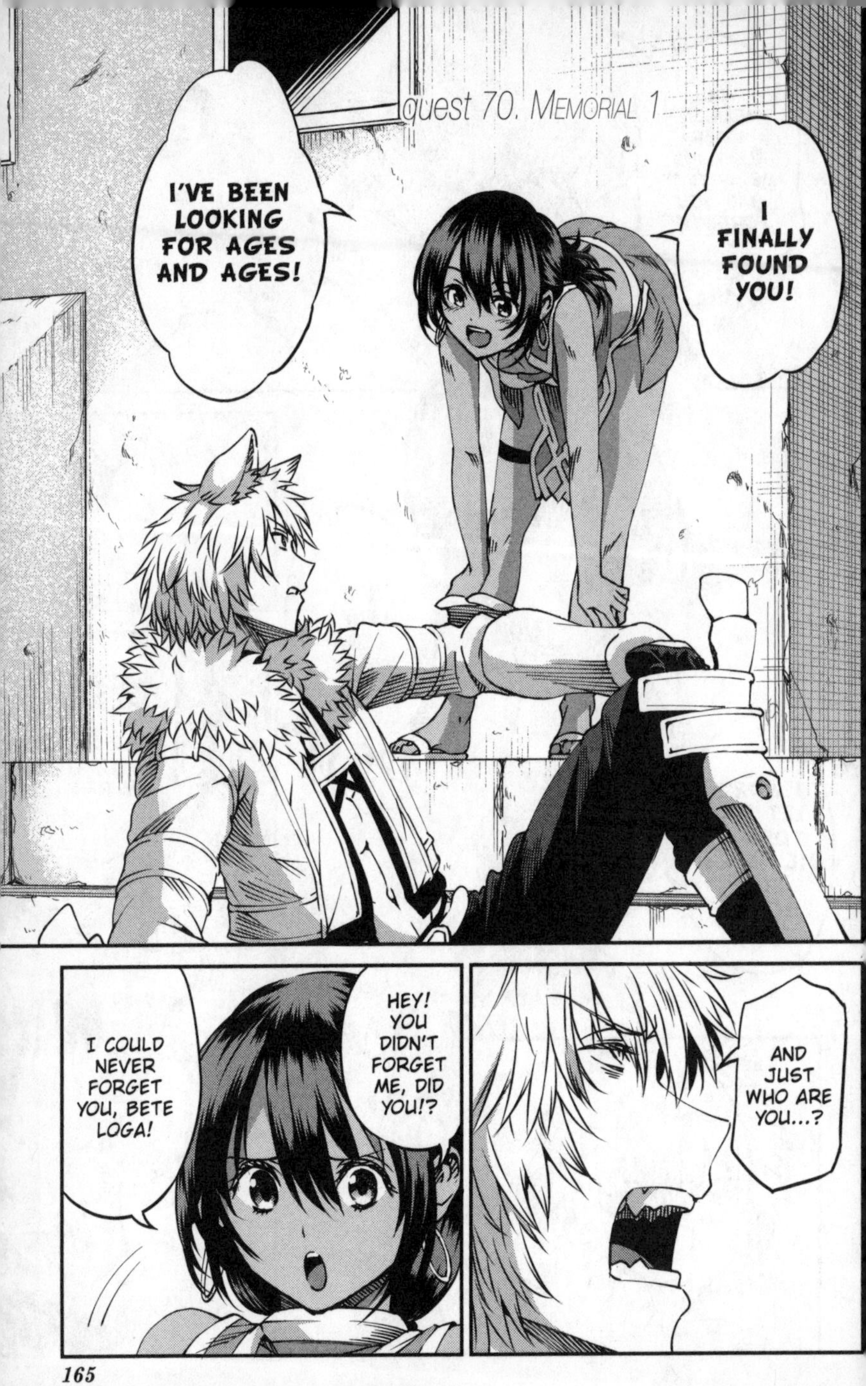
quest 70. Memorial 1
I finally found you!
I've been looking for ages and ages!
And just who are you...?
Hey! You didn't forget me, did you!?
I could never forget you, Bete Loga!

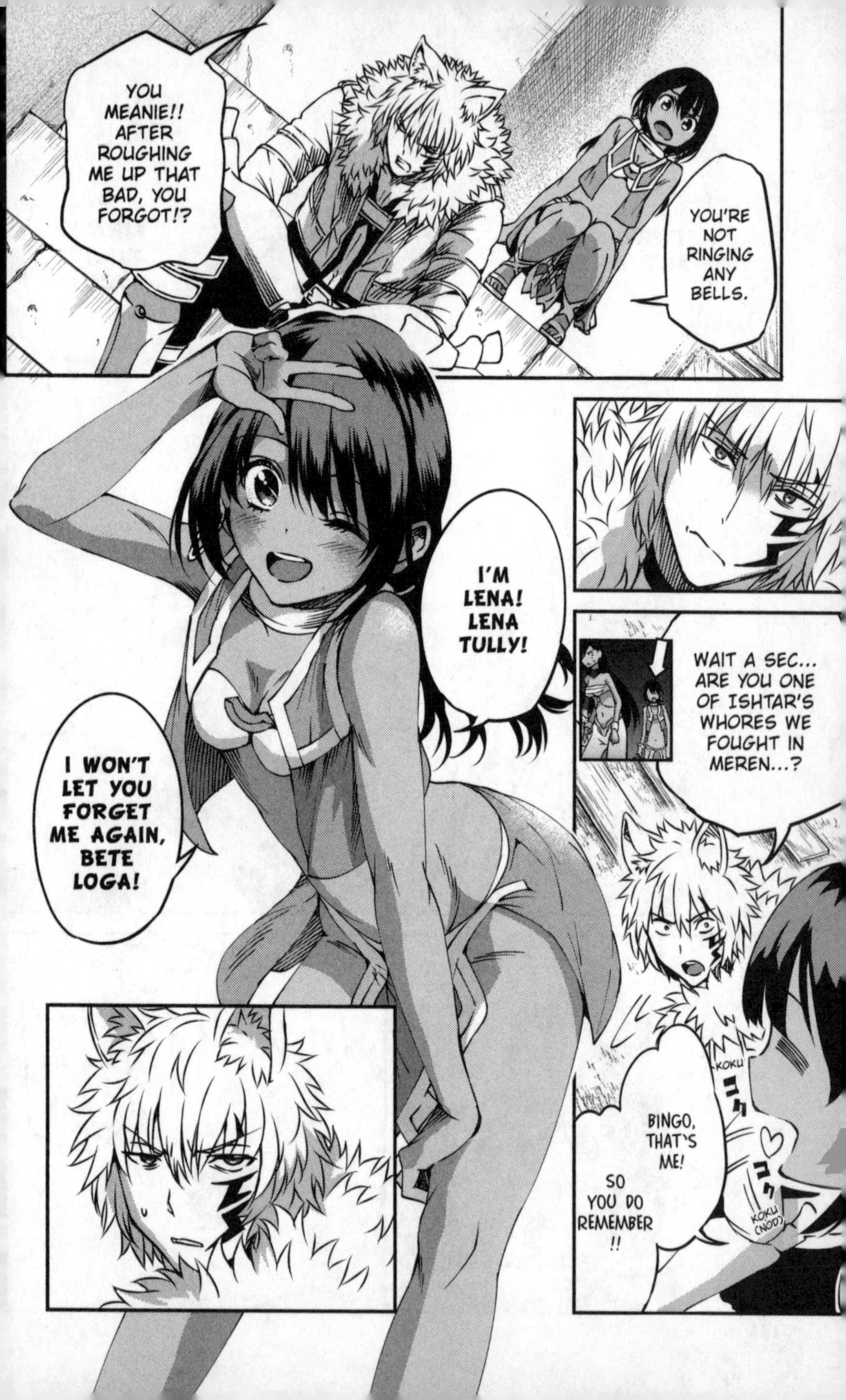
YOU'RE NOT RINGING ANY BELLS.
YOU MEANIE!! AFTER ROUGHING ME UP THAT BAD, YOU FORGOT!?
I'M LENA! LENA TULLY!
I WON'T LET YOU FORGET ME AGAIN, BETE LOGA!
WAIT A SEC... ARE YOU ONE OF ISHTAR'S WHORES WE FOUGHT IN MEREN...?
KOKU
KOKU (NOD)
BINGO, THAT'S ME!
SO YOU DO REMEMBER!!

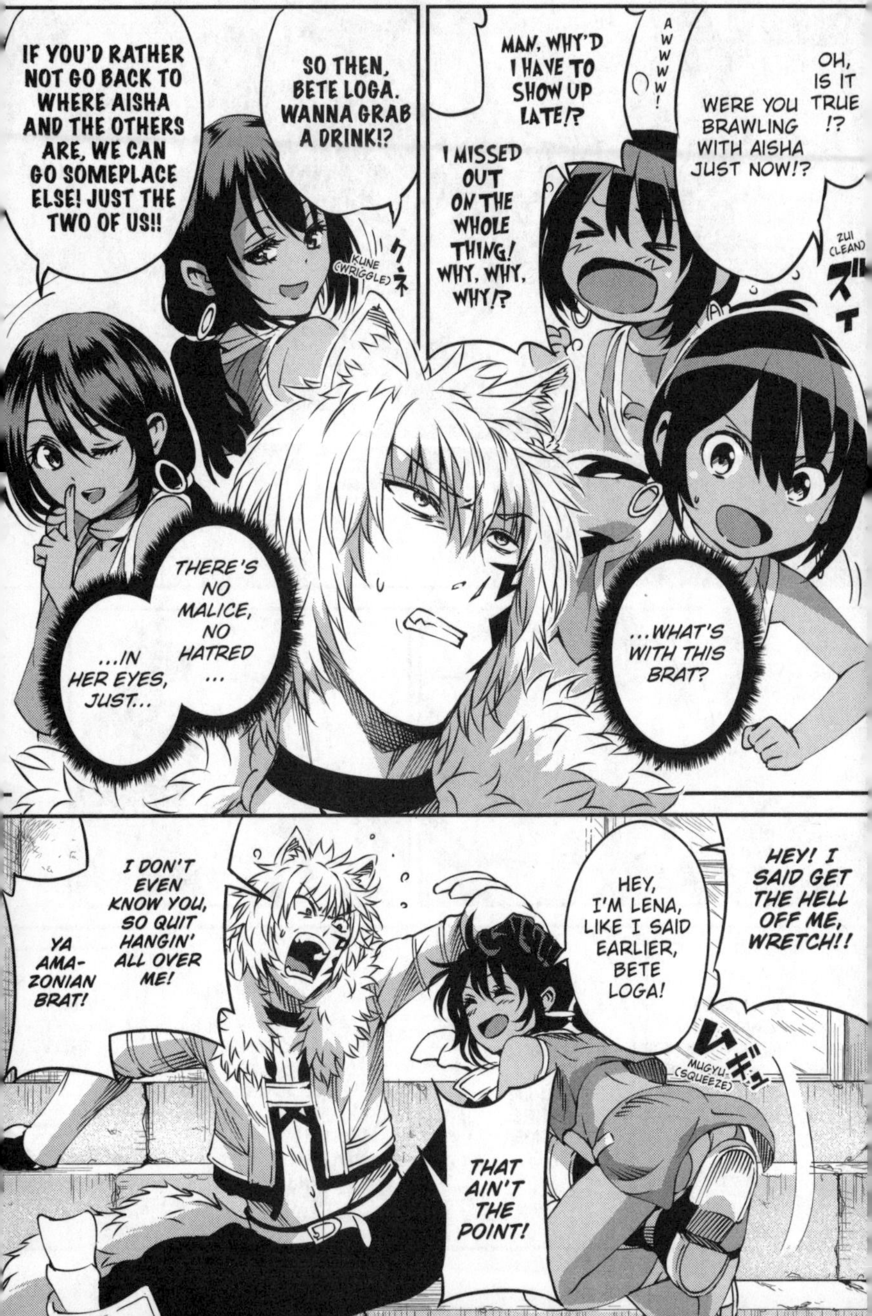
OH, IS IT TRUE!?
WERE YOU BRAWLING WITH AISHA JUST NOW!?
ZUI (LEAN)
AWWWW!
MAN, WHY'D I HAVE TO SHOW UP LATE!?
I MISSED OUT ON THE WHOLE THING! WHY, WHY, WHY!?
SO THEN, BETE LOGA. WANNA GRAB A DRINK!?
KUNE (WRIGGLE)
IF YOU'D RATHER NOT GO BACK TO WHERE AISHA AND THE OTHERS ARE, WE CAN GO SOMEPLACE ELSE! JUST THE TWO OF US!!
...WHAT'S WITH THIS BRAT?
THERE'S NO MALICE, NO HATRED ...
...IN HER EYES, JUST...
HEY! I SAID GET THE HELL OFF ME, WRETCH!!
HEY, I'M LENA, LIKE I SAID EARLIER, BETE LOGA!
MUGYU (SQUEEZE)
THAT AIN'T THE POINT!
I DON'T EVEN KNOW YOU, SO QUIT HANGIN' ALL OVER ME!
YA AMA-ZONIAN BRAT!

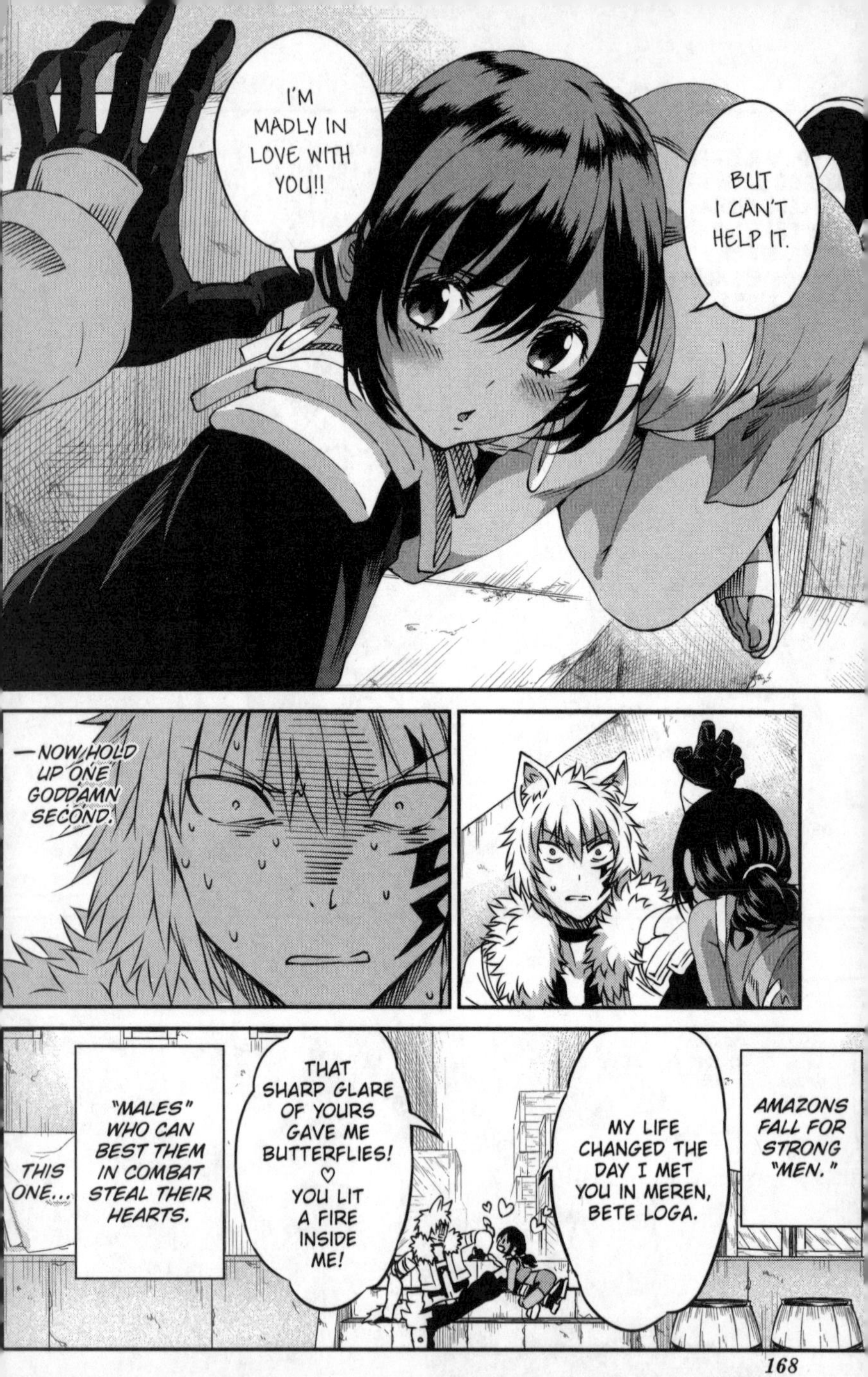
BUT I CAN'T HELP IT.
I'M MADLY IN LOVE WITH YOU!!
—NOW HOLD UP ONE GODDAMN SECOND.
AMAZONS FALL FOR STRONG "MEN."
MY LIFE CHANGED THE DAY I MET YOU IN MEREN, BETE LOGA.
THAT SHARP GLARE OF YOURS GAVE ME BUTTERFLIES! ♡ YOU LIT A FIRE INSIDE ME!
"MALES" WHO CAN BEST THEM IN COMBAT STEAL THEIR HEARTS.
THIS ONE...

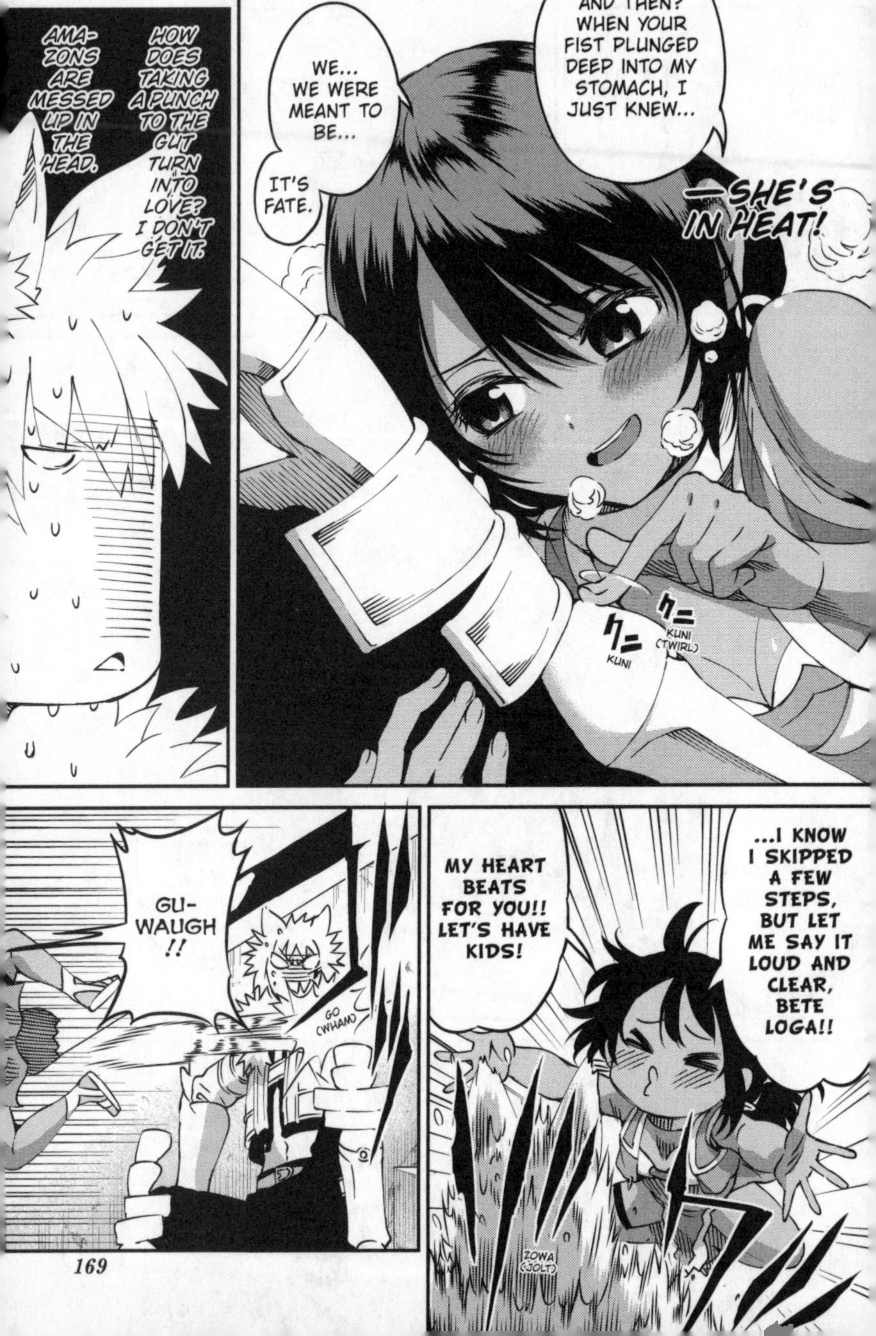

AND THEN? WHEN YOUR FIST PLUNGED DEEP INTO MY STOMACH, I JUST KNEW...
WE... WE WERE MEANT TO BE...
IT'S FATE.
—SHE'S IN HEAT!
クニ KUNI (TWIRL)
クニ KUNI
HOW DOES TAKING A PUNCH TO THE GUT TURN INTO LOVE? I DON'T GET IT.
AMAZONS ARE MESSED UP IN THE HEAD.
...I KNOW I SKIPPED A FEW STEPS, BUT LET ME SAY IT LOUD AND CLEAR, BETE LOGA!!
MY HEART BEATS FOR YOU!! LET'S HAVE KIDS!
ZOWA (JOLT)
GO (WHAM)
GU-WAUGH!!

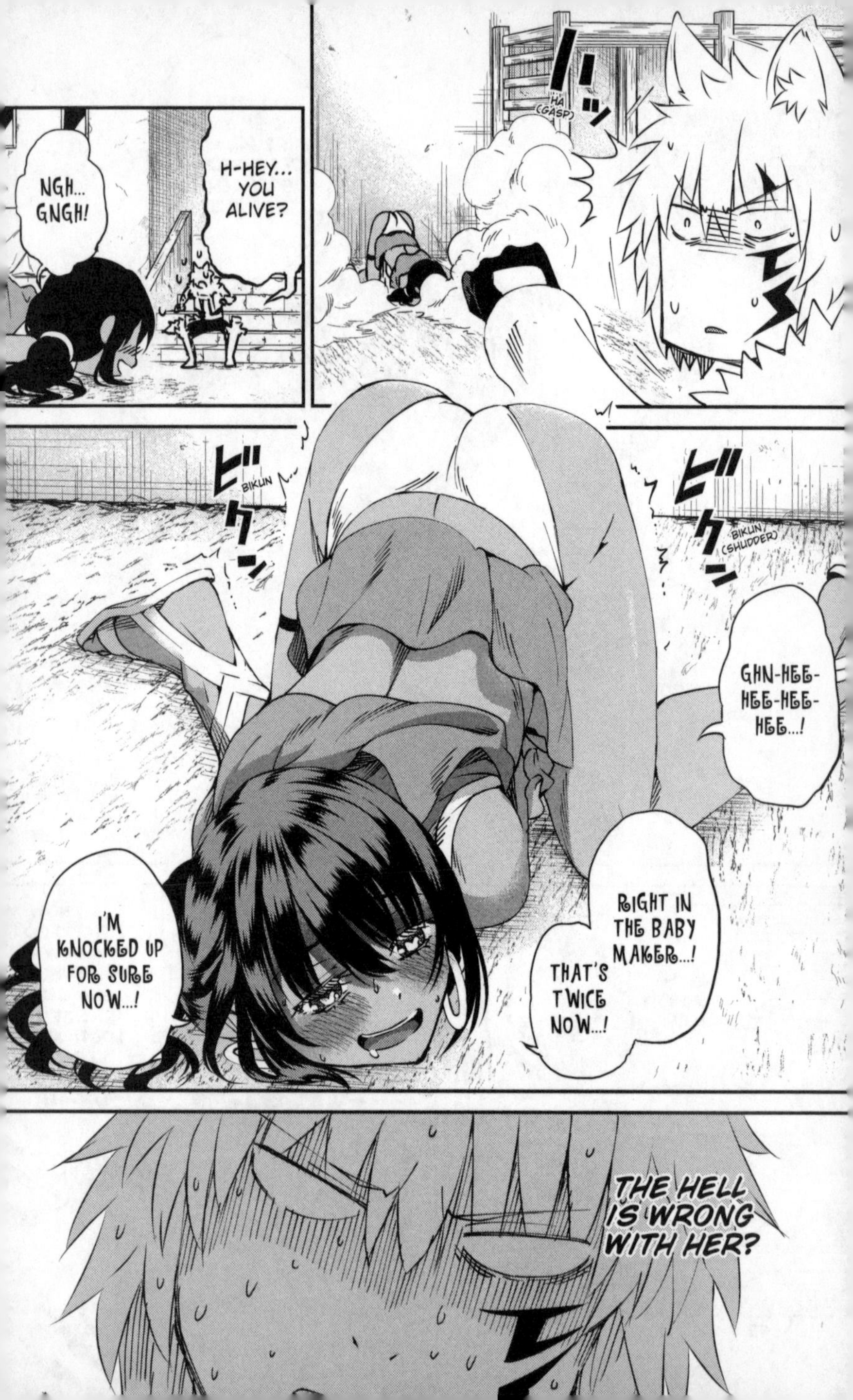

ハッ
HA (GASP)
H-HEY... YOU ALIVE?
NGH... GNGH!
ビクンッ
BIKUN (SHUDDER)
ビクンッ
BIKUN
GHN-HEE-HEE-HEE-HEE...!
RIGHT IN THE BABY MAKER...!
THAT'S TWICE NOW...!
I'M KNOCKED UP FOR SURE NOW...!
THE HELL IS WRONG WITH HER?

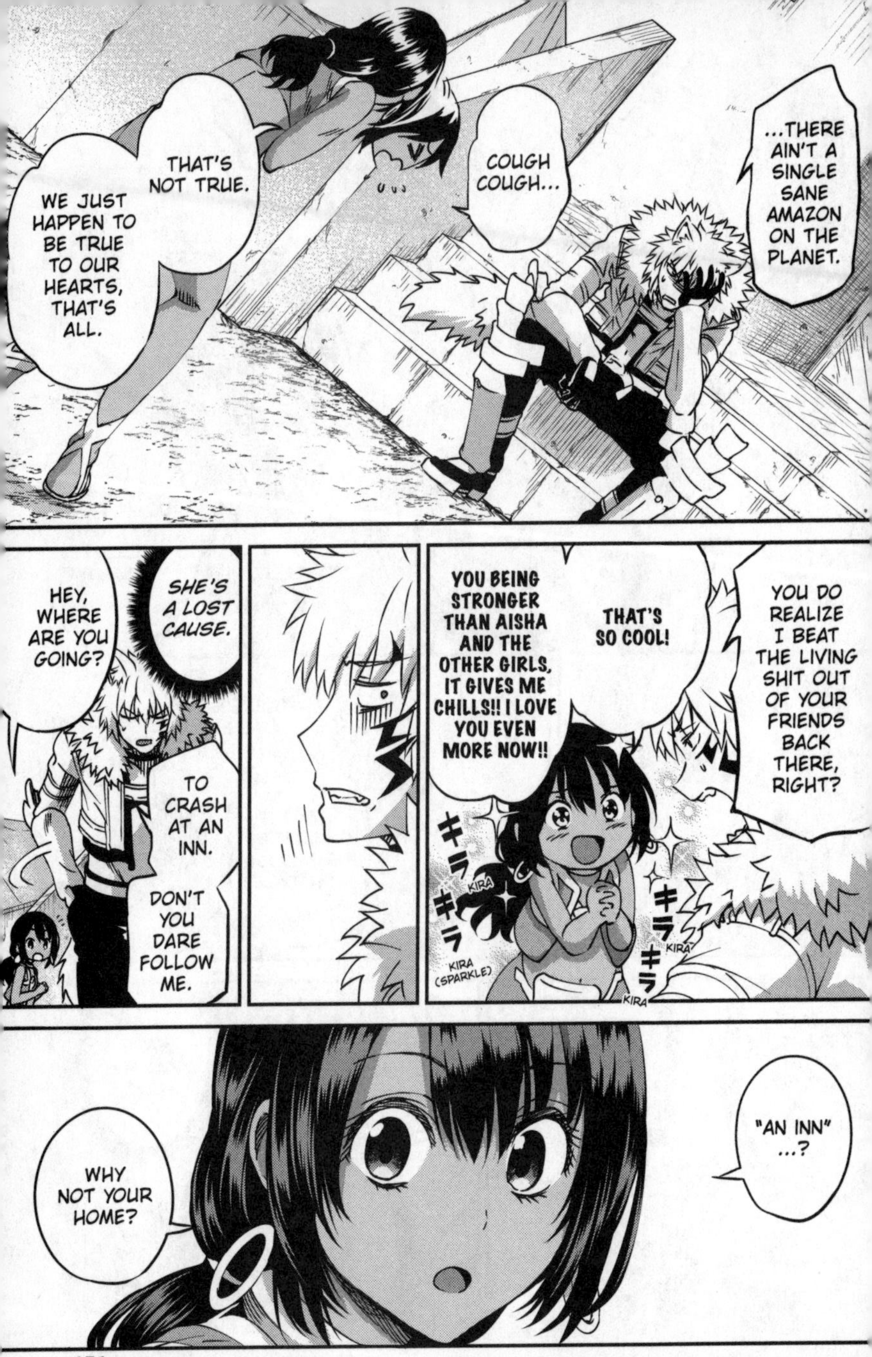
...THERE AIN'T A SINGLE SANE AMAZON ON THE PLANET.
COUGH COUGH...
THAT'S NOT TRUE.
WE JUST HAPPEN TO BE TRUE TO OUR HEARTS, THAT'S ALL.
YOU DO REALIZE I BEAT THE LIVING SHIT OUT OF YOUR FRIENDS BACK THERE, RIGHT?
THAT'S SO COOL!
YOU BEING STRONGER THAN AISHA AND THE OTHER GIRLS, IT GIVES ME CHILLS!! I LOVE YOU EVEN MORE NOW!!
キラ KIRA
キラ KIRA
キラ KIRA
キラ KIRA (SPARKLE)
SHE'S A LOST CAUSE.
HEY, WHERE ARE YOU GOING?
TO CRASH AT AN INN.
DON'T YOU DARE FOLLOW ME.
"AN INN" ...?
WHY NOT YOUR HOME?

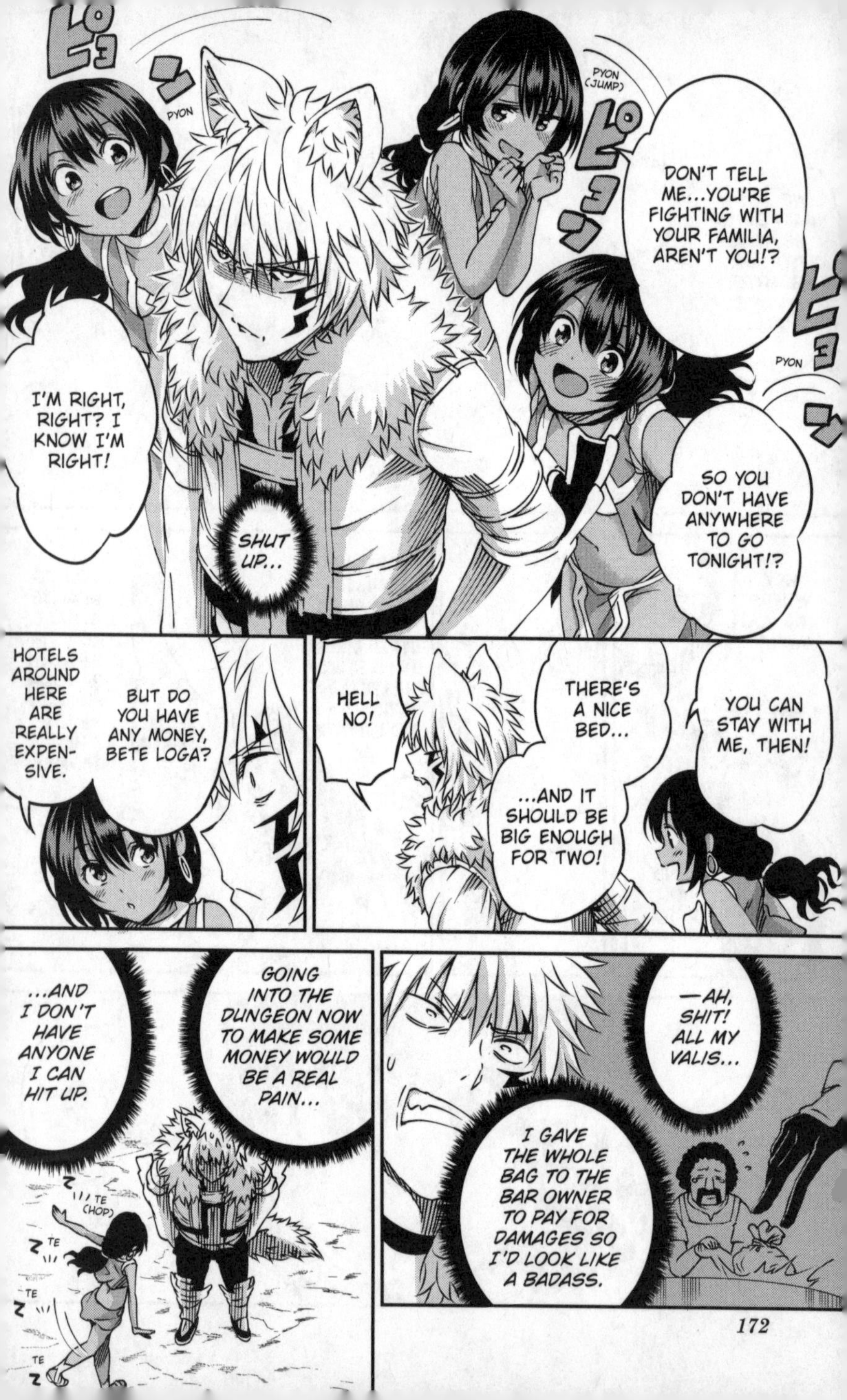
PYON (JUMP)
DON'T TELL ME...YOU'RE FIGHTING WITH YOUR FAMILIA, AREN'T YOU!?
PYON
SO YOU DON'T HAVE ANYWHERE TO GO TONIGHT!?
PYON
I'M RIGHT, RIGHT? I KNOW I'M RIGHT!
SHUT UP...
YOU CAN STAY WITH ME, THEN!
THERE'S A NICE BED...
...AND IT SHOULD BE BIG ENOUGH FOR TWO!
HELL NO!
BUT DO YOU HAVE ANY MONEY, BETE LOGA?
HOTELS AROUND HERE ARE REALLY EXPEN-SIVE.
—AH, SHIT! ALL MY VALIS...
I GAVE THE WHOLE BAG TO THE BAR OWNER TO PAY FOR DAMAGES SO I'D LOOK LIKE A BADASS.
GOING INTO THE DUNGEON NOW TO MAKE SOME MONEY WOULD BE A REAL PAIN...
...AND I DON'T HAVE ANYONE I CAN HIT UP.
TE (HOP)
TE
TE
TE

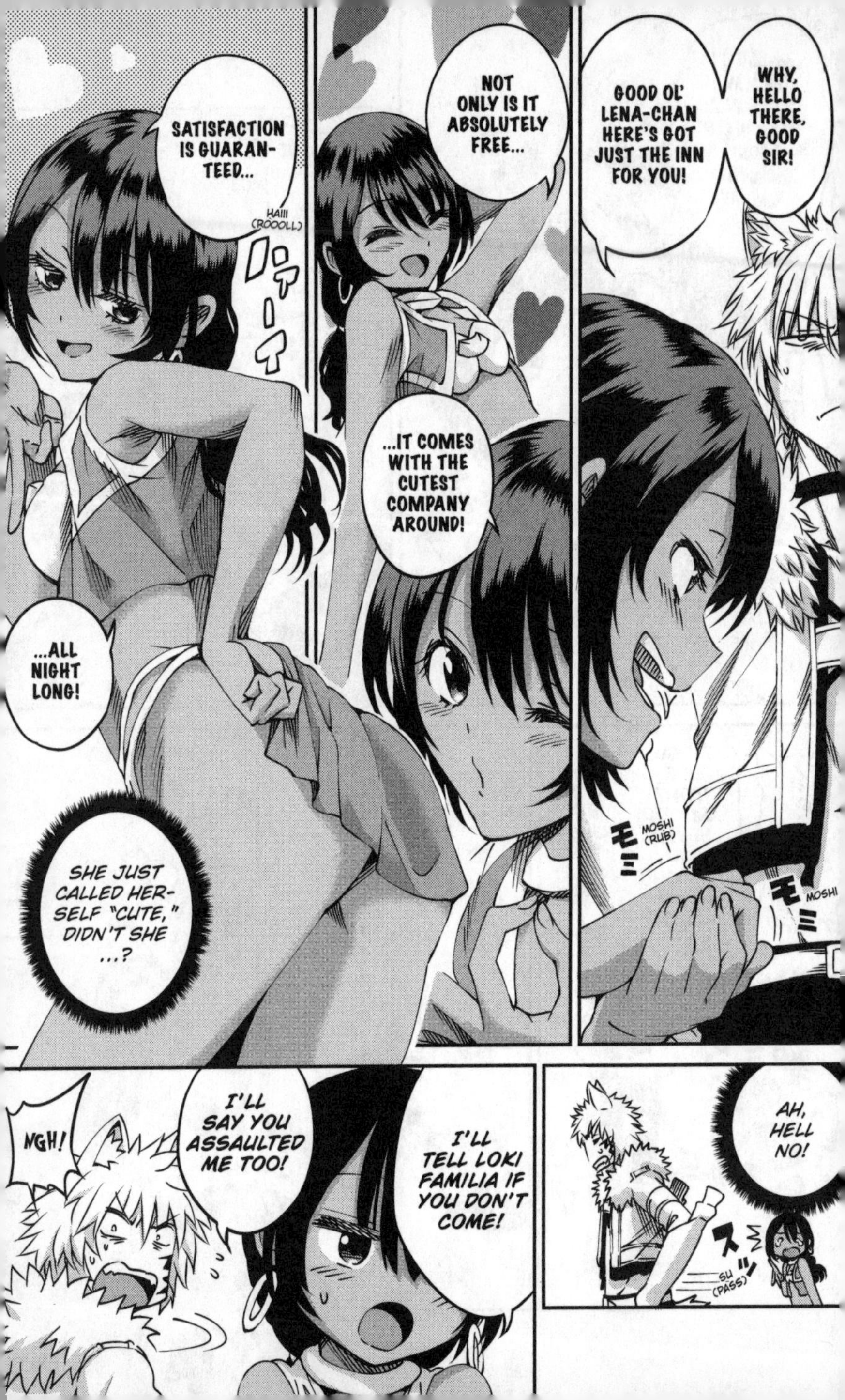

WHY, HELLO THERE, GOOD SIR!
GOOD OL' LENA-CHAN HERE'S GOT JUST THE INN FOR YOU!
MOSHI (RUB)
MOSHI
NOT ONLY IS IT ABSOLUTELY FREE...
...IT COMES WITH THE CUTEST COMPANY AROUND!
SATISFACTION IS GUARAN-TEED...
HAIII (ROOOLL)
...ALL NIGHT LONG!
SHE JUST CALLED HER-SELF "CUTE," DIDN'T SHE ...?
AH, HELL NO!
SU (PASS)
I'LL TELL LOKI FAMILIA IF YOU DON'T COME!
I'LL SAY YOU ASSAULTED ME TOO!
NGH!

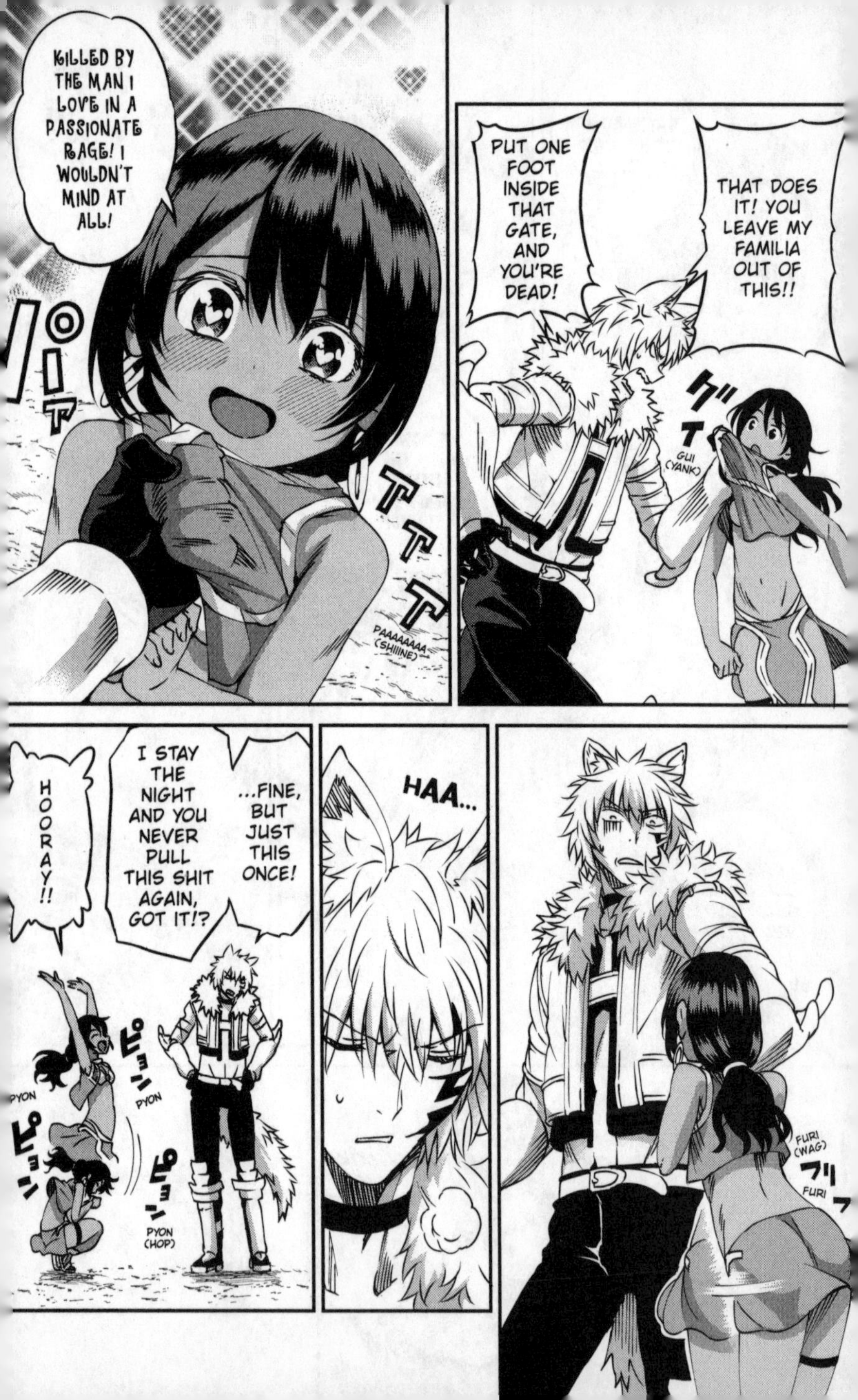
THAT DOES IT! YOU LEAVE MY FAMILIA OUT OF THIS!!
PUT ONE FOOT INSIDE THAT GATE, AND YOU'RE DEAD!
GUI (YANK)
KILLED BY THE MAN I LOVE IN A PASSIONATE RAGE! I WOULDN'T MIND AT ALL!
PAAAAAAAA (SHIIINE)
FURI (WAG)
FURI
HAA...
...FINE, BUT JUST THIS ONCE!
I STAY THE NIGHT AND YOU NEVER PULL THIS SHIT AGAIN, GOT IT!?
HOORAY!!
PYON
PYON
PYON (HOP)

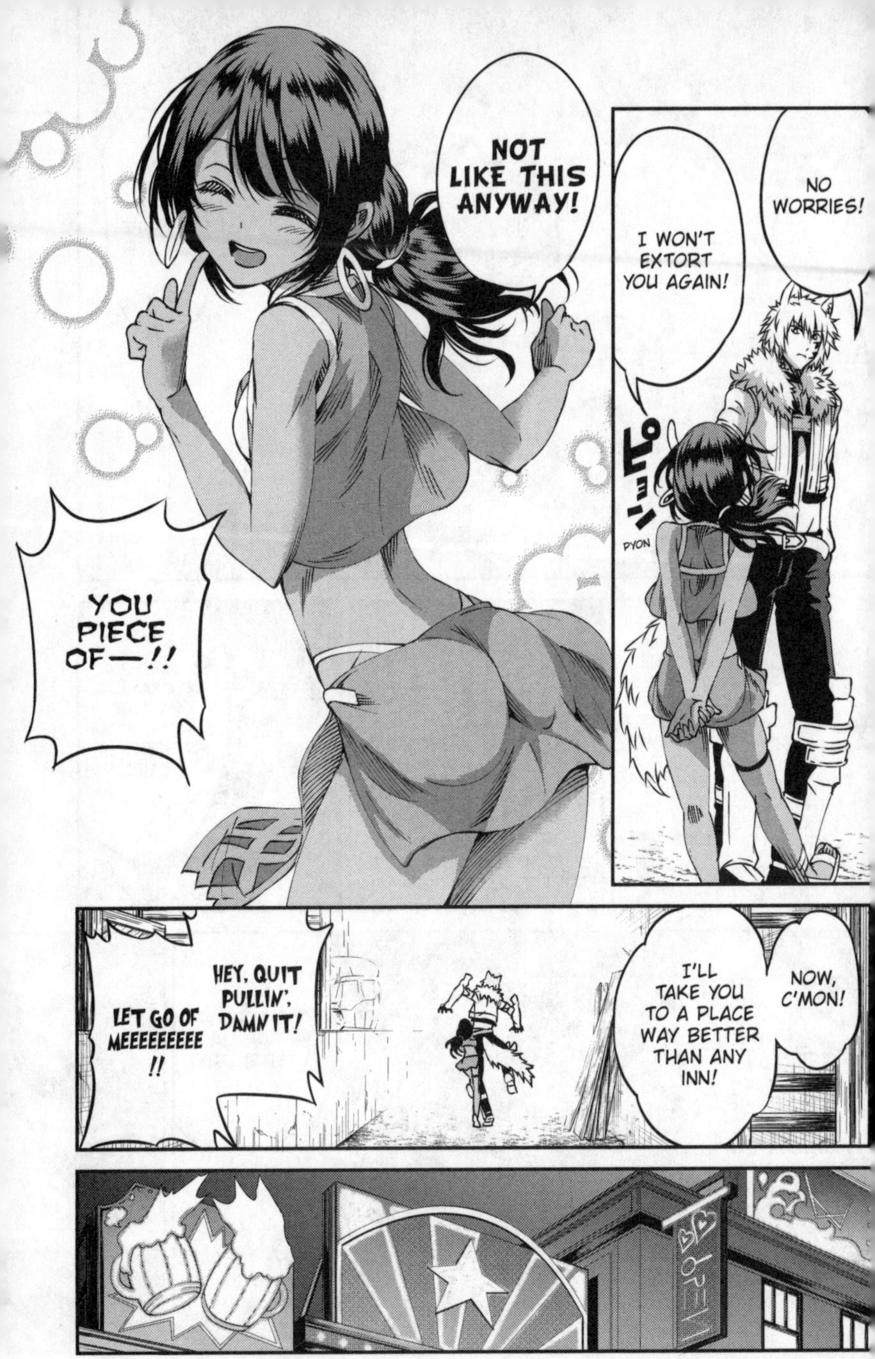
NO WORRIES!
I WON'T EXTORT YOU AGAIN!
ピョン
PYON
NOT LIKE THIS ANYWAY!
YOU PIECE OF—!!
NOW, C'MON!
I'LL TAKE YOU TO A PLACE WAY BETTER THAN ANY INN!
HEY, QUIT PULLIN', DAMN IT!
LET GO OF MEEEEEEEEE!!

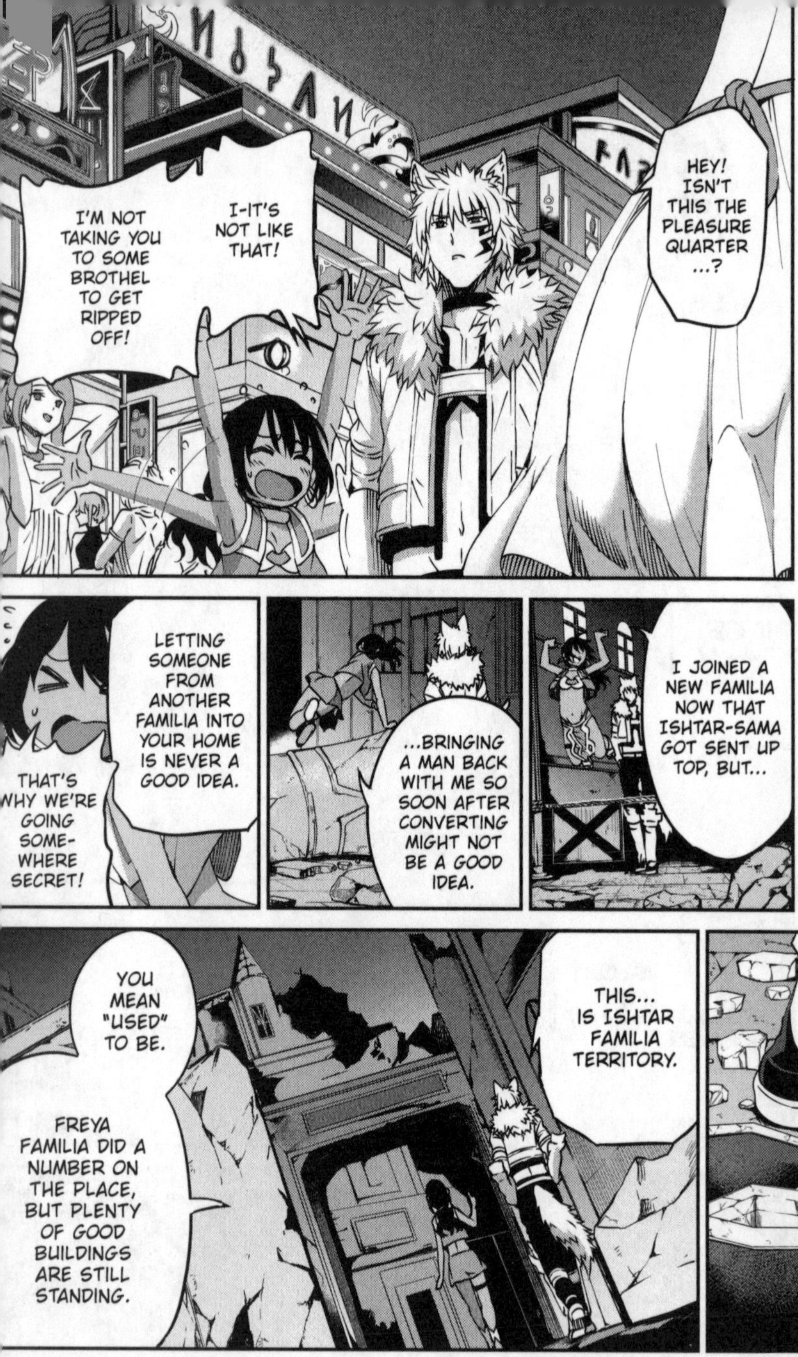
HEY! ISN'T THIS THE PLEASURE QUARTER ...?
I-IT'S NOT LIKE THAT!
I'M NOT TAKING YOU TO SOME BROTHEL TO GET RIPPED OFF!
I JOINED A NEW FAMILIA NOW THAT ISHTAR-SAMA GOT SENT UP TOP, BUT...
...BRINGING A MAN BACK WITH ME SO SOON AFTER CONVERTING MIGHT NOT BE A GOOD IDEA.
LETTING SOMEONE FROM ANOTHER FAMILIA INTO YOUR HOME IS NEVER A GOOD IDEA.
THAT'S WHY WE'RE GOING SOME-WHERE SECRET!
THIS... IS ISHTAR FAMILIA TERRITORY.
YOU MEAN "USED" TO BE.
FREYA FAMILIA DID A NUMBER ON THE PLACE, BUT PLENTY OF GOOD BUILDINGS ARE STILL STANDING.

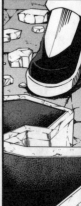

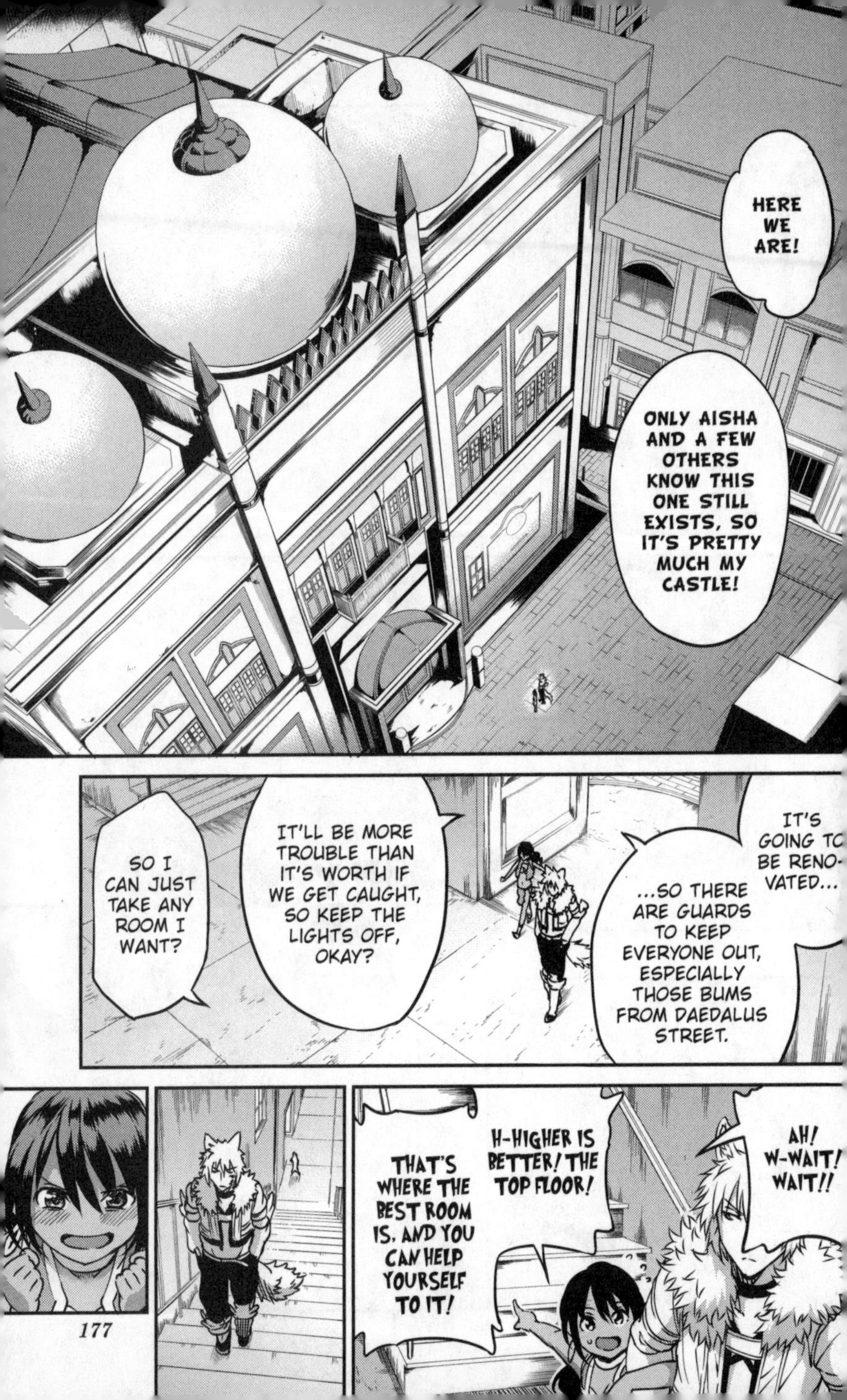
HERE WE ARE!
ONLY AISHA AND A FEW OTHERS KNOW THIS ONE STILL EXISTS, SO IT'S PRETTY MUCH MY CASTLE!
IT'S GOING TO BE RENO-VATED...
...SO THERE ARE GUARDS TO KEEP EVERYONE OUT, ESPECIALLY THOSE BUMS FROM DAEDALUS STREET.
IT'LL BE MORE TROUBLE THAN IT'S WORTH IF WE GET CAUGHT, SO KEEP THE LIGHTS OFF, OKAY?
SO I CAN JUST TAKE ANY ROOM I WANT?
AH! W-WAIT! WAIT!!
H-HIGHER IS BETTER! THE TOP FLOOR!
THAT'S WHERE THE BEST ROOM IS. AND YOU CAN HELP YOURSELF TO IT!

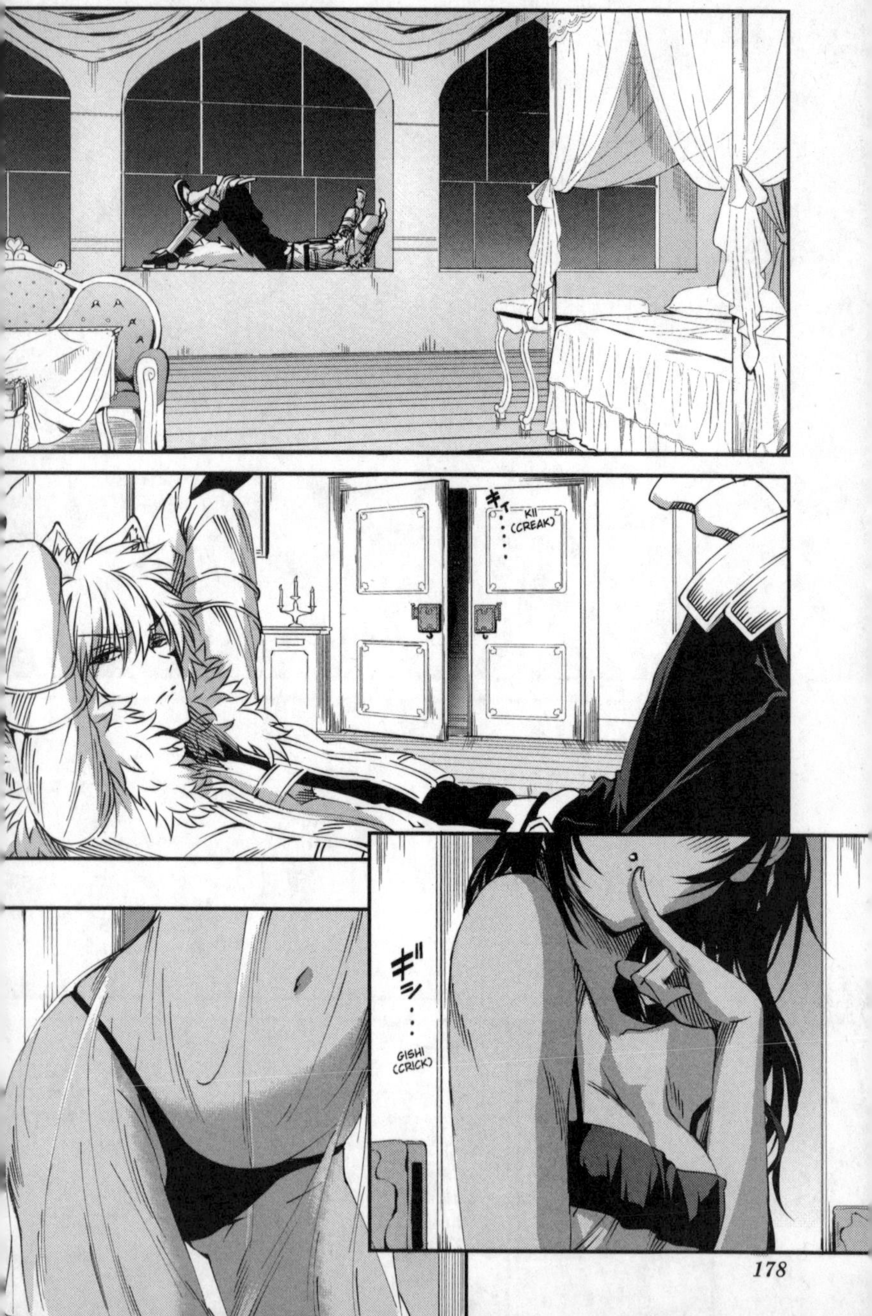
キィ……
KII (CREAK)
ギシ…
GISHI (CRICK)

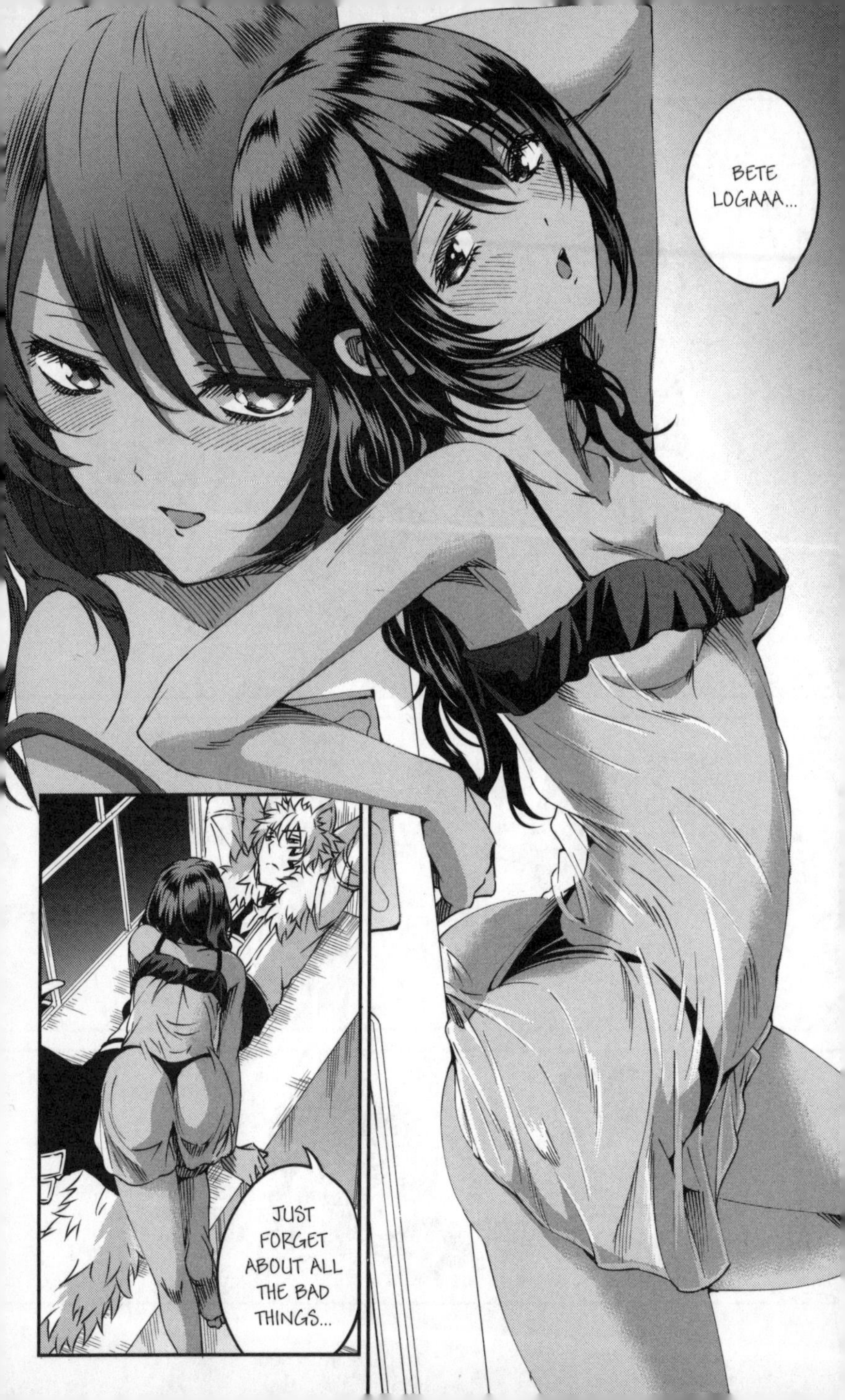
BETE LOGAAA...
JUST FORGET ABOUT ALL THE BAD THINGS...

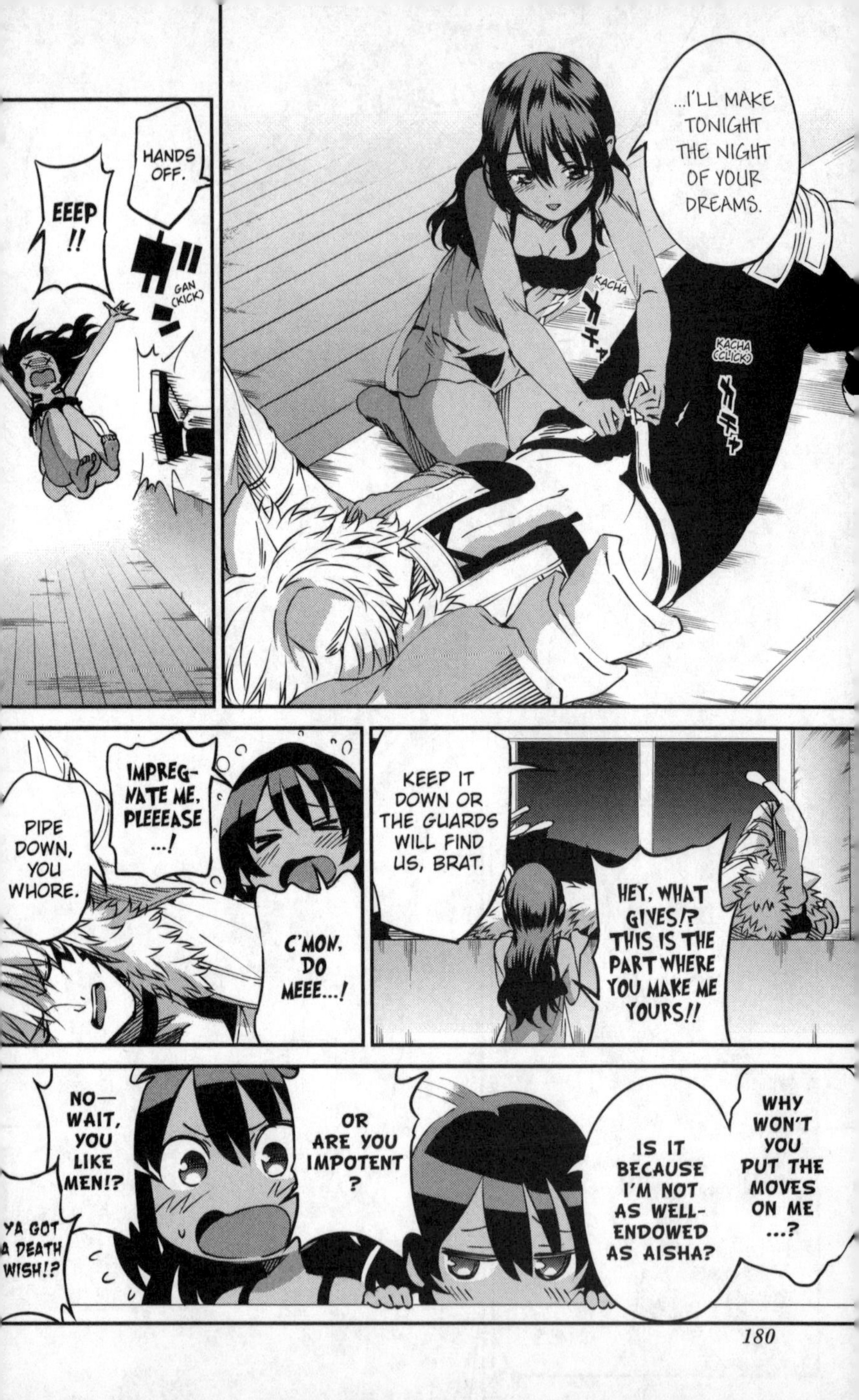
...I'LL MAKE TONIGHT THE NIGHT OF YOUR DREAMS.
KACHA
KACHA (CLICK)
HANDS OFF.
GAN (KICK)
EEEP!!
HEY, WHAT GIVES!? THIS IS THE PART WHERE YOU MAKE ME YOURS!!
KEEP IT DOWN OR THE GUARDS WILL FIND US, BRAT.
IMPREGNATE ME, PLEEEASE...!
C'MON, DO MEEE...!
PIPE DOWN, YOU WHORE.
WHY WON'T YOU PUT THE MOVES ON ME...?
IS IT BECAUSE I'M NOT AS WELL-ENDOWED AS AISHA?
OR ARE YOU IMPOTENT?
NO—WAIT, YOU LIKE MEN!?
YA GOT A DEATH WISH!?

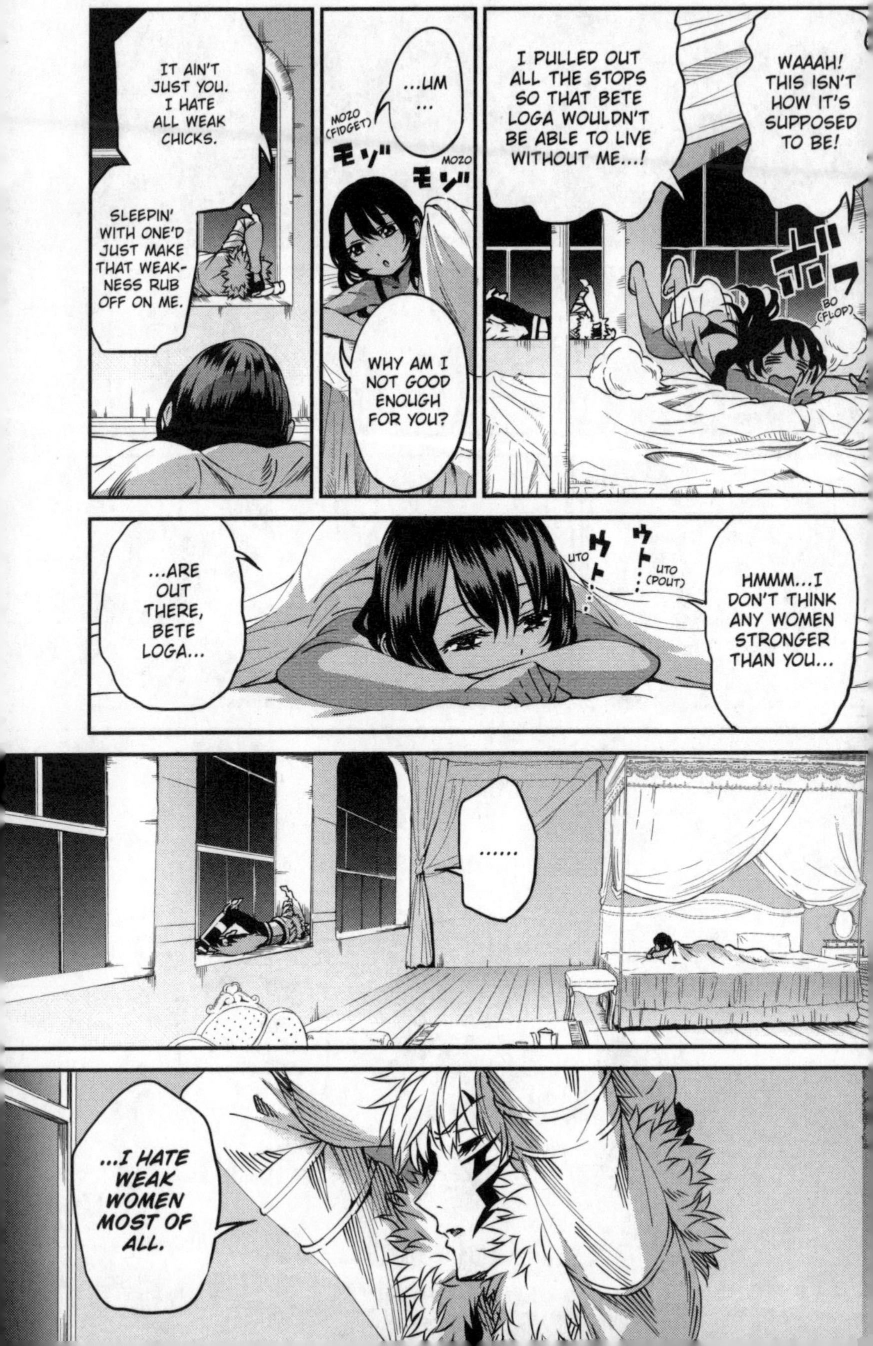
WAAAH! THIS ISN'T HOW IT'S SUPPOSED TO BE!
I PULLED OUT ALL THE STOPS SO THAT BETE LOGA WOULDN'T BE ABLE TO LIVE WITHOUT ME...!
ボフ
BO (FLOP)
...UM ...
モゾ
MOZO (FIDGET)
モゾ
MOZO
WHY AM I NOT GOOD ENOUGH FOR YOU?
IT AIN'T JUST YOU. I HATE ALL WEAK CHICKS.
SLEEPIN' WITH ONE'D JUST MAKE THAT WEAK-NESS RUB OFF ON ME.
HMMM...I DON'T THINK ANY WOMEN STRONGER THAN YOU...
ウト…
UTO (POUT)
ウト…
UTO
...ARE OUT THERE, BETE LOGA...
......
...I HATE WEAK WOMEN MOST OF ALL.

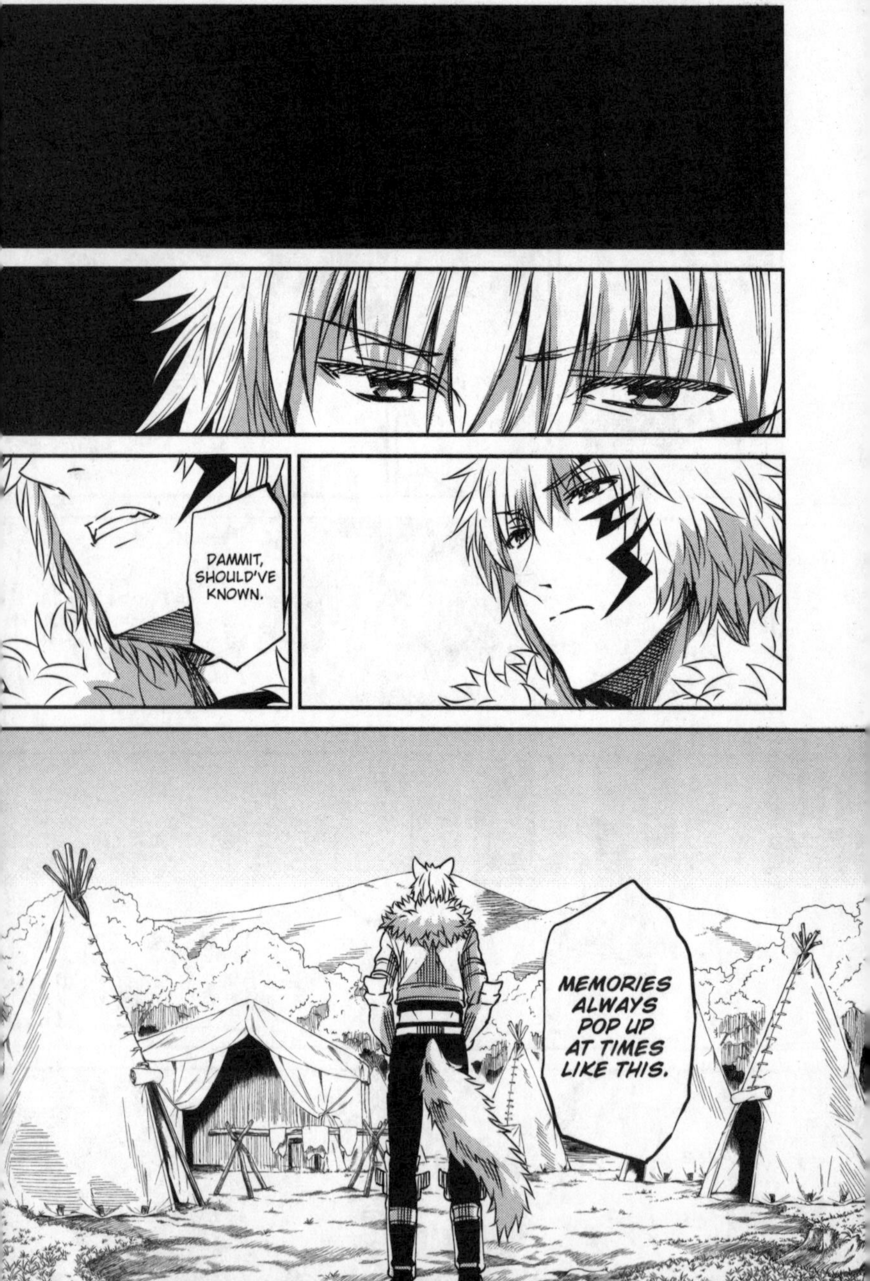
DAMMIT, SHOULD'VE KNOWN.
MEMORIES ALWAYS POP UP AT TIMES LIKE THIS.

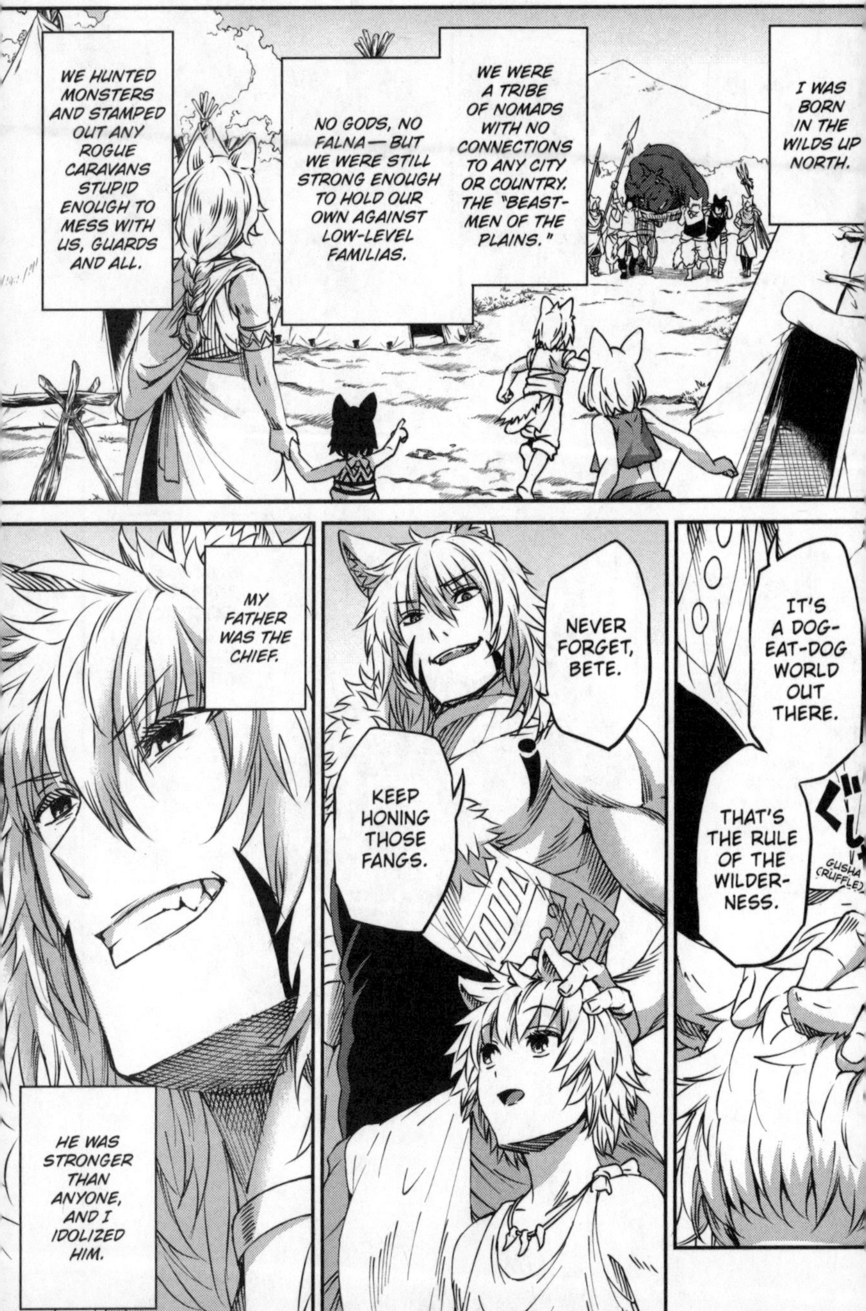
I WAS BORN IN THE WILDS UP NORTH.
WE WERE A TRIBE OF NOMADS WITH NO CONNECTIONS TO ANY CITY OR COUNTRY. THE "BEASTMEN OF THE PLAINS."
NO GODS, NO FALNA—BUT WE WERE STILL STRONG ENOUGH TO HOLD OUR OWN AGAINST LOW-LEVEL FAMILIAS.
WE HUNTED MONSTERS AND STAMPED OUT ANY ROGUE CARAVANS STUPID ENOUGH TO MESS WITH US, GUARDS AND ALL.
IT'S A DOG-EAT-DOG WORLD OUT THERE.
THAT'S THE RULE OF THE WILDERNESS.
GUSHA (RUFFLE)
NEVER FORGET, BETE.
KEEP HONING THOSE FANGS.
MY FATHER WAS THE CHIEF.
HE WAS STRONGER THAN ANYONE, AND I IDOLIZED HIM.

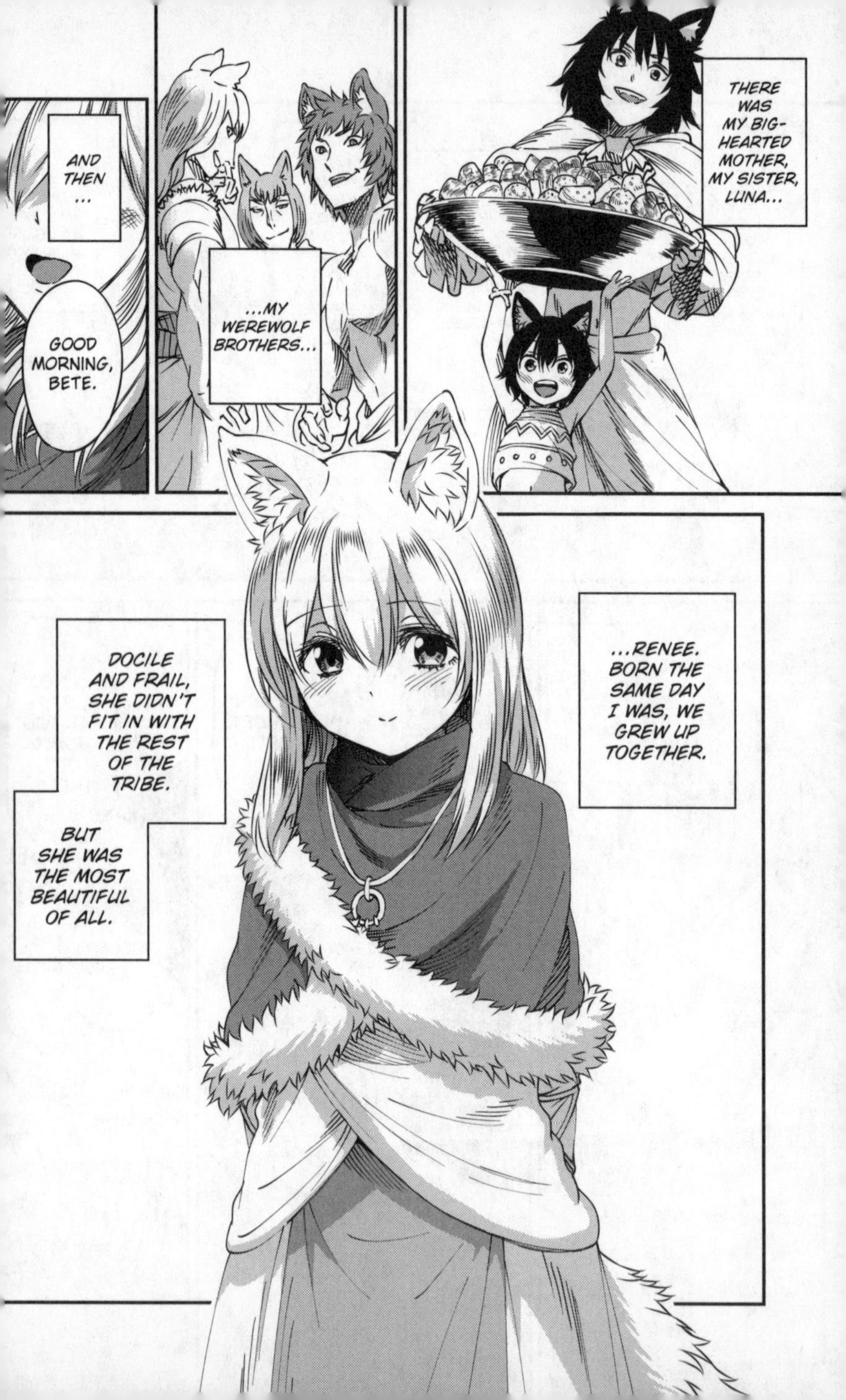
THERE WAS MY BIG-HEARTED MOTHER, MY SISTER, LUNA...
...MY WEREWOLF BROTHERS...
AND THEN ...
GOOD MORNING, BETE.
...RENEE. BORN THE SAME DAY I WAS, WE GREW UP TOGETHER.
DOCILE AND FRAIL, SHE DIDN'T FIT IN WITH THE REST OF THE TRIBE.
BUT SHE WAS THE MOST BEAUTIFUL OF ALL.

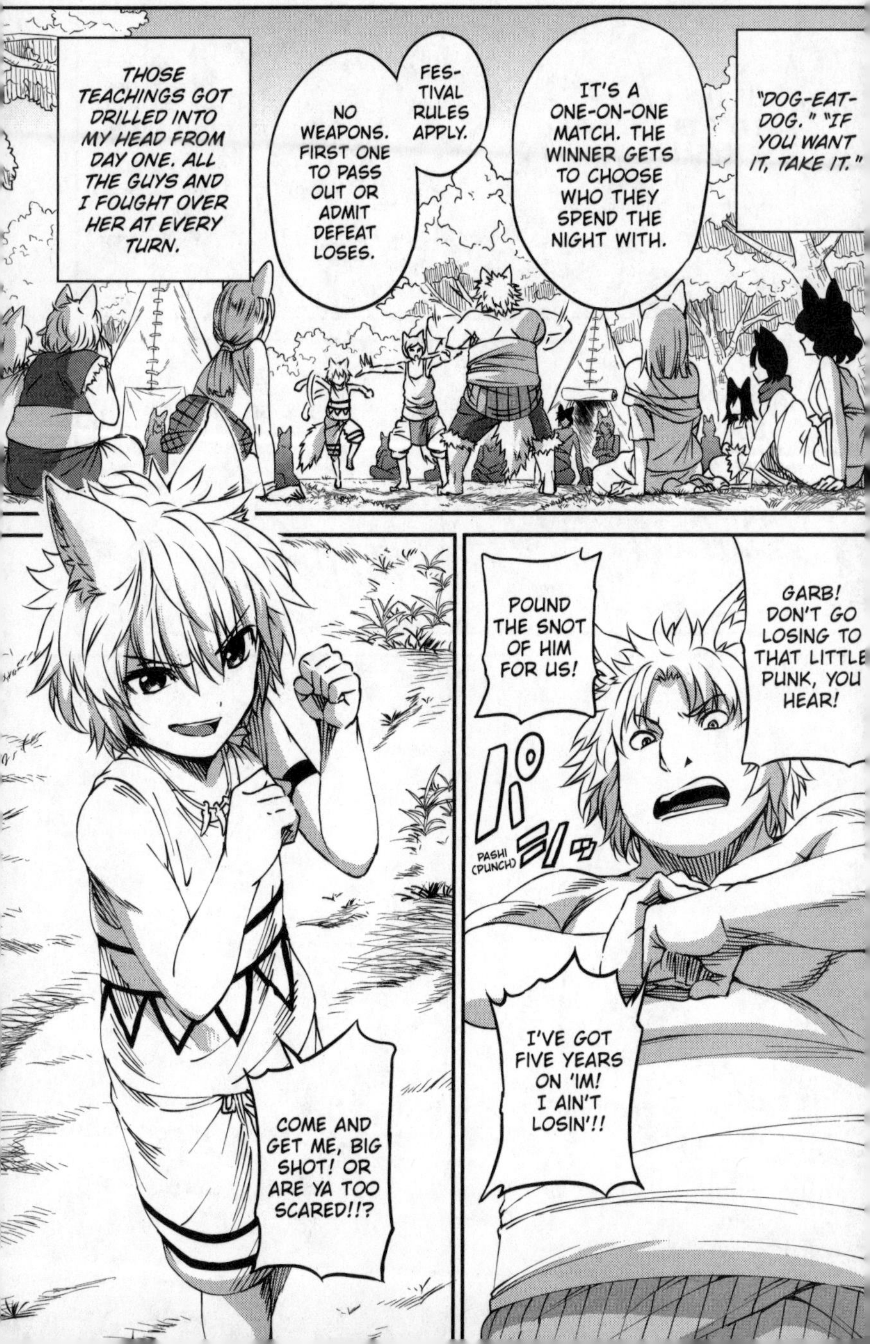
"DOG-EAT-DOG." "IF YOU WANT IT, TAKE IT."
IT'S A ONE-ON-ONE MATCH. THE WINNER GETS TO CHOOSE WHO THEY SPEND THE NIGHT WITH.
FES-TIVAL RULES APPLY.
NO WEAPONS. FIRST ONE TO PASS OUT OR ADMIT DEFEAT LOSES.
THOSE TEACHINGS GOT DRILLED INTO MY HEAD FROM DAY ONE. ALL THE GUYS AND I FOUGHT OVER HER AT EVERY TURN.
GARB! DON'T GO LOSING TO THAT LITTLE PUNK, YOU HEAR!
POUND THE SNOT OF HIM FOR US!
PASHI (PUNCH)
I'VE GOT FIVE YEARS ON 'IM! I AIN'T LOSIN'!!
COME AND GET ME, BIG SHOT! OR ARE YA TOO SCARED!!?

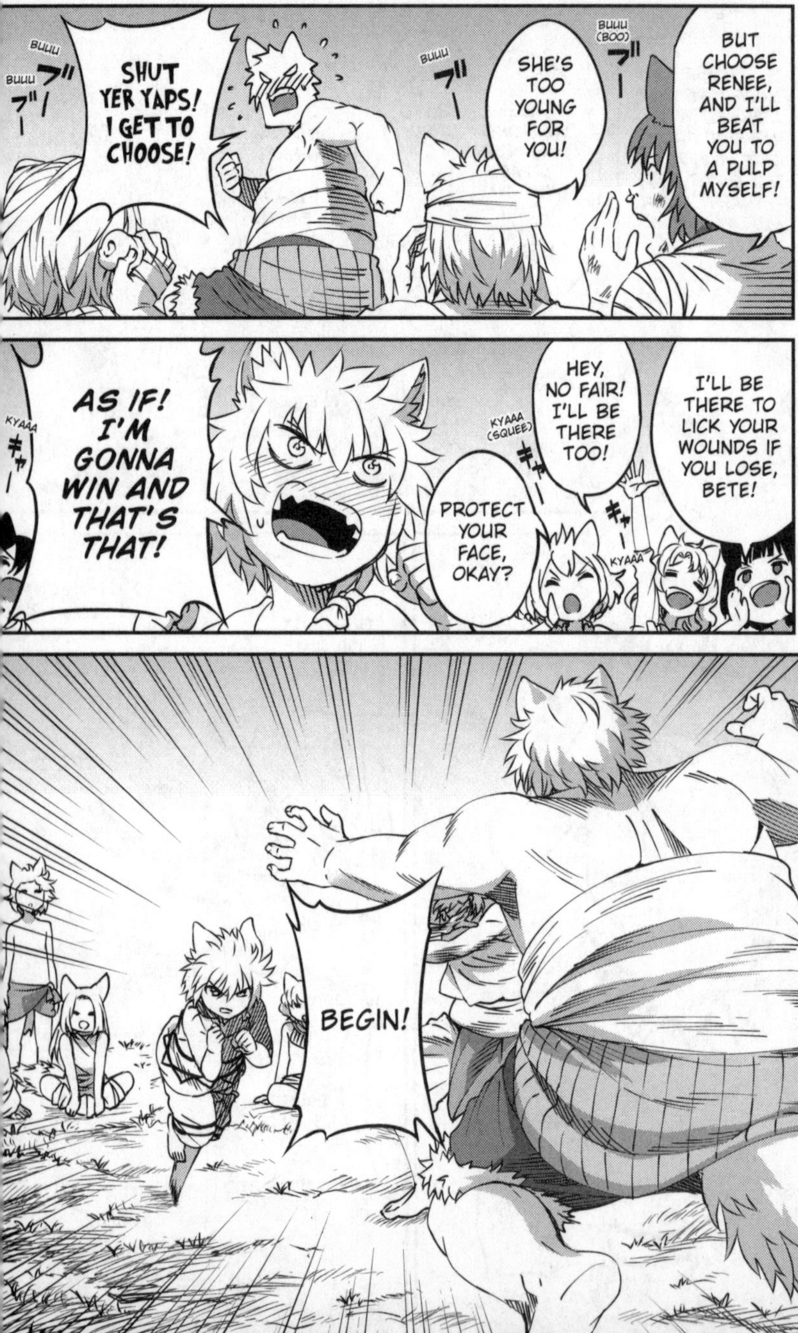
BUT CHOOSE RENEE, AND I'LL BEAT YOU TO A PULP MYSELF!
BUUU (BOO)
SHE'S TOO YOUNG FOR YOU!
BUUU
SHUT YER YAPS! I GET TO CHOOSE!
BUUU
BUUU
I'LL BE THERE TO LICK YOUR WOUNDS IF YOU LOSE, BETE!
HEY, NO FAIR! I'LL BE THERE TOO!
KYAAA (SQUEE)
KYAAA
PROTECT YOUR FACE, OKAY?
AS IF! I'M GONNA WIN AND THAT'S THAT!
KYAAA
BEGIN!

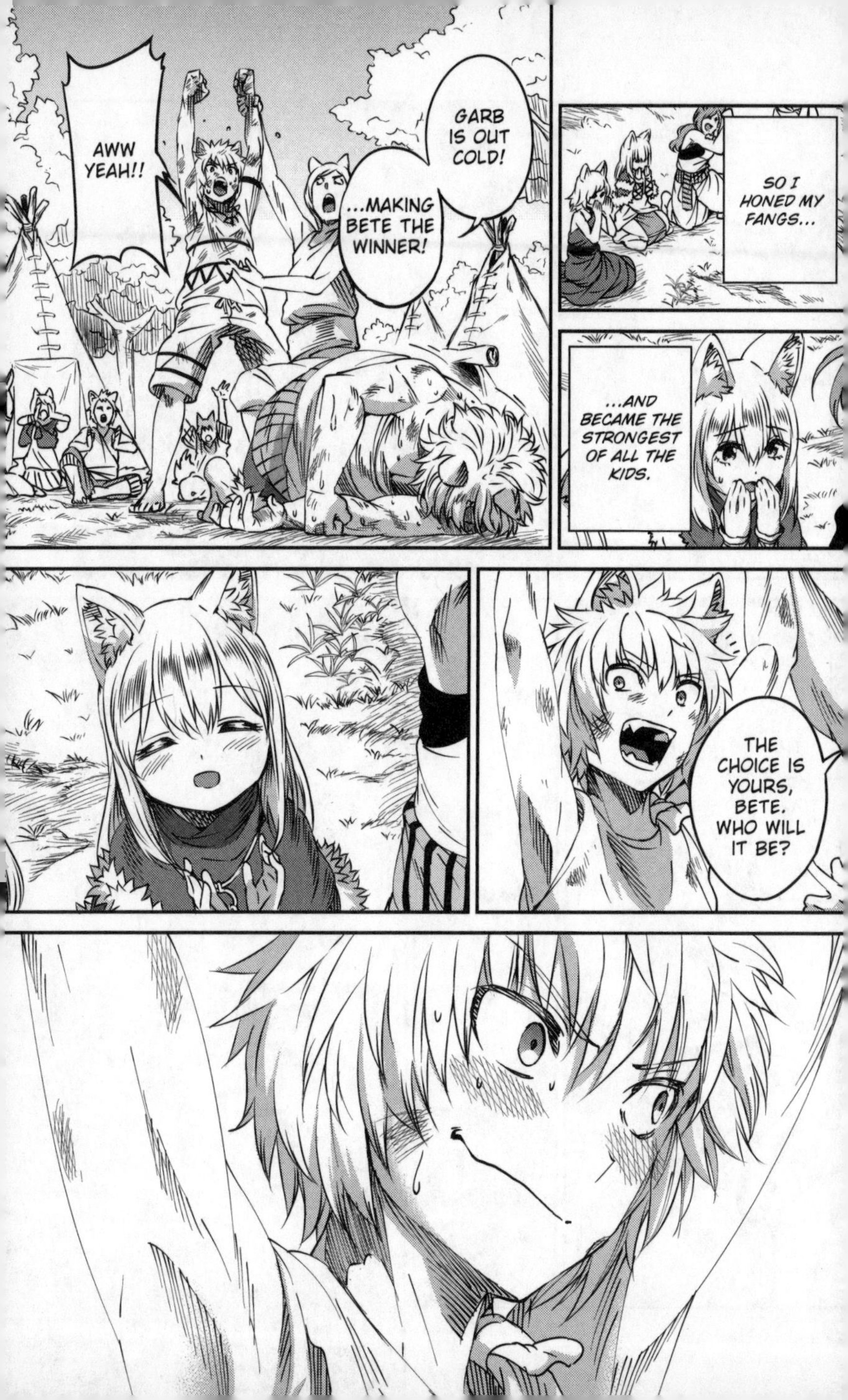
SO I HONED MY FANGS...
...AND BECAME THE STRONGEST OF ALL THE KIDS.
GARB IS OUT COLD!
...MAKING BETE THE WINNER!
AWW YEAH!!
THE CHOICE IS YOURS, BETE. WHO WILL IT BE?

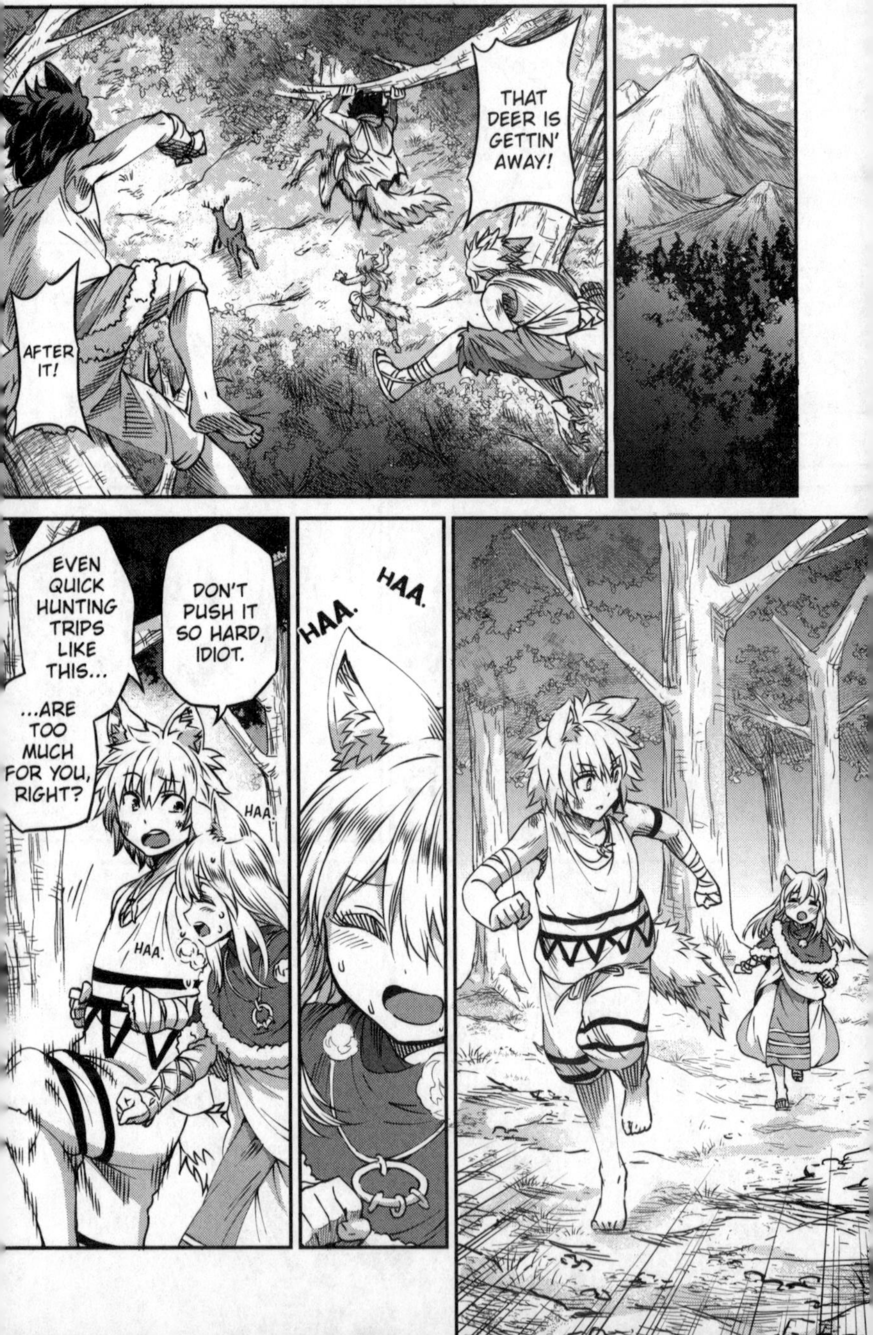
THAT DEER IS GETTIN' AWAY!
AFTER IT!
HAA.
HAA.
DON'T PUSH IT SO HARD, IDIOT.
EVEN QUICK HUNTING TRIPS LIKE THIS...
...ARE TOO MUCH FOR YOU, RIGHT?
HAA.
HAA.

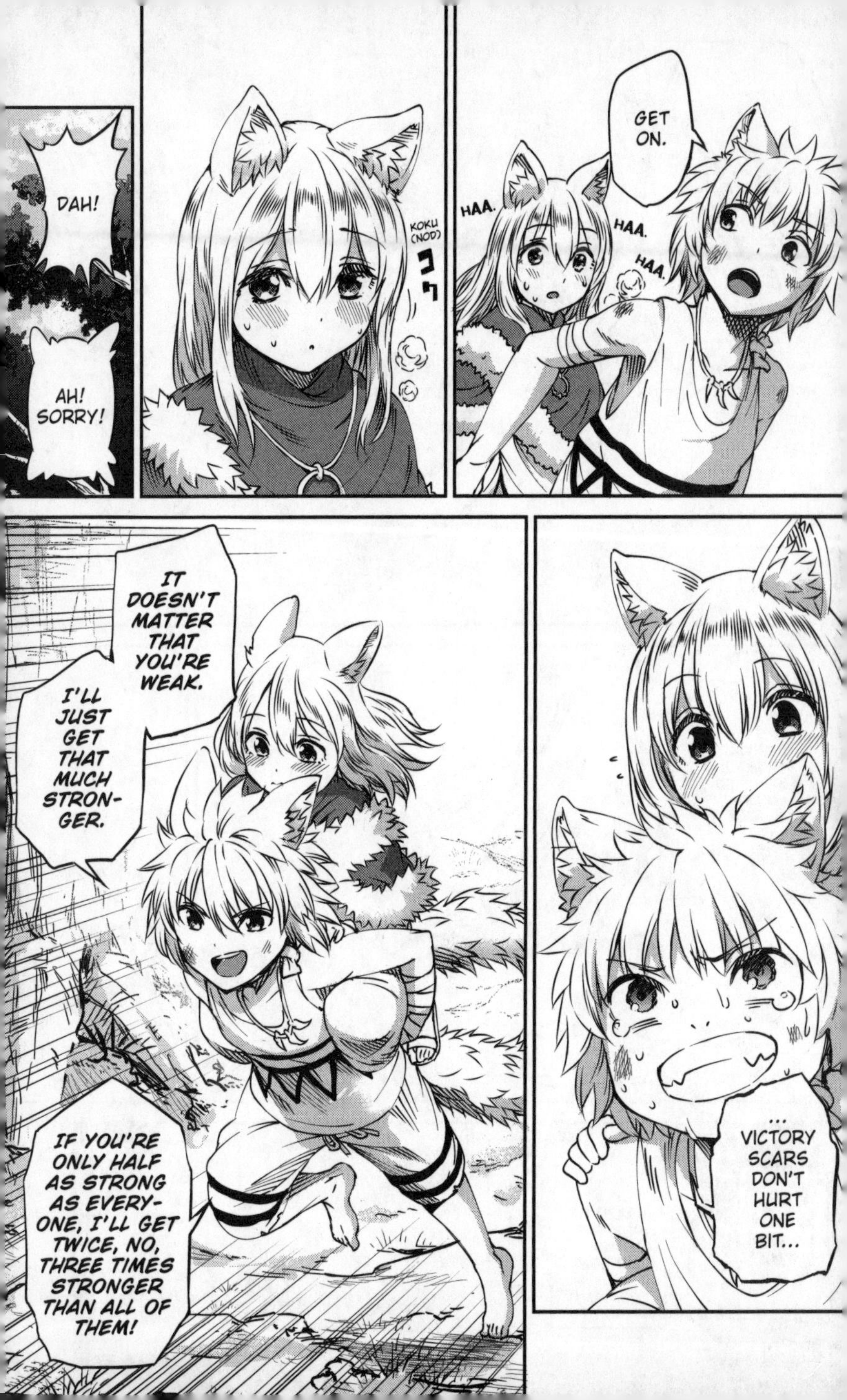
GET ON.
HAA. HAA. HAA.
KOKU (NOD)
コク
DAH!
AH! SORRY!
... VICTORY SCARS DON'T HURT ONE BIT...
IT DOESN'T MATTER THAT YOU'RE WEAK.
I'LL JUST GET THAT MUCH STRONGER.
IF YOU'RE ONLY HALF AS STRONG AS EVERYONE, I'LL GET TWICE, NO, THREE TIMES STRONGER THAN ALL OF THEM!

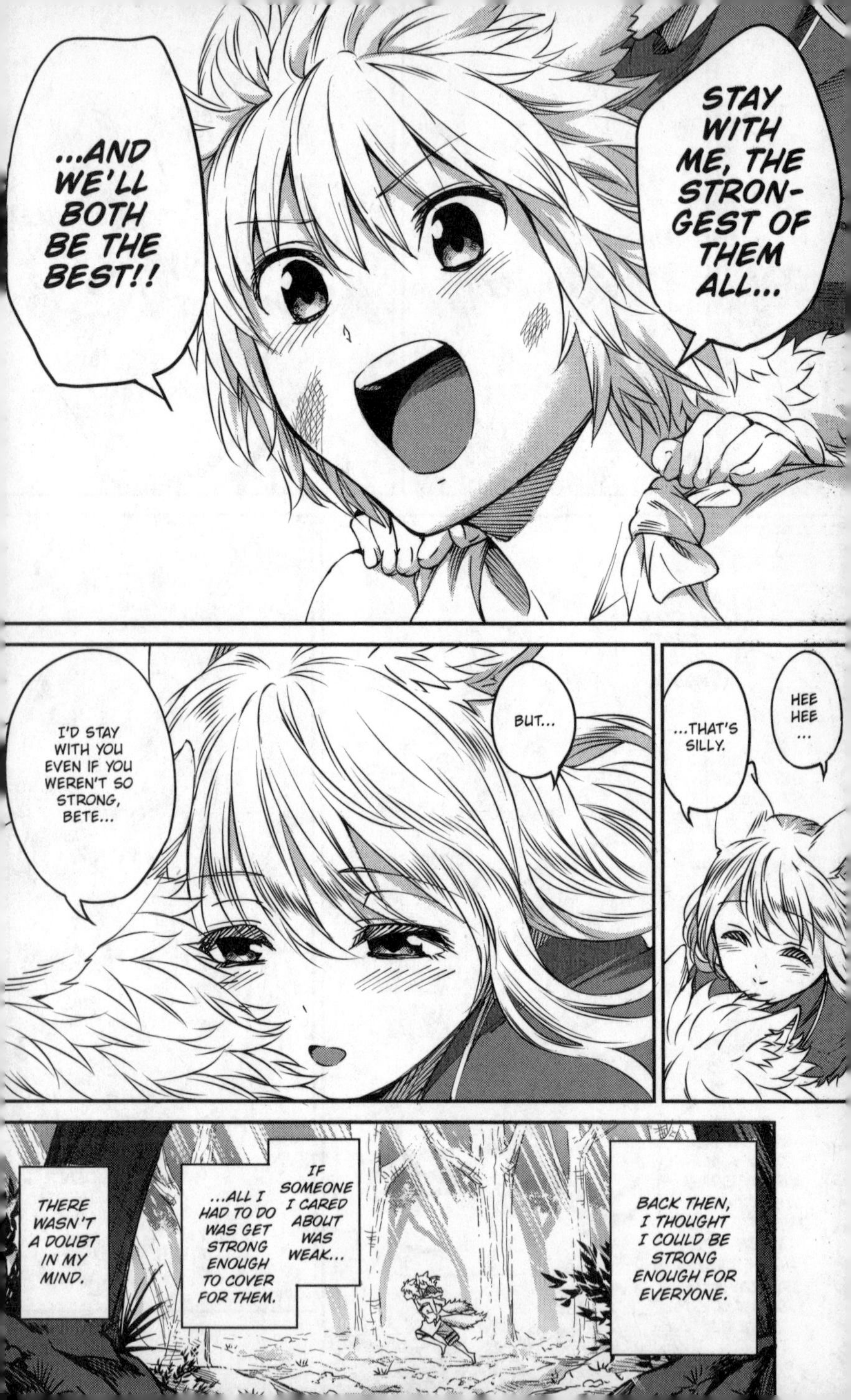
STAY WITH ME, THE STRONGEST OF THEM ALL...
...AND WE'LL BOTH BE THE BEST!!
HEE HEE ...
...THAT'S SILLY.
BUT...
I'D STAY WITH YOU EVEN IF YOU WEREN'T SO STRONG, BETE...
BACK THEN, I THOUGHT I COULD BE STRONG ENOUGH FOR EVERYONE.
IF SOMEONE I CARED ABOUT WAS WEAK...
...ALL I HAD TO DO WAS GET STRONG ENOUGH TO COVER FOR THEM.
THERE WASN'T A DOUBT IN MY MIND.

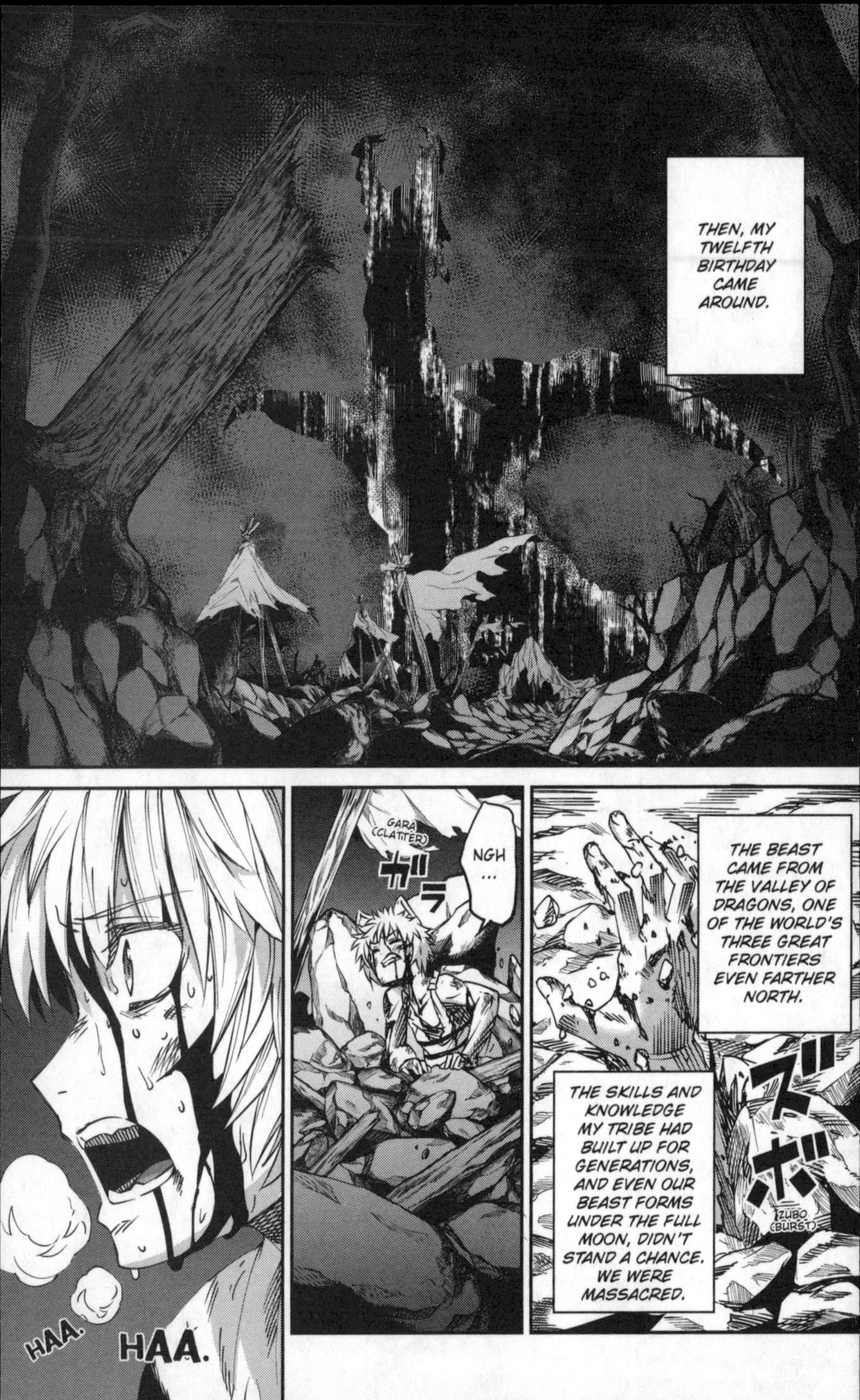
THEN, MY TWELFTH BIRTHDAY CAME AROUND.
THE BEAST CAME FROM THE VALLEY OF DRAGONS, ONE OF THE WORLD'S THREE GREAT FRONTIERS EVEN FARTHER NORTH.
THE SKILLS AND KNOWLEDGE MY TRIBE HAD BUILT UP FOR GENERATIONS, AND EVEN OUR BEAST FORMS UNDER THE FULL MOON, DIDN'T STAND A CHANCE. WE WERE MASSACRED.
ZUBO (BURST)
GARA (CLATTER)
NGH ...
HAA. HAA.

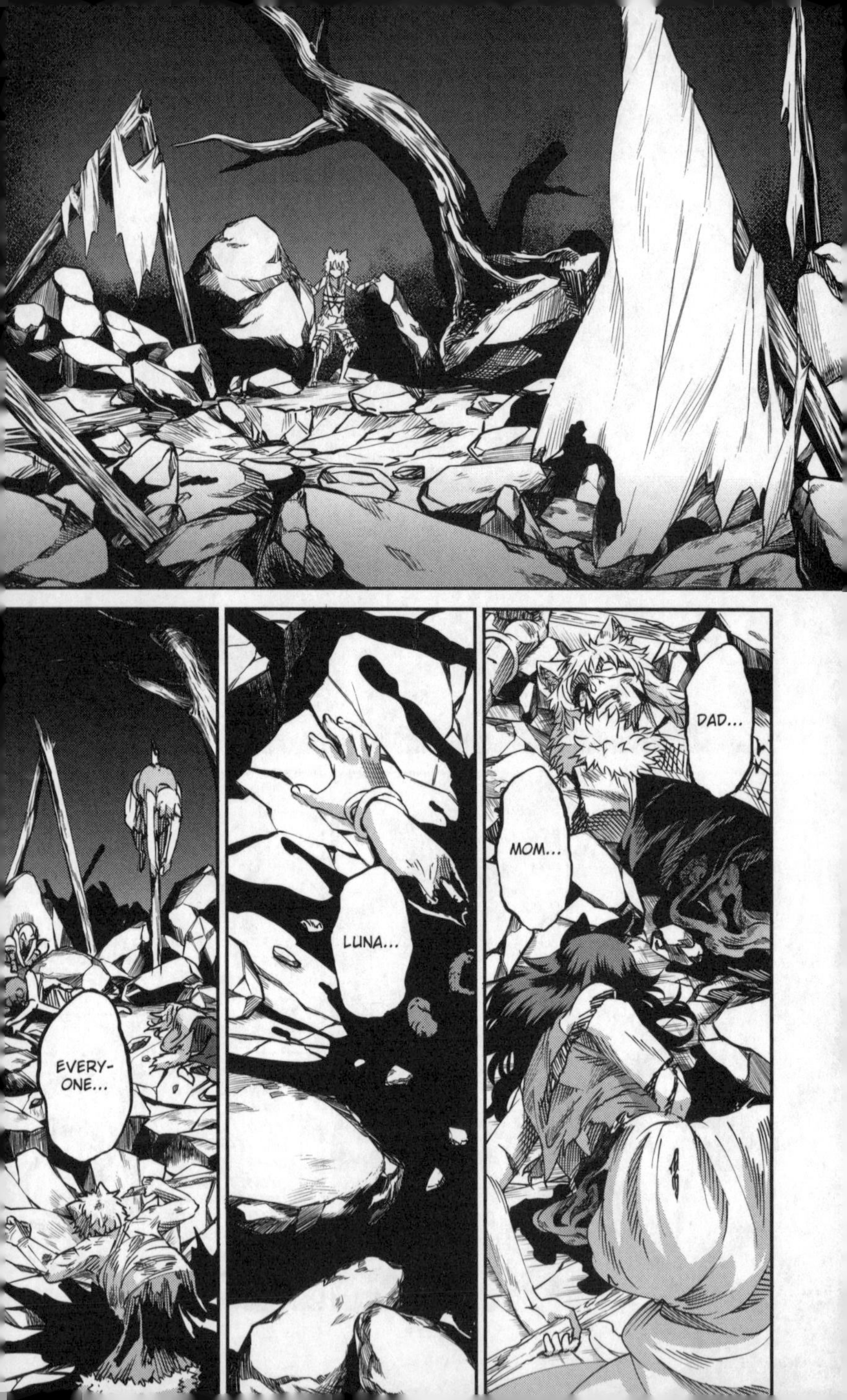
DAD...
MOM...
LUNA...
EVERY-ONE...

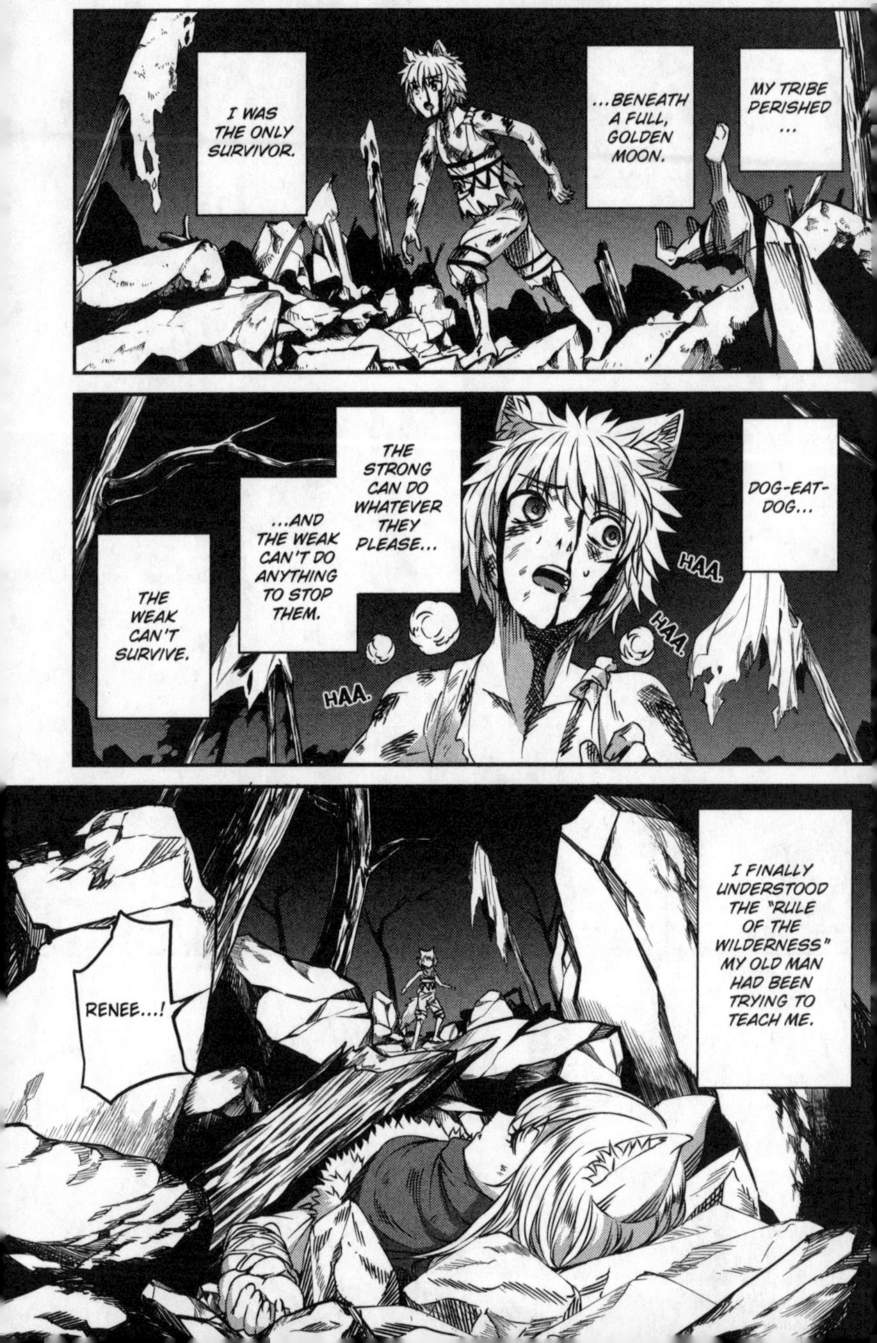
MY TRIBE PERISHED ...
...BENEATH A FULL, GOLDEN MOON.
I WAS THE ONLY SURVIVOR.
DOG-EAT-DOG...
HAA.
HAA.
THE STRONG CAN DO WHATEVER THEY PLEASE...
...AND THE WEAK CAN'T DO ANYTHING TO STOP THEM.
HAA.
THE WEAK CAN'T SURVIVE.
I FINALLY UNDERSTOOD THE "RULE OF THE WILDERNESS" MY OLD MAN HAD BEEN TRYING TO TEACH ME.
RENEE...!

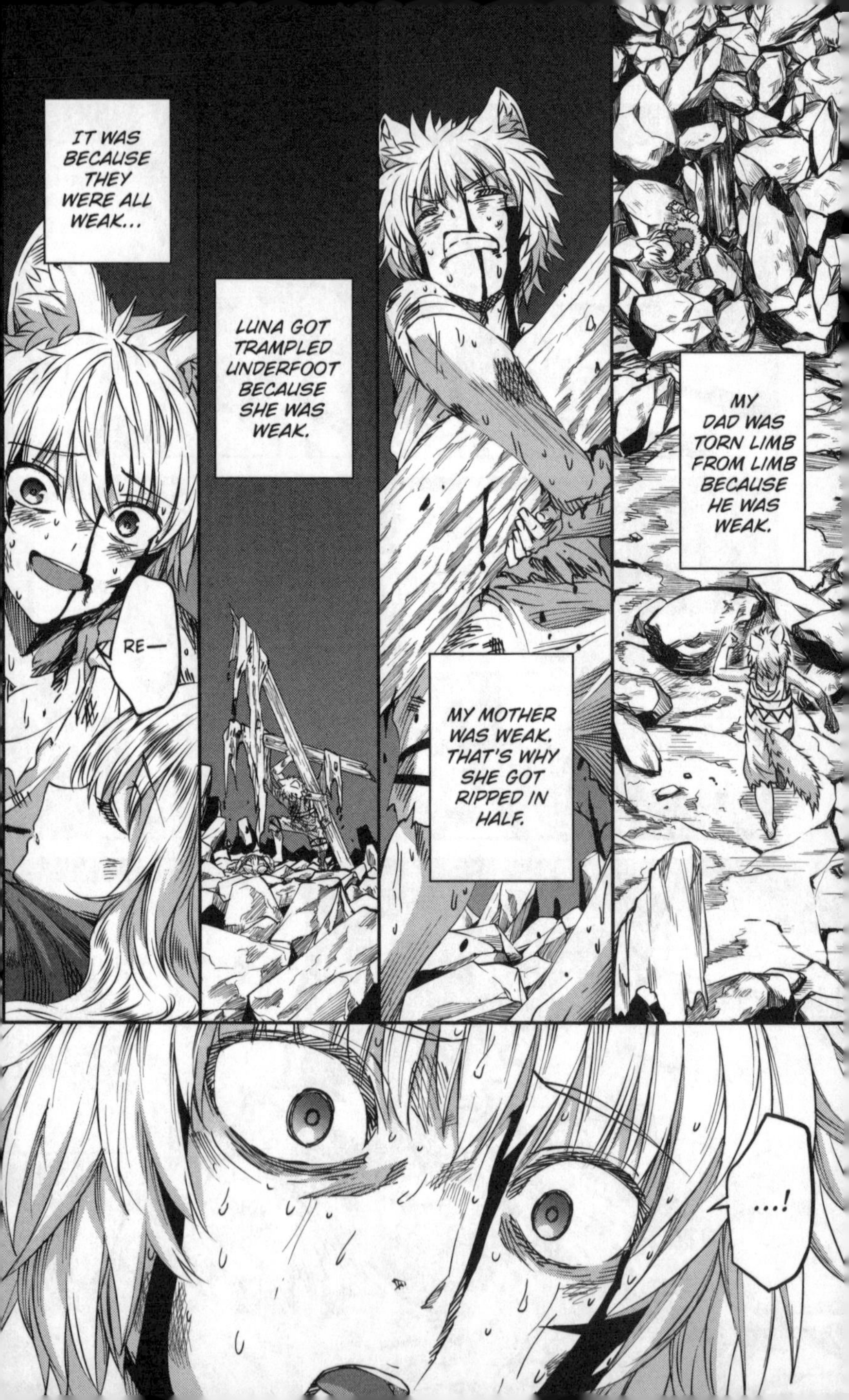
MY DAD WAS TORN LIMB FROM LIMB BECAUSE HE WAS WEAK.
MY MOTHER WAS WEAK. THAT'S WHY SHE GOT RIPPED IN HALF.
LUNA GOT TRAMPLED UNDERFOOT BECAUSE SHE WAS WEAK.
IT WAS BECAUSE THEY WERE ALL WEAK...
RE—
...!

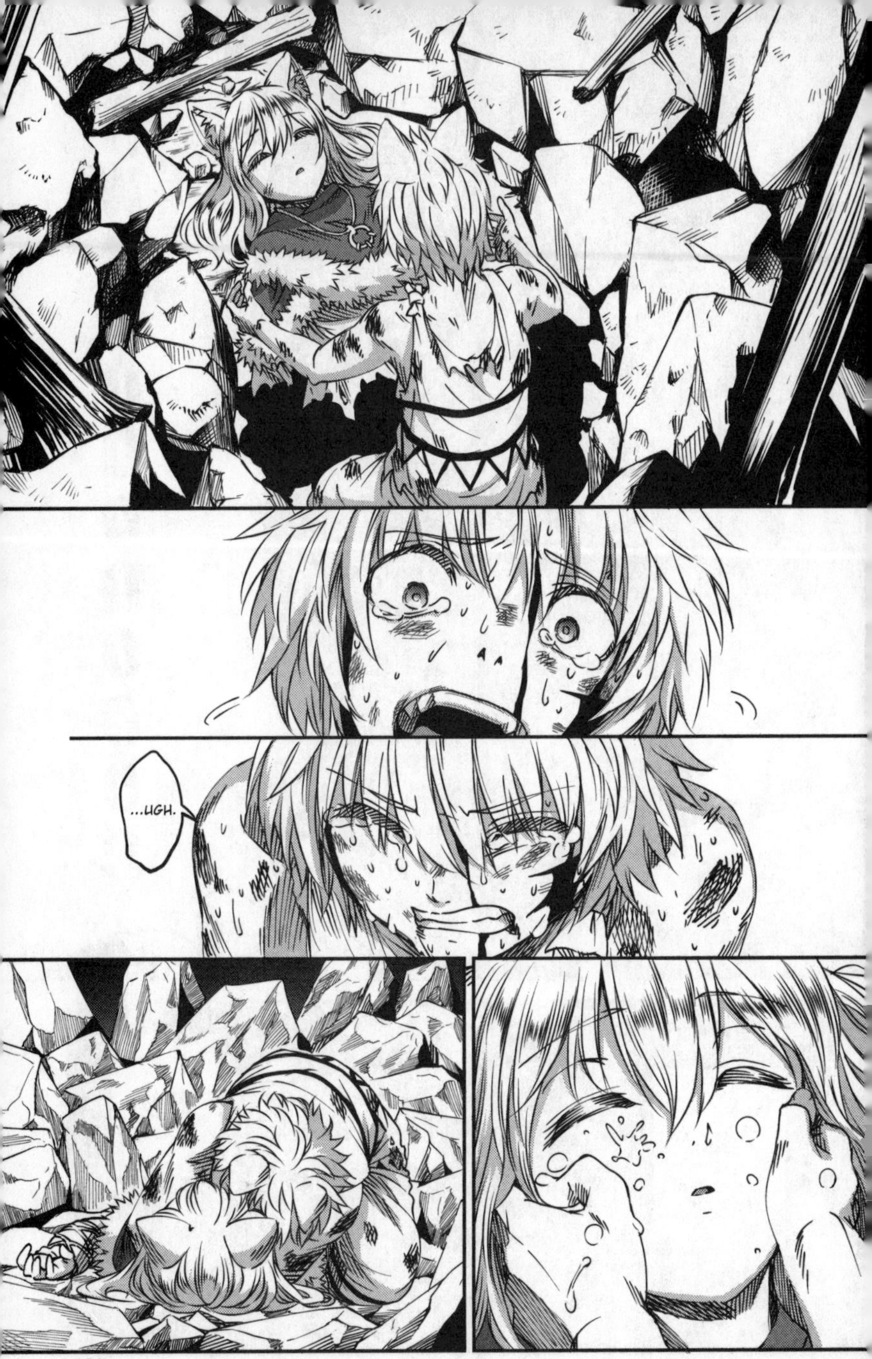
...UGH.

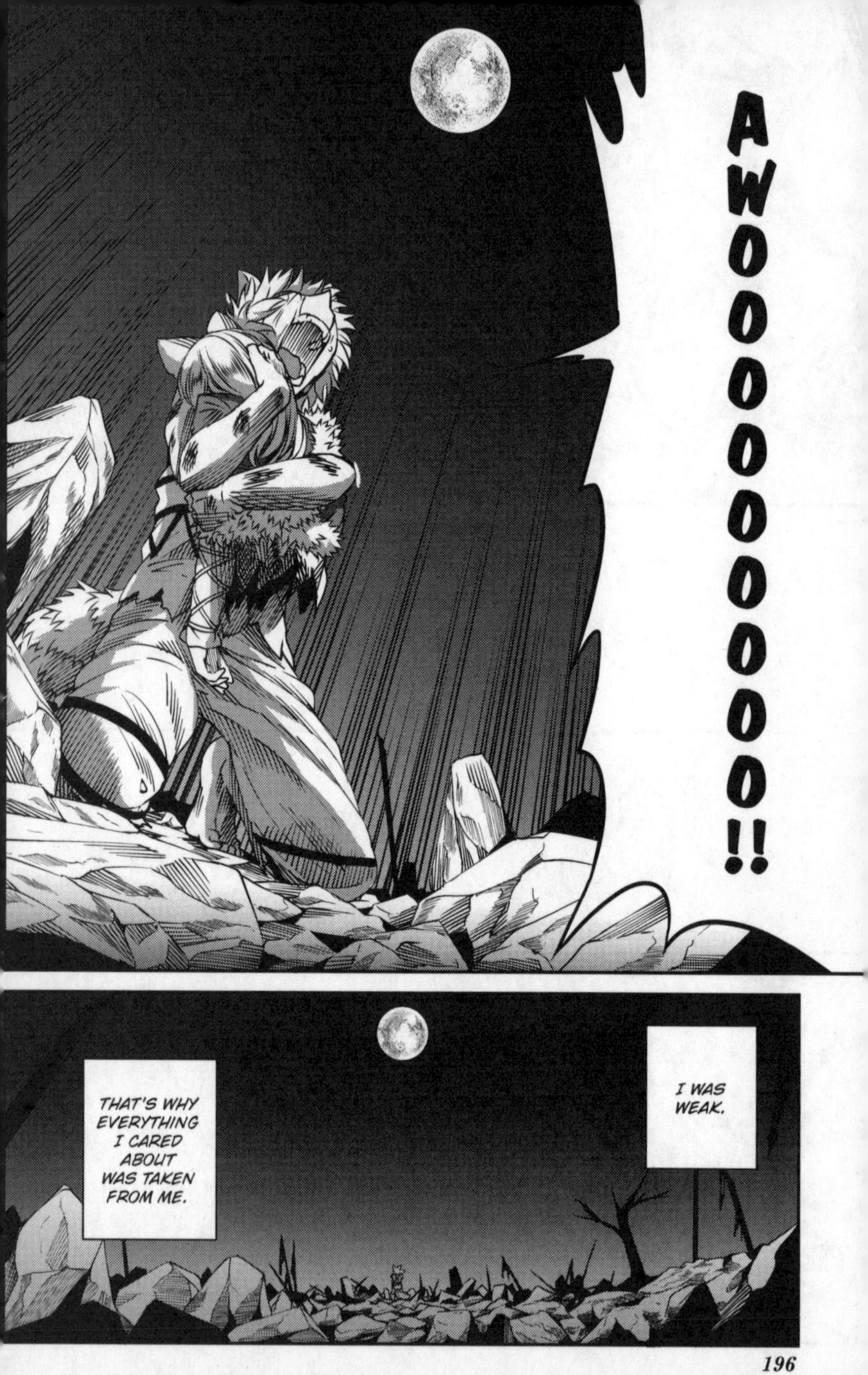

AWOOOOOOOOO!!
I WAS WEAK.
THAT'S WHY EVERYTHING I CARED ABOUT WAS TAKEN FROM ME.

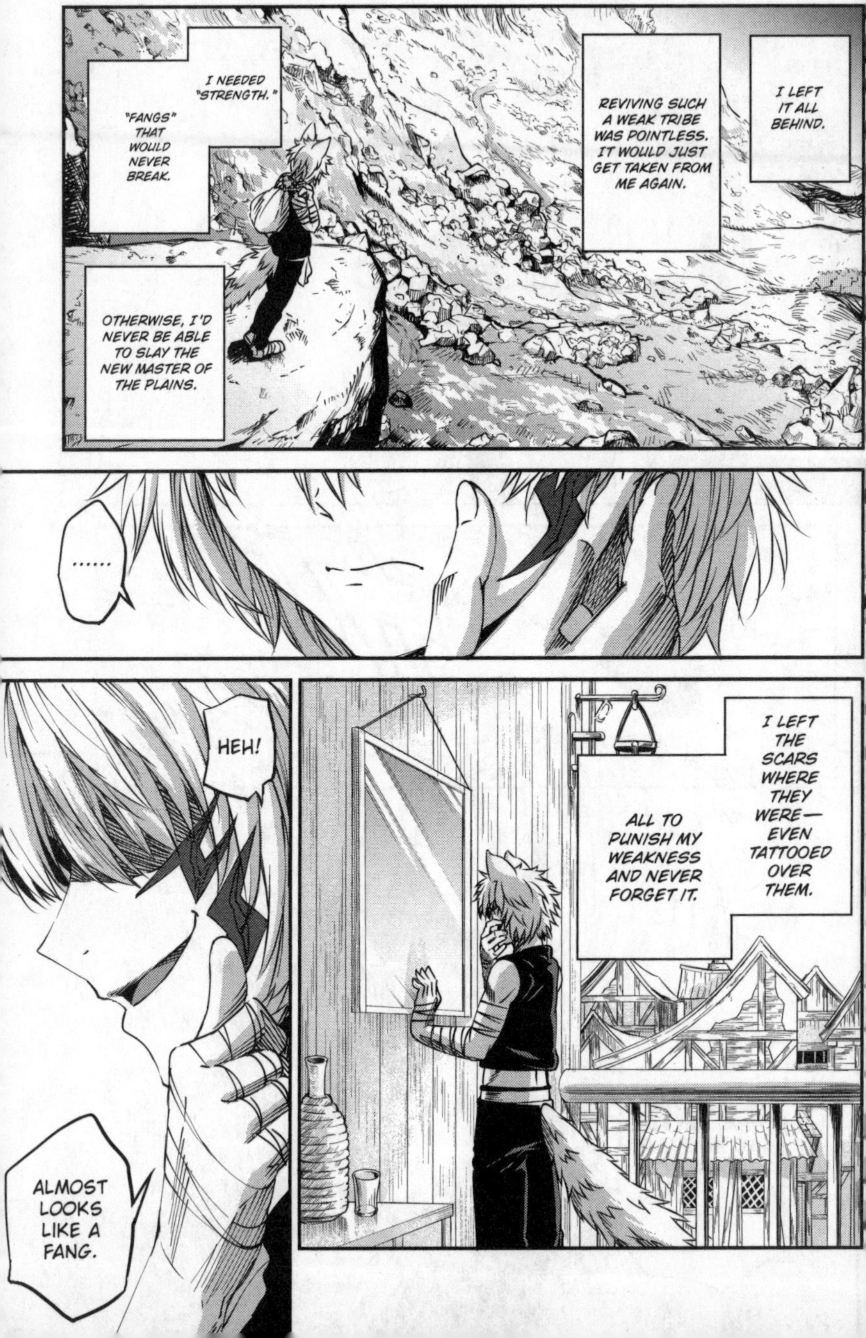
I LEFT IT ALL BEHIND.
REVIVING SUCH A WEAK TRIBE WAS POINTLESS. IT WOULD JUST GET TAKEN FROM ME AGAIN.
I NEEDED "STRENGTH."
"FANGS" THAT WOULD NEVER BREAK.
OTHERWISE, I'D NEVER BE ABLE TO SLAY THE NEW MASTER OF THE PLAINS.
......
I LEFT THE SCARS WHERE THEY WERE—EVEN TATTOOED OVER THEM.
ALL TO PUNISH MY WEAKNESS AND NEVER FORGET IT.
HEH!
ALMOST LOOKS LIKE A FANG.

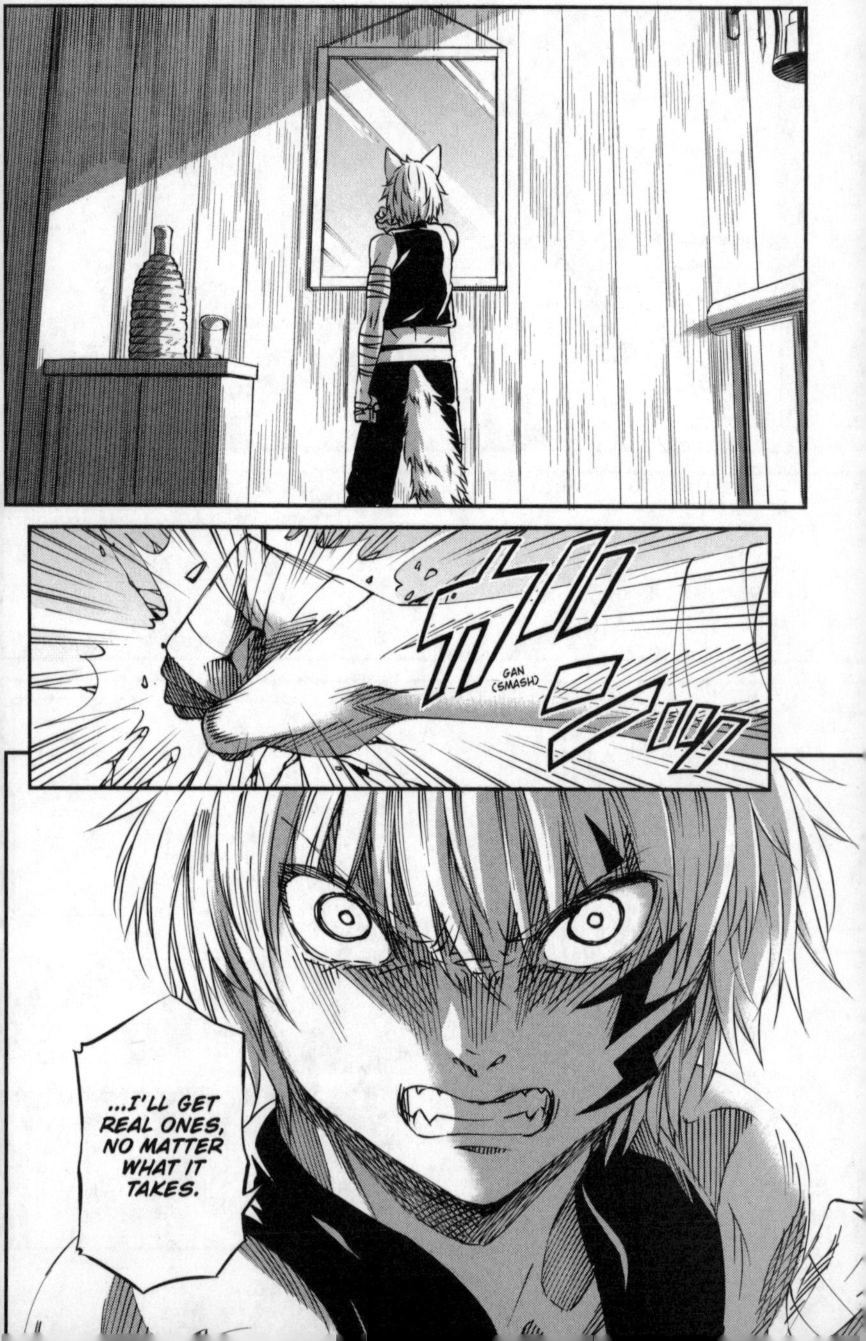
GAN (SMASH)
...I'LL GET REAL ONES, NO MATTER WHAT IT TAKES.

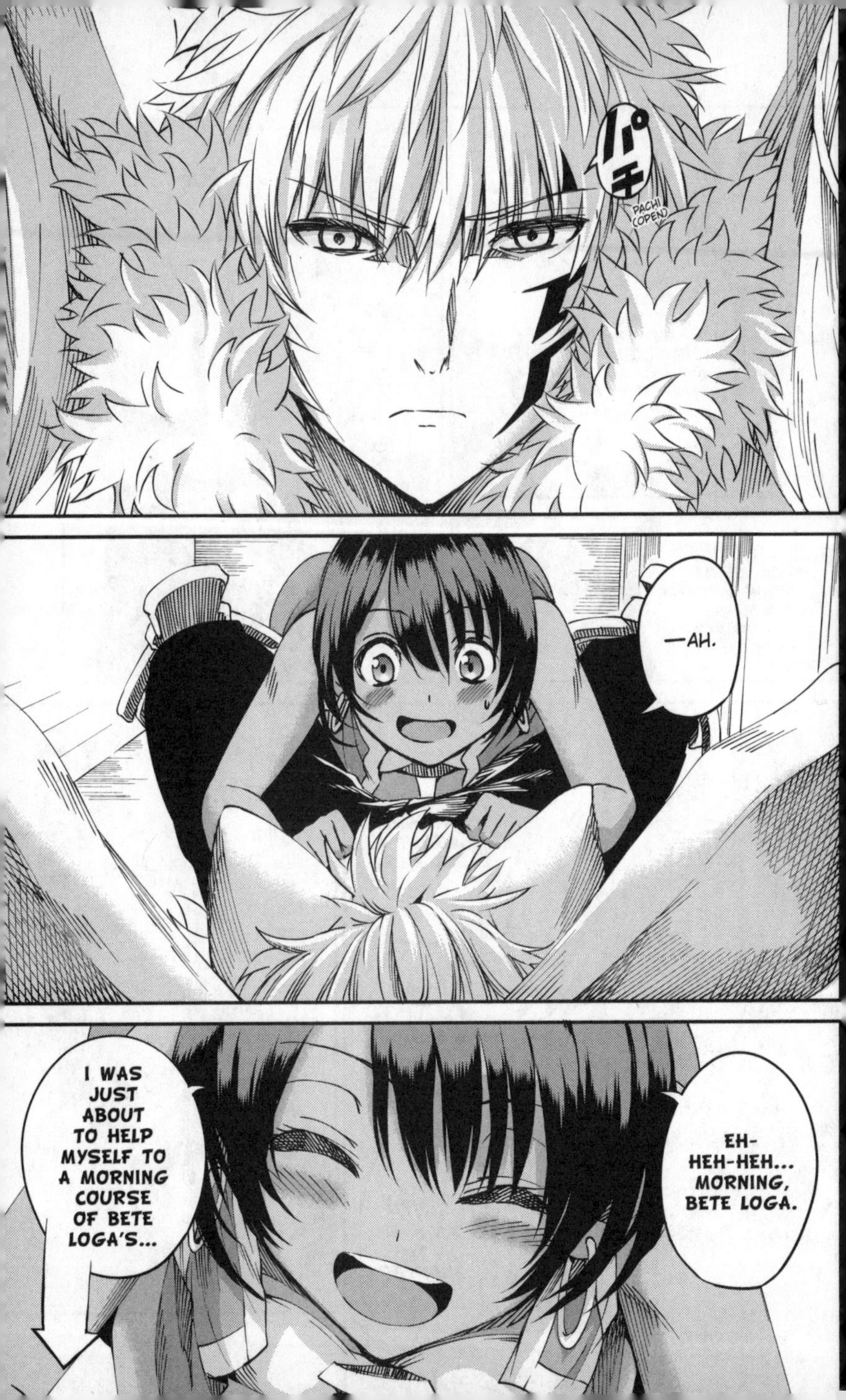
パチ
PACHI (OPEN)
—AH.
EH-HEH-HEH... MORNING, BETE LOGA.
I WAS JUST ABOUT TO HELP MYSELF TO A MORNING COURSE OF BETE LOGA'S...

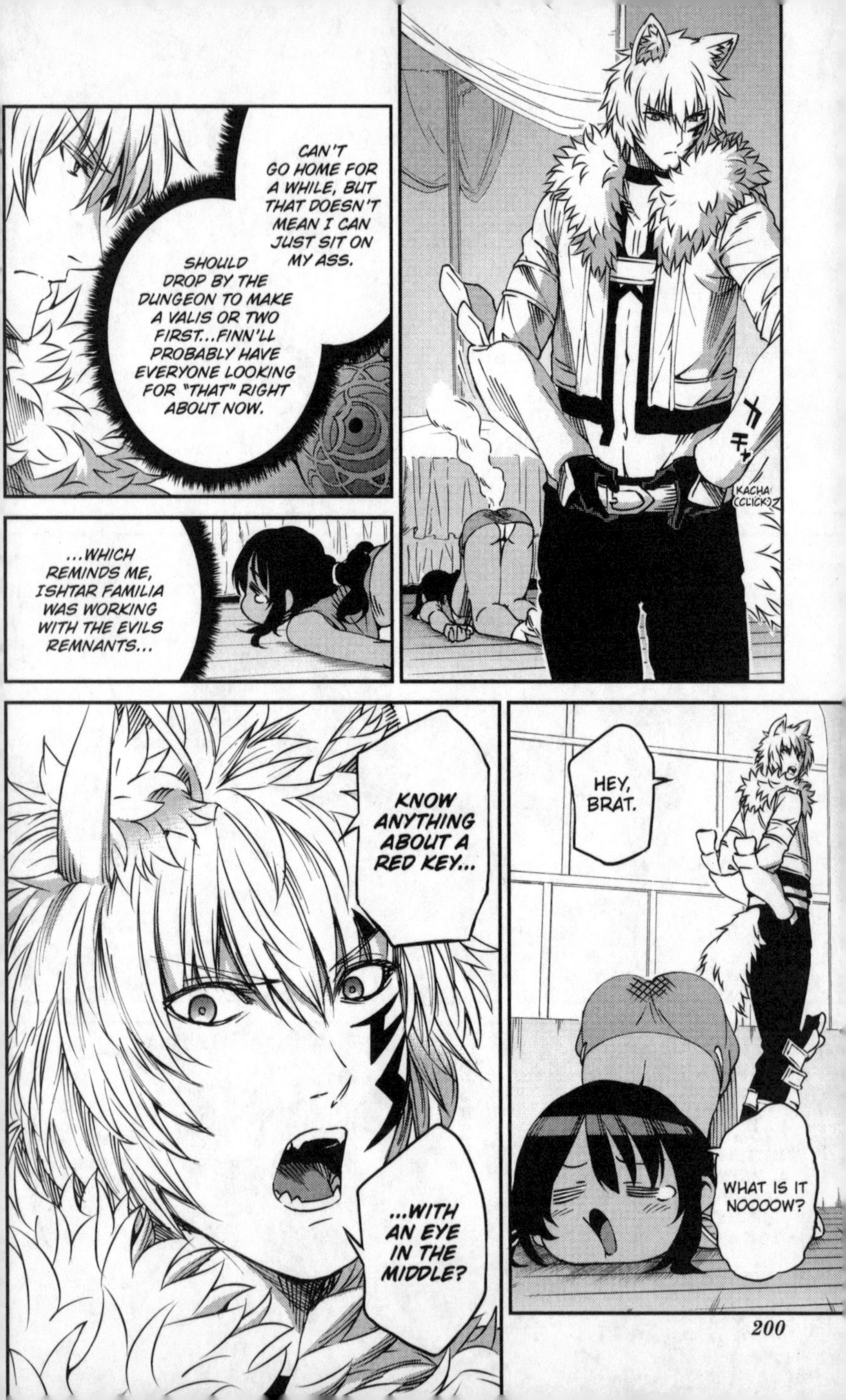
カチャ
KACHA (CLICK)
CAN'T GO HOME FOR A WHILE, BUT THAT DOESN'T MEAN I CAN JUST SIT ON MY ASS.
SHOULD DROP BY THE DUNGEON TO MAKE A VALIS OR TWO FIRST...FINN'LL PROBABLY HAVE EVERYONE LOOKING FOR "THAT" RIGHT ABOUT NOW.
...WHICH REMINDS ME, ISHTAR FAMILIA WAS WORKING WITH THE EVILS REMNANTS...
HEY, BRAT.
WHAT IS IT NOOOOW?
KNOW ANYTHING ABOUT A RED KEY...
...WITH AN EYE IN THE MIDDLE?

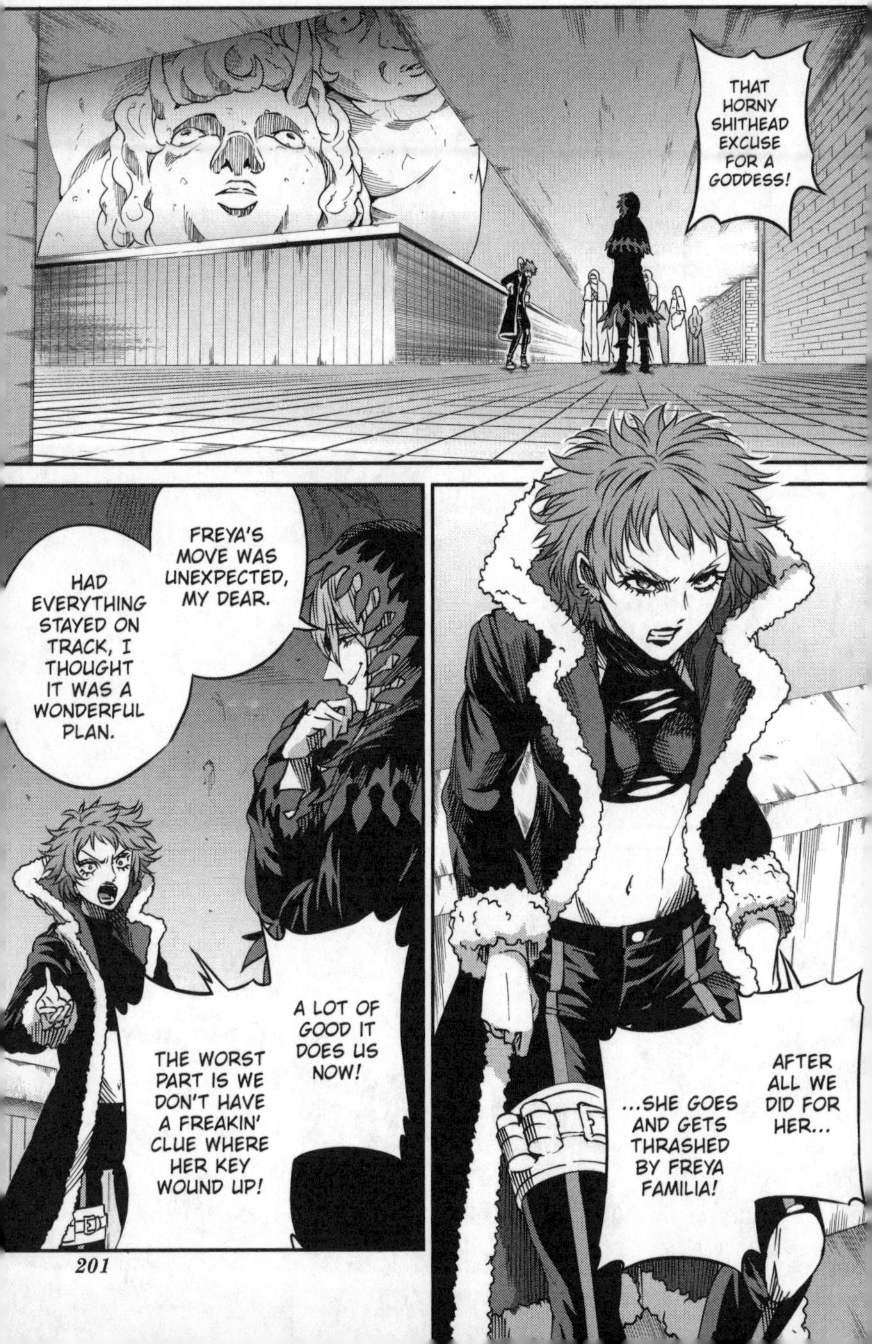
THAT HORNY SHITHEAD EXCUSE FOR A GODDESS!
AFTER ALL WE DID FOR HER...
...SHE GOES AND GETS THRASHED BY FREYA FAMILIA!
FREYA'S MOVE WAS UNEXPECTED, MY DEAR.
HAD EVERYTHING STAYED ON TRACK, I THOUGHT IT WAS A WONDERFUL PLAN.
A LOT OF GOOD IT DOES US NOW!
THE WORST PART IS WE DON'T HAVE A FREAKIN' CLUE WHERE HER KEY WOUND UP!

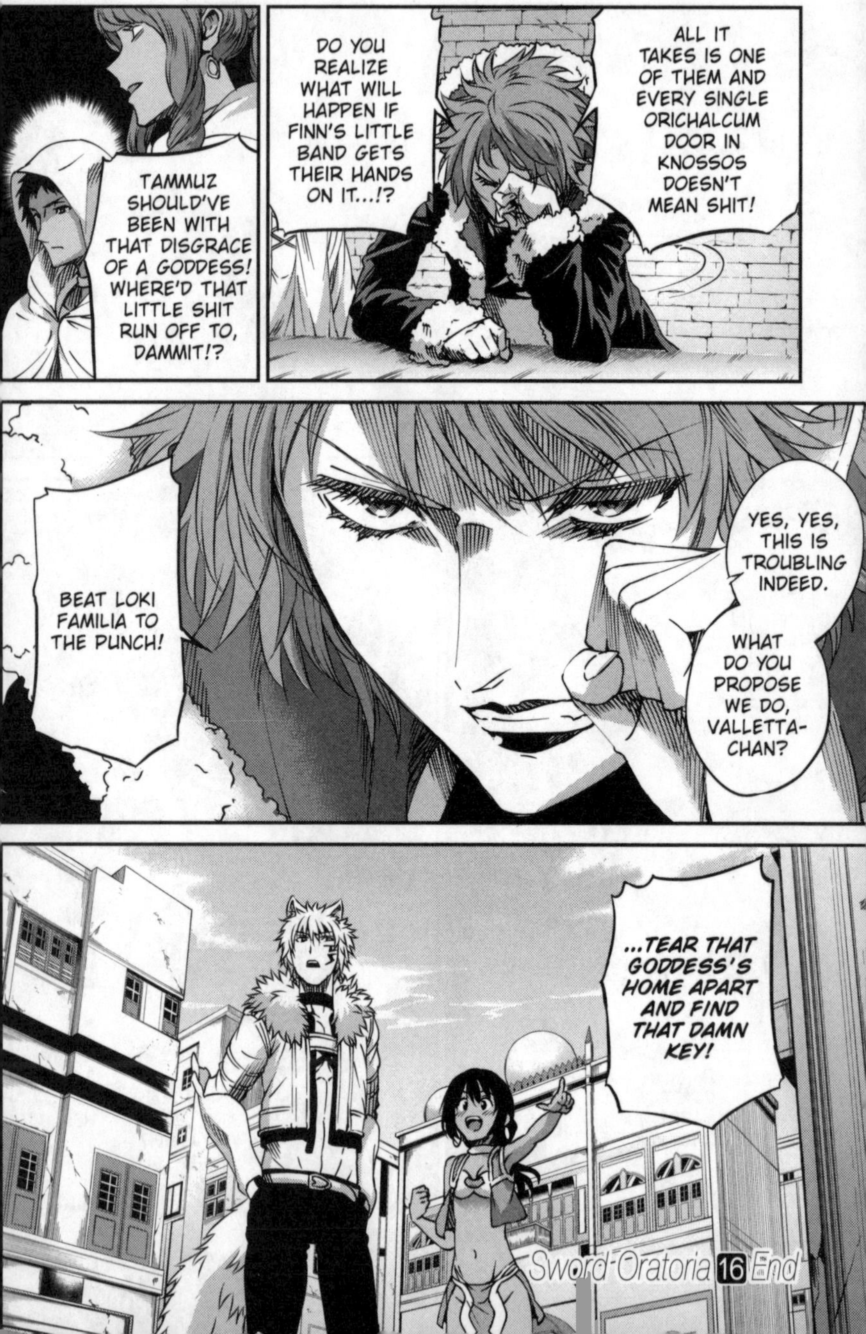
ALL IT TAKES IS ONE OF THEM AND EVERY SINGLE ORICHALCUM DOOR IN KNOSSOS DOESN'T MEAN SHIT!
DO YOU REALIZE WHAT WILL HAPPEN IF FINN'S LITTLE BAND GETS THEIR HANDS ON IT...!?
TAMMUZ SHOULD'VE BEEN WITH THAT DISGRACE OF A GODDESS! WHERE'D THAT LITTLE SHIT RUN OFF TO, DAMMIT!?
YES, YES, THIS IS TROUBLING INDEED.
WHAT DO YOU PROPOSE WE DO, VALLETTA-CHAN?
BEAT LOKI FAMILIA TO THE PUNCH!
...TEAR THAT GODDESS'S HOME APART AND FIND THAT DAMN KEY!
Sword Oratoria 16 End

AFTERWORD

LEENE, THE SECOND CHARACTER AFTER RAUL THAT I WAS ASKED TO DESIGN, MADE HER COVER DEBUT FOR THIS VOLUME. OMORI-SENSEI ASKING ME TO DO THE OFFICIAL DESIGN ALL BUT SEALED HER FATE, SO I KNEW THIS DAY WOULD COME. THAT DIDN'T MAKE IT ANY EASIER TO SAY GOOD-BYE. CHANCES ARE A CRUEL FATE AWAITS MOST OF THE CHARACTERS I DESIGN FOR THIS SERIES, BUT THAT ONLY MAKES ME WANT TO DO THEM JUSTICE ALL THE MORE. RECENTLY, ANYWAY. THERE ARE MORE HEART-WRENCHING TWISTS IN STORE FOR BETE'S ARC IN THE NEXT *SWORD ORATORIA*, SO COME BACK AND SEE WHAT HAPPENS!

TAKASHI YAGI

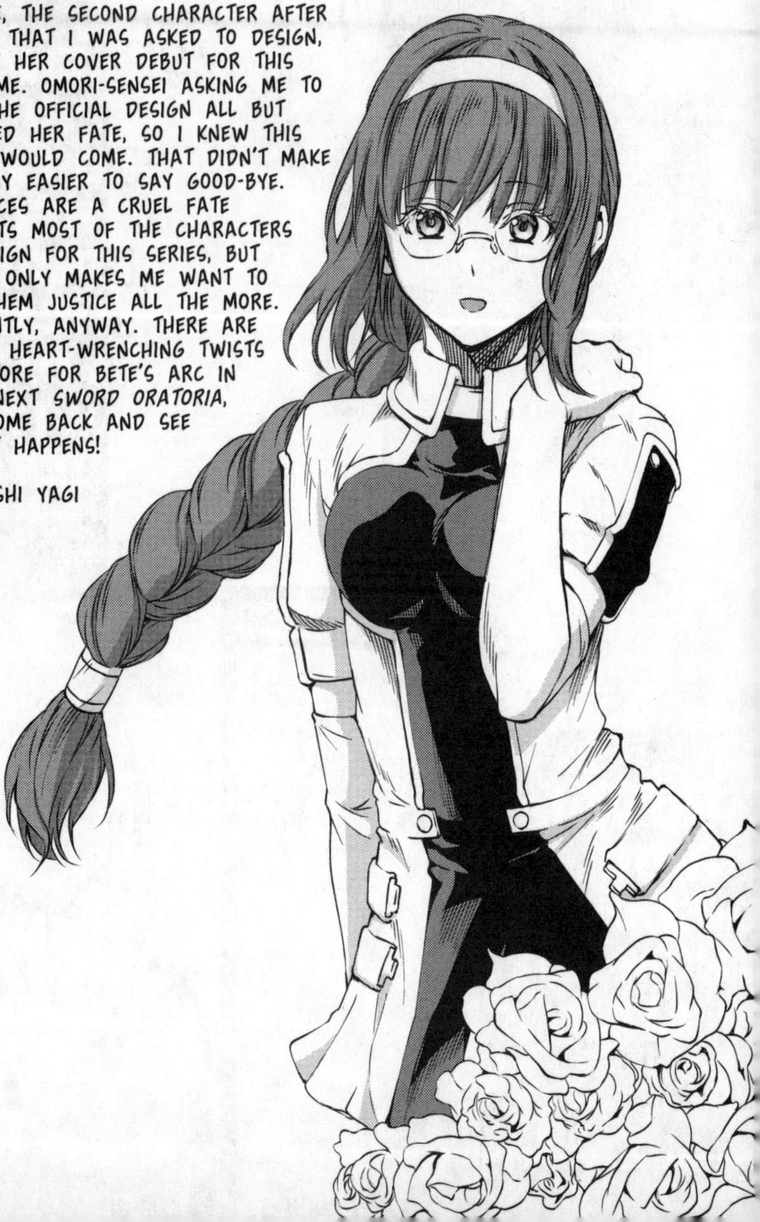

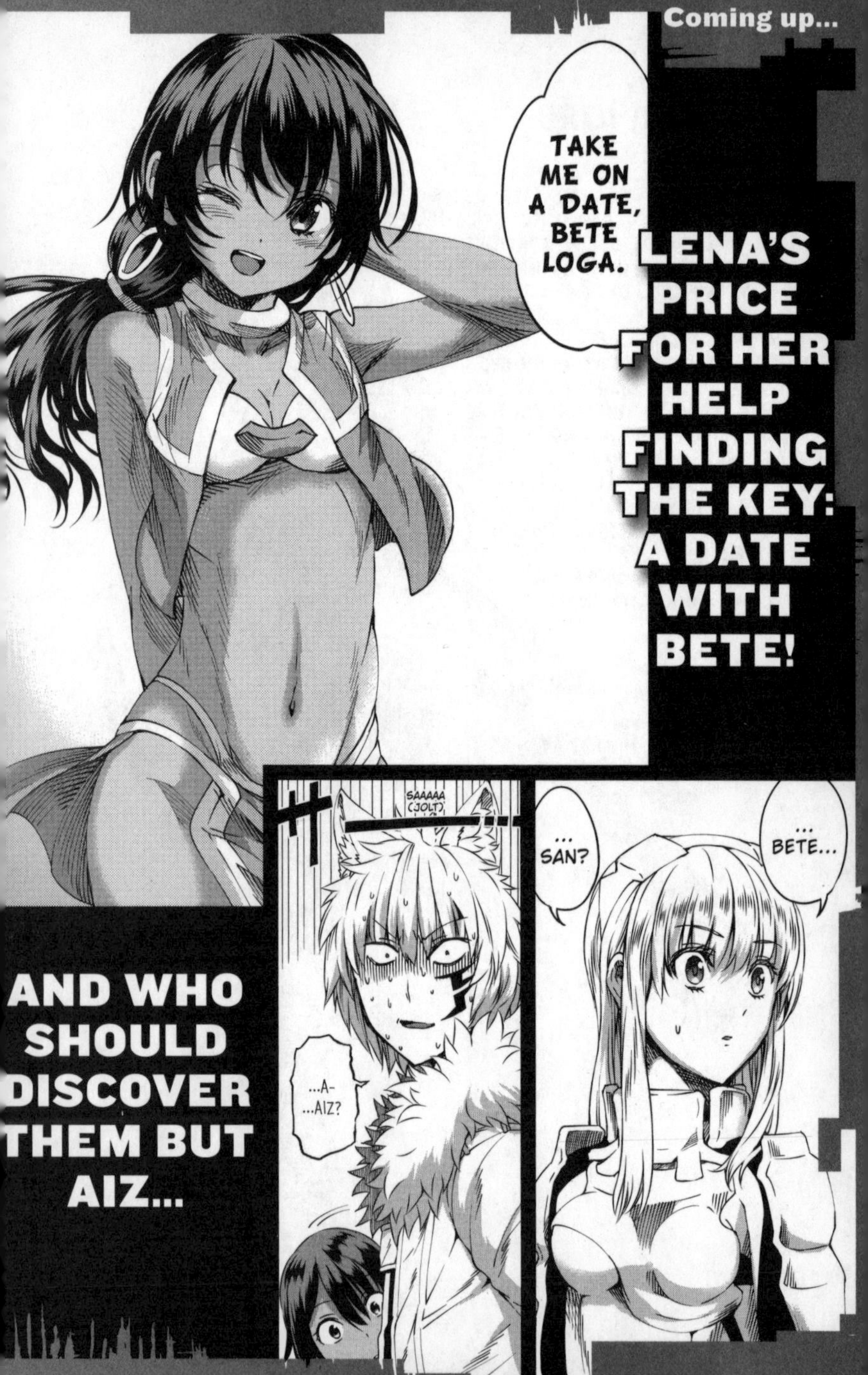
Coming up...
TAKE ME ON A DATE, BETE LOGA.
LENA'S PRICE FOR HER HELP FINDING THE KEY: A DATE WITH BETE!
...BETE...
...SAN?
SAAAAA (JOLT)
...A- ...AIZ?
AND WHO SHOULD DISCOVER THEM BUT AIZ...

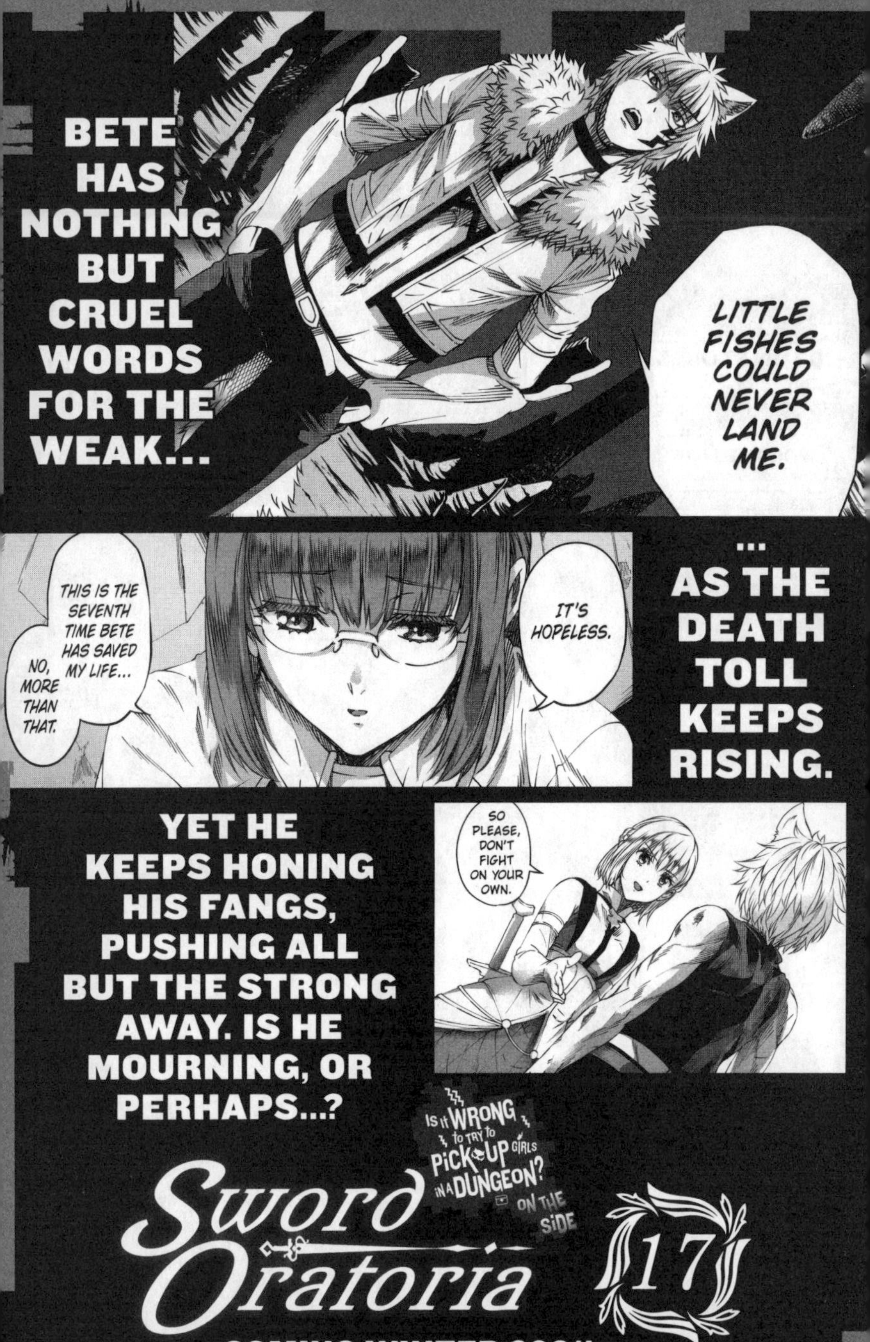
BETE HAS NOTHING BUT CRUEL WORDS FOR THE WEAK...
LITTLE FISHES COULD NEVER LAND ME.
...AS THE DEATH TOLL KEEPS RISING.
IT'S HOPELESS.
THIS IS THE SEVENTH TIME BETE HAS SAVED MY LIFE...
NO, MORE THAN THAT.
SO PLEASE, DON'T FIGHT ON YOUR OWN.
YET HE KEEPS HONING HIS FANGS, PUSHING ALL BUT THE STRONG AWAY. IS HE MOURNING, OR PERHAPS...?
IS IT WRONG TO TRY TO PICK UP GIRLS IN A DUNGEON? ON THE SIDE
Sword Oratoria
17
COMING WINTER 2021!

Toilet-bound Hanako-Kun

At Kamome Academy, rumors abound about the school's Seven Mysteries, one of which is Hanako-san. Said to occupy the third stall of the third floor girls' bathroom in the old school building, Hanako-san grants any wish when summoned. Nene Yashiro, an occult-loving high school girl who dreams of romance, ventures into this haunted bathroom...but the Hanako-san she meets there is nothing like she imagined! Kamome Academy's Hanako-san...is a boy!

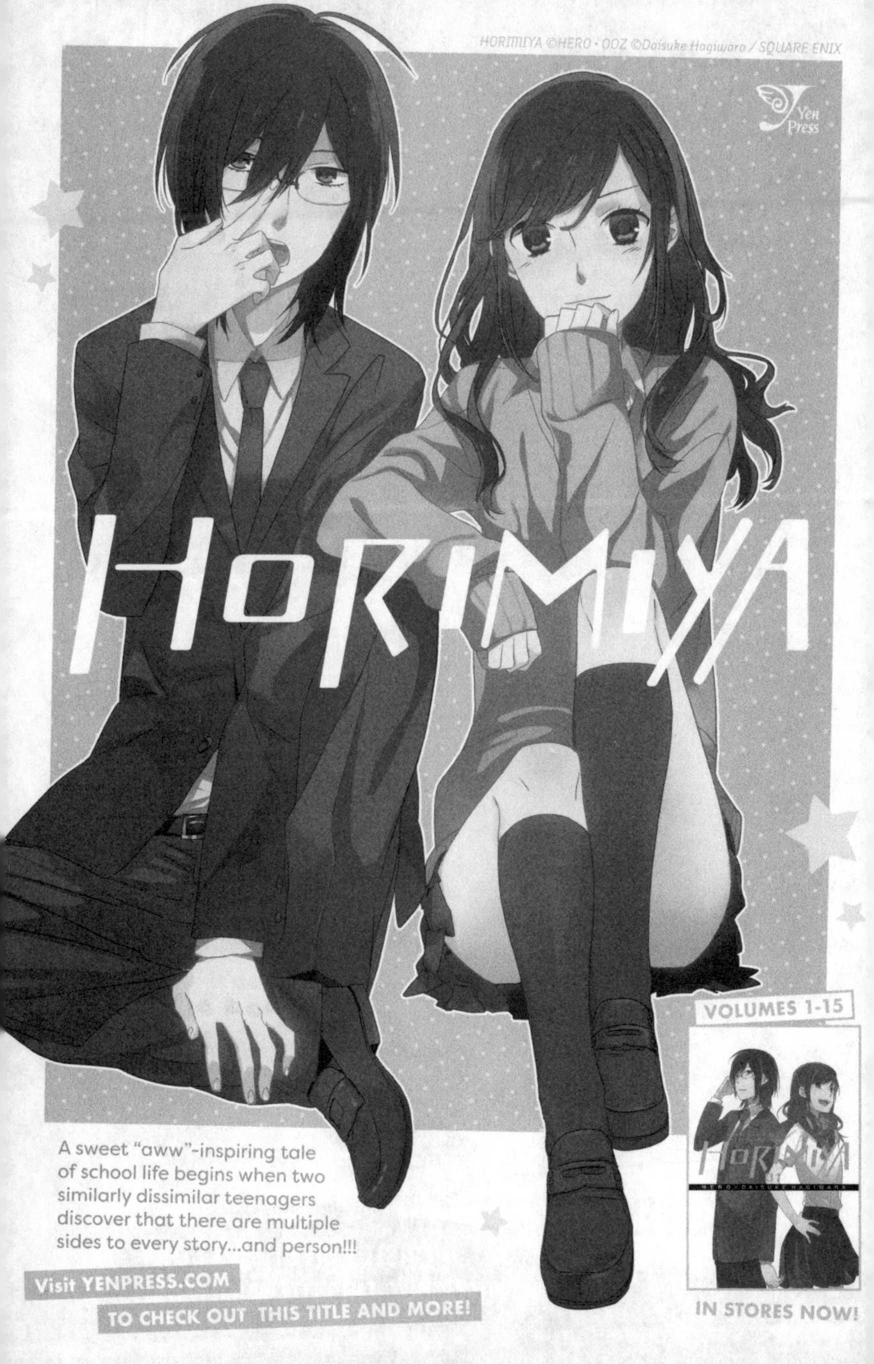
HORIMIYA ©HERO • OOZ ©Daisuke Hagiwara / SQUARE ENIX
Yen Press
HORIMIYA
VOLUMES 1-15
A sweet "aww"-inspiring tale of school life begins when two similarly dissimilar teenagers discover that there are multiple sides to every story...and person!!!
Visit YENPRESS.COM
TO CHECK OUT THIS TITLE AND MORE!
IN STORES NOW!

IS IT WRONG TO TRY TO PICK UP GIRLS IN A DUNGEON? ON THE SIDE: SWORD ORATORIA ⑯

Fujino Omori
Takashi Yagi
Kiyotaka Haimura, Suzuhito Yasuda

Translation: Andrew Gaippe • Lettering: Barri Shrager

DUNGEON NI DEAI WO MOTOMERU NO WA MACHIGATTEIRUDAROUKA GAIDEN SWORD ORATORIA vol. 16
©Fujino Omori/SB Creative Corp.
Original Character Designs:©Kiyotaka Haimura/SB Creative Corp.
Original Character Designs:©Suzuhito Yasuda/SB Creative Corp.
© 2020 Takashi Yagi/SQUARE ENIX CO., LTD.
First published in Japan in 2020 by SQUARE ENIX CO., LTD.
English translation rights arranged with SQUARE ENIX CO., LTD. and Yen Press, LLC through Tuttle-Mori Agency, Inc.

English translation © 2021 by SQUARE ENIX CO., LTD.

Yen Press
150 West 30th Street, 19th Floor
New York, NY 10001

Visit us at yenpress.com
facebook.com/yenpress
twitter.com/yenpress
yenpress.tumblr.com
instagram.com/yenpress

First Yen Press Edition: July 2021

Yen Press is an imprint of Yen Press, LLC.
The Yen Press name and logo are trademarks of Yen Press, LLC.

The publisher is not responsible for websites (or their content) that are not owned by the publisher.

Library of Congress Control Number: 2016946068

ISBNs: 978-1-9753-2129-1 (paperback)
       978-1-9753-2130-7 (ebook)

10 9 8 7 6 5 4 3 2 1

BVG

Printed in the United States of America